The Palm—Tree of Life:
Biology, Utilization and
Conservation

Michael J. Balick, editor

PROCEEDINGS OF A SYMPOSIUM AT THE 1986 ANNUAL MEETING OF THE
SOCIETY FOR ECONOMIC BOTANY HELD AT
THE NEW YORK BOTANICAL GARDEN, BRONX, NEW YORK
13–14 JUNE 1986

Financial support by the World Wildlife Fund—US for international participants
in the symposium is gratefully acknowledged.

This is Volume 6 of ADVANCES IN ECONOMIC BOTANY

Published by The New York Botanical Garden, Bronx, New York 10458, U.S.A.

Issued 3 May 1988

Library of Congress Cataloging-in-Publication Data

Society for Economic Botany (U.S.). Meeting (1986 : New York Botanical Garden)
    The palm—tree of life : biology, utilization, and conservation : proceedings
of a symposium at the 1986 Annual Meeting of the Society for Economic
Botany held at the New York Botanical Garden, Bronx, New York, 13–14
June 1986 / Michael J. Balick, editor.
        p.   cm.—(Advances in economic botany ; v. 6)
    Bibliography: p.
    Includes index.
    ISBN 0-89327-326-0
    1. Palms—Congresses. I. Balick, Michael J., 1952– . II. New York
Botanical Garden. III. Title. IV. Series.
SB317.P3S65   1986
584′.5—dc19   87-36900
                                                                CIP

ISBN 0-89327-326-0
Printed by Allen Press, Lawrence, Kansas, U.S.A.

CONTRIBUTORS

Anthony B. Anderson, Departamento de Botanica, Museu Paraense Emilio Goeldi, Caixa Postal 399, Belém 66.000, Pará, Brazil.

Michael J. Balick, Institute of Economic Botany, The New York Botanical Garden, Bronx, New York 10458.

David M. Bates, L. H. Bailey Hortorium, Cornell University, Ithaca, New York 14853.

Brian M. Boom, The New York Botanical Garden, Bronx, New York 10458.

Charles R. Clement, Instituto Nacional de Pesquisas da Amazônia—INPA, Div. Fruticultura—DCA, Cx. Postal 478, 69.000 Manaus, AM, Brazil.

Lidio Coradin, Centro Nacional de Recursos Genéticos (CENARGEN—EMBRAPA), S.A.I.N., Parque Rural, Caixa Postal 10-2372, CEP 70.770, Brasília-DF, Brazil.

T. Antony Davis, JBS Haldane Research Centre, Nagercoil, 629 004, Tamilnadu, India.

Darleen A. DeMason, Department of Botany and Plant Sciences, University of California, Riverside, California 92521.

John Dransfield, Herbarium, Royal Botanic Gardens, Kew, Richmond, Surrey, TW9 3AB, United Kingdom.

Andrew Henderson, The New York Botanical Garden, Bronx, New York 10458.

Dennis V. Johnson, 605 Ray Dr., Silver Spring, Maryland, 20910.

Francis Kahn, Convenio ORSTOM/IIAP, Apartado Postal 185, Iquitos, Peru.

Eduardo Lleras, Centro Nacional de Recursos Genéticos (CENARGEN—EMBRAPA) Instituto Interamericano de Cooperacion para la Agricultura—IICA, S.A.I.N., Parque Rural, Caixa Postal 10-2372, CEP 70.770, Brasília-DF, Brazil.

Jose Lopez Parodi, Instituto de Investigaciones de la Amazonia Peruana, Centro de Investigaciones—Jenaro Herrera, Apartado Postal 784, Iquitos, Peru.

Kember Mejia C., Instituto de Investigaciones de la Amazonia Peruana, Centro de Investigaciones—Jenaro Herrera, Apartado Postal 784, Iquitos, Peru.

Christine Padoch, Institute of Economic Botany, The New York Botanical Garden, Bronx, New York 10458.

Robert W. Read, National Museum of Natural History, Smithsonian Institution, Washington, D.C. 20560.

Theodore V. St. John, Mycorrhizal Services, P.O. Box 391, Wildomar, California 90395.

Chandra Sekhar, Department of Botany and Plant Sciences, University of California, Riverside, California 92521.

Gail L. Sobel, The New York Botanical Garden, Bronx, New York 10458.

Jeremy Strudwick, The New York Botanical Garden, Bronx, New York 10458.

Natalie W. Uhl, L. H. Bailey Hortorium, Cornell University, Ithaca, New York 14853.

Robert A. Voeks, Department of Geography, California State University, Fullerton, California 92634.

"Man, however, is the animal in the South American forest that utilizes palms in the greatest number of ways . . . . The versatility of palms in the hands of man is astonishing. Houses, baskets, mats, hammocks, cradles, quivers, packbaskets, impromptu shelters, blowpipes, bows, starch, wine, protein from insect larvae, fruit, beverages, flour, oil, ornaments, loincloths, cassava graters, medicines, magic, perfume—all are derived from palms. The importance of man as a biotic factor in the tropical ecosystem has been argued. . . . However, to whatever extent man has been involved in the tropical ecosystem, palms have certainly been a major factor in making possible this involvement and even today, despite the advent of the corrugated tin roof and the rifle, they are of primary importance to many primitive American cultures."

Harold E. Moore
1973

INTRODUCTION

Over the last decade a tremendous interest has developed in the economic utilization of native palm species. Research and domestication programs at many institutions in the tropics and subtropics have focused on palms. As a result, a great deal of information is being obtained about the biology, indigenous utilization, commercial potential and the degree to which wild palm populations have been destroyed as a result of their utilization. In the last five years germplasm banks dedicated to the collection, cultivation, and domestication of underutilized palms have been started in several locations. The recognition of the role that agroforestry can play as an alternative use to cattle raising or monoculture of tropical land has resulted in the need for additional economically attractive, multi-use tree species, and many palms fit this role very well. Increased funding of basic and applied research in rain forest regions has supported work on palms at a number of institutions. Various groups of palm researchers have met in Brazil, Colombia, Costa Rica, the United States and elsewhere to discuss progress and plan collaborative activities on the development of underexploited species. This interest was stimulated further by the publication in April 1985 of a new newsletter, "Useful Palms of Tropical America," that now serves as a forum for exchanging ideas and data on palms. In the Old World, regional meetings and publications on palm resources such as rattan and sago, as well as publications sponsored by the Food and Agricultural Organization of the United Nations, have pointed out the immense value of these plants.

Therefore, it was a very rewarding experience to have convened an international symposium on palm biology, utilization and conservation at the 1986 meeting of the Society for Economic Botany held at The New York Botanical Garden. I am grateful that so many people responded to our invitation, especially since many of them came from great distances, often at their own expense. As a result, symposium speakers were able to participate in a valuable and stimulating exchange of ideas, experiences and perspectives.

The purpose of this symposium was to focus attention on the value of the underexploited palm resources around the world. At the same time it recognized the need for continued studies in both basic and applied biology of palms, as well as the urgent need for conservation of a number of the species presently endangered through over-exploitation and "development" activities.

The published symposium proceedings are divided into four sections. The first, taxonomic overview, consists of a contribution by Drs. Uhl and Dransfield. Their paper discusses a new system of classification of palms.

The second section considers the reproductive biology, ecology and physiology of certain economically useful palms. Drs. DeMason and Sekhar's research on breeding systems in the date palm is an excellent example of the protocol to follow when working with other, lesser-known species.

Dr. Henderson's report on the pollination biology of some of the economically important palms gives economic data on the value of understanding pollination systems of palms. Dr. Kahn focuses on ecological studies of some of the economically important palms in the Peruvian Amazon. Dr. St. John discusses the important role that the vesicular-arbscular mycorrhizae play in the establishment and growth of tropical palms, and how this might be used to support agronomic activities.

The third and largest portion of the book is the section on utilization of palms. Dr. Bates offers a new framework for evaluating the potential economic importance of palms through his concept of "utilization pools." The papers by Drs. Balick and Boom are studies of palm use by several neotropical Indian groups. Dr. Davis discusses the importance of some of the semi-wild palms in the subsistence and commercial economies of Indonesia and elsewhere in South and Southeast Asia. Dr. Lopez-Parodi reports on the use of palms and other plants in the construction of non-conventional, rural housing in the Peruvian Amazon. Dr. Mejia C. discusses how mestizo villagers use palms in a region of the Peruvian Amazon, the Department of Loreto. Dr. Read offers a general look at the utilization of the native palms in the Caribbean. Dr. Anderson describes the way the açai palm is managed in the Amazon Estuary. Dr. Clement focuses on a single species, the pejibaye palm and discusses past and present efforts towards its domestication. Drs. Coradin and Lleras give a broad overview of current activities in Latin America concerning the domestication of native palm species. Dr. Dransfield discusses prospects for cultivation of the economically-valuable rattan palm. Drs. Coradin and Lleras outline the present status of knowledge on native neotropical oil palms and their potential role in Latin America. Dr. Padoch focuses on the aguaje palm and its importance to the economy of Iquitos, Peru. Mr. Strudwick and Ms. Sobel also focus on a single palm, the açai palm, and discuss its use in the region around Belém, Brazil. Dr. Voeks discusses the harvest and management of a palm species greatly valued for its fiber, the piassava palm, in Brazil.

In the final section, on conservation, Dr. Johnson discusses some of the species studied by the other symposium participants and reports on the worldwide endangerment of useful palms.

As a group, the papers in this volume make several important points. Firstly, a great body of information has been generated through recent studies of palms. Contrary to the thinking of some, the lesser-known palms often play important and multiple roles in the local subsistence and commercial economies, as well as making contributions to the global economy. Improved management techniques and the implementation of conservation efforts are the only ways in which some of these palm genera can be saved from extinction forced through over-exploitation. Continued efforts in both basic and applied research on the biology and utilization of palms, as well as more intensive inventory and study of wild palm populations, are priorities for palm research in future years.

I thank all of the participants in the Symposium of the 1986 Annual Meeting of the Society for Economic Botany. The staff of the Institute of Economic Botany, as well as others on The New York Botanical Garden staff worked hard to ensure that this symposium could take place with a minimum of distraction. The Officers and Council of the Society for Economic Botany were very supportive of the idea of a symposium devoted to useful palms, and I am grateful to them for their help and cooperation. J. R. Brooks and Sons, Inc. was kind enough to provide the meeting participants with a selection of unusual tropical fruits to enjoy, an evening which gave many of us a chance to get to know each other a bit better. Drs. Maria Lebron-Luteyn and H. David Hammond of the Scientific Publications Department unselfishly offered their time to help guide me through the many phases of the production of this volume. As each paper was read by three reviewers, I owe my thanks to several dozen people who provided their help and constructive suggestions about the various manuscripts. Elizabeth Pecchia and Rosemary Lawlor tirelessly and without complaint plowed through the typing of several versions of many of the manuscripts. I thank Bobbi Angell for her magnificent drawing which is found on the cover. Finally, none of this would have been possible without the financial support to assemble, house and feed the symposium participants. For their generous support, I thank the World Wildlife Fund–U.S. and The New York Botanical Garden, as well as those individuals who found support from other sources or used personal funds. I thank Dr. Ghillean T. Prance for his invitation to convene this symposium. Last of all I thank my family for their understanding of the fact that so many nights and weekends had to be devoted to the planning, editing and production of this work.

Michael J. Balick
The New York Botanical Garden
4 June 1987

The Palm—Tree of Life:
Biology, Utilization and Conservation

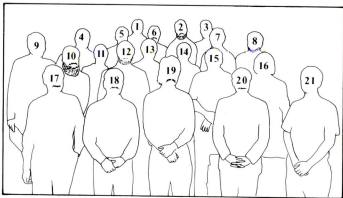

Participants

1. Kember Mejia C.
2. Charles R. Clement
3. Andrew Henderson
4. Jose López Parodi
5. Eduardo Lleras
6. Lidio Coradin
7. Anthony B. Anderson
8. David M. Bates
9. Francis Kahn
10. Jeremy Strudwick

11. Gail L. Sobel
12. Michael J. Balick
13. Natalie W. Uhl
14. Robert W. Read
15. T. Antony Davis
16. Christine Padoch
17. John Dransfield
18. Chandra Sekhar
19. Robert V. Voeks
20. Brian M. Boom
21. Theodore V. St. John

Not shown: Dennis V. Johnson
            Darleen A. DeMason

Genera Palmarum, a New Classification of Palms and Its Implications

NATALIE W. UHL AND JOHN DRANSFIELD

Table of Contents

Abstract

A new classification of palms recognizes 200 genera in six subfamilies: I Coryphoideae, 39 genera; II Calamoideae, 22 genera; III Nypoideae, 1 genus; IV Ceroxyloideae, 11 genera; V Arecoideae, 124 genera; and VI Phytelephantoideae, 3 genera. This reassessment results in 12 genera fewer than the most recent synopsis (Moore, 1973). Some genera are doubtfully distinct. Monographs are needed for more than 80; many of these, including *Phoenix, Borassus,* and *Bactris,* are of primary economic importance. It seems probable that the number of genera may vary somewhat and that the number of species will be further reduced. Fossils indicate that palms are one of the oldest recognizable modern families of monocotyledons, but fossil palms are still very inadequately known. The diversity of palm morphology is remarkable and when better understood seems likely to provide clues to relationships among monocotyledons as a whole. Ecologically palms are extremely varied; they provide excellent subjects for demographic and other studies, particularly those relating to little understood rain forest habitats. Joint appraisals of ecology and utilization are much needed. "Genera Palmarum" will provide a base for future work with newer methods, such as study of flavonoids, isozymes, DNA, and cladistic analyses. This paper includes a discussion of the subfamilies and keys to tribes and subtribes where they occur.

Key words: palms, taxonomy, classification, palm subfamilies, uses of palms

Resumen

Una nueva clasificación de palmas reconoce 200 géneros dentro de seis subfamilias: I Coryphoideae, 39 géneros; II Calamoideae, 22 géneros; III Nypoideae, 1 género; IV Ceroxyloideae, 11 géneros; V Arecoideae, 124 géneros; y VI Phytelephantoideae, 3 géneros. Esta reevaluación resulta en 12 géneros menos del sinopsis más reciente (Moore, 1973). Algunos géneros son dudosamente distintos. Se requieren monografías para más de 80; muchos de estos, incluse *Phoenix, Borassus,* y *Bactris* son de mayor importancia económica. Es probable que el número de géneros puede variar, y por lo tanto, la especie será reducida aún más. Los fósiles indican que las palmas son unas de las familias más viejas que se reconocen como monocotiledones modernos; sin embargo, los fósiles de palmas son muy desconocidos. La diversidad de la morfología de palmas es notable, y, cuando se entiende mejor, es probable que proveerá claves a las relaciones entre los monocotiledones de todas formas. Ecológicamente, las palmas son sumamente variadas. Proveen excelentes ejemplos para estudios demográficos y para otros estudios, particulamrente los que tienen relación con los habitates de las selvas tropicales pocas entendidas. Se requieren estudios entre la ecología y la utilización. "Genera Palmarum" será la base para trabajos en el futuro con nuevos métodos, tal como el estudio de flavonoides, isozimas, DNA, y análisises de clades. Este estudio incluye la discusión de las subfamilias y las claves a tribus y subtribus cuando ocurren.

Palabras claves: las palmas, la taxonomía, la clasificación, subfamilias de palmas, usos de palmas

---

I. Introduction

During the past four and a half years we have reassessed the genera of palms in order to develop a new classification which will be used to determine their arrangement in "Genera Palmarum, a Classification of Palms Based on the Work of Harold E. Moore, Jr." (Uhl & Dransfield, 1987). Recently we published (Dransfield & Uhl, 1986) an outline of the proposed classification, to validate new names and make them available for use before the publication of the book. In this paper we characterize the subfamilies, point out the position of economically important genera, and discuss the implications of the revised classification for future research.

The new system is based on the fifteen major groups of palms defined by Moore (1973). Moore felt that he lacked sufficient information to construct a formal hierarchy, consequently the major groups had no taxonomic status. However, he included a list of unspecialized vs. specialized characters and arranged the groups and the genera within them in order of specialization. The evolutionary sequences used by Moore and further elaborated by Moore and Uhl (1982) are the bases for the new classification.

II. The Subfamilies

The 200 genera are arranged in six subfamilies, which are very unequal with regard to the number of genera placed in them (Tables II–VII). We have made only one significant change in order from Moore's arrangement: Moore's group VI, the caryotoid palms, is now the first tribe in Subfamily V, Arecoideae (Table I). Three considerations were of primary importance in making this change. 1) Flowers in the caryotoid palms are borne in triads, as in all other genera of Arecoideae; 2) the induplicate nature of leaves in Caryoteae seems less significant now that an induplicate leaf (*Guihaia,* Dransfield et al., 1985)

has been discovered in Coryphoideae; 3) the Caryoteae share a number of characters with the Iriarteeae, the second tribe of Arecoideae.

Four characters are of primary importance in delimiting the subfamilies. These are 1) the form of the leaf: whether induplicate (Fig. 1A) or reduplicate (Fig. 3B), palmate, costapalmate, or pinnate, and if pinnate whether divided, bifid, or entire; 2) the number of peduncular bracts, i.e., the number of empty bracts between the prophyll and the first bract that subtends a branch on the main inflorescence axis (Fig. 2D); 3) the flower arrangement: either solitary, in monopodial clusters, or in cincinni (and, if a cincinnus, its form—dyad, triad, or acervulus); 4) the gynoecium, in particular the number and form of the carpels and whether they are apocarpous, syncarpous in various ways, or pseudomonomerous. Characters used to separate tribes and subtribes vary in different subfamilies and are discussed below.

Coryphoideae

Subfamily I, Coryphoideae (Table II), includes 39 subtropical and tropical genera divided into three tribes representing the coryphoid, borassoid, and phoenicoid palms of Moore (1973).

Key to the Tribes of the Coryphoideae

1. Leaves pinnate; basal leaflets modified as spines.
                                                    Phoeniceae.
1. Leaves palmate, costapalmate or entire; acanthophylls absent.
    2. Hermaphroditic, or polygamodioecious, rarely strictly dioecious; if dioecious, flowers not or only slightly dimorphic; rachillae lacking deep pits; endocarp usually thin, crustaceous or cartilaginous.   Corypheae.
    2. Dioecious; flowers usually strongly dimorphic; staminate and sometimes pistillate flowers borne in deep pits formed by connation and adnation of rachilla bracts; endocarp very thick and hard.   Borasseae.

Table I

Major groups formalized

Moore 1973	Position in hierarchy
Coryphoid	Coryphoideae — Corypheae
Borassoid	Coryphoideae — Borasseae
Phoenicoid	Coryphoideae — Phoeniceae
Caryotoid	Arecoideae — Caryoteae
Lepidocaryoid	Calamoideae
Nypoid	Nypoideae
Pseudophoenicoid	Ceroxyloideae — Cyclospatheae
Ceroxyloid	Ceroxyloideae — Ceroxyleae
Chamaedoreoid	Ceroxyloideae — Chamaedoreae
Iriarteoid	Arecoideae — Iriarteeae
Podococcoid	Arecoideae — Podococceae
Arecoid	Arecoideae — Areceae
Cocosoid	Arecoideae — Cocoeae
Geonomoid	Arecoideae — Geonomeae
Phytelephantoid	Phytelephantoideae

A palmate or costapalmate, induplicate leaf (Fig. 1A–C) characterizes all but six of the 39 genera in this subfamily. Exceptions are the induplicate but pinnate leaves of *Phoenix,* the entire leaves of *Johannesteijsmannia* and some species of *Licuala,* the palmate but reduplicate leaves of *Guihaia* (Dransfield et al., 1985), and anomalous splitting superimposed on a basic induplicate structure in leaves of *Rhapis, Rhapidophyllum,* and *Licuala.* We may further note that species in the subfamily have hermaphroditic flowers, or are dioecious, polygamodioecious, or polygamomonoecious, but never monoecious.

The first tribe, Corypheae, contains 31 genera and is divided into four subtribes on the structure of the gynoecium. As the key shows, in Thrinacinae, the carpels are distinct; in Livistoninae, joined by the styles only; in Coryphinae, joined by their bases; and in Sabalinae, united throughout with a single stylar canal.

Key to the Subtribes of the Corypheae

1. Carpels distinct, usually 3 (1–4).   Thrinacinae.
1. Carpels connate, 3.
   2. Carpels basally distinct, united by their styles only.   Livistoninae.
   2. Carpels united basally or throughout.
      3. Carpels united basally, styles free or united, if united then with ±separate stylar canals.   Coryphinae.
      3. Carpels united throughout, with a common stylar canal.   Sabalinae.

The genera of this tribe are of particular importance for two reasons. First, they are of primary interest in evolutionary studies because they include the least specialized palm genera. The flower structure corresponds to that considered basic for monocotyledons as a whole. Flowers are largely trimerous with three sepals, three petals, six stamens in two whorls, and three separate carpels. The carpels are follicular and some have open ventral sutures, thus resembling unspecialized carpels in dicotyledons and other monocotyledons (Uhl & Moore, 1971).

These 31 genera are also of special interest because they exhibit many of the evolutionary trends that also occur independently elsewhere in the family. Variations in leaf form have been noted above. Inflorescences show a reduction series from highly branched to spicate, shoots are hapaxanthic or pleonanthic (see Fig. 1B, C), flowers bisexual or unisexual, perianth parts vary from being all similar, to clearly differentiated into sepals and petals, or with parts united into a single cupule. Stamens have increased from six to many (Uhl & Moore, 1980), carpel number varies from three to one or to more than three, and carpels are free to variously connate.

The second tribe, Phoeniceae, includes the single genus *Phoenix,* distinguished by its unique induplicate but pinnate leaf. *Phoenix,* although dioecious, has apocarpous pistillate flowers which, as also do the staminate, strongly resemble flowers of Thrinacinae in form.

The genera of the third tribe, Borasseae, are

FIG. 1.   Characteristics of the subfamilies. A, *Maxburretia rupicola* (Coryphoideae: Corypheae), note palmate leaf with induplicate (V-shaped) leaflets; B, *Corypha umbraculifera* (Coryphoideae: Corypheae), showing hapaxanthic flowering; C, *Bismarckia nobilis* (Coryphoideae: Borasseae), costapalmate leaf, interfoliar inflorescences (pleonanthic flowering); D, Scaly fruits of *Ceratolobus subangulatus* (Calamoideae: Calameae). Credits: A, D, J. Dransfield; B, W. H. Hodge; C, N. W. Uhl.

FIG. 2. Characteristics of the subfamilies cont. A, *Nypa fruticans* (Nypoideae) showing prostrate stem and erect leaves; B, Same, inflorescence, lateral staminate branches with flowers in bloom, arrow indicating the central pistillate head; C, A bifid leaf of *Chamaedorea brachypoda* (Ceroxyloideae: Hyophorbeae); D, Inflorescence of *Caryota* sp. showing several empty bracts on the peduncle (peduncular bracts). Credits: A, B, C, W. H. Hodge; D, H. E. Moore, Jr.

FIG. 3.   Characteristics of the subfamilies cont. A, *Wodyetia bifurcata* (Arecoideae: Areceae), note lack of bracts within the inflorescence; B, ?*Attalea guaranitica,* note pinnate leaf with reduplicate (tent-shaped) leaflets; C, *Phytelephas macrocarpa* (Phytelephantoideae), staminate tree with inflorescences; D, The strange staminate inflorescence of *Ammandra decasperma,* irregular units are floral receptacles bearing small stamens (Phytele- phantoideae). Credits: A, A. K. Irvine; B, C, W. H. Hodge; D, J. Dransfield.

Table II

Order: Principes. Family: Palmae (conserved name) or Arecaceae (conserved alternative name)

Subfamily I. Coryphoideae

Family: Palmae (conserved name) or Arecaceae (conserved alternative name for the family).

Corypheae

Thrinacinae

1. *Trithrinax* (5) thatch, wood, fruits edible, oil from seeds
2. *Chelyocarpus* (3)
3. *Cryosophila* (8 or less) ornamentals
4. *Itaya* (1) ornamental possibilities
5. *Schippia* (1) rare ornamental
6. *Thrinax* (4) thatch, basketry, ornamentals, posts
7. *Coccothrinax* (49) thatch, brooms, basketry, hats, ornamentals, poles, rope
8. *Zombia* (1) fruits fed to pigs, ornamental
9. *Trachycarpus* (6) wood, fiber, medicines, ornamentals
10. *Rhapidophyllum* (1) ornamental
11. *Chamaerops* (1) fiber, ornamental
12. *Maxburretia* (3)
13. *Guihaia* (1) ornamental possibilities
14. *Rhapis* (12) wood, important ornamentals

Livistoninae

15. *Livistona* (28) wood, thatch, fiber, ornamentals
16. *Pholidocarpus* (6) thatch
17. *Johannesteijsmannia* (4) shelters, thatch
18. *Licuala* (108) thatch, fiber, wood, pith and cabbage edible
19. *Pritchardiopsis* (1) cabbage
20. *Pritchardia* (37 or fewer) leaves for fans and umbrellas
21. *Colpothrinax* (2–more) wood, thatch, inflorescence eaten like pacaya, fruit eaten by pigs
22. *Acoelorraphe* (1) ornamental
23. *Serenoa* (1) ornamental, wax, decoration
24. *Brahea* (16) thatch, fiber, fruits of some edible, ornamentals
25. *Copernicia* (25) thatch, wood, fiber, starch, wax
26. *Washingtonia* (2) ornamentals

Coryphinae

27. *Corypha* (8) thatch, umbrellas, buckets, starch, paper
28. *Nannorrhops* (1) fiber
29. *Chuniophoenix* (3) ornamentals
30. *Kerriodoxa* (1) ornamental

Sabalinae

31. *Sabal* (14) brooms, thatch, ornamentals, Palm Sunday fronds, wood

Phoeniceae

32. *Phoenix* (17) fruit, wood, fiber, and many others

Borasseae

Lataniinae

33. *Borassodendron* (2) cabbage
34. *Latania* (3) wood, thatch, seeds edible, ornamentals
35. *Borassus* (5) wine, syrup, sugar, alcohol, wood, thatch, buckets, baskets, etc.
36. *Lodoicea* (1) thatch, fiber, wood, vegetable ivory, seeds and plants ornamental

Hyphaeninae

37. *Hyphaene* (10) wood, thatch, fiber, wine, fruits edible
38. *Medemia* (1) uses as *Hyphaene*
39. *Bismarckia* (1) wood, thatch, sago

---

[1] In Tables II–VII, the first number refers to genera and the second in parentheses to the approximate number of species. Only the most important uses are listed.

also dioecious. The often large palmate and cos-tapalmate leaves (Fig. 1C) place this tribe in the Coryphoideae. Inflorescences and flowers are specialized with respect to others in the family. The subtribes are separated partly on inflorescence structure. In Hyphaeninae both staminate and pistillate flowers are sunken in pits; in Lataniinae only the staminate flowers are in pits and the genera have an unusual endocarp—large pyrenes (seedlike bodies), formed by the endocarp around the locule of each carpel, enclose the seeds. Flowers are large and structurally complex but show certain similarities to those of Corypheae (Uhl & Moore, 1971). The largest flower in palms, the pistillate flower of *Lodoicea maldivica* belongs here. The pistillate flowers of the tribe often have extremely leathery perianth parts and gynoecia with thick, histologically complex walls. Staminate flowers are exserted from the pits by a remarkable elongation of their receptacles.

Most of the 39 genera of Coryphoideae are valuable as ornamentals. *Chamaerops humilis,* the European fan palm, various cultivars of *Rhapis humilis* (see McKamey, 1983), and several species of *Livistona* are widely grown. *Corypha,* the Talipot palm, is renowned as possessing the largest known inflorescence, estimated to bear ten million flowers (Tomlinson & Soderholm, 1975), and *Lodoicea,* the double coconut, produces the largest known seed. Several other genera are of primary economic importance. *Copernicia prunifera* is the source of carnauba wax. *Phoenix dactylifera,* the date palm, has been known and utilized since antiquity (Johnson, 1983, 1984). *Borassus flabellifer* is important in many areas as a source of sap for sugar and wine and for many other products. Other uses of these palms are listed in Table II.

CALAMOIDEAE

Subfamily II, Calamoideae (Table III), was previously known as Lepidocaryoideae. However, Griffith's (1844) use of "Calamoideae" predates any usage of "Lepidocaryoideae" as a subfamily name. The Calamoideae includes 22 genera long recognized as related because of their scaly fruits (Fig. 1D). The scales develop on the gynoecium and at anthesis provide a tough distal layer that appears to provide protection for the ovules (Uhl & Moore, 1973). The scales represent one of several derived characters that members of the subfamily have in common. Flowers are borne in dyads, sympodial pairs that differ in flower and bract form from the dyads in other Palmae. Bracts, including floral bracteoles, are predominantly tubular in the subfamily. The perianth is distinctive—sepals of flowers are united in a tube and the valvate petals are also often connate. The gynoecium is unique, consisting of three laterally connate carpels with open ventral sutures (Uhl & Dransfield, 1984). Each carpel bears an anatropous ovule which becomes turned inwardly during ontogeny, the micropyles of the three ovules facing the center of the gynoecium at anthesis.

Variation among the genera in the Calamoideae occurs in leaf form, mode of flowering, inflorescence structure, and dyad composition. The two tribes are separated on the basis of leaf structure. The three genera of Lepidocaryeae have palmate but reduplicate leaves, a form found elsewhere in the family only in *Guihaia* (Coryphoideae). Various pinnate forms occur in Calameae which includes 19 genera divided into eight subtribes distinguished by variations in habit, hapaxanthic or pleonanthic shoots, and the sexuality of the flowers comprising each dyad.

Key to the Tribes of the Calamoideae

1. Leaves pinnate or pinnately ribbed; Old World palms (except for one species of *Raphia*).   Calameae.
1. Leaves palmate or briefly costapalmate; New World palms.   Lepidocaryeae.

Key to the Subtribes of the Calameae

1. Flower group consisting of a dyad of hermaphroditic flowers.   Ancistrophyllinae.
1. Flower group not consisting of a dyad of hermaphroditic flowers.
    2. Rachillae catkinlike, bearing either dyads of a hermaphroditic and a staminate flower, or single hermaphroditic flowers.   Metroxylinae.
    2. Rachillae usually not catkinlike (if so then hermaphroditic flowers lacking).

Table III

Subfamily II. Calamoideae 22 (653)

Calameae

Ancistrophyllinae

40. *Laccosperma* (7) cane
41. *Eremospatha* (12) cane

Eugeissoninae

42. *Eugeissona* (6) wood, thatch, sago, endosperm edible

Metroxylinae

43. *Metroxylon* (8) sago, thatch, wood
44. *Korthalsia* (26) cane but has large nodal scars

Calamineae

45. *Eleiodoxa* (1) thatch, sarcotesta sour but edible
46. *Salacca* (15) fruit, thatch, wood
47. *Daemonorops* (15) canes, cabbage
48. *Calamus* (370) canes are the finest, thatch, other items, fruits, medicines
49. *Calospatha* (1) fruit
50. *Pogonotium* (3) rare ornamentals
51. *Ceratolobus* (6) canes weak not used
52. *Retispatha* (1)

Plectocomiinae

53. *Myrialepis* (1) basketry
54. *Plectocomiopsis* (5) cabbage, basketry
55. *Plectocomia* (16) basketry, ornamentation

Pigafettinae

56. *Pigafetta* (1) wood, ornamental

Raphiinae

57. *Raphia* (28 or less) wine, oil, cabbage and seed eaten, fiber, wood, fruits

Oncocalaminae

58. *Oncocalamus* (5) probably cane

Lepidocaryeae

59. *Mauritia* (3) wood, fiber, cork, cabbage, oil, starch
60. *Mauritiella* (14) thatch, fruit
61. *Lepidocaryum* (9) thatch

---

3. Polygamous palms, rachillae bearing single, apparently terminal dyads, each consisting of a hermaphroditic and a staminate flower, but only one flower evident at a time; stamens 20–70; fruit large with very small irregular scales and a thick endocarp with 6 or 12 internal ridges.
   Eugeissoninae.
3. Monoecious or dioecious palms; rachillae various; stamens 6 except in *Raphia* where 6–30; fruit usually with regular scales and lacking an endocarp.
   4. Monoecious palms.
      5. Climbing palm bearing cirri with acanthophylls; rachilla bracts subtending groups of 3–11 flowers, the central pistillate, with two lateral cincinni bearing 0–1 basal pistillate flowers and several distal staminate flowers.
      Oncocalaminae.
      5. Massive acaulescent or tree palms; rachilla bracts subtending solitary flowers, the basal pistillate, the distal staminate.
      Raphiinae.
   4. Dioecious palms.
      6. Pleonanthic, solitary, very tall tree palm; rachillae with minute bracts, in the staminate subtending a dyad of flowers, in the pistillate, solitary flowers.
      Pigafettinae.
      6. Pleonanthic or hapaxanthic, acaulescent, shrubby or climbing palms; rachillae usually with conspicuous bracts.
         7. Hapaxanthic climbing palms, bracts of staminate rachillae subtending paired or solitary flowers, in pistillate rachillae solitary flowers only.
         Plectocomiinae.

7. Hapaxanthic (very rarely and then sterile staminate flowers present) or pleonanthic, climbing or acaulescent palms; staminate inflorescence with paired or solitary flowers; pistillate inflorescence bearing dyads of sterile staminate and pistillate flowers (except in *Salacca* section *Leiosalacca* and *Retispatha* where sterile staminate flower lacking).

Calaminae.

The genera economically most valuable in this subfamily are the rattans including twelve genera: *Oncocalamus, Korthalsia, Laccosperma, Eremospatha, Daemonorops, Calamus, Calospatha, Ceratolobus, Retispatha, Myrialepis, Plectocomiopsis,* and *Plectocomia* (Dransfield, 1979, 1984). *Calamus* is the most important commercially. Several other genera have a wide range of local uses, such as *Metroxylon* and *Eugeissona,* primary sources of sago, *Raphia* which provides fiber and several other products (Table III), and *Salacca* and *Eleiodoxa,* both sources of edible fruits.

NYPOIDEAE

Subfamily III, Nypoideae (Table IV), includes one monotypic genus, the mangrove palm, *Nypa fructicans* (Fig. 2A), which is the earliest known genus of modern palms and one of the first recognizable genera of monocotyledons in the fossil record. Pollen and megafossils of *Nypa* occur in the mid to upper Cretaceous (Daghlian, 1981). *Nypa* differs from all other palms in several characters: in a prostrate, dichotomously branching stem, in an inflorescence with the main axis terminating in a head of pistillate flowers and lateral branches in condensed staminate spikes (Fig. 2B), in similar distinct perianth members in both staminate and pistillate flowers, in having only three stamens united by their filaments, in the cupular form of the three carpels, and in the lack of staminodes and pistillodes (Uhl, 1972).

No characters have yet been found which relate *Nypa* to any other group of palms. The pinnate leaf resembles those of some genera in other subfamilies (except Coryphoideae where leaves are predominantly palmate). The presence on the main inflorescence axis of a prophyll and one peduncular bract is like some genera of Arecoideae, but unlike those genera, other bracts in the inflorescence are fully developed in *Nypa,* a situation paralleled in Calamoideae.

Nypa has a multiplicity of uses (Table IV; Brown & Merrill, 1919; Burkill, 1966). Leaves are an important source of thatch and are of minor value for such things as cigarette papers and fishing floats. Tapping inflorescences yields sugar and alcohol. The large potential of the genus as a stabilizer of estuarine mud and preventer of coastal erosion is also noteworthy.

CEROXYLOIDEAE

Subfamily IV, Ceroxyloideae (Table V), includes 11 genera comprising three tribes. Members of the subfamily are tall or moderate to small, solitary or clustered, and have pinnately divided, bifid, or entire and pinnately veined leaves. Inflorescences bear several peduncular bracts, except for *Wendlandiella* which has only one. One genus, *Pseudophoenix,* the sole member of tribe Cyclospatheae, has hermaphroditic flowers. The other ten genera are monoecious or dioecious, but the staminate and pistillate flowers differ only slightly from each other. The flowers are solitary and spirally arranged or if they are in clusters, flowers are in a linear series with only the proximal flower pistillate, an arrangement termed an acervulus, a form of cincinnus not found elsewhere in the family (Uhl & Moore, 1978). The five genera of Ceroxyleae lack a crownshaft (an apparent extension of the stem formed by tubular bases of the leaf sheaths), are dioecious, and the solitary flowers are open from early in development. Genera of the Hyophorbeae are monoecious or dioecious, with or without crownshafts, and flowers are often in acervuli and are closed in bud. All genera in the subfamily have a rounded, syncarpous, tricarpellate gynoecium with pendulous or laterally attached ovules.

Table IV
Subfamily III. Nypoideae 1 (1)

62. *Nypa* (1) thatch, fiber, sugar, alcohol, salt

Table V

Subfamily IV. Ceroxyloideae 11 (151)

Cyclospatheae
    63. *Pseudophoenix* (4) thatch, fruit for animal food, wine, ornamentals

Ceroxyleae
    64. *Ceroxylon* (20) wax, fruit for cattle food
    65. *Oraniopsis* (1) ornamental
    66. *Juania* (1) cabbage, wood
    67. *Louvelia* (3) cabbage
    68. *Ravenea* (10) cabbage of some, wood, sago

Hyophorbeae
    69. *Gaussia* (4) uncommon ornamentals
    70. *Hyophorbe* (5) important ornamentals
    71. *Synechanthus* (2–3) uncommon also ornamental
    72. *Chamaedorea* (100) inflorescences of some edible, thatch, major ornamentals
    73. *Wendlandiella* (3) rare ornamental

Key to the Tribes of the Ceroxyloideae

1. Proximal flowers on the rachillae bisexual, the distal usually smaller and staminate, all borne on long stalks.   Cyclospatheae.
1. All flowers unisexual, if stalked, then usually briefly so.
    2. Dioecious palms; crownshafts not formed; flowers borne singly on short, usually bracteolate pedicels; flowers open from early in development, the stamens equalling or exceeding the petals.   Ceroxyleae.
    2. Monoecious or dioecious palms; crownshafts present or absent; flowers sessile, usually ebracteolate at anthesis, borne singly or in acervuli of a pistillate and 2 to several staminate, or in lines of staminate flowers, or rarely pistillate flowers (*Wendlandiella*); stamens included within the staminate flower until or sometimes at anthesis. Hyophorbeae.

The Ceroxyloideae have many uses (Table V). *Pseudophoenix* fruits are fed to pigs and trunks used for wood. Species of *Ceroxylon,* an Andean genus, provide wax for candles and matches and the fruits are important as animal food. The apex of *Juania* is edible and the wood has been used for carving, furniture, and other things. *Ravenea* is a source of sago and wood. *Hyophorbe* and *Chamaedorea* are both important ornamentals. *Chamaedorea* (Fig. 2C) is widely grown commercially as a pot plant.

ARECOIDEAE

Nearly two-thirds of the genera and more than half the species of palms belong to the fifth subfamily, the Arecoideae (Table VI). In forming the subfamily we have added the caryotoid palms (Moore, 1973) to five other major groups: the iriarteoid, podococcoid, arecoid, cocosoid, and geonomoid palms (Table I). The resulting 124 genera are characterized by a unique flower cluster, the triad, a cincinnus of two lateral staminate flowers and a central pistillate flower (see Moore & Uhl, 1982 for variations of the triad). The Arecoideae also have pinnate leaves which are reduplicate except in the three genera of Caryoteae where leaves are induplicate. Members of the subfamily are also characterized by inflorescences with a prophyll and one or several peduncular bracts (Fig. 2D) but no adnation of branches. Bracts are reduced elsewhere throughout the inflorescence (Fig. 3A).

Key to the Tribes of the Arecoideae

1. Palms frequently hapaxanthic with basipetal production of inflorescences; leaves pinnate, or doubly pinnate, induplicate, leaflets praemorse; inflorescences bisexual or unisexual by reduction of triads.
    Caryoteae.
1. Palms never hapaxanthic; leaves pinnate or pinnately ribbed, reduplicate, the leaflets various, sometimes praemorse; inflorescences rarely unisexual.

Table VI

Subfamily V. Arecoideae 124 (1466)

Caryoteae
    74. *Arenga* (17) sugar, wine, sago, thatch, fiber, and other products
    75. *Caryota* (12) cabbage, sago, wine, sugar, ornamentals
    76. *Wallichia* (7) thatch, sago

Iriarteeae
  Iriarteinae
    77. *Dictyocaryum* (1–2)
    78. *Iriartella* (2) wood, medicine
    79. *Iriartea* (7) wood, medicine
    80. *Socratea* (12) wood

  Wettiniinae
    81. *Catoblastus* (17) wood
    82. *Wettinia* (9) wood, thatch

Podococceae
    83. *Podococcus* (1)

Areceae
  Oraniinae
    84. *Halmoorea* (1)
    85. *Orania* (17) cabbage, wood

  Manicariinae
    86. *Manicaria* (4) food, wood, medicine, hats, bags

  Leopoldiniinae
    87. *Leopoldinia* (4) thatch, fiber, fruits edible

  Malortieinae
    88. *Reinhardtia* (5) ornamental

  Dypsidinae
    89. *Vonitra* (4) cabbage, fiber, fruit edible
    90. *Chrysalidocarpus* (20) cabbage of some, ornamentals
    91. *Neophloga* (29) ornamentals
    92. *Neodypsis* (14) cabbage, ornamentals
    93. *Phloga* (2) ornamentals
    94. *Dypsis* (21) ornamentals

  Euterpeinae
    95. *Euterpe* (28) wood, thatch, cabbage, fruits
    96. *Prestoea* (28) cabbage, thatch, ornamentals
    97. *Neonicholsonia* (1)
    98. *Oenocarpus* (8) cabbage, oil, wood
    99. *Jessenia* (1) cabbage, oil, fruit, thatch, wood
    100. *Hyospathe* (17) ornamentals

  Roystoneinae
    101. *Roystonea* (10–12) cabbage, fruits for pig food, thatch, wood, ornamentals

  Archontophoenicinae
    102. *Archontophoenix* (2) ornamentals
    103. *Chambeyronia* (2) ornamentals
    104. *Hedyscepe* (1) ornamental
    105. *Rhopalostylis* (3) ornamentals
    106. *Kentiopsis* (1) ornamental
    107. *Mackeea* (1) ornamental
    108. *Actinokentia* (2) ornamental

  Cyrtostachydinae
    109. *Cyrtostachys* (8) ornamentals, wood

TABLE VI
Continued

Linospadicinae

    110. *Calyptrocalyx* (38) rarely as ornamentals
    111. *Linospadix* (11) wood, cabbage, mesocarp eaten
    112. *Laccospadix* (1) ornamental (rare)
    113. *Howea* (2) important ornamentals

Ptychospermatinae

    114. *Drymophloeus* (15) wood, ornamentals
    115. *Carpentaria* (1) important ornamentals
    116. *Veitchia* (18) ornamentals
    117. *Balaka* (7) walking sticks, spears, ornamentals, kernel edible
    118. *Normanbya* (1) wood
    119. *Wodyetia* (1) ornamental
    120. *Ptychosperma* (28) ornamentals, wood
    121. *Ptychococcus* (7) wood, edible seeds
    122. *Brassiophoenix* (2) ornamentals

Arecinae. Type: Areca.

    123. *Loxococcus* (1) seed chewed
    124. *Gronophyllum* (33) wood
    125. *Siphokentia* (2) ornamentals
    126. *Hydriastele* (8) ornamentals, wood
    127. *Gulubia* (9) wood, ornamentals
    128. *Nenga* (5) wood, ornamentals
    129. *Pinanga* (120) wood, seeds chewed, ornamentals
    130. *Areca* (60) endosperm a stimulant, tannin, cabbage, weaving, ornamentals

Iguanurinae

    131. *Neoveitchia* (1) wood, fruit
    132. *Pelagodoxa* (1) endosperm eaten, wood
    133. *Iguanura* (18) minor uses as temporary shelters
    134. *Brongniartikentia* (2)
    135. *Lepidorrhachis* (1) ornamental
    136. *Heterospathe* (32) cabbage, fruit chewed, petioles and leaflets for fiber
    137. *Sommieria* (3) rare ornamentals
    138. *Bentinckia* (2) ornamentals
    139. *Clinosperma* (1)
    140. *Cyphokentia* (1)
    141. *Moratia* (1)
    142. *Clinostigma* (13) ornamentals, wood
    143. *Alsmithia* (1)
    144. *Satakentia* (1) ornamentals
    145. *Rhopaloblaste* (6) ornamentals
    146. *Dictyosperma* (1) ornamental
    147. *Actinorhytis* (2) ornamental, medicinal
    148. *Lavoixia* (1)
    149. *Alloschmidia* (1)
    150. *Cyphophoenix* (2)
    151. *Campecarpus* (1)
    152. *Basselinia* (11) rare ornamentals
    153. *Cyphosperma* (3)
    154. *Veillonia* (1)
    155. *Burretiokentia* (2)
    156. *Physokentia* (7)
    157. *Goniocladus* (1)

Oncospermatinae

    158. *Deckenia* (1) cabbage, fiber
    159. *Acanthophoenix* (1) cabbage
    160. *Oncosperma* (5) cabbage, wood, fiber, ornamentals

TABLE VI

Continued

161. *Tectiphiala* (1) cabbage
162. *Verschaffeltia* (1) wood, ornamental
163. *Roscheria* (1) ornamental
164. *Phoenicophorium* (1) ornamental
165. *Nephrosperma* (1) rare ornamental

Sclerospermatinae

166. *Sclerosperma* (3) thatch, seeds eaten
167. *Marojejya* (2)

Areceae incertae sedis

168. *Masoala* (1)
169. *Carpoxylon* (1)

Cocoeae

Beccariophoenicinae

170. *Beccariophoenix* (1) hat making

Butiinae

171. *Butia* (8) jelly, ornamentals
172. *Jubaea* (1) wine and sugar, ornamental
173. *Jubaeopsis* (1) ornamental, endosperm eaten
174. *Cocos* (1) copra, coir, and many other uses
175. *Syagrus* (32) thatch, wood, wax, edible fruits and seeds, ornamentals
176. *Lytocaryum* (3) ornamentals
177. *Parajubaea* (2) oil from seed, edible fruit
178. *Allagoptera* (5)
179. *Polyandrococos* (2) ornamentals

Attaleinae

180. *Attalea* (22) oil, medicine, and many other products as fiber, thatch, wood
181. *Scheelea* (28) as 180
182. *Orbignya* (20) as 180, wine from terminal bud
183. *Maximiliana* (1) edible fruit, oil from seeds, thatch, basketry

Elaeidinae

184. *Barcella* (1) wood
185. *Elaeis* (2) oil, wine, thatch, wood

Bactridinae

186. *Acrocomia* (26) fiber, fruits for oil and food, medicines
187. *Gastrococos* (1) oil, brooms, rope
188. *Aiphanes* (38) fruit edible, ornamentals
189. *Bactris* (239) fruit edible in some, cabbage, fiber, wood
190. *Desmoncus* (61) fiber, wood
191. *Astrocaryum* (47) fiber, cabbage, fruit for cattle food, oil

Geonomeae

192. *Pholidostachys* (3)
193. *Welfia* (2?) thatch
194. *Calyptronoma* (3+) thatch, fruits for fodder
195. *Calyptrogyne* (5)
196. *Asterogyne* (4) thatch
197. *Geonoma* (75) thatch, ornamentals

2. Leaflets praemorse at the tips and with several principal ribs divergent from the base, or leaflets sometimes divided longitudinally into 1–several ribbed parts; inflorescence with a prophyll and more than 2 large peduncular bracts.

3. Inflorescence rarely spicate, usually branched to 1–2 orders; flowers sessile, not sunken in pits.

Iriarteeae.

      3. Inflorescence spicate; flowers sunken in pits and exserted at anthesis on elongate receptacles.
                                                              Podococceae.
   2. Leaflets usually acute, or if praemorse or longitudinally divided, the inflorescence with a prophyll and (0) 1 (2) large peduncular bracts.
      4. Flowers always sunken in pits in the rachillae; petals of both staminate and pistillate flowers connate basally in a soft tube, the lobes valvate, styles elongate, conspicuous.   Geonomeae.
      4. Flowers usually superficial, rarely enclosed in pits; petals of staminate flowers free and valvate; pistillate petals imbricate with minutely to conspicuously valvate apices, rarely basally connate or valvate, styles not elongate.
         5. Gynoecium usually pseudomonomerous, only very rarely triovulate, when triovulate, the fruit rarely more than 1-seeded, if so then fruit lobed; fruit with a thin or rarely thick endocarp, sometimes with a basal operculum but lacking 3 or more pores.   Areceae.
         5. Gynoecium trilocular, triovulate, the fruit never lobed; fruit almost always with a thick bony endocarp enclosing 1–3, rarely more, seeds and with 3, or rarely more, clearly defined pores.
                                                              Cocoeae.

The first tribe, Caryoteae, is distinguished by induplicate, praemorse leaflets, and by doubly pinnate leaves in one genus (*Caryota*). Hapaxanthic shoots (see Fig. 1B) also occur in the Caryoteae. Members of the second tribe, Iriarteeae, have stilt roots and reduplicate praemorse leaflets, with leaves secondarily divided by longitudinal splitting of the primary leaflets in some genera. These two tribes share several characters—multiple inflorescences in some genera, numerous peduncular bracts, praemorse leaflets, and secondary division in the leaves—and seem more closely related to each other than to the other tribes. Of the two subtribes of Iriarteeae, Iriarteinae have solitary inflorescences and apical styles, and Wettiniinae multiple inflorescences and basal styles.

Key to the Subtribes of the Iriarteeae

1. Inflorescences solitary, bisexual; gynoecium with apical styles and stigmas.   Iriarteinae.
1. Inflorescences multiple, rarely solitary by abortion, usually unisexual; gynoecium with basal styles and stigmas.   Wettiniinae.

The third tribe, Podococceae, includes only the monotypic genus, *Podococcus*, which on the basis of leaf structure seems related to Iriarteeae, but the inflorescence has pits enclosing flowers structurally different from those of Iriarteeae, and there are also differences in fruit structure.

The largest tribe, Areceae, with 84 genera, is divided into 15 subtribes. Except for the five genera comprising the first five subtribes, all Areceae are pseudomonomerous, having gynoecia in which only one carpel is fertile, bearing an often large ovule, but parts of the other two carpels, usually the styles and stigmas and sometimes vestigial locules, are present.

The first four subtribes of Areceae include the five triovulate genera whose relationships are not clear at present. The position of these genera seems likely to change as more information accrues. Relationships of the remaining 11, pseudomonomerous subtribes are also not fully understood. The following key will show the identifying characters of the subtribes.

Key to the Subtribes of the Areceae

1. Gynoecium triovulate.
   2. Leaf very large, undivided, or irregularly divided; inflorescence at anthesis entirely enclosed by a netlike prophyll and peduncular bract; fruit corky warted.   Manicariinae.
   2. Leaf pinnate or if entire rather small; inflorescence not enclosed by prophyll and peduncular bract at anthesis; fruit smooth.
      3. Prophyll very much smaller than peduncular bract(s), usually obscured by the leaf sheaths; peduncular bracts large, woody, usually beaked.   Oraniinae.
      3. Prophyll and peduncular bract similar; peduncular bract membranous or coriaceous but scarcely woody, not conspicuously beaked.
         4. Moderate palms with stems obscured by sheath fibers; inflorescence with numerous spreading branches of up to the 4th order; staminate flowers rounded with 6 stamens; fruit lenticular or ovoid, stigmatic remains basal.   Leopoldiniinae.
         4. Diminutive to moderate palms with slender stems not obscured by sheath fibers; inflo-

rescence spicate, or with few ±approximate branches of 1, rarely 2 orders; staminate flowers pointed with 8–40 stamens; fruit ovoid to ellipsoidal, stigmatic remains apical.

Malortieinae.

1. Gynoecium pseudomonomerous, rarely 2 abortive carpels present.
   5. Endocarp with a well defined operculum covering the embryo.
      6. Spines present, at least in juvenile stages.   Oncospermatinae.
      6. Spines absent.   Iguanurinae.
   5. Endocarp lacking a well defined operculum.
      7. Petals of pistillate flower connate; staminodes connate in a cupule adnate to the petals.

Roystoneinae.

      7. Petals of pistillate flower free, imbricate, very rarely connate (*Siphokentia*); staminodes tooth-like, not forming a cupule.
         8. Leaf large, bifid or irregularly divided; inflorescence spicate or branched to 1 order, congested, bearing 1 large complete and 2–several small, incomplete peduncular bracts; staminate sepals narrow, separated in bud.   Sclerospermatinae.
         8. Leaves various; inflorescence usually lacking incomplete peduncular bracts, variously branched, congested or not; staminate sepals imbricate, valvate, or connate, not widely separate.
            9. Flowers borne in pits or depressions in long pedunculate, interfoliar spikes, spikes solitary or several together in a leaf axil; staminate flowers symmetrical or nearly so; sepals rounded, broadly imbricate; stigmatic remains apical.   Linospadicinae.
            9. Flowers superficial or if in pits, inflorescence branched, infrafoliar; flowers symmetrical or asymmetrical; sepals various; stigmatic remains various.
               10. Flowers borne in pits with prominent, rounded lips; inflorescence infrafoliar, branched to 3 orders; peduncle very short; basal branches sharply divaricate; crownshaft well developed.   Cyrtostachydinae.
               10. Flowers not borne in pits or if so, then staminate flower with acute sepals and/ or fruit with lateral stigmatic remains and the inflorescence branching to 1 order only; inflorescence infra- or interfoliar, branched to several orders, rarely spicate, peduncle short to moderate; basal branches not sharply divaricate; crownshaft present or absent.
                  11. Staminate flowers strictly symmetrical, rounded or bullet-shaped.
                     12. Leaflet tips almost always entire; inflorescences usually interfoliar, spicate or branched up to 4 orders; staminate flowers often very small, ±rounded apically in bud with sepals nearly half as long as the petals in bud; stamens 6 or 3; gynoecium often trilocular but uniovulate; stigmatic remains basal.   Dypsidinae.
                     12. Leaflet tips praemorse; inflorescence infrafoliar, branched to 4 orders; staminate flowers moderate, bullet-shaped in bud with sepals less than half as long as the petals; stamens numerous; gynoecium unilocular; stigmatic remains apical.   Ptychospermatinae.
                  11. Staminate flowers usually asymmetrical, if symmetrical then inflorescence bracts 1 only, or staminate flower not rounded or bullet-shaped.
                     13. Inflorescence branched to 1 order, sometimes hippuriform, rarely spicate, peduncular bract slightly to markedly exserted from the prophyll; staminate flower usually with filaments markedly inflexed; stigmatic remains apical, basal, or lateral. New World.   Euterpeinae.
                     13. Inflorescence spicate or branched to 3 orders, peduncular bract if present not exserted from the prophyll; staminate flowers with filaments inflexed or not; stigmatic remains always apical. Old World.
                        14. Inflorescence branches either bearing a prophyll only or, if also bearing a peduncular bract, triads usually borne along the entire length of the rachilla (except *Loxococcus*), branches usually not widely spreading, rachillae straight, scarcely zigzag, not irregularly angled; flowers borne spirally, distichously, or in whorls, or on one side of the rachilla only; staminate flowers usually more or less 3 times as long as the pistillate or more when inflorescence bract(s) open, if not then peduncular bract lacking.   Arecinae.
                        14. Inflorescence always bearing a prophyll and a peduncular bract, branches spreading widely, sometimes pendulous, rachillae usually distinctly zigzag, irregularly angled, flowers spirally inserted; staminate flowers only slightly larger than the pistillate when bracts open.   Archontophoenicinae.

Table VII
Subfamily VI. Phytelephantoideae 3 (14)

198. *Palandra* (1) vegetable ivory
199. *Phytelephas* (12) vegetable ivory, thatch, immmature fruits and seeds edible
200. *Ammandra* (1–2) vegetable ivory

The distinguishing character of the fifth tribe, Cocoeae, is the presence in the hard endocarp of three or rarely more pores. Two bracts are predominant on the inflorescence; the prophyll is usually rather small but the peduncular bract is usually large, often woody, and sometimes cowl-like. Flowers of this tribe resemble those of many Areceae but the gynoecium in Cocoeae always has three or rarely more carpels. The tribe is divided into five subtribes. Four of these are distinguished by inflorescence characters. In Beccariophoenicinae the peduncular bract is borne at the tip of the peduncle and appears to be deciduous at anthesis. The peduncular bract is fibrous or woody in Elaeidinae, and the staminate, and in *Elaeis* the pistillate, flowers also, are enclosed in pits. In Attaleinae and Butiinae the peduncular bract is woody; the subtribes are distinct by the separation of flowers into androgynous, staminate, and sometimes pistillate inflorescences in Attaleinae and lack of such differentiation in Butiinae.

Key to the Subtribes of the Cocoeae

1. Spiny palms, armed in some or all parts with soft to mostly stout spines, or when rarely unarmed (some spp. of *Bactris*), then the petals of pistillate flowers connate. Bactridinae.
1. Unarmed palms except for the sometimes sharply toothed petiole margins, petals of pistillate flowers always free and broadly imbricate.
    2. Peduncular bract fibrous or woody; pistillate flowers deeply sunken in the rachillae; endocarp with pores at or above the middle. Elaeidinae.
    2. Peduncular bract woody; pistillate flowers superficial; endocarp with pores at or below the middle, or not evident.
        3. Peduncular bract borne at the tip of the peduncle, circumscissile and deciduous at anthesis; endocarp pores not distinct. Beccariophoenicinae.
        3. Peduncular bract borne just above the insertion of the prophyll, splitting longitudinally, usually cowl-like, persistent; endocarp pores conspicuous.
            4. Inflorescences normally of more than one kind on the same plant, androgynous and staminate, or sometimes also pistillate; pistillate flower sometimes with more than 3 carpels. Attaleinae.
            4. Inflorescences not normally differentiated into androgynous and staminate; pistillate flower always trilocular and triovulate. Butiinae.

Members of the sixth tribe, the Geonomeae, are clearly distinguished by the existence in the inflorescence axes of deep pits, each enclosing a triad of flowers.

The Arecoideae have many uses (Table VI)—in particular certain Cocoeae are most important—the coconut, *Cocos nucifera,* the African and American oil palms, *Elaeis oleifera* and *E. guineensis,* other oil producing palms belonging to the Attaleinae, and the genera *Bactris* and *Acrocomia* which provide fiber, edible fruits, medicines, and other products.

Phytelephantoideae

Subfamily VI, Phytelephantoideae (Table VII), includes only three genera but adds considerable diversity to the family. Distinguishing characters are dioecy, and dimorphic inflorescences on staminate and pistillate trees, monopodial flower clusters, and multiparted flowers. A distinctive syncarpous gynoecium with long styles and stigmas (Uhl & Dransfield, 1984) and centrifugal stamen development (Uhl & Moore, 1977) are other specialized features. The perianth in two genera, *Palandra* and *Phytelephas* has been shown by developmental studies to be four parted (Uhl & Dransfield, 1984). The three genera are separated on the structure of the staminate flowers: in *Palandra,* four flowers are united by long stalks, in *Phytelephas* (Fig. 3C), staminate flowers are sessile but in groups of four on the spicate inflorescence axis, and in *Ammandra,* staminate flowers are borne on short terete branches (Fig. 3D). Stamen numbers range from over 900 in *Palandra,* to 400–500 in *Ammandra,* and about 200 in *Phytelephas.*

The three genera are the "ivory" palms of South America. Other uses are noted for *Phytelephas* (see Table VII).

III. Some Implications for Future Research in Palms

The development of a formal classification has led to some insights with respect to both the past history and the direction of future research on palms. We believe that the subfamilies as outlined here are natural, well defined groups. The Coryphoideae is more diverse than the other subfamilies. It includes most of the evolutionary trends seen elsewhere as well as the least specialized flowers, and seems to be a basic and perhaps older group in the family.

Some of the genera of palms are not clearly defined. Our survey has shown that the greatest lack in knowledge lies with the genera of Madagascan palms, where several new ones are indicated. We are working toward a treatment of the palms of that island. Several genera, including the economically important *Euterpe* and *Prestoea* and the genera of the Attaleinae, also are not well circumscribed. Other genera are clearly delimited, but their species are not yet well understood. In all, about 80 genera are in need of monographic treatment, of which some are currently in progress.

Research on many other aspects of palms is needed. Palms are among the most diverse as well as the oldest seed plants. Studies of their morphology, anatomy, and development have contributed greatly to the new classification. Nevertheless, many genera have not been investigated and further research in these areas is certain to be rewarding. Fossil records of specimens relatable to modern genera of palms go back to the Upper Cretaceous, about 65 million years ago (Daghlian, 1981). It is also noteworthy that many fossils, while recognizable as palms, cannot be identified with modern genera. The fossil record and present distribution suggest that palms were widespread before the continents of Laurasia and Gondwana were much separated and that many palms became rafted to their present positions as the continents broke up and moved apart. The delimitation of the subfamilies provides some clues to dispersal routes, but detailed studies of fossils and phytogeography are much needed. Such studies would certainly contribute significantly to our knowledge of the evolution of palms and perhaps of monocotyledons as a whole.

Palms are proving to be excellent subjects for ecological studies which, although in their infancy, are most promising. Some topics being investigated are the physiological and morphological bases of shade tolerance in understory palms, demography with respect to clonal palms and for use in understanding community dynamics, and the mechanical architecture of arborescent palms [see Principes 30(3), 1986, Ecology Issue, for papers summarizing recent work].

When all genera of palms are considered (Tables II–VIII), two things regarding their economic importance stand out. First, the multiple uses to which they are put is particularly impressive. Palms have long been considered second to grasses and possibly legumes in economic importance, but certainly palms are important sources of more different products than the other families. Major products are wood, fiber, starch, sugar, edible fruits, and oil. A relatively large number of palms supply one or more of these while certain palms are important sources of particular products. Joint considerations of utilization and ecology, as presented by many papers in this symposium, are now particularly timely. We need to understand how local peoples are using palms and relate utilization to the demography of specific genera. Further investigations of chemistry, including flavonoids and isozymes, DNA, and other modern approaches are also vital. We must know palms better in order to efficiently utilize and preserve their remarkable diversity.

IV. Acknowledgments

We are very grateful for comments by M. Balick, A. Henderson, R. W. Read, and P. B. Tomlinson who reviewed the manuscript.

V. Literature Cited

Brown, W. H. & E. D. Merrill. 1919. Philippine palms and palm products. Bull Bur. Forest. Philipp. Islands, No. 18.

Burkill, I. H. 1966. A dictionary of the economic products of the Malay Peninsula, 2nd ed. Vol. II.

Ministry of Agriculture and Cooperatives, Kuala Lumpur, Malaysia.

Daghlian, C. P. 1981. A review of the fossil record of monocotyledons. Bot. Rev. 47: 517–555.

Dransfield, J. 1979. A manual of the rattans of the Malay Peninsula. Malaysian Forest Records No. 29. Forest Department, Kuala Lumpur, Malaysia.

———. 1984. The rattans of Sabah. Sabah Forest Records No. 13. Forest Department, Sabah.

———, S. K. Lee & F. N. Wei. 1985. *Guihaia,* a new coryphoid genus from China and Vietnam. Principes 29(1): 3–12.

——— & N. W. Uhl. 1986. An outline of a classification of palms. Principes 30(1): 3–11.

Griffith, W. 1844. The palms of British India. Calcutta J. Nat. Hist. 5: 1–103.

Johnson, D. V. 1983. A bibliography of graduate theses on the date and other *Phoenix* species. Date Palm J. 2(2): 257–267.

———. 1984. Additional graduate theses on the date palm and other *Phoenix* species. Date Palm J. 3(2): 437.

McKamey, L. 1983. Secret of the Orient: Dwarf *Rhapis excelsa.* Grunwald Printing Company, Corpus Christi, Texas.

Moore, H. E., Jr. 1973. The major groups of palms and their distribution. Gentes Herb. 11(2): 27–141.

——— & N. W. Uhl. 1982. Major trends of evolution in palms. Bot. Rev. 48(1): 1–69.

Tomlinson, P. B. & P. K. Soderholm. 1975. The flowering and fruiting of *Corypha elata* in South Florida. Principes 19(3): 83–99.

Uhl, N. W. 1972. Inflorescence and flower structure in *Nypa fruticans* (Palmae). Amer. J. Bot. 59: 729–743.

——— & J. Dransfield. 1984. Development of the inflorescence, androecium and gynoecium with reference to palms. Pages 397–449 *in* R. A. White & W. C. Dickison (eds.), Contemporary problems in plant anatomy. Academic Press, New York.

——— & ———. 1987. Genera palmarum: A classification of palms based on the work of Harold E. Moore, Jr. The International Palm Society and the L. H. Bailey Hortorium, Ithaca, New York.

——— & H. E. Moore, Jr. 1971. The palm gynoecium. Amer. J. Bot. 58: 945–992.

——— & ———. 1973. The protection of pollen and ovules in palms. Principes 17(4): 111–149.

——— & ———. 1977. Centrifugal stamen initiation in phytelephantoid palms. Amer. J. Bot. 64: 1152–1161.

——— & ———. 1978. The structure of the acervulus, the flower cluster of chamaedoreoid palms. Amer. J. Bot. 65: 197–204.

——— & ———. 1980. Androecial development in six polyandrous genera representing five major groups of palms. Ann. Bot. (London), ser. 2, 445: 57–75.

The Breeding System in the Date Palm (*Phoenix dactylifera* L.) and Its Recognition by Early Cultivators

DARLEEN A. DEMASON AND K. N. CHANDRA SEKHAR

Table of Contents

Abstract

Phoenix dactylifera L., the date palm, is a dioecious species and has dimorphic flowers: the staminate flowers have large petals, six stamens and three pistillodes and pistillate flowers have short petals, six staminodes and three separate carpels. The earliest remains of cultivated dates are from approximately 4000 B.C. A stylized depiction of date pollination in an Assyrian relief is the earliest documented evidence that primitive man recognized sexuality in plants. Date palm culture has had significant economic, social and religious impact on peoples of the Middle East since the beginnings of civilization. Structural studies of flower development and the occasional occurrence of male plants with apparently bisexual flowers suggest that the genus evolved from bisexual ancestors, possibly through gynodioecy. Researchers have suggested that auxin and gibberellic acid control sexuality. The pollen variety used for pollination not only influences the size and shape of the resulting seed (xenia) but also has a direct effect on the size, shape, weight, and time of ripening of the resulting fruit (metaxenia). Some pollen varieties induce small, early ripening fruit and others induce large, late-ripening fruit. Metaxenia has since been shown to be of importance in other crop plants. Date pollen is small, reticulate, monosulcate and is released in the two-celled state. The cytoplasm of the vegetative cell is dense and contains mitochondria, plastids, numerous small vacuoles and stores lipids in lipid bodies. The generative cell is small, and the nuclei of both cells are distinguishable by their size, shape and staining characteristics. Pollen is easily collected and stored, and germinates well in vitro. Pollen from different male clones show differences in size and in amount of protein. The authors hope to correlate differences in pollen structure, biochemistry and physiology with metaxenic effect.

Key words: date, *Phoenix,* dioecy, pollen, metaxenia, palms, Arecaceae

Résumé

Phoenix dactylifera L., le dattier, est une espèce dioïque à dimorphisme floral: les fleurs staminées possèdent des pétales allongés, six étamines et trois pistillodes, tandis que les fleurs pistillées se caractérisent par des pétales courts, 6 staminodes, et trois carpelles non-soudés. Les vestiges les plus anciens de dattes cultivées datent d'environ 4.000 ans avant J.C. Une représentation stylisée de la pollinisation des dattiers dans un bas-relief de la période Assyrienne constitue l'indication la plus ancienne que l'homme primitif avait connaissance de l'existence de phénomènes sexuels parmi les plantes. La culture du palmier-dattier a eu un impact économique, social et religieux considérable sur les peuples du Moyen-Orient depuis l'origine de notre civilisation. Des études structurales du developpement floral et l'apparition occasionnelle de fleurs apparemment bisexuées semblent indiquer que le genre *Phoenix* a évolué à partir d'un ancêtre bisexué, peut-être par l'intermédiaire de la gynodioécie. Certains chercheurs out suggéré que les auxines et l'acide giberellique contrôlent la sexualité. Le cultivar utilisé comme source de pollen (cultivar pollinisateur) influence non seulement la taille et la forme des semences (xénie) mais également la taille, la forme, le poids et la rapidité de maturation du fruit (métaxénie). Certains cultivars pollinisateurs induisent la production de fruits de petite taille à maturation précoce, tandis que d'autres induisent la production de fruits de grande taille à maturation tardive. Des effets marqués de métaxénie ont également été observés chez d'autres plantes cultivées. Le pollen du dattier est de petite taille, réticulé, monosulqué et est libéré au stade bicellulaire. Le cytoplasme de la cellule végétative est dense et contient des mitochondries, des plastes, de nombreuses petites vacuoles et des lipides. La cellule générative est de taille réduite; les noyaux des deux cellules peuvent être distingués par leur taille, leur forme, et leurs charactéristiques de coloration histologique. Le pollen est récolté et emmagasiné de manière aisée; il germe bien *in vitro*. Le pollen de différents clones mâles se différencient par la taille, la forme et la teneur en protéines. Les auteurs espèrent corréler les differences structurales, biochimiques, et physiologiques du pollen avec les effets de métaxénie.

I. Introduction

Many reviews have been written in the last few decades on the cultural, historical and botanical aspects of the date palm, *Phoenix dactylifera* L. Popenoe (1924, 1973), Nixon (1951), and Goor (1967) have written extensively on the history of its cultivation. Nixon and Carpenter (1978) have written on cultural techniques practiced in the United States. Reuveni (1985, 1986) has recently reviewed various aspects of flowering and fruit set. As one would expect, most attention has been directed to the pistillate flowers, on fruit development and ripening, and on varieties of fruits. These are all aspects of the female plant's biology in this dioecious species. We, however, are interested in the breeding system of the date palm and, particularly, the male contribution to the breeding system. It has been well documented in field trials that the pollen parent affects the morphology and development of the fruit in the date palm. This phenomenon has been termed "metaxenia." We have initiated both structural/ultrastructural and physiological/biochemical studies of date pollen with the hope of adding to our knowledge of the poorly understood phenomenon of metaxenia. In this review of the breeding system in the date, we will recount the historical aspect of man's recognition of sexuality in the species, emphasize the complex aspects of the expression of dioecy and metaxenia, review the recent work which has been done on in vitro and in vivo pollen germination, present new data on the structure and ultrastructure of the pollen, and finally present some initial experiments on differences between pollen from different male clones which may have a bearing on the phenomenon of metaxenia.

II. General Features of *Phoenix dactylifera* L.

The vegetative characteristics which distinguish *Phoenix dactylifera* L. from other members of the palm family include a multistemmed pleonanthic habit, leaves in a spiral phyllotaxis, and induplicately imparipinnate leaves with lower pairs of pinnae modified into spines (Figs. 1–3) (Fisher, 1985; Moore, 1973, 1982). Seedling plants go through a sequence from juvenility to maturity in the expression of the axillary buds. Very young seedlings produce no axillary buds associated with the juvenile leaves; during subsequent growth, axillary buds are mainly vegetative and grow into sucker shoots, commonly called offshoots, and finally mature plants produce axillary buds which mainly produce inflorescences. Offshoots themselves go through a similar developmental sequence, producing sterile buds, vegetative buds, and finally inflorescence buds (Bouguedoura, 1983; Hilgeman, 1954). Commercial propagation of the date palm is done by separating offshoots from the parent trunk. Clonal propagation in this way is currently the only way to obtain fruit or pollen qualities true to the cultivar.

Characteristics of the reproductive structures can also be used to identify the date palm. The species is dioecious. Male plants are vegetatively similar to female plants, but the flowers are dimorphic. Both male and female inflorescences are borne interfoliarly within a flattened, woody prophyll, commonly called a spathe (Fig. 2). They have a single flattened central rachis which bears generally unbranched rachillae in a somewhat spiral arrangement (Figs. 3, 4). Staminate flowers have three connate sepals, three petals much exceeding the sepals in length, six stamens with short filaments, and linear erect anthers. Three reduced carpels or pistillodes occur in the center of the male flowers (Figs. 5, 7). The pistillate flowers are globose, sepals are connate in a 3-lobed cupule, petals are short and imbricate; three carpels are separate, ovoid and narrow to a recurved, exerted stigma. Pistillate flowers contain six reduced stamens or staminodes (Figs. 6, 8). A single basal, anatropous ovule occurs per carpel but only one carpel per flower matures into a one-seeded fruit (Fig. 4). The fruit is ovoid to oblong with a smooth epicarp, fleshy mesocarp and papery endocarp. The seed is elongate and deeply grooved with intruded testa. The embryo is lateral under a circular depression and consists of a single cotyledon, root pole and an epicotyl which is oriented in the same plane as the root-cotyledon axis (DeMason & Thomson, 1981). The endosperm is homogeneous and consists of living, nucleate cells with thick, mannan-rich walls and which are filled with protein and lipid bodies (DeMason et al., 1983).

Phoenix dactylifera L. is best adapted to tropical or subtropical climates where minimum temperatures of 20°F (−6.7°C) or below seldom occur. Fruit can mature properly only in areas of the world where the average daily maximum temperature, May to October inclusive, is well above 95°F (35°C) and the rainfall from July to October inclusive is less than one-half inch (Nixon, 1951). However, the date palm requires an abundance of water. The finest dates are grown in oases which receive a continuous and dependable supply of water, either by gravity from high bordering mountains or from artesian sources or are under constant, large-scale irrigation (Nixon, 1951).

The taxonomic relations within the genus *Phoenix* are not well-defined. There are in the genus approximately 17 species, which are distributed in Africa, Arabia, and from India to Malaya and Sumatra (Beccari, 1890). These species are distinguished mainly on vegetative characters. *Phoenix* has been placed in its own tribe within the subfamily Coryphoideae (Dransfield & Uhl, 1986).

III. Early Cultivation and Recognition of Sexuality

The date palm is one of the Holy Land's most ancient fruit trees. It has been in cultivation in the Near East probably as early as Neolithic time, and it is a symbol of fertility and harvest in the three major world religions emanating from that area, Judaism, Christianity, and Islam. Remains of cultivated dates have been found as early as 4000 B.C. in Lower Mesopotamia (D. Zohary & Spiegel-Roy, 1975; M. Zohary, 1982). The species, or a related wild one, was probably native and widely dispersed in oases, along riverbeds and in saline or semi-saline plant communities in the dry regions of the Middle East. The species is well suited to cultivation due to the easily stored and transported dry fruit and to the long-term viability of and easily germinated seed, uncharacteristic of the palm family in general. Primitive peoples had many uses for the palm: the fruit, edible both fresh and dried, could be used to make sweets, syrup, fermented liquor and vinegar; the tender terminal bud could be eaten; sap could be made into a fresh or fermented beverage; the leaves could be used to thatch dwellings or woven into mats, baskets and other household utensils; the fibers on the trunk could be used for cordage; spines could be used for needles and pins; while the wood could be used for fences, roofs and rafts (Nixon, 1951; M. Zohary, 1982). From the Bronze Age on, date cultivation seems to have been well established in warm areas of the Near East (D. Zohary & Spiegel-Roy, 1975). Phoenician traders carried dates and date culture to all parts of the Mediterranean. The genus name 'Phoenix' is thought to have been coined by the Greeks because the plant and fruits were exported from the date palm cultures of the coastal region of Phoenicia (Popenoe, 1973; M. Zohary, 1982).

Cultivation of the date palm supplies the earliest documented evidence that man recognized sexuality in plants. The palm is shown abundantly in artistic designs on pottery and in relief on architecture in Assyria (about the ninth century B.C.). A monograph of many such designs

FIGS. 1–4.   Habit, flowering and fruiting structures. 1. A young male tree showing spirally arranged leaf bases and two offshoots. 2. Spathe or prophyll which encloses male or female inflorescences. Note spines on leaf bases. 3. Staminate inflorescences at anthesis. 4. Young developing fruits. OS = offshoot, SP = spathe.

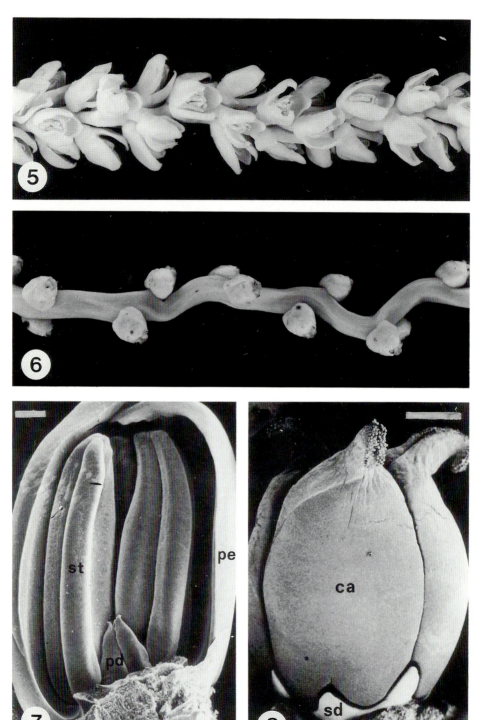

was assembled by Danthine (1937). Among these Assyrian designs are human-griffin chimeras pollinating female palm trees with male inflorescences. Even before this time, the date palm symbolized fertility to the early Semites. The date palm symbolized the fabled "Tree of Life." Two well-known deities of the Semites mentioned in the Old Testament—Baal, meaning an unirrigated palm or god of unirrigated land, and Ishtar (Astarte), a fertile palm or goddess of irrigated soil and fertility—were considered false gods by the early Hebrews (Goor, 1967; Popenoe, 1924).

Even so, the Hebrews considered the date palm to have a central place in their culture and agriculture. The date palm has been grown in the Jordan and Aravah Valleys, the Dead Sea area, and the El Arish and Gaza districts from very early times. The date palm symbolized the state of Judea on coins and signified righteousness, honor, and beauty (Goor, 1967). The Hebrews knew the significance and art of date pollination, and they understood that there were male and female palms and knew that there could be no perfect dates without fertilization. The method of tying a spikelet of the male inflorescence above the female spathe such that the wind would carry the pollen to the female flowers was described in the Babylonian Talmud Shabbat, 47a (Goor, 1967). Date palm leaves are among the "four species" carried by Jews for the Feast of the Tabernacles.

The date palm is a particularly important symbol for the people of Islam. Mohammed lived in a date-growing area and mentioned date palms often in his teachings. There are 26 references to date palms in the Koran (Popenoe, 1924). The following quote summarized by Qazwini (in Popenoe, 1924) shows that he understood the breeding system in dates:

> ... The date palm bears a striking resemblance to Man, in the beauty of its erect and lofty stature, its division into two distinct sexes, male and female, and the property which is peculiar to it of being fecundated by a sort of copulation ...

The great dependency of people in the Near East on products from the date palm gave them the opportunity to become intimately familiar with the plant's life cycle. These people thus discovered sexuality in dates many centuries before it was generally recognized in plants.

IV. Expression of Dioecy in *Phoenix dactylifera*

The date palm is functionally dioecious and little is known about the control of sex expression in the species. Although sex chromosomes have not been observed, seedling plants are approximately half male and half female (Beal, 1937; Nixon & Carpenter, 1978). Pistillate flowers set fruit consistently only after pollination. Certain minor exceptions to the rule and developmental studies of the flower suggest, however, that the date palm evolved from a bisexual ancestor. Staminate and pistillate flowers are provided with pistillodes and staminodes, respectively. A recent histological and SEM study of flower development showed that staminate and pistillate flowers are identical in early development in that they both produce, in succession, sepals, petals, stamens (or staminodes) and carpels (or pistillodes). Both staminate and pistillate flowers are identical morphologically and histologically up to the point of carpel (or pistillode) initiation (Figs. 9, 10). Subsequently, the two flower types diverge in their development. The staminate flowers show a continuation in the development of the stamens and a lack of normal growth in the pistillodes (Figs. 11, 13, 15) whereas the pistillate flowers show a continuation in the development of the carpels and a truncation of staminode development (Figs. 12, 14, 16). The staminate flowers show more development of the pistillodes than the pistillate flowers do of the staminodes. The pistillodes, although smaller in size than normal carpels, do show some development of stigmatic papillae on their tips (DeMason et al., 1982). This greater tendency toward bisexuality in the staminate flowers is further documented by the occasional occurrence

←

FIGS. 5–8. Staminate and pistillate flowers. 5. Rachilla with crowded, long-petalled staminate flowers at anthesis. 6. Rachilla with widely-spaced short-petalled pistillate flowers at anthesis. 7. Scanning electron microscope image of dissected preanthesis staminate flowers (sepals, one petal and three stamens removed). 8. Scanning electron microscope image of dissected pistillate flower at anthesis (calyx and corolla removed). Bars are 0.5 mm. ca = carpel, pd = pistillode, pe = petal, sd = staminode, st = stamen.

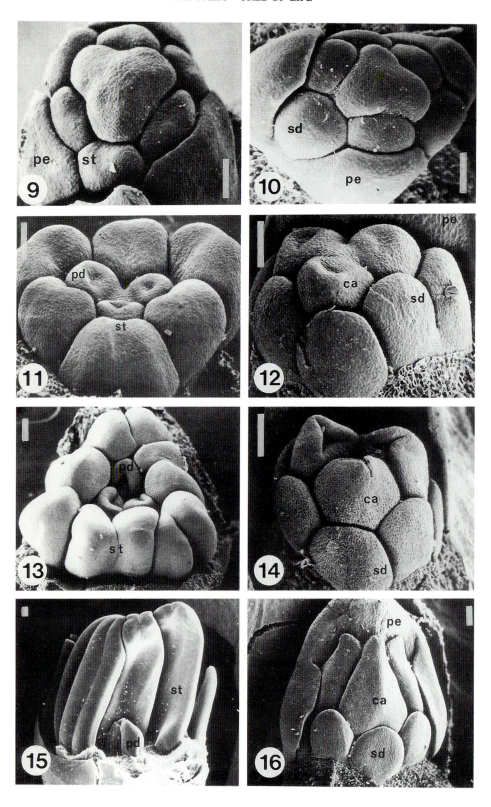

of sterile bisexual flowers on male trees (De-Mason & Tisserat, 1980; Reuveni, 1986). These flowers look like typical staminate flowers in superficial characteristics such as petal length and flower arrangement on the rachillae. However, upon closer inspection one notes well-developed carpels in the center of the flowers. These carpels usually contain no ovules, but can develop into parthenocarpic fruit. When parthenocarpic fruit does develop, it resembles the occasional parthenocarpic fruit which can occur on female trees, that is, three instead of one carpel develops per flower and the resulting fruit is dry and papery. On rare occasions, fertile fruit have been observed on male trees (Beal, 1937).

Gynodioecy has been defined as the condition in which female plants are relatively constant and male plants are inconstant and are often morphologically and functionally bisexual (Lloyd, 1976; Richards, 1986). All morphological and developmental evidence in date points to stability in the control of pistillate flowers and female plants, but to some instability in the control of staminate flowers and male plants. This evidence leads us to believe that in the genus *Phoenix,* dioecy evolved through gynodioecy as an intermediate state. Dioecy is uncommon in flowering plants (approximately 4% of all species) but it seems that it usually has evolved from gynodioecy (Richards, 1986).

It is generally thought that sexual expression in plants is controlled by hormone balance. Two studies have been recently conducted to determine the mechanism of this control in date. The results of the two studies are conflicting, which suggests that further work in this area would be profitable. Leshem and Ophir (1977) studied endogenous levels of gibberellic acid and found that higher activity levels of this hormone were present in female plants than in male plants although flowering on both sexes was associated with a drop in gibberellic acid activity. This study suggests that gibberellic acid activity is associated

with "femaleness." On the other hand, DeMason and Tisserat (1980) found that if young male flowers were placed in culture, increased carpel development was associated with higher levels of auxins (2,4-D and p-CPA), which suggests "femaleness" is associated with auxin levels.

V. Xenia and Metaxenia—The Direct Effect of Pollen on Fruit

Investigators in the U.S. and elsewhere have shown by very careful field studies that, within certain limits, the pollen used for pollination not only influences the size and shape of the resulting seed (xenia), but also has a direct effect on the size, shape, and weight, as well as time of ripening of the resulting fruit (metaxenia) (Nixon, 1926, 1927, 1928, 1931, 1934a, 1934b, 1935; Osman et al., 1974; Ream, 1976; Reuveni, 1986; Schroeder & Nixon, 1958). These studies demonstrated the first evidence of a direct effect of pollen on tissues outside the embryo and endosperm. Since the initial discovery of metaxenia by Swingle (1928), it has been observed in other crops—including apple, chestnuts, citrus, coconut, cotton, peaches, pear and persimmon (Osman et al., 1974). Pollen from more than 200 species and from male date clones have been tested for their metaxenic effects on California fruit varieties. The male clone 'Fard 4' has consistently produced dates that are smaller, lighter, and earlier-ripening than all other male clones tested. Male clones which have consistently produced large, heavier but later-ripening fruit, include 'Mosque', 'Boyer', and 'Crane'. The effect of the pollen parent on the timing of fruit ripening has had economic benefits in the marginal date growing areas in California where early ripening is desired because there is insufficient heat for proper maturation of the fruit (Nixon, 1931; Nixon & Carpenter, 1978; Whittlesey, 1933). Among the other *Phoenix* species tested for their

←

FIGS. 9–16. Early development of staminate and pistillate flowers. 9. Young staminate flower initiating pistillodes. 10. Young pistillate flower initiating carpels. 11. Young staminate flower with developing stamens and pistillodes. 12. Young pistillate flower with developing carpels. Note that there has been no further development of staminodes. 13. Young staminate flower with bilobed stamens and developing pistillodes. 14. Young pistillate flowers with developing carpels. 15. Young staminate flowers with elongating stamens and continued development of pistillodes. 16. Pistillate flower with elongating carpels. Bars = 100 μm. ca = carpel, pd = pistillode, pe = petal, sd = staminode, st = stamen. (From DeMason et al., 1962, with permission from journal.)

metaxenic effect on *P. dactylifera, P. sylvestris* (L.) Roxb. pollen produces fruit and seed more normal in size, shape, etc., than any other species tested. This may indicate that *Phoenix sylvestris* is more closely related to the date palm than other species in the genus.

The physiological or genetic basis for the phenomenon of metaxenia is not known. Osman et al. (1974) attempted to determine if a genetic component was involved in metaxenia by comparing not only means of fruit characteristics but distribution around the means for the pollen types tested. They felt that a significant part of the spread around the means in size, in time of ripening and in other characters was related to the heterozygosity of the pollen clone used. They also reported that flowers pollinated by 'Fard 4' pollen showed delayed suppression of abortive carpels in comparison to that of the dominant carpel. 'Boyer' pollen, on the other hand, caused almost complete cessation of growth of abortive carpels within one week of pollination. These differences might suggest that pollen exhibits some sort of hormonal or physiological control upon fruit growth.

VI. Pollen Structure and Characteristics

There has been a great deal of interest in the structure of pollen in flowering plants. Taxonomists have used pollen wall features for taxonomic purposes. Embryologists have been interested in pollen development. And, recently, there has been a great interest among reproductive biologists in the ultrastructure of mature pollen and of growing pollen tubes. Structural studies can give some clues as to the natural mode of pollination. The authors feel that *Phoenix* represents a model system for studying pollen structure, cytochemistry, and protein biochemistry, as well as the physiological controls of pollen tube growth.

Recently, an SEM study was done of pollen from a number of species in the genus and a number of male date clones (Tisserat & DeMason, 1982). The pollen was found to be fairly uniform in size, shape and exine structure and sculpture. Fresh pollen is elliptical or boat-shaped, monosulcate and the exine exhibits a tectate-perforate structural pattern (the exine consists of small holes in the tectum in which the pores were smaller in diameter than the muri between them) (Fig. 17). The grains ranged from 17.2 to 26.7 μm in length. A small amount of wax-like or lipid-like deposit occurs on the surface of the exine in most pollens examined. The uniformity in pollen grain morphology and structure does not allow pollen features to be useful in taxonomic or phylogenetic determinations, but small differences in length to width ratio and size and shape of pores in the tectum do allow identification of species or cultivars from the SEM image of *Phoenix* pollen.

When fresh or dried pollen is placed in an aqueous solution (fixative or stain) it becomes spherical (Figs. 18–21). Date pollen is shed in a two-celled state and consists of a large vegetative cell which completely surrounds the smaller generative cell. The grain is surrounded by a relatively thin intine, except in the area of the aperture where the intine is very thick and the exine is very thin or non-existent (Fig. 18). The vegetative cell nucleus and the generative cell are usually in close proximity to one another and both are usually located on the opposite side of the grain from the aperture (Figs. 18, 19, 21).

The cytoplasm of the vegetative cell is very dense and contains numerous mitochondria, plastids, vacuoles, lipid bodies, rough endoplasmic reticulum and individual ribosomes (Figs. 18, 21–23). The mitochondria have well developed internal membranes, whereas the plastids do not (Fig. 22). The plastids also do not contain starch. Small inclusions often occur in the vacuoles, including dark deposits. Occasionally, long fibrous bundles of presumably proteinaceous composition are present in the cytoplasm. These have also been described in the pollen of *Nicotiana alata* (Cresti et al., 1985). These authors speculated that the bundles consisted of proteinaceous materials utilized for cytoplasmic streaming during pollen germination. However, we have also observed similar bundles in cotyledonary parenchyma in date embryos (DeMason & Thomson, 1981). We feel that the bundles are more likely to be a storage form of protein or enzymes. The vegetative cell nucleus is elongate and densely-staining at the light microscope level with toluidine blue and DAPI (Figs. 18, 19). In the electron microscope, the vegetative cell nucleus is lighter staining and contains small amounts of heterochromatin. The nuclear mem-

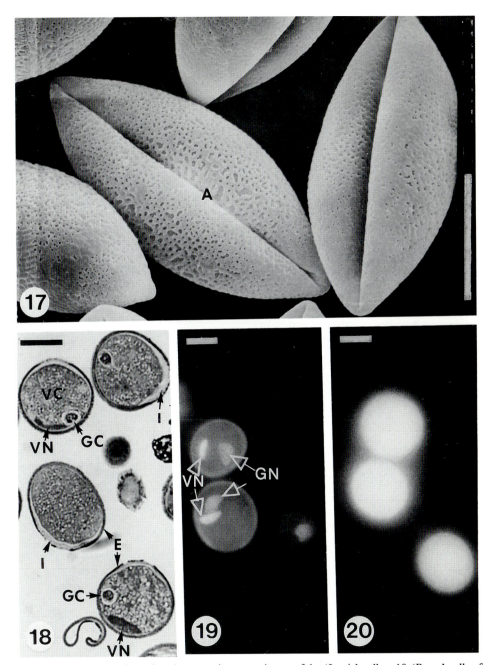

FIGS. 17–20   Pollen. 17. Scanning electron microscope image of dry 'Jarvis' pollen. 18. 'Boyer' pollen fixed (2% glutaraldehyde in 50 mM phosphate buffer pH 7.6), dehydrated, embedded in methacrylate (Polysciences), and stained in 1% toluidine blue. 19. Fresh 'Boyer' pollen stained with 0.0005 aqueous DAPI (Polysciences). 20. Fresh 'Fard 4' pollen stained with fluorocein diacetate (Heslop-Harrison & Heslop-Harrison, 1970). Bar = 10 μm. A = aperture, E = exine, GC = generative cell, GN = generative cell nucleus, I = intine, VN = vegetative cell nucleus.

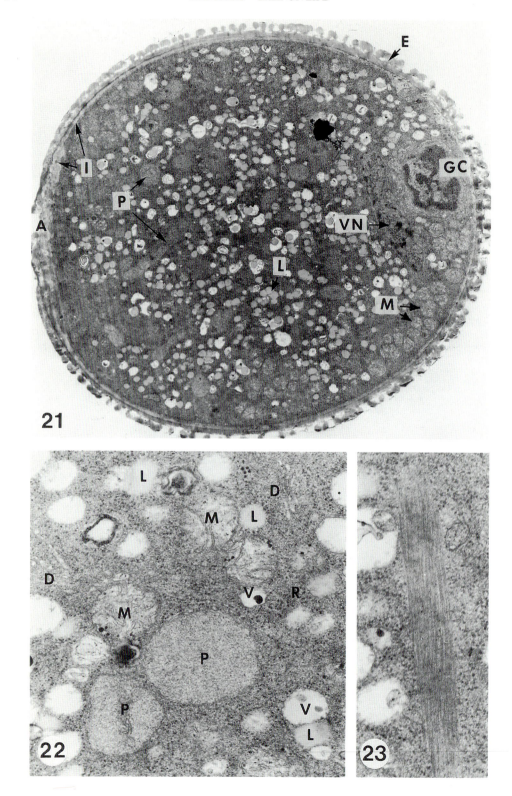

brane is smooth (Fig. 21). This is quite different from the image of the vegetative nucleus in pollen of other species where it contains little heterochromatin and has a very convoluted outline (Cresti et al., 1985; Knox, 1984; Mogensen, 1986).

The generative cell contains a very large nucleus and a small amount of surrounding cytoplasm (Figs. 21, 24, 25). The cell is enclosed by a very undulate plasma membrane and either lacks a surrounding wall or the wall is very thin (Platt-Aloia et al., 1986) (Figs. 24, 25). The plasma membrane of the generative cell is sometimes seen pulled away from that of the vegetative cell (Fig. 24), but more often the two membranes are appressed (Fig. 25). The cytoplasm of the generative cell is also very dense and contains endoplasmic reticulum, ribosomes, some organelles (probably mitochondria) and abundant microtubules (Figs. 24, 25). These characteristics are similar to those of generative cells in other species, except that most pollen contains generative cells surrounded by a wall (Cresti et al., 1984, 1985; Nakamura & Miki-Hirosige, 1985; Owens & Westmuckett, 1983). *Hippeastrum,* like date, also contains a generative cell with no surrounding cell wall (Mogensen, 1986). The nucleus in the generative cell is variable in shape from wide and spindle-shaped to ovate. It is light-staining with toluidine blue and DAPI, and contains much heterochromatin at the EM level (Figs. 18, 19, 21, 24, 25). In most other pollens studied, the generative cell is elongate and cresent-shaped or spindle-shaped (Burgess, 1970; Cresti et al., 1984, 1985; Echlin, 1972).

An initial study of pollen among the various cultivars of the date palm showed no qualitative differences in the structure or ultrastructure. The study of pollen grain length (Tisserat & DeMason, 1982) suggested that pollen of different male cultivars may vary in size. We suspended pollen of four male date varieties in fluorocein diacetate and measured the area of viable (fluo-

rocein accumulating) grains (Fig. 20) projected on the graphics tablet of a microcomputer. The results are presented in Table I, which shows that 'Fard 4' had the largest pollen and 'Crane' the smallest in the sample we selected. The pollen size seems to correlate with our initial study of protein content of the male date varieties. Pollen was ground in buffer and protein content was measured via the Peterson reaction on a gram fresh weight basis (Peterson, 1977). Again, 'Fard 4' had the greatest amount of protein, whereas 'Crane' had the least (Table I).

Although man has artificially pollinated dates from early times, the genus *Phoenix* is commonly reported to be wind-pollinated in the wild (McCurrach, 1960). The lack of extensive stigmatic surface on the female flowers might lead one to doubt this hypothesis, and the presence of bees and other insects on staminate flowers has been reported (McGregor, 1976; and pers. obs.). Uhl and Moore (1977) studied the histology of *Phoenix* flowers and found no correlation between anatomy and anemophily. Henderson (1986) reviewed the literature on pollination in the genus and felt that the evidence was stronger for entomophily rather than for anemophily. Pollen grain characteristics provide another line of evidence to distinguish entomophily from anemophily. Wind-borne pollen has a number of characteristic structural features: the size ranges from 20 μm to 40 μm (Whitehead, 1969) it is starchy (rather than lipid-rich) (Baker & Baker, 1979, 1983), has a thin exine which is relatively smooth and lacks a sticky pollen-coat (Knox, 1984). Although there is some ambiguity in the presence of lipid rather than starch in date pollen, we feel that date pollen fits the description of wind-borne pollen better than that of insect-borne pollen. It is at the lower range of the wind size class, has a thin, relatively smooth exine and a non-sticky surface. Our field observations and experience lead us to believe that anemophily is

$\leftarrow$

FIGS. 21–23. Transmission electron microscope image of pollen. Pollen was fixed in 2% glutaraldehyde in 50 mM phosphate buffer, post-fixed in 1% osmium tetroxide in same buffer, dehydrated through acetone and embedded in Spurr's epoxy resin. 21. Section through whole pollen grain with aperture, generative cell and vegetative cell nucleus. ×8200. 22. Cytoplasm of vegetative cell with plastids, mitochondria, lipid bodies, dictyosomes, vacuoles and ribosomes. ×32,000. 23. Cytoplasm of vegetative cell with a fibrous bundle of possibly proteinaceous composition. ×44,000. A = aperture, D = dictyosome, E = exine, GC = generative cell, I = intine, L = lipid body, M = mitochondrion, P = plastid, R = ribosome, V = vacuole, VN = vegetative cell nucleus.

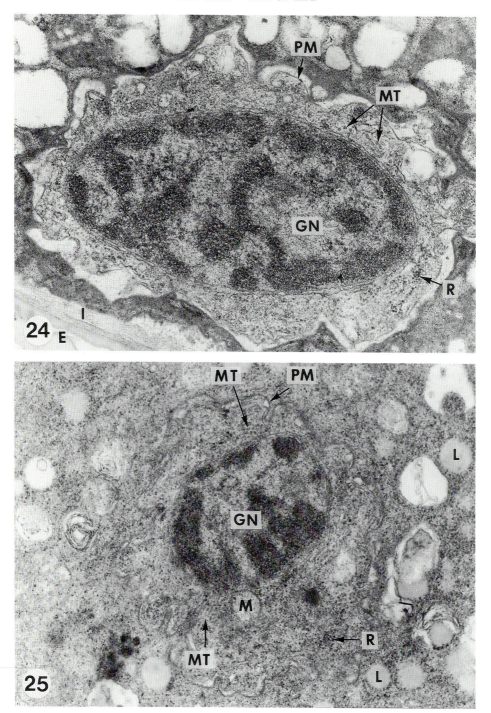

FIGS. 24, 25.   Generative cell. 24. Generative cell showing space between its plasmalemma and that of the vegetative cell. Small fibers in space indicate some polysaccharide may be present. ×33,000. 25. Generative cell which has no space between it and vegetative cell. This seems to be a more typical image. ×33,000. E = exine, GN = generative cell nucleus, I = intine, L = lipid body, M = mitochondrion, MT = microtubule, R = ribosome, PM = plasma membrane.

Table I

Size and protein composition of pollen from four male date cultivars

Cv.	Pollen size (μm^2)[1] (mean $\pm$ SE)	Ranked order and significance[2]	μg protein/mg fresh wt. (mean $\pm$ SE)[3]
Crane	354.6 $\pm$ 17.7	A	17.52 $\pm$ 2.67
Jarvis 1	403.6 $\pm$ 20.2	B	23.13 $\pm$ 4.17
Boyer 11	406.8 $\pm$ 20.3	B	19.29 $\pm$ 3.26
Fard 4	427.8 $\pm$ 21.4	C	33.13 $\pm$ 4.17

[1] Sample size = 50.
[2] Duncan's Multiple Range Test; means with different letters are significantly different at 1% level; results of ANOVA were df = 3,185; F value = 20.95; $P < 0.0001$.
[3] Sample size = 6.

a viable means of pollen transfer in uncultivated trees of *Phoenix dactylifera*.

VII. In Vitro and In Vivo Pollen Germination

In commercial date gardens, male trees in the ratios of 1 to 30–50 female trees are grown from which inflorescences or pollen are collected for artificial pollination. An enormous quantity of pollen is required for artificial pollination. It is estimated that for mechanically pollinating 50 female plants, approximately 2.8 liters of dry pollen are required (Brown, 1983). Growers routinely store pollen from one year to the next. Studies on the viability of stored date pollen go back to the 1930's. Albert (1930) showed that the germination percentage of pollen stored for one year at 38°F (3.3°C) was greater than that of pollen stored at room temperature. In a detailed study, Crawford (1938) found that the percentage of fruit set after pollination of the female flowers with pollen stored for one year at room temperature was very low (3%), whereas no significant differences in fruit set were observed between fresh pollen (65%) and that stored for one year at 8°F (-13.3°C) (69%).

Pollen germination in vitro has been used for over 20 years as a test of viability. Using modified Brewbaker and Kwack medium (1963), Furr and Enriquez (1966) were able to obtain a high percentage of in vitro pollen germination. Also, the authors observed differences in germination rate on changing the concentrations of sucrose, calcium, or boron in the growth medium. A few studies have been done on the effects of temperature on in vitro pollen germination. For ex-

ample, Furr and Ream (1968) achieved optimum in vitro germination (88%) by incubating pollen in germination medium at 80° F (26.6°C). Germination rate was low at both low [52°F (11.1°C): 22%] and high [110°F (43.3°C): 43%] temperatures. This agrees well with an in vivo study done in Israel. Detached pistillate flowers were cultured at different temperatures. A higher rate of pollen tube penetration occurred in flowers cultured at 25 or 28°C than in flowers cultured at 15 or 20°C (Reuveni, 1986). A natural question one might then ask is whether pollen germination and pollen tube growth rate vary in the different male cultivars. Results of our preliminary experiments show that they might. 'Fard 4' pollen seems to germinate slower than the other varieties tested thus far. If this result holds up under further examination, a whole new realm of experiments can be done. For example, one could test whether the pollen from different cultivars vary in their response to calcium, boron, and sugar in the medium. And to assist commercial growers, one could test the available male cultivars for pollen that has higher germination rates and more rapid pollen tube growth rates at lower temperatures than the males used currently either alone or, usually, in a mixture from several males.

The many aspects of the breeding system of the date palm, such as its dioecious nature, the documented existence of the phenomenon of metaxenia in the species, the fact that plants produce large inflorescences from which one can collect large quantities of pollen, the good storage potential of the pollen, and the ease in which pollen can be germinated in vitro and in vivo, make this a unique model system for studying many aspects of pollen biology. Information obtained on the species would be of value for commercial growers, for those studying the breeding system of other palms, and possibly for studies of other crop and native plants.

VIII. Acknowledgments

The authors thank Jim Stillman and Mark Wilson for technical assistance, and Cliff Brown and John Carpenter for use of the USDA date variety collection. We also thank John Carpenter for critically reading the manuscript. Dr. Paul Gepts translated the abstract into French.

IX. Literature Cited

Albert, D. W. 1930. Viability of pollen and receptivity of pistillate flowers. Rep. Date Growers' Inst. 7: 5–7.

Baker, H. G. & I. Baker. 1979. Starch in angiosperm pollen grains and its evolutionary significance. Amer. J. Bot. 66: 591–600.

——— & ———. 1983. Some evolutionary and taxonomic implications of variation in the chemical reserve of pollen. Pages 43–52 in D. L. Mulcahy & E. Ottaviano (eds.), Pollen: Biology and implications for plant breeding. Elsevier Biomedical, New York.

Beal, J. M. 1937. Cytological studies in the genus *Phoenix*. Bot. Gaz. 99: 400–407.

Beccari, O. 1890. Revisa monografica delle species del genere *Phoenix* Linn. Malesia 3: 344–416.

Bouguedoura, N. 1983. Development and distribution of axillary buds in *Phoenix dactylifera* L. Proceedings of the First Symposium on the Date Palm. King Faisal University, Saudi Arabia. 1: 40–44.

Brewbaker, J. L. & B. H. Kwack. 1963. The calcium-ion and substances influencing pollen growth. Pages 143–151 in H. F. Linskens (ed.), Pollen physiology and fertilization. North-Holland Publishing, Amsterdam.

Brown, G. K. 1983. Date production mechanization in the U.S.A. Proceedings of the First Symposium on the Date Palm. King Faisal University, Saudi Arabia. 1: 2–12.

Burgess, J. 1970. Cell shape and mitotic spindle formation in the generative cell of *Endymion nonscriptus*. Planta 95: 72–85.

Crawford, C. L. 1938. Cold storage of date pollen. Rep. Date Growers' Inst. 15: 20.

Cresti, M., F. Ciampolini & R. N. Kapil. 1984. Generative cells of some angiosperms with particular emphasis on microtubles. J. Submicrosc. Cytol. 16: 317–326.

———, ———, D. L. M. Mulcahy & G. Mulcahy. 1985. Ultrastructure of *Nicotiana alata* pollen, its germination and early tube formation. Amer. J. Bot. 72: 719–727.

Danthine, H. 1937. Le palmier-dattier et les arbres sacrés dans l'iconographie de l'asie occidentale ancienne. Biblioth. Archéol. Hist. 25: 1–277.

DeMason, D. A., R. Sexton & J. S. G. Reid. 1983. Structure, composition and physiological state of the endosperm of *Phoenix dactylifera* L. Ann. Bot. 52: 71–80.

———, K. Stolte & B. Tisserat. 1982. Floral development in *Phoenix dactylifera*. Canad. J. Bot. 60: 1437–1446.

——— & W. W. Thomson. 1981. Structure and ultrastructure of the cotyledon of date palm (*Phoenix dactylifera* L.). Bot. Gaz. 142: 320–328.

——— & B. Tisserat. 1980. The occurrence and structure of apparently bisexual flowers in the date palm, *Phoenix dactylifera* L. (Arecaceae). J. Linn. Soc., Bot. 181: 283–292.

Dransfield, J. & N. W. Uhl. 1986. An outline of a classification of palms. Principes 30: 3–11.

Echlin, P. 1972. The ultrastructure and ontogeny of pollen in *Helleborus foetidus* L. IV. Pollen grain maturation. J. Cell Sci. 11: 111–129.

Fisher, J. B. 1985. Palmae (Arecaceae). Pages 337–343 in A. H. Halevy (ed.), Handbook of flowering. Vol. I. CRC Press, Boca Raton, Florida.

Furr, J. R. & V. M. Enriquez. 1966. Germination of date pollen in culture media. Rep. Date Growers' Inst. 43: 24–27.

——— & C. L. Ream. 1968. The influence of temperature on germination of date pollen. Rep. Date Growers' Inst. 45: 7–9.

Goor, A. 1967. The history of the date through the ages in the Holy Land. J. Econ. Bot. 21: 320–340.

Henderson, A. 1986. A review of pollination studies in the Palmae. Bot. Rev. 52: 221–259.

Heslop-Harrison, J. & Y. Heslop-Harrison. 1970. Evaluation of pollen viability by enzymatically induced fluorescence: Intracellular hydrolysis of fluorescein diacetate. Stain Technol. 45: 115–120.

Hilgeman, R. H. 1954. The differentiation, development, and anatomy of the axillary bud, inflorescence and offshoot in the date palm. Rep. Date Growers' Inst. 31: 6–10.

Knox, R. B. 1984. The pollen grain. Pages 198–271 in B. M. Johri (ed.), Embryology of angiosperms. Springer-Verlag, Berlin.

Leshem, Y. & D. Ophir. 1977. Differences in endogenous levels of gibberellin activity in male and female partners of two dioecious tree species. Ann. Bot. 41: 375–379.

Lloyd, D. G. 1976. The transmission of genes via pollen and ovules in gynodioecious angiosperms. Theor. Population Biol. 9: 299–316.

McCurrach, J. C. 1960. Palms of the world. Harper, New York.

McGregor, S. E. 1976. Insect pollination of cultivated crop plants. U.S. Dept. Agric. Handb. #496.

Mogensen, H. L. 1986. Juxtaposition of the generative cell and vegetative nucleus in the mature pollen grain of amaryllis (*Hippeastrum vitatum*). Protoplasm 134: 67–72.

Moore, H. E., Jr. 1973. The major groups of palms and their distribution. Gentes Herbar. 11: 27–141.

———. 1982. Major trends of evolution in palms. Bot. Rev. **48**: 1–69.

Nakamura, S. & H. Miki-Hirosige. 1985. Fine-structural study on the formation of the generative cell wall and intine-3 layer in a growing pollen grain of *Lilium longiflorum*. Amer. J. Bot. **72**: 365–375.

Nixon, R. W. 1926. Experiments with selected pollens. Rep. Date Growers' Inst. **3**: 11–14.

———. 1927. Further evidence of the direct effect of pollen on the fruit of the date palm. Rep. Date Growers' Inst. **4**: 7–9.

———. 1928. The direct effect of pollen on the fruit of the date palm. J. Agric. Res. **36**: 97–128.

——— 1931. The commercial utilization of differences of ripening of dates due to pollen. Rep. Date Growers' Inst. **8**: 5–6.

———. 1934a. Metaxenia in dates. Proc. Amer. Soc. Hort. Sci. **32**: 221–226.

———. 1934b. Recent pollination experiments. Rep. Date Growers' Inst. **11**: 9–11.

——— 1935. Metaxenia and interspecific pollination in *Phoenix*. Proc. Amer. Soc. Hort. Sci. **33**: 21–26.

———. 1951. The date palm—"Tree of Life"—in the subtropical deserts. J. Econ. Bot. **5**: 274–301.

——— & J. B. Carpenter. 1978. Growing dates in the United States. USDA Agric. Inform. Bulletin #207.

Osman, A. M. A., W. Reuther & L. C. Erickson. 1974. Xenia and metaxenia studies in the date palm *Phoenix dactylifera* L. Rep. Date Growers' Inst. **51**: 6–16.

Owens, S. J. & A. D. Westmuckett. 1983. The structure and development of the generative cell wall in *Gibasis karwinsky, G. venustula* and *Tradescantia blossfieldiana* (Commelinaceae). Pages 149–157 *in* D. L. Mulcahy & E. Ottaviano (eds.), Pollen: Biology and implications for plant breeding. Elsevier Biomedical, New York.

Peterson, G. L. 1977. A simplification of the protein assay method of Lowrey et al., which is more generally applicable. Anal. Biochem. **83**: 346–356.

Platt-Aloia, K. A., E. M. Lord, D. A. DeMason & W. W. Thomson. 1986. Freeze fracture observations on membranes of dry and hydrated pollen from *Collomia, Phoenix,* and *Zea*. Planta **168**: 291–298.

Popenoe, P. 1924. The date palm in antiquity. Sci. Monthly **XIX(3)**: 313–325.

———. 1973. The date palm. Field Research Projects, Coconut Grove, Miami, Florida.

Ream, C. L. 1976. Metaxenia effect of pollen from inbred male palms on ripening of date fruit. Rep. Date Growers' Inst. **53**: 21–22.

Reuveni, O. 1985. *Phoenix dactylifera*. Pages 343–349 *in* A. Halevy (ed.), Handbook of flowering. Vol. I. CRC Press, Boca Raton, Florida.

———. 1986. Fruit set and fruit development of the date palm (*Phoenix dactylifera* L.). Pages 119–144 *in* S. P. Monselise (ed.), Handbook of fruit set and development. CRC Press, Boca Raton, Florida.

Richards, A. J. 1986. Plant breeding systems. Allen & Unwin, Ltd., London.

Schroeder, C. A. & R. W. Nixon. 1958. Morphological effects of pollens and thinning on fruit of 'Deglet Noor' dates. Rep. Date Growers' Inst. **35**: 17–18.

Swingle, W. T. 1928. Metaxenia in the date palm, possibly a hormone action by the embryo or endosperm. J. Heredity **19**: 257–268.

Tisserat, B. & DeMason, D. A. 1982. A scanning electron microscope study of pollen of *Phoenix* (Arecaceae). J. Amer. Soc. Hort. Sci. **107**: 883–887.

Uhl, N. & H. E. Moore, Jr. 1977. Correlations of inflorescence, flower structure, and floral anatomy with pollination in some palms. Biotropica **9**: 170–190.

Whitehead, D. R. 1969. Wind pollination in the angiosperms: Evolutionary and environmental considerations. Evolution **23**: 28–35.

Whittlesey, H. R. 1933. Ripening dates earlier by using different pollen. Rep. Date Growers' Inst. **10**: 9.

Zohary, D. & P. Spiegel-Roy. 1975. Beginnings of fruit growing in the Old World. Science **187**: 319–327.

Zohary, M. 1982. Plants of the Bible. Cambridge University Press, London.

Pollination Biology of Economically Important Palms

Table of Contents

Abstract

The pollination systems of four economic palms are reviewed. These palms are two well-established crops, *Elaeis guineensis* and *Cocos nucifera,* and two species with high economic potential, *Orbignya phalerata* and *Bactris gasipaes.* All are believed to be insect pollinated. The importance of understanding pollination systems is stressed, particularly in relation to fruit yield, pest control, germplasm transfer, and insect-transmitted disease. Economically inspired research on palm pollination is also shown to have much academic interest, especially concerning evolution of sexual systems and pollination systems.

Key words: palms, pollination, *Elaeis guineensis, Cocos nucifera, Orbignya phalerata, Bactris gasipaes*

Resumen

Los mecanismos de polinización en cuatro palmas con valor económico son revisados. Estas palmas incluyen dos especies tradicionalmente cultivadas, *Elaeis guineensis* y *Cocos nucifera,* asi mismo como otras dos taxa con gran potencial económico, *Orbignya phalerata* y *Bactris gasipaes.* Se cree que las cuatros son polinizados por insectos. La importancia del conocimiento de mecanismos de polinización es enfatizado, particularmente en la producción de frutos, control de insectos, transferencia de semillas, y enfermedades transmitidas por insectos. Investigacion en polinización de palmas motivada por razones económicas se muestra que también tiene valor académico, especialmente lo concerniente a evolución de los mecanismos sexuales y de polinización.

I. Introduction

The most important products of many economic palms come from their fruit. An important process in fruit development is pollination. These statements are obvious, and yet it is curious that, until recently, most palms, especially economic palms, were considered to be wind pollinated. However, it is now known that many palms are pollinated by insects (review by Henderson, 1986). In this paper I consider the importance of understanding the pollination mechanisms of economic palms, not only for the obvious reason of fruit yield, but also for less obvious reasons such as pest control, germplasm transfer, insect-transmitted disease, and knowledge of evolutionary trends in palms.

I will concentrate on four species: *Elaeis guineensis* Jacq., *Cocos nucifera* L., *Orbignya phalerata* Mart., and *Bactris gasipaes* H.B.K., chosen for several reasons. The first two are well-established as economically important species, and

Advances in Economic Botany 6: 36–41, 1988
© 1988 The New York Botanical Garden

36

the latter two have much economic potential. Their pollination systems are relatively well-known, and represent two common syndromes among palms, bee pollination and beetle pollination. They are all cocosoid palms, and their relatedness makes comparison of their pollination systems of interest.

In a recent review of palm pollination (Henderson, 1986) I characterized two insect pollination syndromes that appear common in palms. The first was a protogynous beetle pollination syndrome (found in *Elaeis, Orbignya,* and *Bactris*), and the second a protandrous bee pollination syndrome (found in *Cocos*). The beetle pollination syndrome involves two groups of beetles, curculionids and nitidulids. The curculionids all belong to a pantropical tribe, the Derelomini, and are apparently only known from palm inflorescences. The nitidulids, in the neotropics at least, belong to the genus *Mystrops,* and are also usually only known from palm inflorescences. Both groups consist of small active beetles, which appear to have rather intricate associations with palms.

II. *Elaeis guineensis*

This species is widely cultivated in plantations throughout the tropical areas of the world for its oil-yielding fruit (Hartley, 1977).

The sexual system of *E. guineensis* is monoecy, with unisexual inflorescences. It is out-breeding, since anthesis on succeeding inflorescences does not overlap (Hartley, 1977). It produces either staminate or pistillate inflorescences in alternating cycles of several months' duration (Williams & Thomas, 1970). During changes in the cycle hermaphrodite inflorescences are commonly produced.

Inflorescence morphology has been described and illustrated by Purseglove (1972) and Moore (1973). Inflorescences are enclosed in bud by a prophyll and peduncular bract. The peduncle bears a rachis with numerous rachillae. Staminate flowers are solitary, and are surrounded by connate bracteoles. They are trimerous and have a pistillode. Pistillate flowers are in triads, although the lateral staminate flowers usually abort early in development. Pistillate flowers are also bracteolate, trimerous, and have a staminodal ring.

Inflorescence development at flowering time has been described by Purseglove (1972) and Syed (1979). Hermaphrodite inflorescences are protogynous (Hardon, 1976). The peduncular bract of staminate inflorescences splits two to three weeks before anthesis. Anthesis is acropetal, and is completed within two to four days. Staminate flowers are anise scented. Anthesis in pistillate inflorescences also begins on proximal flowers. Pistillate flowers also produce an anise scent, but intermittently during the day. Pistillate anthesis lasts 24 hours.

Elaeis guineensis has been usually considered to be wind pollinated (Hartley, 1977), but recently Syed (1979) has shown pollination to be by beetles. Syed found large numbers of insects, especially derelomine weevils (*Elaeidobius* spp.), visiting staminate inflorescences. On pistillate inflorescences few insects were continually present, but swarms arrived at irregular intervals and then soon left. Amongst these were large numbers of *Elaeidobius* spp., and several, especially *E. kamerunicus,* carried large numbers of *Elaeis* pollen grains. Syed (1981) has described the association between *Elaeis* and *Elaeidobius.* The weevils feed and breed on staminate inflorescences. Adults eat flower tissue, but not pollen, while larvae feed on flowers decomposing after anthesis. Adults visit pistillate flowers but spend little time there. *Elaeidobius* is restricted to *Elaeis guineensis,* and even *Elaeis oleifera* is not so attractive to them, much less other palms. Up to six species co-exist on the same inflorescences, and do so by having different oviposition sites. The relative abundance of each changes according to different climatic regimes.

The understanding of the pollination system in *Elaeis guineensis* has had great economic consequences. The species is native to West Africa, and problems of low yield due to poor pollination had never been encountered there. It has been introduced and widely planted in southeast Asia, where yields had generally been lower, and assisted pollination necessary (Greathead, 1983). Following introduction from West Africa to southeast Asia of one species of pollinator, *Elaeidobius kamerunicus,* fruit yields increased by 20% in Malaysia and 53% in Sabah (Syed et al., 1982). The beetle has now been introduced throughout the region. In West Africa alternative methods of insect pest control are now being developed, since it is realized that chemical control of insect pests was having a deleterious effect on *Elaeidobius* populations, and decreasing yield (Greathead, 1983).

III. *Cocos nucifera*

The coconut is widely cultivated throughout tropical areas of the world, usually on smallholdings, for the multiple useful products from its fruit (Child, 1974).

The sexual system of *Cocos* is monoecy, with inflorescences bearing both staminate and pistillate flowers. It is usually out-breeding, since in most varieties staminate and pistillate anthesis does not overlap, either on the same or succeeding inflorescences. However, some varieties are regularly selfed (Child, 1974).

Inflorescence morphology has been described by Purseglove (1972). Inflorescences are enclosed in bud by a prophyll and peduncular bract. The peduncle bears a rachis with numerous simple rachillae. Flowers are borne in triads, or in a derived pattern. Triads are born proximally on the rachillae, with paired or solitary staminate flowers distally. Flowers are dimorphic and trimerous. Staminate flowers have a pistillode, and pistillate flowers have staminodes.

Inflorescence development during flowering has been described by Purseglove (1972) and Sholdt and Mitchell (1967). The bright cream-colored inflorescence is protandrous, and anthesis basipetal. Staminate anthesis begins on distal flowers, and takes place during the morning. Nectar is produced by the pistillode. Flowers fall from the inflorescence soon after anthesis. Staminate anthesis continues for a maximum of 38 days. Usually staminate anthesis finishes before pistillate anthesis begins. Pistillate anthesis lasts for a maximum of 12 days, usually less, and also begins with distal flowers. Pistillate flowers also produce nectar.

Pollination has been attributed to wind, insects, or both. The subject has been reviewed by Child (1974), Furtado (1924), Menon and Pandalai (1958), and Sholdt and Mitchell (1967). Most authors cited in these reviews have stressed the role of flies and bees in pollination. The most detailed study is that of Sholdt and Mitchell (1967). These authors concluded that in Hawaii coconuts were either cross- or self-pollinated. Wind pollination occurred to a limited extent, but the main pollinating agents were insects, especially honey bees.

The origin of *Cocos nucifera* is in the islands of southeast Asia (Harries, 1978). Wild type populations have recently been discovered in Australia and the Philippines (Buckley & Harries, 1984; Gruezo & Harries, 1984). Pollination of wild type populations is not known, but there is good evidence that in cultivation the coconut is bee pollinated. McGregor (1976, and refs. therein) reported that in areas where bees were kept on coconut estates, yields were remarkably high, and he considered that introduction of honey bees into plantations could increase yields. He cited the Philippines as an area of low yield and low bee population.

IV. *Orbignya phalerata*

Fruits of the babassú palm are widely used by local people in Brazil for oil, extracted from the seeds (Anderson, 1983; Balick, 1979).

The sexual system of *Orbignya phalerata* is functional dioecy. Inflorescences are either all staminate, or with staminate and pistillate flowers. However, in the latter type only pistillate flowers are functional. The species is therefore an obligate outcrosser (Anderson et al., in press).

Inflorescences are enclosed in bud by a prophyll and thick, woody peduncular bract. The peduncle bears a rachis with numerous rachillae. On staminate inflorescences flowers are paired or solitary. On hermaphrodite inflorescences pistillate flowers are borne at the base of the rachillae. Flowers are dimorphic and trimerous, and the staminate polyandrous (Anderson et al., in press).

The inflorescence is protogynous. In staminate inflorescences anthesis begins soon after bract opening, and an odor is produced. In hermaphrodite inflorescences pistillate anthesis begins immediately after bract opening, and can continue for 48 hours (Anderson et al., in press).

Pollination has been described by Anderson et al. (in press). The only insect abundant on both staminate and pistillate inflorescences is the nitidulid beetle *Mystrops mexicanus*. Pollen is found on specimens collected on pistillate inflorescences at anthesis.

Orbignya phalerata is currently widely used by local people within its current natural range in

South America. Because of its high potential, efforts are being made to domesticate it (Balick, 1984). Understanding of the pollination is clearly important to such domestication. Anderson et al. (in press) indicated that wind pollination could be effective in open, disturbed habitats, but it is not known how effective wind could be in an artificial environment, or what effect absence of its natural pollinators would have on yield. As domestication proceeds, account will have be taken of possible detrimental effects from absence of pollinators.

V. *Bactris gasipaes*

Bactris gasipaes, the pejibaye palm, has edible fruits, which are widely eaten by local people throughout Central and South America (Mora-Urpí et al., 1984). Intensive efforts are currently being made to cultivate pejibaye on a commercial scale.

The sexual system of *Bactris gasipaes* is monoecy, with inflorescences bearing both staminate and pistillate flowers. It is out-breeding, since pistillate and staminate anthesis do not overlap.

Inflorescence morphology has been described by Beach (1984) and Mora-Urpí and Solís (1980) Inflorescences are enclosed in bud by a prophyll and spiny peduncular bract. The peduncle bears a rachis with numerous simple rachillae, with most flowers being paired or solitary staminate interspersed with triads. Flowers are dimorphic and trimerous.

Inflorescence development during flowering time has also been described by Beach and Mora-Urpí and Solís. The inflorescence is protogynous. The peduncular bract splits between 16:00 and 17:20 hr. Pistillate flowers are at anthesis immediately, and remain so for 24 hours, producing a musky odor. At 17:00 the next day staminate anthesis begins and after a few minutes staminate flowers fall from the inflorescence.

Pollination likewise has been described by Beach and Mora-Urpí and Solís. Large numbers of derelomine weevils (*Phyllotrox* sp.) and scarab beetles (*Cyclocephala* sp.) arrive as soon as the peduncular bract splits, and leave the inflorescence 24 hours later, at or soon after staminate anthesis. Beach emphasized the role of the scar-

abs, while Mora-Urpí and Solís emphasized the role of the derelomine weevils.

The natural home of the pejibaye is not known for certain, but is believed to be the eastern Andean foothills of Peru (Prance, 1984). Pollination of possible wild populations is not known, but in cultivation it is either by weevils or scarab beetles, or both. The relatively high fruit yield of pejibaye seems to indicate that pollination is effective even in artificial environments. It may be that pollinators have spread with the palm while it has been transported by man throughout the neotropics. However, if current efforts to introduce pejibaye into the old world tropics are successful (Balick, pers. comm.), then lack of effective pollinators could become a problem.

VI. Discussion

Knowledge of pollination of economic palms, especially those grown for their fruit, is obviously important. This has clearly been demonstrated in the case of the oil palm, *Elaeis guineensis.* Understanding the pollination system of this species has not only increased yields and eliminated the necessity of assisted pollination, but also demonstrated an important point. This is that if germplasm is to be transferred from a wild to a cultivated state, then beneficial symbionts should be simultaneously transferred. As complex tropical ecosystems become more and more disturbed, and as more and more palms are raised in plantations, then management of pollinators will become an important issue. A further area of importance is pest control. Clearly, insect pollinators must be protected against indiscriminate use of insecticides. As Wood (1976) has emphasized, an integrated approach to pest control involves developing the fullest possible understanding of interactions between insects and palms. Similarly, in the case of insect-transmitted diseases, those potential vectors must be distinguished from beneficial pollinators.

Finally, I want to discuss how economically inspired research can be of great academic interest. I refer to the evolution of sexual systems and pollination systems. The four species discussed are all cocosoid palms, and their sexual and pollination systems are summarized in Table I. This group is characterized by having flowers in triads, or a derived pattern. *Cocos nucifera,*

Table I

Summary of sexual systems and pollination systems

	Sexual system	Flower arrangement	Receptivity	Direction of anthesis	Pollinator
Elaeis guineensis	Monoecious, inflorescences unisexual, flowers unisexual	In ♂ inflorescences paired or solitary; in ♀ inflorescences solitary pistillate	Protogynous (in ♂ inflorescences)	Acropetal	Derelomine weevils
Cocos nucifera	Monoecious, inflorescences hermaphroditic, flowers unisexual	Few triads at base of rachillae, paired or solitary staminate above	Protandrous	Basipetal	Honey bees
Orbignya phalerata	Functionally dioecious, inflorescences either staminate or hermaphroditic (then functionally pistillate)	In ♂ inflorescences triads at base of rachillae	Protogynous	Not known	Nitidulid beetles
Bactris gasipaes	Monoecious, inflorescences hermaphroditic, flowers unisexual	Few triads scattered on rachillae, rest paired or solitary staminate	Protogynous	Not known	Scarab beetles; derelomine weevils

Elaeis guineensis, Bactris gasipaes, and *Orbignya phalerata* all show a tendency, common in cocosoid palms, for distal areas of the rachillae to bear paired or solitary staminate flowers only. In *C. nucifera* this tendency is clear, and pistillate flowers are only found at the base of the rachillae. In *E. guineensis* this tendency may have led to unisexual inflorescences, since hermaphrodite inflorescences have proximal pistillate flowers. Similarly in *O. phalerata,* this tendency may have led to the occurrence of unisexual inflorescences, and this may be a stage in the evolution of dioecy. *Bactris gasipaes* exhibits a condition, common in the genus, of scattered triads, but even they tend to be in a proximal position. Furthermore, all four species are dichogamous, and because of the relative position of the flowers, outlined above, dichogamy is based on the direction of anthesis. In *Cocos nucifera* anthesis is basipetal and thus the inflorescence is protandrous. In *Elaeis guineensis* anthesis is acropetal and (hermaphrodite) inflorescences protogynous. The direction of anthesis is not known for *B. gasipaes* or *O. phalerata,* but may be almost simultaneous in staminate flowers. The question arises as to what selective pressures among these related palms would lead from protandrous mellitophily

to protgynous cantharophily (or vice versa). This question can be rephrased, and it can be asked what selective pressure would lead from basipetal to acropetal anthesis (or vice versa). The answer may lie, in part, in insect behavior.

Bawa and Beach (1981) considered that sexual systems were fundamentally linked to pollination biology, and could only be understood in this context. They considered that protandry was the commonest condition in angiosperms, and that the evolution of protogyny could, in part, be attributed to the life histories of pollinators. In this context it can be seen that a basipetal anthesis (i.e., protandry) is better suited to bee behavior, since initially flowers at anthesis are in an exposed, accessible position. On the other hand, acropetal anthesis (i.e., protogyny) would be better suited to beetle behavior, since initially flowers at anthesis are in a concealed position. Further, in protogynous systems inflorescence development can be related to insect behavior. In *Bactris gasipaes,* beetles arrive in the evening, bearing pollen, and contact stigmas. They are not active during the day, but leave the following evening, bearing pollen, immediately after staminate anthesis. On the other hand, the behavior of the pollinating beetles of *E. guineensis* is quite different. They are confined to staminate inflorescences and are active during the day only, when they make short intermittent visits to pistillate inflorescences. Thus, inflorescence development of *E. guineensis* and *B. gasipaes* can be seen to be directly related to, if not caused by, pollinator behavior. The initial stages of the evolution of one or the other system, protogyny or protandry, may depend on local abundance and effectiveness of insect pollinators.

Clearly there is still a lot to learn about the fascinating association between palms and their pollinators. The study of pollination systems in economic palms will continue to contribute greatly to the solution of both economic and academic problems.

VII. Acknowledgments

I am grateful to Drs. Michael Balick, Brian Boom, Julie Denslow, Scott Mori, Michael Nee, and Ghillean Prance for their comments on earlier versions of the manuscript.

VIII. Literature Cited

Anderson, A. B. 1983. The biology of *Orbignya martiana* (Palmae), a tropical dry forest dominant in Brazil. Ph.D. Thesis. University of Florida, Gainesville.

————, **W. Overall & A. Henderson.** (In press). Pollination ecology of forest dominant palm (*Orbignya phalerata* Mart.) in northern Brazil. Biotropica.

Balick, M. J. 1979. Amazonian oil palms of promise: A survey. Econ. Bot. **33:** 11–28.

————. 1984. Palms, people and progress. Horizons **3(4):** 33–37.

Bawa, K. S. & J. H. Beach. 1981. Evolution of sexual systems in flowering plants. Ann. Missouri Bot. Gard. **68:** 254–274.

Beach, J. H. 1984. The reproductive biology of the peach or "pejibayé" palm (*Bactris gasipaes*) and a wild congener (*B. porschiana*) in the Atlantic lowlands of Costa Rica. Principes **28:** 107–119.

Buckley, R. & H. Harries. 1984. Self sown wild type coconuts from Australia. Biotropica **16:** 148–151.

Child, R. 1974. Coconuts, 2nd ed. Longman, London.

Furtado, C. X. 1924. A study of the coconut flower and its relation to fruit production. Gard. Bull., Singapore **3:** 261–273.

Greathead, D. J. 1983. The multi-million dollar weevil that pollinates oil palms. Antenna **7:** 105–107.

Gruezo, W. S. & H. C. Harries. 1984. Self sown, wild type coconuts in the Philippines. Biotropica **16:** 140–147.

Hardon, J. J. 1976. Oil palm breeding—Introduction. Pages 89–109 *in* R. H. V. Corley, J. J. Hardon & B. J. Wood (eds.), Oil palm research. Elsevier Scientific Publishing Company, New York.

Harries, H. C. 1978. The evolution, dissemination and classification of *Cocos nucifera* L. Bot. Rev. **44:** 265–319.

Hartley, C. W. S. 1977. The oil palm, 2nd ed. Longman, London.

Henderson, A. 1986. A review of pollination studies in the Palmae. Bot. Rev. **52(3):** 221–259.

McGregor, S. E. 1976. Insect pollination of cultivated crop plants. USDA Agricultural Research Service.

Menon, K. P. V. & K. M. Pandalai. 1958. The coconut palm. A monograph. Indian Central Coconut Committee, Ernakulam, India.

Moore, H. E., Jr. 1973. The major groups of palms and their distribution. Gentes Herb. **11:** 27–141.

Mora-Urpí, J. & E. M. Solís. 1980. Polinización en *Bactris gasipaes* H.B.K. (Palmae). Rev. Biol. Trop. **28:** 153–174.

————, **E. Vargas, C. A. López, M. Villaplana, G. Allón & C. Blanco.** 1984. The pejibaye palm (*Bactris gasipaes* H.B.K.). FAO, Rome.

Prance, G. T. 1984. The pejibaye, *Guilielma gasipaes* (H.B.K.) Bailey, and the papaya, *Carica papaya* L. Pages 87–104 *in* D. Stone (ed.), Pre-Columbian plant migration. Harvard University Press, Cambridge.

Purseglove, J. W. 1972. Tropical crops. Monocotyledons. Longman, London.

Sholdt, L. L. & W. A. Mitchell. 1967. The pollination of *Cocos nucifera* L. in Hawaii. Trop. Agric., Trinidad **44:** 133–142.

Syed, R. A. 1979. Studies on oil palm pollination by insects. Bull. Entomol. Res. **69:** 213–224.

————. 1981. Insect pollination of oil palm: Feasibility of introducing *Elaeidobius* spp. into Malaysia. Pages 263–289 *in* E. Pushparajah & Chew Poh Soon (eds.), The oil palm in agriculture in the eighties: A report on the International Conference on oil palm in agriculture in the eighties. Kuala Lumpur, Malaysia.

————, **I. H. Law & R. H. V. Corley.** 1982. Insect pollination of oil palm: Introduction, establishment and pollinating efficiency of *Elaeidobius kamerunicus* in Malaysia. Planter, Kuala Lumpur **58:** 547–561.

Williams, C. N. & R. L. Thomas. 1970. Observations on sex differentiation in the oil palm, *Elaeis guineensis* L. Ann. Bot. **34:** 957–963.

Wood, B. J. 1976. Pests—Introduction and ecological considerations. Pages 333–346 *in* R. H. V. Corley, J. J. Hardon & B. J. Wood (eds.), Oil palm research. Elsevier Scientific Publishing Company, New York.

Ecology of Economically Important Palms in Peruvian Amazonia

FRANCIS KAHN

Table of Contents

Abstract

Most palm species are used by Amazonian natives and provide a variety of products, such as edible fruits, oil, palm heart, building materials, and basketry. However, only a few species have significant economic potential. These palms occur essentially in seasonal swamp forests on waterlogged soils covering vast areas in Peruvian Amazonia, or on sandy soils. Three especially promising species—*Jessenia bataua, Mauritia flexuosa* and *Euterpe precatoria*—constitute dense populations on these soils, which are generally considered as unfit for agriculture. The management of promising palm populations will contribute to increasing the economic value of such soils by transforming seasonal swamp forests into productive agroforestry fields.

Key words: palms, forest management, waterlogged soils, Amazonia, Peru

Resumen

La mayoría de las palmas son utilizadas por el selvático Amazónico forneciendo una variedad de productos como frutas, aceite, chonta, materiales de construcción y cestería. Sin embargo, pocas son las especies que tienen un buen potencial económico. Estas palmeras se encuentran principalmente en los suelos hidromórficos, periódicamente inundados, que cubren gran parte de la Amazonia Peruana, y también en los suelos arenosos. Tres especies promisoras—*Jessenia bataua, Mauritia flexuosa* y *Euterpe precatoria*—forman poblaciones muy densas en estos suelos, generalmente considerados como muy pobres para la agricultura. El manejo de las poblaciones de palmeras promisoras contribuirá a mejorar la potencialidad económica de tales suelos transformando estas vegetaciones en agroselvas productivas.

I. Introduction

Population density and species richness of palms are generally high in Amazonian forests (Boom, 1986; Kahn, 1986a; Kahn & Castro, 1985; Marmillod, 1982; Sist, 1985). Palms are generally abundant in upland forests, with a large number of understory species and a few arborescent forms (Kahn, 1986b). In contrast, seasonal swamp forests are dominated by arborescent palms (Granville, 1976, 1978; Kahn & Castro, 1985). Palms also occur in areas flooded by rivers and on sandy soils (campinas in Brazil, chamizales in Peru), generally with lower species richness in both cases.

Native Amerindians of Amazonia use most of the Amazonian palm species (Anderson, 1978; Balick, 1979, 1985; Boom, 1986; Braun, 1968; Cavalcante, 1974; Kahn & Mejia, 1987; Lévi-Strauss, 1950; Mejia, 1983; Schultes, 1974, 1977; Wallace, 1853). All parts of palms can be used: leaves (thatching, basketwork, house walls, fibers), petiole (building parts, arrows), trunk (house walls, floors, doors, starch, blowpipes), fruit (edible fruit, oil, charcoal), palm heart, and sometimes roots (medicine). While palm uses and exploitation are supplementary economic activities, some species can be more important (e.g., *Mauritia flexuosa* L.f., see Padoch, this volume).

Although there are a lot of uses for palms, only a few species have significant economic potential. This is the case for species with high yields of edible fruit, rich oil composition, palm hearts acceptable for canning, and/or starch production. Other, related species are also of great interest as potential sources of germplasm for genetic improvement.

II. Promising Palms in Peruvian Amazonia

The economic potential of several Peruvian palms is evaluated (one to three asterisks) in the following list by considering the value of the product (e.g., oil quality, fruit or palm heart acceptability), frequency and density of natural populations, and potential of soils on which they are generally found (good soils are used more for crops than for native palms; on poorly drained soils there is an increased potential for forest management). Most of these palms also offer products of purely local importance, e.g., as building materials or fibers (see Lopez Parodi and Mejia C., this volume). We will discuss here only those products of economic importance in the local marketplace.

OIL PALMS

*** *Elaeis oleifera* (H.B.K.) Cortés (poloponta) is a stemmed, but creeping palm. Populations of this species are being prospected throughout

Amazonia for further improvement and hybridization with the African oil palm, *E. guineensis* Jacq., as well as a separate breeding program. The Amazonian species offers a high quality oil, lower height because of its creeping trunk, and better resistance to diseases (Meunier, 1976; Ooi et al., 1981).

*** *Jessenia bataua* (Mart.) Burret (ungurahui) is a monocaulous, arborescent palm, 25 m in height. *Jessenia* oil is similar to olive oil (Balick, 1981, 1982), with high quality protein in the presscake (Balick & Gershoff, 1981). Natives use *Jessenia* oil for cooking and make a drink from the pulp (Schwyzer, 1981).

* *Oenocarpus* spp. (sinamillo) are medium, mono- or multi-stemmed palms, 10–15 m in height. These species are part of a genetic complex including *Jessenia* (Balick, 1981, 1986; Forero, 1983; Martin & Guichard, 1979). They are occasionally used by natives to make a drink from the pulp, and are promising species for a *Jessenia–Oenocarpus* gene bank.

EDIBLE FRUITS AND STARCH

* *Astrocaryum chambira* Burret (chambira) is a monocaulous, arborescent palm, 15–25 m in height. The endosperm is drunk or eaten as with coconut. The epidermis of the pinnae of young leaves is used for fibers (hammocks, bags).

*** *Bactris gasipaes* H.B.K. (pijuayo) is a multi-stemmed palm, 15–20 m in height. It is cultivated in Amazonia for its fruit (food and drink), and is never found in natural populations (see Clement, this volume).

*** *Mauritia flexuosa* L. f. (aguaje) is a monocaulous, arborescent palm, up to 30 m in height, and the most popular in Peruvian Amazonia. Its fruit (also an ice cream made from it) is sold in all the streets of Iquitos, constituting a rather important, but local, commercial trade (see Padoch, this volume). The species is dioecious and only female plants are harvested. At present, male plants are used only as sources of "suri" (beetle larvae). However, the trunk of *Mauritia flexuosa* contains a high concentration of starch and its production would permit the economic use of male plants. Today starch is extracted only by the Warao Indians of the Orinoco delta (Heinen & Ruddle, 1974), but *Mauritia flexuosa* could become an important source of starch for the

Table I

Population structure of four palm species with economic potential found in a survey area in upland forest on well-drained soils in the lower Ucayali River basin, Peruvian Amazonia

	On slope (0.43 ha)	On plateau (0.28 ha)
Jessenia bataua		
Stemmed palms	0	0
Acaulescent juveniles (≥ 1 m)	128	67
Seedlings (< 1 m)	95	58
Euterpe precatoria		
Stemmed palms	0	0
Acaulescent juveniles (≥ 1 m)	7	1
Seedlings (< 1 m)	22	6
Oenocarpus cf. *bacaba*		
Stemmed palms	3	1
Acaulescent juveniles (≥ 1 m)	3	4
Seedlings (< 1 m)	4	2
Astrocaryum chambira		
Stemmed palms	0	0
Acaulescent juveniles (≥ 1 m)	1	0
Seedlings (< 1 m)	0	0

Amazonian region as a whole (Ruddle et al., 1978).

is responsible for the destruction of the large populations of huasai in the region.

PALM HEART

** *Euterpe precatoria* Mart. (huasai) is a monocaulous, arborescent palm, 20 m in height. Traditionally used to produce palm heart in Peruvian Amazonia, this species is less suitable for canning than multi-stemmed species such as *E. oleracea* Mart. or *Bactris gasipaes*. Nevertheless, a canning factory in Iquitos uses this palm and

III. Ecology of Promising Palms in the Lower Ucayali River Basin

Forest ecosystems are very diversified in Amazonia (Pires, 1974): upland (terra firme) forests (Oldeman, 1974; Prance et al., 1976; Takeuchi, 1960), seasonal swamp forests on waterlogged soils (Granville, 1978; Kahn & Castro, 1985), forests periodically flooded by rivers (Prance,

Table II

Population structure of four promising palm species in a 1 ha area of "sacha aguajal" in the lower Ucayali River basin, Peruvian Amazonia (ad: adult; trj: trunked juvenile; acj: acaulescent juvenile; N: total number of palms; BA: basal area in m^2/ha)

	ad	trj	acj	N (h $\geq$ 1 m)	BA (DBH $\geq$ 0.15 m)
Mauritia flexuosa	18	53	179	250	6.94 (72.59%)
Jessenia bataua	28	73	260	361	2.16 (22.59%)
Euterpe precatoria	45	62	143	250	0.46 (4.81%)
Oenocarpus mapora	3	7	30	40	— —
					9.56 (100%)

Total BA (DBH $\geq$ 0.15 m) = 26.34
Dicot BA (DBH $\geq$ 0.15 m) = 16.78 (63.71%)
Palm BA (DBH $\geq$ 0.15 m) = 9.56 (36.29%)

Table III

Population structure of three promising palm species in a 1 ha area of "aguajal" in the lower Ucayali River basin, Peruvian Amazonia. This parcel is only inundated by the river during the years of highest flood (legend see Table II)

	ad	trj	acj	N (h ≥ 1 m)	BA (DBH ≥ 0.15 m)
Mauritia flexuosa	138	92	415	645	16.53 (96.55%)
Euterpe precatoria	35	7	8	50	0.59 (3.45%)
Oenocarpus mapora	18	36	67	121	– –
					17.12 (100%)

Total BA (DBH ≥ 0.15 m) = 31.11
Dicot BA (DBH ≥ 0.15 m) = 13.99 (44.97%)
Palm BA (DBH ≥ 0.15 m) = 17.12 (55.03%)

1980), and low forests on sandy soils (Anderson, 1981). All these ecosystems are found in the lower Ucayali River basin (Encarnación, 1985).

PROMISING PALMS IN UPLAND FORESTS

The economically promising palms discussed above are infrequent in the upland forests on well-drained soils (orthic acrisol), where species richness and density of palms are very high. In the lower Ucayali basin 0.71 ha of forest were surveyed; 29 species and a density of 5625 palms (or axes for multi-stemmed species) greater than 1 m in height were found. Only four of the promising species were encountered in the survey area (Table I). *Oenocarpus* cf. *bacaba* Mart. (*Kahn & Mejia 1723*, NY) is only found on well-drained soils, but generally at low density. *Astrocaryum chambira* is rarely encountered in these forests; dense populations occur in secondary vegetation and near villages where it is propagated by man. This species has potential for agroforestry on well-

drained soils. Only juveniles of *E. precatoria* and *J. bataua* are found in these upland forests.

PROMISING PALMS IN SEASONAL SWAMP FORESTS

The natives usually distinguish two palm swamp forest formations: a mixed *Jessenia bataua–Mauritia flexuosa* formation called "sacha aguajal," and an almost pure *Mauritia flexuosa* formation called "aguajal."

1. Sacha aguajal

In the lower Ucayali valley, this formation stands on low terraces that are never flooded by the Ucayali River; inundations are caused by rains. The soil is a gleysol, with organic matter concentrated near the surface. A total of 18 palm species (2380 axes greater than 1 m in height) were found on the 1 ha surveyed, but among them were only four promising species: *M. flexuosa*, *J. bataua*, *E. precatoria* and *O. mapora*

Table IV

Population structure of two promising palm species of a 0.5 ha area of "aguajal" annually affected by river flooding in the lower Ucayali River basin, Peruvian Amazonia (legend see Table II)

	ad	trj	acj	N (h ≥ 1 m)	BA (DBH ≥ 0.15 m)
Mauritia flexuosa	19	23	33	75	9.57 (100%)
Euterpe precatoria	2	–	3	5	– –
					9.57 (100%)

Total BA (DBH ≥ 0.15 m) = 11.10
Dicot BA (DBH ≥ 0.15 m) = 1.53 (13.78%)
Palm BA (DBH ≥ 0.15 m) = 9.57 (86.22%)

Table V

Relationship between the population structure of *Jessenia bataua* and gleyic podzol in the lower Ucayali River basin, Peruvian Amazonia

	Gleyic podzol (0.1 ha)[a]	Gleyic acrisol transition zone (0.1 ha)[b]	Well drained orthic acrisol (0.1 ha)[c]
Adults	13	5	0
Trunked juveniles	5	2	0
Acaulescent juveniles (≥ 1 m)	87	57	27
Seedlings (< 1 m)	209	173	22
Respectively from a—0.27 ha, b—0.19 ha, c—0.71 ha surveyed.			

Karst. subsp. *mapora,* the former three in dense populations. Relative basal area of palms reaches 36.29% (Table II) on this site. The American oil palm, *E. oleifera,* occurs infrequently on such sites, but can form dense populations.

2. Aguajal

Mauritia flexuosa formations have been mentioned by Spruce (1871), Bouillenne (1930) and Moore (1973), and cover vast areas from the Andean piedmont to the Atlantic coast, always on waterlogged soils. In French Guiana, *M. flexuosa* formations occur almost exclusively in coastal savannah (Granville, 1978).

These formations are particularly extensive in Peruvian Amazonia. An analysis of Landsat survey data (ONERN, 1977) concluded that they cover 21% of 311,970 ha near Iquitos and 34% of 66,560 ha in the Marañon River valley.

Mauritia flexuosa reaches very high densities in natural populations. An average of 246 trunked palms per ha (CV: 24.7%) was found by Salazar and Roessl (1977) based on 10 plots of 0.5 ha surveyed along the Itaya River near Iquitos. In the upper Huallaga valley, Gonzálcs (1971–1974) found an average per ha of 351 trunked palms (CV: 26%) and 297 acaulescent juveniles (CV: 43%) based on 20 plots of 0.05 ha surveyed.

In the lower Ucayali valley such formations

Table VI

Summary of the occurrence of economically promising palm species in the forest ecosystems of Peruvian Amazonia (H: high; M: medium; L: low)

Forest ecosystems	Promising species	Population density	Population frequency
1. Upland forests, on well drained, orthic acrisol.	*Astrocaryum chambira* Burret	L	M
	Oenocarpus cf. *bacaba* Mart.	L	M
	Bactris gasipaes H.B.K.	(cultivated)	
2. Seasonal swamp forests, on gleysol, periodically inundated by rains.	*Jessenia bataua* (Mart.) Burret	H	H
	Euterpe precatoria Mart.	H	H
	Mauritia flexuosa L. f.	M	H
	Oenocarpus mapora Karst.	M–H	H
	Elaeis oleifera (H.B.K.) Cortés	H	L
3. Seasonal swamp forests, on distric histosol, inundated by rains and by river during the years of highest flood.	*Mauritia flexuosa* L. f.	H	H
	Euterpe precatoria Mart.	M	H
	Oenocarpus mapora Karst.	M–H	H
4. Swamp forests, on distric histosol, flooded by river each year.	*Mauritia flexuosa* L. f.	H	H
	Euterpe precatoria Mart.	L	H
5. Forests on gleyic podzol.	*Jessenia bataua* (Mart.) Burret	H	H
	Euterpe precatoria Mart.	L	M
6. Forests on alluvial soils (eutric fluvisol).	*Euterpe precatoria* Mart.	M	M
	Oenocarpus mapora Karst.	M	M
	Bactris gasipaes H.B.K.	(cultivated)	

Table VII

Sex ratio in three populations of *Mauritia flexuosa* in the lower Ucayali River valley, which reveals the economic destruction caused by current collection methods

	Sacha aguajal (1 ha)	Aguajal (1 ha)	Aguajal (0.5 ha)
Male plants	15 (83.33%)	100 (72.46%)	13 (68.42%)
Female plants	3 (16.66%)	23 (16.67%)	4 (21.05%)
Sex unknown	– –	15 (10.86%)	2 (10.53%)
Totals	18	138	19

stand on the lowest terraces. The soil is a distric histosol, composed of organic matter, several meters in depth; soil water is acid (pH: 3.5). The organic matter is essentially *M. flexuosa* litter: fallen leaves, male inflorescences and infructescences. *Jessenia bataua* does not occur in this vegetation type.

The structures of two parcels are presented. The first area is inundated by rains and by the river only during the years of highest flood. A total of 11 palm species (1184 axes greater than 1 m in height were found on 1 ha surveyed, among them only three promising species. Total basal area (for DBH greater than 15 cm) is high, with 31.11 m²/ha, of which 53.13% corresponds to *M. flexuosa* (Table III). The second area is flooded by the river each year. The part of the vegetation that is most exposed to the river includes numerous dead palms. Eight palm species were found on 0.5 ha surveyed, with only two promising species. The canopy is mainly composed of *M. flexuosa* with a few *E. precatoria*; a few dicotyledons are also present (Table IV).

PROMISING PALMS ON PODZOLS

In the lower Rio Negro valley the association of *J. bataua–Mauritia carana* Wallace–*Euterpe controversa* Barb. Rodr. is found on orthic podzol (pers. obs.). A preliminary study on the lower Ucayali River indicates a relationship between the density of *J. bataua* populations and gleyic podzol (Table V).

IV. Palms and Forest Management

All the data presented here clearly show that several of the most promising palm species in Peruvian Amazonia form large and dense populations on waterlogged and poorly drained soils (Table VI). These soils are generally unfit for agriculture. Covering vast areas as they do, they seriously limit the economic development of this region. While we do not believe that the management of palm populations on waterlogged soils can lead to any major industrial use and development, it could be important as part of a regional ecodevelopment program. The objective is to transform the seasonal swamp forests into productive agroforestry fields, to increase the economic value of such regions. The three species with the highest densities in Peruvian Amazonia—*J. bataua*, *M. flexuosa* and *E. precatoria*—can be used integrally; in addition to their economic potential described above, they also serve as sources of building materials.

In all tropical countries, palms of waterlogged soils are commonly used. In Brazilian Amazonia, Anderson et al. (1985) described the integration of *Euterpe oleracea* in an agroforestry system. Examples from Asia and Pacific islands are given respectively by Ruddle et al. (1978) and Barrau (1959). Uses of African *Raphia* swamps are listed by Profizi (1983), who proposes a rational management system of these swamps based on palms.

Two preliminary points must be resolved if any management plan is to succeed. First, rational management of these natural palm populations can begin only with a change in fruit-collecting practices. At present, fruit is collected by cutting down palms, and as a result the native vegetation is progressively losing its economic potential. In the case of the dioecious *Mauritia flexuosa*, there is currently a preponderance of male plants among adult palms, reflecting past collecting practices (Table VII). In contrast, Salazar and Roessl (1977) found 111 males and 69 females per ha in slightly-disturbed vegetation. This management problem also exists in other Amazonian countries. Granville (1985) has campaigned against the cutting down of palms for fruit-collecting in French Guiana. Second, it is necessary to introduce new palm uses. In Peru, starch production from the trunk of *M. flexuosa* is unknown. A technological transfer from Asia or the Orinoco delta should be attempted.

V. Acknowledgments

This study was supported by the international convention ORSTOM, France/IIAP, Peru. I am indebted to C. Padoch for her helpful assistance on the English text. Information on soils was given by L. Veillon. Field studies on seasonal swamp forests in the lower Ucayali River basin were made with the collaboration of K. Mejia. Conclusions are my own, however.

VI. Literature Cited

Anderson, A. B. 1978. The names and uses of palms among a tribe of Yanomama Indians. Principes **22(1):** 30–41.
———. 1981. White sand vegetation of Brazilian Amazonia. Biotropica **13(3):** 199–210.
———, **A. Gély, J. Strudwick, G. L. Sobel & M. G. C. Pinto.** 1985. Um sistema agroflorestal na várzea do estuario amazônico (ilha das onças, Município de Barcarena. Estado do Pará). Acta Amazonica. **15(1–2):** 195–224.
Balick, M. J. 1979. Economic botany of the Guahibo. I. Palmae. Econ. Bot. **33(4):** 361–376.
———. 1981. *Jessenia bataua* and *Oenocarpus* species: Native Amazonian palms as new sources of edible oil. Pages 145–155 *in* F. H. Pride, L. H. Princen & K. D. Mukherjee (eds.), New sources of fats and oils. Amer. Oil Chem. Soc., Champaign.
———. 1982. Palmas neotropicales. Nuevas fuentes de aceite comestible. Interciencia **7(1):** 25–29.
———. 1985. Useful plants of Amazonia: A resource of global importance. Pages 339–367 *in* G. T. Prance & T. E. Lovejoy (eds.), Key environments: Amazonia. Pergamon Press, New York.
———. 1986. Systematics and economic botany of the *Oenocarpus–Jessenia* (Palmae) complex. Adv. Econ. Bot. **3:** 1–140.
——— **& S. N. Gershoff.** 1981. Nutritional evaluation of the *Jessenia bataua* palm. Source of high quality protein and oil from tropical America. Econ. Bot. **25(3):** 261–271.
Barrau, J. 1959. The sago palms and other food plants of marsh dwellers in the South Pacific islands. Econ. Bot. **13:** 151–162.
Boom, B. M. 1986. The Chácobo Indians and their palms. Principes **30:** 63–70.
Bouillenne, R. 1930. Un voyage botanique dans le bas Amazone. Arch. Inst. Bot. Univ. Liège **8:** 1–185, pls. 1–34.
Braun, A. 1968. Cultivated palms of Venezuela. Principes **12:** 39–103, 111–136.
Cavalcante, P. B. 1974. Frutas comestíveis da Amazônia. Publicações avulsas 27. MPEG, Belém, Brazil.
Encarnación, F. 1985. Introducción a la flora y vegetación de la Amazonia Peruana: Estadio actual de los estudios, medio natural y ensayo de una clave de determinación de las formaciones vegetales en la llanera Amazónica. Candollea **40(1):** 237–252.
Forero, P. L. E. 1983. Anotaciones sobre bibliografía seleccionada del complejo *Jessenia–Oenocarpus* (Palmae). Cespedesia **12(45–46):** 21–49.
Gonzáles, R. M. 1971–1974. Estudio sobre la densidad de poblaciones de aguaje (*Mauritia* sp.) en Tingo María, Perú. Rev. For. Perú **5(1–2):** 46–54.
Granville, J.-J. de. 1976. Notes guyanaises: Quelques forêts sur le grand Inini. Cah. ORSTOM, sér. Biol. **XI(I):** 23–24.
———. 1978. Recherches sur la flore et la végétation guyanaises. Thèse Doctorat d'Etat. Univ. of Montpellier, France.
———. 1985. Cueillir sans détruire. SEPANGUY, Cayenne (poster).
Heinen, H. D. & K. Ruddle. 1974. Ecology, ritual and economic organization in the distribution of palm starch among the Warao of the Orinoco delta. J. Anthropol. Res. **30:** 116–138.
Kahn, F. 1986a. Les palmiers des forêts tropicales humides du bas Tocantins (Amazonie brésilienne). Rev. Ecol. (Terre et Vie) **41(1):** 3–14.
———. 1986b. Life forms of Amazonian palms in relation to forest structure and dynamics. Biotropica **18(3):** 214–218.
——— **& A. de Castro.** 1985. The palm community in a forest of central Amazonia, Brazil. Biotropica **17(3):** 210–216.
——— **& K. Mejia.** 1987. Notes on the biology, ecology and use of a small Amazonian palm: *Lepidocaryum tessmannii*. Principes **31(1):** 14–19.
Lévi-Strauss, C. 1950. The use of wild plants in tropical South America. Handbook of South America Indians **6:** 465–486. Cooper Square Publishers, New York.
Marmillod, D. 1982. Methodik und Ergebnisse von Untersuchungen über Zusammensetzung und Aufbau eines Terrassenwaldes in peruanischen Amazonien. These Doktorgrades. Georg-August Univ. of Göttingen, Fed. Rep. Germany.
Martin, G. & Ph. Guichard. 1979. A propos de quatre palmiers spontanés d' Amérique latine. Oléagineux **34:** 375–381.
Mejia, K. 1983. Palmeras y el Selvícolo Amazónico. Univ. Nac. Mayor San Marcos. Mus. Hist. Nat. Lima.
Meunier, J. 1976. Les prospections de palmacées. Une nécessité pour l'amélioration des palmiers oléagineux. Oléagineux **31:** 153–157.
Moore, H. E. 1973. Palms in the tropical forest ecosystems of Africa and South America. Pages 63–88 *in* B. J. Meggers, E. S. Ayensu & W. D. Duckworth (eds.), Tropical forest ecosystems in Africa

and South America: A comparative review. Smithsonian Institution Press, Washington, D.C.

Oldeman, R. A. A. 1974. L'architecture de la forêt guyanaise. Mém. 73, ORSTOM, Paris.

ONERN. 1977. Use of remote sensing systems evaluating the potential of the aguaje palm tree in the Peruvian jungle. ONERN, Lima.

Ooi, S. C., E. B. da Silva, A. A. Müller & J. C. Nascimiento. 1981. Oil palm genetic resources. Native *Elaeis oleifera* populations in Brazil offer promising sources. Pesq. Agropec. Bra. Brasilia 16(3): 385–395.

Pires, J. M. 1974. Tipos de vegetação da Amazônia. Br. Flor. 5(17): 48–58.

Prance, G. T. 1980. A terminologia dos tipos de florestas amazonicas sujeitas a inundação. Acta Amazonica 10(3): 499–504.

———, W. A. Rodrigues & M. F. da Silva. 1976. Inventário florestal de um hectare de mata de terra firme km 30 da estrada Manaus-Itacoatiara. Acta Amazonica 6(1): 9–35.

Profizi, J. P. 1983. Contribution à l'étude des palmiers *Raphia* du Sud Bénin. Botanique. Ecologie. Ethnobotanique. Thèse Doctorat de spécialité. Univ. of Montpellier, France.

Ruddle K., D. Johnson, P. K. Townsend & Y. D. Rees.

1978. Palm sago. A tropical starch from marginal lands. The University Press of Hawaii, Honolulu.

Salazar, A. & J. Roessl. 1977. Estudio de la potencialidad industrial del aguaje. Proyecto ITINTEC 3102 UNA-IIA, Lima.

Schultes, R. E. 1974. Palms and religion in the Northwest Amazon. Principes 18: 3–21.

———. 1977. Promising structural fiber palms of the Colombian Amazon. Principes 21: 72–82.

Schwyzer, A. 1981. Producción casera del aceite de ungurahui (*Jessenia polycarpa*). Proyecto de Asentamiento Rural Integral—Jenaro Herrera, Iquitos, Perú. Bol. Tec. 11.

Sist, P. 1985. Régénération et dynamique des populations de quelques espèces de palmiers en Guyane française. DEA, Univ. of Paris VI.

Spruce, R. 1871. Palmae Amazonicae, sive Enumeratio Palmarum in itinere suo per regiones Americae aequatoriales lectarum. J. Linn. Soc. 11: 65–183.

Takeuchi, M. 1960. A estrutura da vegetação na Amazonia. 1. A mata pluvial tropical. Bol. Mus. Paraense E. Goeldi, N. S. Bot. 6: 1–17 pp.

Wallace, A. R. 1853. Palm trees of the Amazon and their uses. John van Voorst, London.

Prospects for Application of Vesicular-Arbuscular Mycorrhizae in the Culture of Tropical Palms

T. V. St. John

Table of Contents

Abstract

Vesicular-arbuscular mycorrhizae are a type of symbiosis between plants and beneficial fungi. Most wild and cultivated plants are mycorrhizal hosts. The effects of mycorrhizae include improved transplant recovery and survival, enhanced growth rate, and heightened drought resistance. These effects are thought to be directly or indirectly due to the ability of the fungus to aid in uptake of phosphorus. Mycorrhizae are known to occur in several palm genera, including *Bactris, Oenocarpus, Phoenix,* and *Jessenia.* They have been experimentally shown to be of significance in *Jessenia* and *Bactris,* but future experiments will undoubtedly indicate that the palms in general tend to be quite dependent on these symbionts. Experiments are now in progress with *Euterpe, Jessenia,* and *Bactris,* and will soon be initiated with *Orbignya* and *Oenocarpus.* Artificial inoculation in palm culture is indicated because nursery conditions often exclude native symbionts through use of sterilized soil, use of biocides, over-fertilization, or any of several other incompatible practices. The use of mycorrhizae in tropical nurseries will require modification of existing practices and special training of field personnel. For now inoculum must be produced or gathered locally, although commercial sources are becoming available. Realistically, we may expect inoculated nursery stock to survive and perform better after transplanting, and anticipate that in some cases inoculated plants will require less time in the nursery.

Key words: mycorrhiza, VAM, nursery, transplant, *Jessenia, Bactris*

Resumo

Micorrizas do tipo vesicular-arbuscular são simbioses de raízes com fungos benéficos, encontradas na maioria das plantas nativas e cultivadas. Entre os efeitos das micorrizas incluem-se melhor recuperação, taxa de crescimento acelerada e elevada resistência à seca, após o transplantio. Tais efeitos atribuem-se direta- ou indiretamente à capacidade do fungo de ajudar na absorção do fósforo. Micorrizas são conhecidas em vários gêneros das palmeiras, inclusive de *Bactris, Oenocarpus, Phoenix,* e *Jessenia.* Experimentalmente, tem sido demonstrada a importância desta simbiose em *Jessenia* e *Bactris,* mas experimentos no futuro provavelmente poderão indicar que as palmeiras em geral são dependentes desta simbiose. Estão em andimento experimentos com *Euterpe, Jessenia,* e *Bactris,* e estão sendo iniciados com *Orbignya* e *Oenocarpus.* A inoculação artificial em cultura de palmeiras é indicada, porque em condições de viveiro, quase sempre os simbiontes nativos são excluidos pelo uso de solo esterilizado, de pesticidas, superfertilização e várias outras práticas incompatíveis com a micorriza. A aplicação das micorrizas em viveiros tropicais exige modificação das práticas atuais e treinamento especial do pessoal do campo. Por enquanto, o inóculo está senso produzido ou colhedo no local, mas fontes comerciais já se tournam disponíveis. Podemos antecipar que as plantas inoculadas exigirão menos tempo no viveiro.

Table I

Mycorrhizal growth responses of selected plant species

Species	Mycorrhizal/control	Growth parameter	Authority
Apple	60	Dry weight	Geddeda et al., 1984
Avocado	2.5	Dry weight	Menge et al., 1980
Black Cherry	58	Dry weight	Kormanik et al., 1982
Black Walnut	5.1	Dry weight	Kormanik et al., 1982
Cranberry	7.2	Dry weight	Read, 1983
Rough Lemon	25	Dry weight	Kleinschmidt & Gerdemann, 1972
Cleopatra Mandarin	22	Dry weight	Kleinschmidt & Gerdemann, 1972
Troyer Citrange	5.3	Dry weight	Kleinschmidt & Gerdemann, 1972
Keen Sour Orange	2.4	Dry weight	Kleinschmidt & Gerdemann, 1972
Papaya	1.3	Height	Ramirez et al., 1975
Bactris gasipaes	3.0	No. of leaves	Janos, 197.
Jessenia bataua	1.8	Dry weight	St. John, unpubl.

I. The Mycorrhizal Symbiosis

We classify mycorrhizal symbioses into several distinct types, each of which involves a different kind of fungus and host plant. The most widespread types of mycorrhizae are vesicular-arbuscular mycorrhizae (VAM), found in palms and most other plants, and Ectomycorrhizae (ECM), found in certain forest trees. Mycorrhizae that are distinct from the two main kinds are found in the Ericaceae, Orchidaceae, and several small tropical families. VAM are the most widespread, and are the mycorrhizae of crop plants and most annual and woody natives (Gerdemann, 1968). VAM fungi are the most abundant microorganisms in most native soils (Hayman, 1978). The fungal partners of VAM are markedly unselective with regard to host plant; for example, the same species of fungus may be associated with liverworts, ferns, palms, and garden vegetables.

The fungi of VAM are recognized by the morphology of their large resting spores. Until a few years ago, the few recognized forms were known by descriptive names (Mosse & Bowen, 1968). Later, Gerdemann and Trappe (1974) placed the VAM-forming fungi in four genera of the family Endogonaceae. There are three large genera, *Glomus, Gigaspora,* and *Scutellospora.* The family includes three less common genera that form VAM, one that forms ECM, and others about which little or nothing is known. The number of species in the VAM genera has increased at a bewildering rate since 1974.

Our knowledge of tropical species is very limited. Many of the species described from Florida and elsewhere (Schenck & Smith, 1982; Trappe, 1982) are also found in the tropics. As with most other groups of organisms, there are undoubtedly many species, found only in the tropics, remaining to be described.

The role of mycorrhizae in the tropical rain forest has been the subject of discussion in recent years (Jordan, 1982; Went & Stark, 1968). The fungal symbionts are presumed to provide the same services for their host plants in the tropics that they provide in temperate forests (St. John, 1985).

II. The Beneficial Effects of Mycorrhizae

Mycorrhizae have been shown to improve plant growth over that of nonmycorrhizal controls; a few of the many examples are shown in Table I. The magnitude of the mycorrhizal growth response depends heavily on such factors as the species of plant and the native fertility of the soil used in the experiment. The way in which the growth response is brought about is clearly nutritional in most cases. VAM can greatly improve uptake of phosphorus and certain micronutrients, especially zinc and copper.

Among the more useful effects of VAM are the findings that mycorrhizal plants suffer less transplant injury (Menge et al., 1980) and are better able to withstand drought than nonmycorrhizal controls (Safir et al., 1971, 1972). Mycorrhizal plants may also be more resistant to certain

Table II

Mycorrhizal status of palm species

Species	VAM	Origin	Authority
Areca catechu	−	arboretum	Alwis & Abeynayake, 1980
Arecastrum romanzoffianum	+	field	Hood, 1970
Arenga engleri	+	field	Asai, 1934; Maeda, 1954
Bactris gasipaes	+	field	Janos, 1977
Bactris gasipaes	+	greenhouse	St. John, unpubl.
Calamus sp.	+	field	Janse, 1897
Caryota urens	+	arboretum	Alwis & Abeynayake, 1980
Chamaerops humilis	+	greenhouse	Kryuger, 1970
Cocos nucifera	+	field	Johnston, 1949
Cocos nucifera	+	field	Lily, 1975
Cocos nucifera	−	nursery	St. John, unpubl.
Elaeis guineensis	+	field	St. John, unpubl.
Euterpe edulis	+	field	St. John, unpubl.
Euterpe oleracea	+	field	St. John, unpubl.
Euterpe oleracea	+	greenhouse	St. John, unpubl.
Jessenia bataua	−	field	St. John, unpubl.
Jessenia bataua	+	greenhouse	St. John, unpubl.
Livistona chinensis	+	field	Asai, 1934; Maeda, 1954
Oenocarpus bacaba	+	field	St. John, 1980
Phoenix dactylifera	−, +	field	Trappe, 1981
Phoenix roebelenii	−	greenhouse	Stanczak-Boratynska, 1954
Rhapis excelsa	+	greenhouse	Stanczak-Boratynska, 1954
Rhapis humilis	+	greenhouse	Maeda, 1954
Roystonea elata	+	field	Baradas & Halos, 1980
Sabal palmetto	+	field	Hood, 1970; Meador, 1977
Syagrus sp.	−	field	St. John, 1980
Washingtonia filifera	+	field	St. John, unpubl.

pathogens (Schenck, 1981). Phosphorus fertilization in itself can bring about a wide range of physiological effects, including most of those attributed to the mycorrhizal condition, and there is reason to suspect that most or all effects of VAM may be side benefits of improved phosphorus nutrition.

The mycelium of the VAM fungus extends from the root, where it enters the cortical cells, into the surrounding soil. The internal hyphae penetrate the cortex of the finest rootlets, where they form structures that are diagnostic of the symbiosis. Oil storage organs called vesicles can form inside or outside the roots, and the haustoria-like arbuscules form within cortical cells. The arbuscules appear to be the site of much, but probably not all, of the metabolite exchange between host and fungus (Hayman, 1983).

The external mycelium extends into the soil, where it takes up phosphorus that is unavailable to the unaided root. The remarkable improvement that mycorrhizae bring about in phosphorus nutrition is a result of the spatial distribution of the hyphae. Since phosphate moves

very slowly in soil, it cannot diffuse to the root as rapidly as it is taken up. A zone of depletion forms, isolating the root surface from most of the soil volume. Mycorrhizal hyphae cross the depletion zone, take up phosphorus that is beyond the reach of the root, and transport it to the cortex (Tinker, 1978).

The external hyphae consist of coarse, thick-walled trunk hyphae, and fine, short-lived side branches. These lateral branches proliferate locally near nutrient-rich microsites, such as decomposing insect remains or subterranean deposits of decomposing organic matter (Nicolson, 1959). The localized concentration of hyphae in effect shortens the average pathway along which phorphorus ions must diffuse, greatly improving the rate of uptake over that which would be possible if the hyphae were distributed randomly through the soil (St. John et al., 1983).

III. Mycotrophy in Palms

Mycorrhizae are known to occur in several palm genera (Table II). The significance of these symbionts to the palms is known only for *Bactris gasipaes* (Janos, 1977) and *Jessenia bataua* (St. John, unpubl.); however, on indirect evidence it appears likely that most or all palms benefit from the association. The morphology of the fine absorbing roots provides this evidence. The relative dependence, or "mycotrophy," of a species is indicated in part by the presence and character of root hairs, and by the diameter of the finest roots (Baylis, 1975). The function of mycorrhizal hyphae is paralleled to some extent by root hairs, and those plant species lacking root hairs tend to be the most mycotrophic. Root hairs are uncommon or absent among the palms. Went and Darley (1953) established experimentally that *Phoenix dactylifera* L. is incapable of producing root hairs, and *Cocos nucifera* has also been reported to lack them (Murray, 1977; Purseglove, 1972). Although Tomlinson (1962) stated that palms bear root hairs, he gave no example.

IV. Artificial Inoculation in Palms

Artificial inoculation of palms may be necessary when nursery conditions exclude native symbionts, or when native fungi are relatively ineffective in phosphorus absorption. Such conditions may be rather common (St. John, unpubl. obs.). An important factor may be the high soil temperatures often encountered in unshaded nurseries and new plantings. Temperatures near 35°C can inhibit formation of the symbiosis (Parke et al., 1983), although species capable of colonizing host roots at temperatures up to 41°C were found in Florida (Schenck & Schroder, 1974). Temperatures above 52.5°C for ten minutes were lethal to inoculum of *Glomus fasciculatum* in California (Menge et al., 1979). The soil temperature of surface layers in clearings in the tropics may temporarily surpass 50°C (Longman & Jenik, 1974). Soil temperatures in unshaded nursery containers, often black in color, could potentially go even higher.

There are several other possible reasons for failure or scarcity of mycorrhizae in palm nurseries. The soil may have been initially sterilized, or its source or handling may have been such that any native inoculum was destroyed. Because large spores are not normally carried by the wind, and the hyphae do not grow through the soil unless associated with a suitable host plant, VAM are very slow to reestablish once lost. Other potential difficulties include the use of biocides or large doses of fertilizer. Thus tropical palms may be transplanted into phosphorus-deficient tropical soils without their natural means of obtaining phosphorus. If the new planting site has also been cleared, as is often the case, the soil may have very low native populations of mycorrhizal fungi. Early reintroduction of the native fungi in the nursery is the only rapid and certain way to ensure the important advantages of mycorrhizae when the seedlings are transplanted.

The establishment of mycorrhizae in tropical nurseries will require modification of existing practices and special training of field personnel. In order to minimize labor costs, inoculation may be carried out when the plants are being handled for other reasons. If inoculated at the time of planting, the seedlings will become mycorrhizal at the earliest possible time and will be better able to withstand later handling in the nursery. However, two important disadvantages may be overriding in certain circumstances. First, some seeds always fail, and plant mortality is always highest in the earliest stages, so a certain amount of expensive inoculum and labor will be wasted. Second, where damping off is a problem, potentially useful fungicides may have to be withheld to protect the mycorrhizal inoculum.

The nursery practices that may have to be modified are over-fertilization and use of pesticides. Fertilization will have to be held to the minimum consistent with good plant growth, since high levels of phosphorus and nitrogen sometimes can inhibit mycorrhiza formation. Certain slow release fertilizers work well, and can be applied as a single dose at the time of planting. Many pesticides can be inhibitory to the symbiosis (Trappe et al., 1984); care should be taken in selecting and applying any pesticides that must be used. Where containerized or outplanted seedlings are grown without shade, a mulch should be used to control extreme and fluctuating soil temperatures.

For now inoculum must be produced or gathered locally. The open pot culture method (Ferguson & Woodhead, 1982) can be used as a routine part of nursery operation, or inoculum may be collected from suitable local sources. In using pot cultures one is able to select fungi that produce a favorable growth response in the local conditions. The disadvantages of these cultures include the several-month period required to produce them and the poor quality inoculum, sometimes infested with pathogens, that may result from casual efforts. Local collection of inoculum has the advantage of being relatively rapid. Such materials as cacao leaf litter, the roots of pasture grasses, or the litter layers of forests are rich in mycorrhizal inoculum. However, no selection of beneficial fungi can be made and there is a danger of introducing plant pathogens.

Commercial sources of VAM inoculum are now becoming available (Native Plants Incorporated, Salt Lake City, Utah). At present only temperate zone fungi are offered. However, we may take encouragement from the fact that techniques exist for producing large quantities of quality, pathogen-free inoculum. If a demand develops for tropical inoculum, appropriate material can no doubt be brought to market in a fairly short time.

V. Expectations from Artificial Inoculation

While there is cause for enthusiasm about inoculating palms with VAM fungi, it is important to identify realistically both the potential and the limitations of artificial inoculation. We can introduce symbionts where they were entirely lacking, or we can introduce more beneficial isolates at a high propagule density. However, we will realize little additional benefit if good symbionts are already present in the soil. Compared with nonmycorrhizal plants, mycorrhizal seedlings in phosphorus-deficient soil will grow more rapidly and survive transplanting with less mortality. The magnitude of the benefits depends heavily on the plant species, the soils involved, and a number of other factors. When nursery conditions are such that mycorrhizal fungi are absent or ineffective, the use of artificial inoculation may lead to faster turn around of seedlings and better early performance after outplanting.

VI. Acknowledgments

Preparation of this manuscript and attendance at the symposium were supported by USAID grant No. DPE–5542–G–SS–4061–00. I thank Sr. and Sra. Osvaldo Manoel Santos for the Portuguese summary, and Dr. J. M. Trappe for useful suggestions on an earlier draft of this paper.

VII. Literature Cited

Alwis, D. P. & K. Abeynayake. 1980. A survey of mycorrhizae in some forest trees of Sri Lanka. Pages 146–153 in P. Mikola (ed.), Tropical mycorrhiza research. Clarendon Press, Oxford.

Asai, T. 1934. Über das Vorkommen und die Bedeutung der Wurzelpilze in den Landpflanzen. Jap. Jour. Bot. 7: 107–150.

Baradas, S. N. & P. M. Halos. 1980. Selection of mycorrhizal isolates for biological control of *Fusarium solani* f. *phaseoli* on *Vigna unguiculata*. Pages 247–248 in P. Mikola (ed.), Tropical mycorrhiza research. Clarendon Press, Oxford.

Baylis, G. T. S. 1975. The magnolioid mycorrhiza and mycotrophy in root systems derived from it. Pages 373–389 in F. E. Sanders, B. Mosse & P. B. Tinker (eds.), Endomycorrhizas. Academic Press, London.

Ferguson, J. J. & S. H. Woodhead. 1982. Increase and maintenance of vesicular-arbuscular mycorrhizal fungi. Chapter 5a, pages 47–54 in N. C. Schenck (ed.), Methods and principles of mycorrhizal research. The American Phytopathological Society, St. Paul, Minnesota.

Ferwerda, J. D. 1977. Oil palm. Chapter 13, pages 351–382 in P. de T. Alvim & T. T. Kozlowski (eds.), Ecophysiology of tropical crops. Academic Press, New York.

Geddeda, Y. I., J. M. Trappe & R. L. Stebbins. 1984. Effects of vesicular-arbuscular mycorrhizae and phosphorus on apple seedlings. Jour. Amer. Soc. Hort. Sci. 109: 24–27.

Gerdemann, J. W. 1968. Vesicular-arbuscular mycorrhiza and plant growth. Ann. Rev. Phytopathol. 6: 397–418.

——— & J. M. Trappe. 1974. The Endogonaceae in the pacific northwest. Mycologia Memoir no. 5: 1–76. N.Y. Bot. Gard., Bronx, New York.

Hayman, D. S. 1978. Endomycorrhizae. Chapter 10B, pages 401–442 in Y. R. Dommergues & S. V. Krupa (eds.), Interactions between non-pathogenic soil organisms and plants. Elsevier Scientific Publishing Company, Amsterdam.

———. 1983. The physiology of vesicular-arbuscular endomycorrhizal symbiosis. Canad. Jour. Bot. 61: 944–963.

Hood, S. C. 1970. A classification of the symbiotic relation of fungi with plant roots. Hood Laboratory, Tampa, Florida. 32 pp.

Janos, D. P. 1977. Vesicular-arbuscular mycorrhizae affect the growth of *Bactris gasipaes.* Principes 21: 12–18.

Janse, J. M. 1897. Les endophytes, radicaux de quelques plantes Javanaises. Ann. Jard. Bot. Buitenzorg 14: 53–212.

Johnston, A. 1949. Vesicular-arbuscular mycorrhiza in Sea Island cotton and other tropical plants. Trop. Agric. (Trinidad) 26: 118–121.

Jordan, C. F. 1982. Amazon rain forests. Amer. Sci. 70: 394–401.

Kleinschmidt, G. D. & J. W. Gerdemann. 1972. Stunting of *Citrus* seedlings in fumigated nursery soil related to the absence of endomycorrhizae. Phytopathology **62**: 1447–1453.

Kormanik, P. P., R. C. Schultz & W. C. Bryan. 1982. The influence of vesicular-arbuscular mycorrhizae on the growth and development of eight hardwood tree species. Forest Sci. **28**: 531–539.

Kryuger, L. V. 1970. Mikoriza komnatnykh rasteniy. Učen. Zap. Permsk. Gosud. Pedagog. Inst. **80**: 39–49.

Lily, V. G. 1975. Note on the development of vesicular-arbuscular mycorrhiza *Endogone fasciculata* in coconut root. Curr. Sci. **44**: 201–202.

Longman, K. A. & J. Jenik. 1974. Tropical forest and its environment. Longman, London.

Maeda, M. 1954. The meaning of mycorrhiza in regard to systematic botany. Kumamoto Jour. Sci., Ser. B **1954(3)**: 57–84.

Maedor, R. E. 1977. The role of mycorrhizae in influencing succession on abandoned Everglades farmland. Master of Science Thesis. University of Florida, Gainesville. 100 pp.

Menge, E. L. V. Johnson & V. Minassian. 1979. Effect of heat treatment and three pesticides upon the growth and reproduction of the mycorrhizal fungus *Glomus fasciculatus*. New Phytol. **82**: 473–480.

———, J. A., J. LaRue, C. K. Labanauskas & E. L. V. Johnson. 1980. The effect of two mycorrhizal fungi upon growth and nutrition of avocado seedlings grown with six fertilizer treatments. Jour. Amer. Soc. Hort. Sci. **105**: 400–404.

Mosse, B. & G. D. Bowen. 1968. A key to the recognition of some *Endogone* spore types. Trans. Brit. Mycol. Soc. **51**: 469–481.

Murray, D. B. 1977. Coconut palm. Chapter 14, pages 383–407 *in* P. de T. Alvim & T. T. Kozlowski (eds.), Ecophysiology of tropical crops. Academic Press, New York.

Nicolson, T. H. 1959. Mycorrhiza in the Gramineae. I. Vesicular-arbuscular endophytes, with particular reference to the external phase. Trans. Brit. Mycol. Soc. **42**:421–438.

Parke, J. L., R. G. Linderman & J. M. Trappe. 1983. Effect of root zone temperature on ectomycorrhiza and vesicular-arbuscular mycorrhiza formation in disturbed and undisturbed forest soils of southwest Oregon. Canad. Jour. Bot. **13**: 657–665.

Purseglove, J. W. 1972. Tropical crops. Monocotyledons 2. John Wiley & Sons, Inc., New York.

Ramirez, B. N., D. J. Mitchell & N. C. Schenck. 1975. Establishment and growth effects of three vesicular-arbuscular mycorrhizal fungi on papaya. Mycologia **67**: 1039–1041.

Read, D. J. 1983. The biology of mycorrhiza in the Ericales. Canad. Jour. Bot. **61**: 985–1004.

Safir, G. R., J. S. Boyer & J. W. Gerdemann. 1971. Mycorrhizal enhancement of water transport in soybean. Science **172**: 581–583.

———, ——— & ———. 1972. Nutrient status and mycorrhizal enhancement of water transport in soybean. Pl. Physiol. **49**: 700–703.

St. John, T. V. 1980. Uma lista de plantas Brasileiras tropicais infestadas por micorrizas do tipo vesicular-arbuscular. (A list of tropical Brazilian plant species infected with vesicular-arbuscular mycorrhizae.) Acta Amaz. **10**: 229–234.

———. 1985. Mycorrhizae. Chapter 13 *in* G. T. Prance & T. E. Lovejoy (eds.), Amazon rain forest. Key Environment Series, Pergamon Press, New York.

——— & D. C. Coleman. 1983. The role of mycorrhizae in plant ecology. Canad. Jour. Bot. **61**: 1005–1014.

———, ——— & C. P. P. Reid. 1983. The association of vesicular-arbuscular mycorrhizal hyphae with soil organic particles. Ecology **64**: 957–959.

Schenck, N. C. 1981. Can mycorrhizae control root disease? Pl. Dis. Reporter **65**: 231–234.

——— & V. N. Schroder. 1974. Temperature response of *Endogone* mycorrhiza on soybean roots. Mycologia **66**: 600–605.

——— & G. S. Smith. 1982. Additional new and unreported species of mycorrhizal fungi (Endogonaceae) from Florida. Mycologia **74**: 77–92.

Stanczak-Boratynska, W. 1954. Badania anatomiczne mykorhizy egzotycznych roslin Palmiarni Poznanskiej. Ann. Univ. Mariae Curie-Skłodowska, Sect. 3, Biol. **9**: 1–60.

Tinker, P. B. H. 1978. Effects of vesicular-arbuscular mycorrhizas on plant nutrition and plant growth. Physiol. Veg. **16**: 743–751.

Tomlinson, P. B. 1962. Essays on the morphology of palms. VIII. The root. Principes **6**: 122–124.

Trappe, J. M. 1981. Mycorrhizae and productivity of arid and semiarid rangelands. Pages 581–599 *in* J. T. Manassah & E. T. Briskey (eds.), Advances in food producing systems for arid and semiarid lands. Academic Press, Inc., New York.

———. 1982. Synoptic keys to the genera and species of Zygomycetous mycorrhizal fungi. Phytopathology **72**: 1102–1107.

———, R. Molina & M. Castellano. 1984. Reactions of mycorrhizal fungi and mycorrhiza formation to pesticides. Ann. Rev. Phytopathol. **22**: 331–359.

Went, F. & E. Darley. 1953. Root hair development on date palms. Rep. Date Grower's Inst. **29**: 3–5.

——— & N. Stark. 1968. Mycorrhiza. BioScience **18**: 1035–1039.

Utilization Pools: A Framework for Comparing and Evaluating the Economic Importance of Palms

DAVID M. BATES

Table of Contents

Abstract

The widespread occurrence of palms in tropical and warm-temperature regions of the world and their extensive integration into the economies of peoples populating these regions make them ideal subjects for cross-cultural comparisons and models for examining interesting questions concerning human/plant interactions. Effective comparisons require a consistent means of evaluting palm use in societies of widely different cultures and levels of technology. This problem is addressed and suggestions are made for employing utilization pools in making comparisons. Factors affecting future plant utilization are discussed, and predictions are made concerning palm utilization and, by inference, that of other kinds of plants in mankind's future.

Key words: Palmae, palm, use, future

Resumen

La extensa incidencia de palmas en tropicales y templadas regiones del mundo y su extensiva integración en las economías de los habitantes de estas regiones se las hacen sujetos ideales para comparaciones a través de varias culturas y modelos para examinar interesantes cuestiones de las interacciones entre los humanos y las plantas. Comparaciones efectivas requieren un método consistente para evaluar el uso de palmas en sociedades de vastas diferencias de culturas y niveles tecnología. Se enfrenta con esta problema y se hacen sugerencias para usar los niveles de utilización al hacer comparaciones. Se discuten los factores que afectan la futura utilización de las plantas, y se hacen predicciones de la utilización de palmas y, por inferencias, la de otros tipos de plantas en el futuro de los hombres.

Palabras claves: Palmae, palmas, uso, futuro

I. Introduction

As economic botanists, we have a vested interest in the wise use of the plant resources that nurture and give sustenance to mankind. Curiosity about ourselves and our surroundings, coupled with a realization that the natural world, of which we are a part, is undergoing accelerating modification, has given a sense of urgency to studies of indigenous plant use in subsistence and near-subsistence economies. Our forays into these societies and others of a simple technological base are designed, in part, to record human knowledge of the plant world with hope that the understanding gained will be helpful in assuring humanity's future.

What does the future hold for plant utilization? Which of the multitude of plants constituting our worldly flora will humans depend upon in the future? Will they be those that currently dominate agriculture and related production sciences, or will now obscure species rise to prominence? To what degree will the techniques of subsistence farming and woodland management be integrated into general agricultural or agroforestry practice? From our present understanding of plant use can we make rational predictions concerning the future?

Some years ago, caught up in Harold E. Moore, Jr.'s infectious enthusiasm for palms, I realized that this remarkable group of plants had potential value as an example for examining the kinds of questions posed above. Early thoughts on some aspects of palm-based economies (Bates, 1982) were further developed in a more broadly phrased consideration of plant utilization (Bates, 1985). In the present paper I return to palms to use these remarkable plants as focus for comparing roles of plants among peoples of differing cultures and technology and for making predictions concerning future uses of plants.

II. Palms as Role Models

There is a special essence to palms, captured by E. J. H. Corner (1966), who wrote, "Of all the land plants the palm is the most distinguished." In our mind's eye we tend to visualize palms as spires capped by spreading green crowns set against a tropical backdrop, but an appreciation of the value and uses of palms to humans depends on more than an idealized view of them. It flows from a knowledge of the basic aspects of palm biology and an understanding of the features of palms that suit them to broad scale comparative analyses of plant/human interactions, especially in tropical subsistence economies and those associated with developing nations. Here attention is given to the latter, and the following paragraphs provide a summary of palm characteristics and relationships with humanity that make the family so useful in comparative studies.

1. Palms are ubiquitous elements of hydric to xeric, tropical to warm-temperate environments. Biologically, they are indicators as well as functional elements of the ecosystems of these regions, and in their broad range of adaptations they interface with a large proportion of the world's population.

2. Palm distribution is largely coincident with that of third world countries or developing nations. Hence, palms are integral elements of these cultures and economies. Their future utilization can be tied to the development of these nations.

3. Palms provide humans with an enormous array of useful products and thus touch upon many aspects of the human condition, ranging from food procurement to production of industrial commodities.

4. Palms are elements of many different subsistence patterns, extending from hunting-gathering to subsistence and industrialized plantation agriculture. As such, they exemplify a broad array of approaches to plant utilization.

5. Palms are perennial, generally "woody," and predominantly trees. They provide a contrast to annual crops and opportunities to develop perennial production systems or those that integrate annual and perennial species.

6. The ability to use palms in a wide variety of tropical studies has potential advantages for temperate zone agriculture. By extension, models related to human/plant interactions in the tropics might be applied to temperate zone situations, especially in developing agroforestry practices and polycropping systems for marginal lands.

III. Knowledge of Palm Uses

As with any group of plants, the basic foundation of palm ethnobotany and economic botany is a comprehensive inventory of uses. For palms a complete inventory remains unwritten, but the rich store of information that now exists is nevertheless sufficient to establish much detail about the usefulness of these plants. Accounts of palm uses abound in the botanical and anthropological literature, being found in early writings, such as Wallace (1853), standard references, including Burkill (1935), and in many recent papers, e.g., those of Balick (1980, 1984), Fox (1977), Hodge (1975), Kitzke and Johnson (1975), Plotkin and Balick (1984), Ruddle et al. (1978),

Schultes (1974), Weinstock (1983), and Wilbert (1976).

The number of palm products that are basic or esoteric items of human subsistence is probably greater than those attributable to any other plant family. The coconut palm (*Cocos nucifera* L.) is said popularly to have 1000 uses; while 801 uses were ascribed to the palmyra palm (*Borassus flabellifer* L.) in the Tamil poem *Tala Vilasam* (Seemann, 1856). Other palms, for instance, the sugar palm (*Arenga pinnata* (Wurmb) Merrill) in the Old World (Miller, 1964) and the moriche and temiche (*Mauritia flexuosa* L. f. and *Manicaria saccifera* Gaertn.) in the New World (Wilbert, 1976), provide more strongly defined examples of use. For purposes of this paper, however, the details of use are less important than is recognition that palms are ubiquitous providers of shelter, food, fibers, construction materials, utensils, fuel, and medicinals and are elemental sources of mythology and spiritual awareness.

IV. Palm Utilization Patterns

The variety and richness of palm use stands in tribute to human ingenuity and creativeness, but when palm use is considered collectively with that of other plants in cultural and environmental contexts, it takes on added dimensions. There is a patterning to human utilization of plants that indicates use is under strong selective pressures (Bates, 1985). Selection reflects socio-economic conditions, levels of technological achievement, degrees of interaction with other peoples, beliefs, and other factors that affect the human condition, the outcome of which may be likened to a grand, all-embracing expression of optimized foraging [see Winterhalder & Smith (1982) for relevant discussion].

In simple hunting-gathering societies the patterns of utilization and use themselves are direct measures of the constraints imposed by natural habitats. Technological innovations and other changes in societies alter the parameters of selection by modifying the effects of natural environments. Under these conditions utilization patterns become more complex, but they remain analyzable in the same terms as those of simpler societies. As tangible evidences of selection, patterns of utilization provide a basis for making cross-cultural comparisons and have predictive value concerning the future use of plants.

Dependence on individual plant species in given societies differs: some are staples, others are complementary or augmentative to staples, while still others are of minor or no direct importance. Patterns of utilization, which are the collective expressions of plant usage in particular societal contexts, may be used to differentiate **utilization pools,** the concept of which was introduced and defined by Bates (1985). Thus, the staples of a society constitute the primary utilization pool. Species that directly augment or complement primary pool species form the secondary pool; while those that have only marginal significance make up the tertiary pool.

The pool concept is useful in at least four contexts. First, it focuses attention on the collective nature of plant use and the interplay of factors that are its determinants. Second, it can be applied at all levels of human organization from that of bands to tribes or nations, or to humanity as a whole. Third, it has no set time dimension. Utilization may be analyzed in terms of daily to annual cycles or in terms of changes that occur over extended periods of time. Fourth, it illustrates that plant utilization patterns are not static, but instead represent dynamic systems of change in which species membership in a given pool is always under a number of selective pressures of varying intensity and direction.

To illustrate utilization patterns and the application of the pool concept and to set the stage for consideration of palms in the future, palms are placed in worldwide utilization contexts.

Primary Pool

The competitive realm of international agriculture determines the composition of the primary pool. Species of this pool are the staples of mankind, e.g., the cereals, wheat (*Triticum* spp.), rice (*Oryza sativa* L.), and maize (*Zea mays* L.). Of the 100 species or so constituting the pool, many are cultigens. About 25 are food plants; the remainder provide a variety of basic commodities. Two oil-yielding palms, the coconut and the African oil palm (*Elaeis guineensis* Jacq.), are members of this select group. Although oil production is the obvious determinant for these species, the coconut also enters the pool because of its many other uses, including that of wood (Haas & Wilson, 1985).

SECONDARY POOL

Species constituting the secondary pool sometimes have a broadly international flavor, but more commonly are of national or regional importance. A few are cultigens. Most are cultivated or occur in managed stands, yet some remain wild and unmanaged. This pool consists of perhaps 1000 species, of which less than 20 species or species groups are palms. These palms, identified from Johnson's (1983) agroforestry assessment and references such as Hodge (1975), are utilized primarily as sources of fiber, sugar, starch, oil, or edible fruits and palm hearts. As is true of many palms, most have uses beyond those for which they are recognized here and are significant components of subsistence economies.

The best known palm species in the secondary pool is the date palm (*Phoenix dactylifera* L.). This ancient cultigen, perhaps arguably a member of the primary pool, is grown in both the Old and New Worlds. Except as ornamentals, the other palms of this pool are restricted to either one or the other of these hemispheres. Asiatic and Pacific island taxa include the betel palm (*Areca catechu* L.), the sugar palm, the palymra or lontar palm, the sago palm (*Metroxylon sagu* Rottb.), the rattans (*Calamus* and *Daemonorops* spp.), and the nipa palm (*Nypa fruticans* Wurmb). Species less certainly ascribable to the secondary pool today are the talipot and gebang (*Corypha umbraculifera* L. and *C. utan* Lam.), the fishtail palm (*Caryota urens* L.), and the salac (*Salacca zalacca* (Gaertn.) Voss). African raffia palms (*Raphia* spp.) may also belong in this Old World list.

Central and South American species of secondary pool character include the babassú (*Orbigyna phalerata* Mart.), the peach palm or pejibaye (*Bactris gasipaes* H.B.K.), the carnauba wax palm (*Copernicia prunifera* (Mill.) Moore), the jucara and açaí (*Euterpe edulis* Mart. and *E. oleracea* Mart.), the piassavas (*Attalea funifera* Mart. and *Leopoldinia piassaba* Wall.), and perhaps the ouricuri (*Syagrus coronata* (Mart.) Becc.).

Although some species extend beyond the boundaries of either Brazil or Amazonia, this Latin American group of secondary palms is especially a Brazilian/Amazonian phenomenon. It represents an industrialization of essentially wild stands and provides a significant proportion of Brazil's oil and fiber needs, some edibles, and an exported wax (Johnson, 1982). Insofar as the Brazilian agricultural economy is concerned, the babassú is a component of its primary pool, being the principal source of palm kernel oil (FAO, 1984). The carnuaba wax palm may also reach this status, as might the combined sources of piassava and the jucara and açaí. Other multipurpose Brazilian palm species, which worldwide would be of tertiary importance at most, could be regarded as secondary pool members, for example, the tucum (*Astrocaryum aculeatum* Mart.) and related species and the buriti, referred to above as moriche. Considerations of Brazilian palms at various levels of utilization are found in Cavalcante (1977), Hodge (1975), Johnson (1982), Kitzke and Johnson (1975), May et al. (1985), Mors and Rizzini (1966), and Pesce (1985).

TERTIARY POOL

Palm species constituting the worldwide tertiary pool probably number more than half those of the family. Their astounding variety of products are generally derived from wild stands and marketed locally, if at all. In these contexts the palms of this pool may be staple resources around which many subsistence peoples organize their lives.

Accounts of palm use amongst subsistence or essentially subsistence peoples are rich in variety. A sample is found in the studies of Balick (1984), Blanc-Pamard (1980), Bodley and Benson (1979), Dransfield (1976), Fox (1977), Weinstock (1983), and Wilbert (1976, 1980). In other instances information about palms is integrated into generalized studies of life and plant utilization, as done recently by Alcorn (1984) for the Huastec Maya and Rodin (1985) for the Kwanyama Ovambo of southwestern Africa. The latter provides a simple but illustrative example.

The Kwanyama occupy the northern reaches of Ovamboland, a desert region forming the northern boundary of Namibia. The subsistence pattern of these peoples is based on the cultivation of a small number of crops, particularly pearl millet [*Pennisetum americanum* (L.) K.

Schum., (*in* Rodin, 1985, as *P. typhoides* (Burm.) Stapf & C. E. Hubb.)] and Kaffir corn [*Sorghum bicolor* (L.) Moench, Caffrorum Group (as *S. caffrorum* var. *ondongas* (Koern.) Snowdon)], raising cattle and goats, fishing in ephemeral pans, and the wide harvest of native plants.

Rodin enumerates a Kwanyama-named flora of slightly more than 400 taxa, of which about three quarters are ascribed some human use other than as animal feed. While the data are not particularly suited for analyses, descriptive information indicates a primary pool consisting principally of cultivated grains and legumes and selected indigenous plants. Among the gathered wild plants is the single species of palm indigenous to the region, a doum palm [*Hyphaene petersiana* (Klotzsch) Mart. (*in* Rodin, 1985, as *H. ventricosa* Kirk)] known among the Kwanyama as omulunga.

Rodin reports that omulunga, which occurs in a scattered distribution, is "Considered [the] most useful plant in Ovamboland," and he records a significant number of uses for it. The trunks are hollowed out to make watering troughs or containers for Kaffir beer. The cabbage is an edible delicacy. The leaf blades are the premier raw materials for basketry, and their fibers may also be extracted. Basketry and fibers are used in all manner of utilitarian ways, and even become part of girls' adornment during puberty rites. The petioles enter light construction and are used as carrying poles, to fashion bows and ladles, or as fuel for cooking fires. The inflorescences may be tapped and the sap fermented to make wine, which also may be distilled. The fleshy, fibrous mesocarp of the fruit is eaten raw, and the outer, fleshy layers of the seed, like the sap, are fermented and distilled. The stony endosperm is a vegetable ivory and twin-seeded fruits may be made into dolls. Despite this impressive inventory of uses, the patterns of plant utilization by the Kwanyama are changing, and many of these uses are best thought of in the past tense, a point returned to in the discussion.

LIMITATIONS OF POOL CONCEPTS

Having introduced utilization pools in three situations and having argued their value in describing, analyzing, and predicting plant use, caveats are nevertheless in order. For the present, concepts of utilization pools must remain largely philosophical, a way of looking at human/plant interactions rather than a means for definitive analyses. The reasons for this are straightforward.

Criteria by which individual species are placed in a particular utilization pool are not defined, except as generalized perceptions. This is a vexing problem, yet rigidly defined criteria applicable to food plants and all other kinds of plants, to economies ranging from subsistence to industrialized, and to time periods of varying duration seem certain to be nonsensically cumbersome. A reasonable balance between definitions too strong or too weak probably will emerge in broadly phrased statements that can be used as guidelines. While use per se is the starting point, the emphasis must be on comparisons and relative values within the plant resource base of the societies being considered.

Data relevant to this comparative approach are difficult or impossible to extract from the literature in consistent ways. Overall, data are incomplete, of uneven quality, or lacking comparability. The absence of current, synonymized floras covering broad phytogeographical regions of the world, to which ethnobotanical studies may be related, is a basic problem. Beyond that, most ethnobotanical or economic botany accounts are phrased too narrowly to provide the full flavor of the many interactions of a society with their plant resource base, a notable recent exception being Alcorn's "Huastec Mayan Ethnobotany" (1984). Enumerations of use alone are not sufficient. Patterns, however, are more difficult to describe than use, and even when done with insight, as by Tanaka (1980) for the Kalahari San, they tend to focus on food plants rather than resource utilization as a whole. As societies become more complex, the number of variables that affect plant utilization increases. Hence, the need for a broader data base also increases, and deficiencies in it have more pronounced effects.

V. Palms in the Future

Implicit in predicting utilization of palms and other plants are the views we hold about the future of the earth and the nature of human subsistence. Views are likely to vary as interpretations and emphasis of evidence are colored by one's experiences and the points that one wishes to make. Yet, it is apparent that little attention has been given to testing hypotheses or establishing parameters in which predictions might be realized. Such pursuits are not merely academic. They are essential to one's case. How can one validly argue the future use of the omulunga among the Kwanyama, that of sago or sugar palms among Indonesians, or that of indigenous or introduced palms by any group of people without considering the future subsistence of the peoples concerned? Since our predictions ultimately must be based on our understanding of human/plant interactions, the need to focus on utilization patterns is reinforced.

The assumptions on which this palm reading are based represent one set of possibilities. They are projections of what are perceived as established trends. Basic to all others are the assumptions that, in the foreseeable future, the human population will continue to grow and the level at which it eventually stabilizes will be greater than that which now populates the planet. Population increases, in turn, suggest ever greater humanization of the earth, in the sense of Dubos (1973), ever greater management of the earth's biotic resources, and ever greater dependence on domesticated plants, rather than those collected in the wild. Agriculture and related production sciences are certain to become more, not less, reliant on applications of technology, which will encompass not only genetic manipulations but also ecologically appropriate agronomic practices. The plant resources base is destined to become genetically less diverse, and primary and secondary utilization pools more strongly defined, with the secondary pool smaller and more international in character. The isolation and independence of subsistence economies will decrease with increasing regionalization and internationalization of economic systems.

An earlier analysis of utilization trends (Bates, 1985) placed predictions of the foregoing kind in an indefinite time frame, but existing conditions present immediate concerns that need to be factored into our view of palm utilization. First, many peoples of the world now face immediate, severe, and compelling subsistence problems. For these peoples long-term trends and future events are irrelevant. Second, worldwide patterns of wealth and poverty and related conditions are unlikely to change dramatically. As a corollary, much of the world's population will continue to practice some form of subsistence agriculture. Third, opportunities to sample, select, and preserve desired germplasm are short-term at best. Hence, the options for developing new crops for agriculture, using a full range of genetic diversity, are also limited.

In the context of these assumptions and the special characters and utilization patterns of palms, the future of palms appears to vary from dismal to bright. In a most basic sense, palms are important and often dominant elements of tropical and subtropical ecosystems. Corner (1966) stresses that palms provide more carbohydrate and oil, in the form of leaves, pollen, honey, and fruits, to the wildlife of the tropics than any other family of plants. The continued diminution in the extent of natural vegetation has led to the extinction of some palms and threatens many others (Moore, 1977). The implications for the biosphere are obvious, widely considered, and represent a major challenge to mankind (Myers, 1984). In mitigation is the expectation that many palm species will remain or become significant components of managed tropical ecosystems, whether these are forest preserves or agroforestry systems. In a related context palms, even now, are significant components of the world's ornamental flora, a flora that may be expected to become increasingly pervasive in the coming years.

In the more traditional sense of use and utilization patterns, what is the prognosis for palms? The economics of world commerce suggest that the entry of additional palm species into the primary pool of staples is doubtful, although not impossible, especially if oil production from the African oil palm or the coconut should falter because of disease or the potential oil productivity of *Acrocomia* species, as described by Lleras (1985), should be realized. The competitiveness of agriculture at the international level, however, already has led to the exclusion of individual palm species as worldwide sources of carbohydrates and fibers, and were it not for the coconut, and again arguably the date, foods as well. In those areas of plant use where primary international utilization pools have yet to be defined, e.g., fodder and perhaps even biocrude, palms would not be expected to dominate, for their intrinsic nature does not suit them to these uses. Predictions regarding exotic chemicals are not possible, exotic implying just that; however, present evidence does not suggest palms are an especially rich source of unique compounds.

In contrast to a limited potential within the primary pool, palms could be major contributors in the development and internationalization of the secondary pool. Selection, which heretofore has operated less broadly and more fortuitously in defining the composition of this pool, would seem to favor expanded utilization of selected palms in situations or circumstances less favorable to primary pool species. Expansion of agriculture into tropical forests and deserts and the promise of integrated plantings and sustainable production systems of low energetic cost in these environments are principal selection factors. Events of these kinds, however, should not be seen as simple extensions of subsistence agriculture, but as major changes in agrarian traditions, involving among others increased capital investment, development of marketing infrastructures and transportation systems, inputs of agricultural technology, and selection and breeding for superior strains, both conventionally and through applications of biotechnology. Competitiveness within this emerging arena of agriculture is certain to become intense, with species favored to the extent they are adaptable at all stages from production to marketing and consumption, not only within their area of origin but also in similar situations or in markets worldwide.

Among the palms, the future of dates seems assured and that of the betel nut will be, as long as the chewing habit persists. Rattans have major promise in agroforestry systems and presumably could be cultivated in the New World tropics as well as in those of the Old. Among edibles, palm hearts are unique and production could expand in cultivation. Less certain is the future of edible fruits, such as the pejibaye and salac, which must compete with an array of desirable tropical alternatives. In the long term they may have significance only where tradition is strong. Similarly, the future of palm fibers is problematical. Coir, as another product of the coconut, has advantages in the mat and brush market. While other palm fibers have specialty and regional importance, e.g., raffia and piassava, cultivation and increased production are unlikely without stronger markets.

As secondary pool members, the potential for palms seems greatest as sources of oils, and secondarily as sources of carbohydrates. Further, since palms collectively represent important sources of wood and construction materials, uses in those contexts could expand as corollaries to others. Palms adaptable either to xeric regions in which irrigation is not feasible or to waterlogged soils in which conventional cultivation is difficult are those with greatest promise. Combinations of sugar-producing and oil-yielding palms in xeric regions seem entirely feasible; whereas starch and oil combinations have potential in swampy regions, although the data of Wilbert (1976) and Ruddle et al. (1978) cast some doubts on the competitiveness of sago-producing palms. The extent to which palms or other plants provide other products, e.g., wood, fibers, or fuel, or services, e.g., soil stabilization, will also be factors in determining use, for one of the goals of integrated plantings is to provide agricultural self-sufficiency in marginal habitats. In this sense the utilization of the babassú in Brazil (May et al., 1985) and the lontar on the islands of Roti and Savu (Fox, 1977) have particular relevance.

The strengthening and definition of the secondary pool and concomitant expansion of cultivation and managed lands indicate continuing decline in the use of wild species and thus contraction of tertiary pools, whether defined locally or worldwide. The example of the Kwanyama and the omulunga is indicative of such changes.

Through their recorded history the Kwanyama have been subsistence agriculturists, relying on the integration of cultivated and wild plants for much of their sustenance. From the account of Rodin (1985) and others that he cites, however, it is evident that the recent development of a cash economy and introduction of goods from outside are having major effects on the social structure of these people and their use of wild plants. Many of the traditional uses of the omulunga and much accompanying ritual focus on it have lessened or have ceased. Were it not for the continuing importance of the leaves of this species as a source of basketry materials and fibers and seasonal use of its fruits for wine the role of the omulunga would be minor in a culture that once was highly dependent on it. The future of omulunga depends on the extent that basketry persists or develops in the changing socio-economic state of the Kwanyama. In an expanding market cultivation or management are possible, as is competition with other fiber sources, including more productive palms.

VI. Conclusions

The uses of plants in given cultural contexts reflects the needs and technologies of those cultures and are under strong selective pressures. The results of selection may be represented in utilization pools of ranked value. Conceptually, utilization pools emphasize interrelatedness of plant resources and provide a basis for evaluating and comparing the role of plants in different societies. Because palms are conspicuous elements of tropical ecosystems and economies, providing humans with an array of products, they are broadly representative of utilization patterns and pools and are useful as models for considering evolution of plant utilization.

Present utilization of palms finds two species, the coconut palm and African oil palm, among the primary staples of world agriculture and commerce. About 20 taxa, including the date palm, betel palm, and babassú, are of major regional or market significance; and an uncounted number of species are of importance to local, tropical subsistence economies.

Within the parameters established, predictions of future palm utilization do not identify particular palm species as potential primary pool companions of the coconut or African oil palms or suggest the use of palm products derived from wild species will do other than decline. Palms, however, are expected to be significant contributors to cultivated and managed environments, with strong secondary pool potential in basic commodities, especially oils and carbohydrates, and specialty items, such as rattan and palm hearts. Conclusions drawn from palm analyses are applicable to other groups of plants when modified to suit their peculiarities.

VII. Acknowledgments

I wish to thank the reviewers of this paper for their thoughtful and constructive comments and suggestions and Paula Twomey for her Spanish translation of the abstract.

VIII. Literature Cited

Alcorn, J. B. 1984. Huastec Mayan ethnobotany. University of Texas Press, Austin, Texas.

Balick, M. J. 1979. Amazonian oil palms of promise: A survey. Econ. Bot. 33: 11–28.

———. 1980. Economic botany of the Guahibo. I. Palmae. Econ. Bot. 33: 361–376.

———. 1984. Ethnobotany of palms in the Neotropics. Adv. Econ. Bot. 1: 9–23.

Bates, D. M. 1982. The economic potential of palms. Seminar on underexploited economic plants. 13–18 December. Taipei, Taiwan.

———. 1985. Plant utilization: Patterns and prospects. Econ. Bot. 39: 241–265.

Blanc-Pamard, C. 1980. De l'utilisation de trois espèces de palmiers dans le sud du 'V Baoule' (Côte d'Ivoire). Cah. O.R.S.T.O.M. Sér. Sci. Hum. 17: 247–255.

Bodley, J. H. & F. C. Benson. 1979. Cultural ecology of Amazonian palms. Reports of Investigations 56. Laboratory of Anthropology, Washington State University, Pullman, Washington.

Burkill, I. H. 1935. A dictionary of the economic products of the Malay Peninsula. 2 vols. Crown Agents for the Colonies, London.

Cavalcante, P. B. 1977. Edible palm fruits of the Brazilian Amazon. Principes 21: 91–102.

Corner, E. J. H. 1966. The natural history of palms. Weidenfeld and Nicolson, London.

Dransfield, J. 1976. Palms in the everyday life of west Indonesia. Principes 20: 38–47.

Dubos, R. 1973. Humanizing the earth. Science 179: 769–772.

FAO. 1984. 1983 FAO production year book. Food and Agricultural Organization of the United Nations, Rome.

Fox, J. J. 1977. Harvest of the palm. Harvard University Press, Cambridge, Massachusetts.

Haas, A. & L. Wilson (eds.). 1985. Coconut wood: Processing and use. Forestry Paper 57. Food and Agricultural Organization of the United Nations, Rome.

Hodge, W. H. 1975. Oil-producing palms of the world—A review. Principes 19: 119–136.

Johnson, D. V. 1982. Commercial palm products of Brazil. Principes 26: 141–143.

———. 1983. Multi-purpose palms in agroforestry: A classification and assessment. Int. Tree Crops J. 2: 217–244.

Kitzke, E. D. & D. V. Johnson. 1975. Commercial palm products other than oils. Principes 19: 3–26.

Lleras, E. 1985. Acrocomia um gênero com grande potencial. Newsletter: Useful palms of tropical America 1: 3–5.

May, P., A. B. Anderson, M. J. Balick & J. M. F. Frazão. 1985. Subsistence benefits from the babassu palm. Econ. Bot. 39: 113–129.

Miller, R. H. 1964. The versatile sugar palm. Principes 8: 115–147.

Moore, H. E., Jr. 1977. Endangerment at the specific

and generic levels in palms. Pages 267–282 *in* G. T. Prance & T. S. Elias (eds.), Extinction is forever. New York Botanical Garden, New York.

Mors, W. B. & C. T. Rizzini. 1966. Useful plants of Brazil. Holden-Day, San Francisco, California.

Myers, N. 1984. The primary source: Tropical forests and our future. Norton, New York.

Pesce, C. 1985. Oil palms and other oil seeds of the Amazon. Translated and edited by D. V. Johnson from the original, Oleaginosas da Amazonia. 1941. Oficinas Graficas da Revista da Veterinaria, Belém. Reference Publications, Algonac, Michigan.

Plotkin, M. J. & M. J. Balick. 1984. Medicinal uses of South American palms. J. Ethnopharm. 10: 157–179.

Rodin, R. J. 1985. The ethnobotany of the Kwanyama Ovambos. Missouri Bot. Gard. Monogr. Syst. Bot. 9: 1–163.

Ruddle, K., D. V. Johnson, P. K. Townsend & J. D. Rees. 1978. Palm sago. A tropical starch from marginal lands. University of Hawaii Press, Honolulu, Hawaii.

Schultes, R. E. 1974. Palms and religion in the northwest Amazon. Principes 18: 3–21.

Seemann, B. 1856. Popular history of the palms. Lovell Reeve, London.

Tanaka, J. 1980. The San: Hunter-gatherers of the Kalahari. University of Tokyo Press, Tokyo.

Wallace, A. R. 1853. Palm trees of the Amazon and their uses. John van Voorst, London.

Weinstock, J. A. 1983. Rattan: Ecological balance in a Borneo rainforest swidden. Econ. Bot. 37: 58–68.

Wilbert, J. 1976. *Manicaria saccifera* and its cultural significance among the Warao Indians of Venezuela. Bot. Mus. Leafl. 24: 275–335.

———. 1980. The palm-leaf sail of the Warao Indians. Principes 24: 162–169.

Winterhalder, B. & E. A. Smith (eds.). 1982. Hunter-gatherer foraging strategies. Ethnographic and archeological analyses. University of Chicago Press, Chicago, Illinois.

The Use of Palms by the Apinayé and Guajajara Indians of Northeastern Brazil

Michael J. Balick

Table of Contents

Abstract

The use of palms by two tribes of Indians in Northeastern Brazil, the Apinayé and Guajajara, was studied to determine both specific uses and the overall degree of dependence of these people on palms in their daily lives. Three indigenous reserves in Brazil were visited: Caru and Pindaré in the State of Maranhão, and São José in Goiás. Dependence on palms was inversely related to the people's degree of acculturation. As the natural resource base declined (including the availability of palms), people began to cultivate the so-called "modern crops" and reduce their utilization of wild palms. Seventeen species of palms were found to be used by these two groups of Indians, of which *Orbignya phalerata,* the babassu palm, was of greatest value, yielding a variety of important products. In this area palms provide food, fuel, shelter, fiber, construction materials, medicine, magic and other basic necessities of life. Loss of knowledge concerning palm uses indicates the urgency with which plant usage must be catalogued among indigenous groups.

Key words: palms, ethnobotany, Apinayé Indians, Guajajara Indians, Brazil

Resumo

Foi estudado o uso que fazem das palmeiras, duas tribos de índios do Nordeste do Brasil— os Apinayé e os Guajajara—com a finalidade de conhecer tanto os usos específicos como, de um modo geral, o grau de dependência destes povos quanto às palmeiras, na sua vida diária. Três reservas indígenas foram visitadas: Caru e Pindaré no Estado do Maranhão e São José, em Goiás. O grau de aculturação destes povos está diretamente relacionado ao uso que fazem das palmeiras. Assim que o ambiente natural em torno deles se declina (inclusive a disponibilidade de palmeiras), começam a cultivar as chamadas "culturas modernas," com a redução do uso de palmeiras. Encontrou-se que dezessete espécies de palmeiras são usadas por estes dois grupos de índios; *Orbignya phalerata,* o babaçu, é a de maior valor. Nesta área, as palmeiras fornecem alimento, combustível, abrigo, fibras, material de construção, remédios, elementos de magia e demais coisas básicas da vida. Os esudiosos devem continuar registrando a notável diversidade de uso de plantas pelos indígenas, pois estes conhecimentos estão sendo perdidos em ritmo acelerado.

I. Introduction

This paper reports on a survey of the use of palms by two tribes of Brazilian Indians, the Apinayé and Guajajara, carried out during August– September 1983. The purpose of the fieldwork was to collect germplasm of the babassu palm (*Orbignya phalerata* Mart.), as part of a long-term study of the domestication of this genus for oil, charcoal and meal production. The study team comprised scientists from the New York Botanical Garden (NYBG), the Centro Nacional de Recursos Genéticos (CENARGEN), Brasília, and the former Instituto Estadual do Babaçu (INEB), once located in São Luís, Maranhão. We carried out in-depth studies on the taxonomy, utilization and folk-classification of the palms in the Apinayé and Guajajara territory. Additionally, collections were made of other useful indigenous plants as well as of crop plants; these will be the subject of a forthcoming paper.

II. The Apinayé

The Apinayé are one of the indigenous groups of Northeastern Brazil. They speak a language of the Gê Family; Apinayé is very similar to other dialects of Northern Kayapó (Davis, 1966).

The Apinayé presently live in two settlements ("aldeias"), Mariazinha and São José (6°30'S; 47°30'W). These are located in the Municipality of Tocantinópolis, in Northern Goiás (Fig. 1). Nimuendajú (1983) wrote that during his first visit to the area in 1928, this group lived in four aldeias: Cocal, Gato Prêto, Bacaba and Mariazinha. According to Pereira (1982), the Apinayé comprised 4200 people in 1823, declined to a low of 150 in the late 1800's and early 1900's, and in recent times (1981) numbered 448. Epidemics of smallpox, fever and other health problems are blamed for much of the decline in population. Our work was carried out at São José, as the people there utilize babassu and other palms to a far greater degree than at Mariazinha.

The Fundação Nacional do Índio (FUNAI) reserve consists of a total of about 101,000 hectares of land. The absence of a land survey has led to conflict with the settlers inhabiting the region around Tocantinópolis, the major urban center for the area. The Trans-Amazon highway passes some 3 km from the aldeia of São José. This has changed the community, and there is presently a substantial trade of producing handicrafts for sale to the travellers along that road.

Traditionally, the Apinayé depended heavily on the babassu forests that cover their land. Farming, hunting and fishing were also important, although the latter is of less importance at present. Today, a cooperative for the collection and sale of babassu exists, and this is probably the major gathering activity of the people. In addition, a great deal of leaves of jaborandi (*Pilocarpus jaborandi,* Rutaceae) is collected for sale to pharmaceutical laboratories for processing into the drug pilocarpine, used to treat glaucoma. During the period of our visit, the inhabitants collected jaborandi leaves one or two days per week on a large scale basis. A truck, operated by a person acting as a middleman, periodically collects the dried leaves.

In 1980, FUNAI developed a cooperative project of rice, corn and bean production (Pereira, 1982). According to our observations, present day agriculture includes the cultivation of a large quantity of rice, beans, cassava and corn. Other cultivated crops include sweet potatoes (*Ipomoea batatas*), yams (*Dioscorea* spp.), banana (*Musa sapientum*) and pineapple (*Ananas comosus*).

The most complete account of the culture of this group was written by Nimuendajú earlier in this century; this reference has been recently reprinted by the Museu Paraense Emílio Goeldi in Belém, Pará (1983). There have also been studies by Da Matta (1973), Maybury-Lewis (1960), Pereira (1982), Oliveira (1930), Lowie (1946), and others. Information on the language has been gathered by FUNAI working in collaboration with the Summer Institute of Linguistics (SIL). They have prepared a four volume set of language primers (1975a, 1975b, 1975c, 1976).

According to the Indians, the present site of habitation was recently settled only six months or so prior to our visit. It contains several dozen palm thatch houses constructed in a circle around an open field, to one side of which is a small stream used for bathing, drinking and irrigation (Figs. 2, 3). The former site, a few kilometers away (but within the reserve), did not have enough water for their needs and was abandoned. That site was said to have been occupied for "many years."

III. The Guajajara

The Guajajara were visited at two sites. The first location was the FUNAI post, Caru, along the Rio Pindaré near the junction of the Rio Caru and Rio Pindaré (3°40'S; 46°05'W) (Fig. 1). This is in the Municipality of Bom Jardim, Maranhão state. Caru is a more isolated site, recently made more accessible by nearby construction of the

FIG. 1. Location of the three reserves visited: Caru, Pindaré and São José.

FIGS. 2, 3.   FIG. 2. Side view of Apinayé houses at São José. House walls and roof are made from *Orbignya phalerata*. Note circular placement of village houses. FIG. 3. Front view of Apinayé house. Note dense stand of *Orbignya phalerata* behind houses.

Carajás railway. We entered Posto Indígena Caru by driving for many miles along the uncompleted railway bed and crossed the Rio Pindaré by foot to reach the village. Several days after our arrival we were informed that the railroad bridge between us and the only accessible road would be closed to vehicular traffic within a day or so, and railroad ties installed across it. Had we stayed in Caru, there would have been no way of returning with our vehicle, except by building a barge on the river four to six months in the future when the water level had risen to an adequate height. We chose, therefore, to leave this post and travel to Posto Indígena Pindaré, another site of Guajajara habitation. This is also located in the Municipality of Bom Jardim, along the Rio Pindaré, about 15 kilometers west of the town of Santa Inêz (3°30′S; 45°30′W) (Fig. 1). As Posto Indígena Pindaré is near a paved road, the reserve has much more infrastructure and facilities, such as electricity for a portion of the night. Consequently, due to this accessibility, there is a high degree of acculturation among the group, and less primary forest in the region as a result of past exploitation.

Posto Indígena Caru was founded in 1975. According to the most recent census, 84 people live in the village. There appears to be a great deal of intermarriage between Indians and local settlers, much more so than at any of the other reserves visited during this study.

The development of the Carajás railway system has an impact upon the lives of the villagers in Caru. In return for the use of their land, the Indians report that they were provided with consumer goods, such as refrigerators. In addition, a well was dug for drinking water and a pump installed, forests were cleared and fenced for pasture, and other improvements made in the community. A cement block structure serves as a community center and school, and is staffed by a full-time teacher (Fig. 4).

We were not able to get information on the size of the Caru reserve. Services provided, in addition to those previously mentioned, include some health care, electricity (although the generator was not functioning when we were there), and sanitary services. The population at Caru came originally from Pindaré. There is also some minimal contact with another tribe, the Guajá, in an area near to the reserve. The Guajajara we spoke to estimated that, over the past 15 years,

perhaps 20 persons have settled in a provisional FUNAI post (Posto Indígena Awá) with an undetermined number of Guajá still living in the forest. The Guajá, much more dependent than the Guajajara on babassu palms for subsistence, obtain starch, protein, oil, fiber, and fuel from the wild stands of palms.

The crops grown in the Caru reserve include rice, corn, cassava and beans, as well as yams and peanuts. Local varieties of these crops are still grown, and, according to our informants, modern varieties of rice and corn have also been introduced and accepted.

The FUNAI representative at P.I. Pindaré noted that the most recent census counted 87 families in the village, 195 females and 192 males. The post was founded around 1914, and probably as a result is relatively developed. In contrast to the palm thatch/mud huts found in the other reserves visited, the Guajajara of Pindaré have cement houses provided by the government (Fig. 5). Interestingly enough, however, many of these houses have additions built of palm thatch. People report that the traditional type construction remains much cooler in the hot weather, and therefore choose to live in palm thatch huts.

Cultivated plants at P.I. Pindaré include rice, corn, manihot, banana, beans and cucurbits. Material of these and other crops for the CENARGEN germplasm bank was collected here, as well as in the nearby village of Jurongo a few kilometers away. People were very eager to share their indigenous cultivars with us, and refused to accept compensation. Collections of traditional varieties included *Arachis, Cucurbita, Dioscorea, Oryza, Ipomoea, Manihot, Phaseolus, Ricinus, Sesamum, Vigna,* as well as *Orbignya.*

Much ethnological information on the Guajajara is found in Wagley and Galvão (1948, 1949). During fieldwork in 1941–1942, the authors estimated the population of the Guajajara to number more than 2000. The Guajajara refer to themselves as Tenetehara, and are part of the Tupí-Guaraní linguistic family. The Guajajara are very much involved in shamanism and with divinities. The shamans cure by means of sucking or massaging, to remove the harmful element from the person afflicted. We found that the Guajajara claimed to use greater numbers of plants in ritual baths and ceremonies for stimulating healing than did the Apinayé. However, in view of the short duration of our visits, it would be

FIGS. 4, 5.   FIG. 4. Main avenue of village at Caru. Note cement school house/town hall. FIG. 5. Typical house at Pindaré; note that one section is constructed from cement block while the addition is constructed from *Orbignya phalerata.*

presumptuous to attempt an accurate comparison of medicinal and magic plants between these groups, as this area of knowledge is often the most closely guarded and secret, while we were primarily interested in food plants. We had contact with two shamans from São José, one Apinayé, as well as a Shavanté from the same region.

Boudin (1978) provides much information on the language spoken by the Guajajara in his "Dicionário de Tupi Moderno." Included in this work are plant names.

Gomes (1977) provided a great deal of information on the Guajajara, based on his fieldwork in the region in 1975. Several chapters in his study are devoted to the economy of these people, and a number of extractive plant products are mentioned: babassu kernels (*Orbignya phalerata*), copaíba oil (*Copaifera langsdorffii*), jutaicica and jatobá resins (*Hymenaea* spp.), almecega resin (*Protium* sp.) and cumaru nuts (*Diopteryx odorata*).

The use of *Cannabis indica* by the Guajajara, as reported by Wagley and Galvão (1948) has continued to the present. These authors noted that native tobacco (presumably *Nicotiana rustica*) and *Cannabis* are smoked as a "general pastime," and that native tobacco is frequently used by shamans to treat illness. We did not observe frequent use of the *Cannabis* in either village, although workers who have had contact with Guajajara in other areas report *Cannabis* smoking to be a traditional activity. In general, the traditional use of hallucinogens or stimulants seemed to be minimal relative to the use of these substances by Indians elsewhere in lowland Amazônia.

IV. Palm Utilization

To simplify the presentation of the data on palms, the species used by both the Apinayé and Guajajara will be presented together, in a list arranged alphabetically by Latin binomial. Comments on the morphology of the palm, the common names by which it is known, uses, and voucher specimens are included under each binomial heading. Apinayé and Guajajara (Tenetehara) names for palm species are transcribed using symbols mostly from the International Phonetic Alphabet. Voucher specimens have been deposited at CEN and NY; these two institutions

also have duplicate material that will be distributed in the future.

Acrocomia aculeata (Jacq.) Loddiges ex Mart.

Portuguese: Macauba.
Guajajara: Pãrena, mukazá.
Apinayé: Řóni.

This is a tall palm to 6 m in height or more. The trunk is covered with spines. Large panicles, to ca. 1 m in length contain hundreds of round fruits ca. 3.5 cm in diam., that turn green-yellow when mature.

Use: The yellowish fruit mesocarp is said to be very nutritious and contains an edible oil. The endocarp is woody and durable, and surrounds an oil-rich endosperm similar in consistency to coconut. The endocarps are boiled in water or roasted directly on the fire, cracked and eaten. For oil extraction, the ripe fruits are cracked open and the oleaginous endosperm macerated with a mortar and pestle, releasing the oil. The air-dried kernel contains 53–65% oil (Balick, 1979). According to the Guajajara at Caru, this oil is preferred to oil from babassu.

In previous times the Guajajara would find a stem that had already fallen and strip off the outer portion. The central portion was then burned and the resulting ash used to fertilize crops such as rice, corn and manihot.

Voucher specimens: *Balick et al. 1556, 1623.*

Allagoptera leucocalyx (Drude) Kuntze.

Portuguese: Coco de chapada.
Apinayé: Gračaré.

This low growing, acaulescent palm is common in the scrub savanna on sandy soil (vegetation known in Brazil as "chapada"), where it is often found in association with *Orbignya eichleri*. Small panicles of fruit are borne in the center of the rosette of leaves.

Use: The fruits are eaten when ripe or when still green.

Voucher specimen: *Balick et al. 1572.*

Astrocaryum campestre Mart.

Portuguese: Tucum da chapada.
Apinayé: Řoře.

This acaulescent palm grows to ca. 0.5 m tall and has spiny, gracefully pinnate leaves. Small panicles of fruit appear from the center of the rosette of leaves, subtended by a papery prophyll and a sturdy bract ca. 50 cm long × 6.5 cm wide. It is common in the chapada area of the Apinayé reserve, growing in association with *Orbignya eichleri.*

Use: The Apinayé use the dried fruits to make beads and ornaments for necklaces. The endocarps are carefully polished and carved into a variety of figures (Fig. 6). The fruits are edible, with a tasty nut-like endosperm. This palm is harvested as a source of palm heart (palmito). The leaves furnish a purported cure for venereal disease. To prepare this cure, leaves of řoře are collected, macerated and made into a tea with water. The concoction is put outside the house at night, and consumed early the next morning. The young leaves are made into thread by stripping the bundles of fiber from the leaves and rolling them together. This thread is used for many purposes.

Voucher specimen: *Balick et al. 1586.*

Astrocaryum munbaca Mart.

Portuguese: Marajá.
Guajajara: Marazu'a.

This palm is commonly found in the Pindaré reserve, growing in association with *Orbignya phalerata.* Marazu'a is a caespitose palm, bearing thin trunks to ca. 4 cm in diam., and growing to 4 m tall. The stem is covered with rings of flattened brown spines.

Use: The Guajajara use this palm as a source of edible fruit. When green, the entire fruit can be eaten; when ripe, only the endosperm is edible.

Voucher specimen: *Balick et al. 1479.*

Astrocaryum vulgare Mart.

Portuguese: Tucum.
Guajajara: Tucumã.
Apinayé: Řoindí.

This is another caepitose species of *Astrocaryum.* The trunk is much more substantial than the other two species collected during this study, growing to 10–17 cm in diam. Tucumã grows to 4–5 m or more in height, and is common in old fields (capoeira), near dwellings and in the forest in both Caru and São José. The heavy panicles

are 1–1.4 m in length and bear many globose fruits ca. 5 cm long × 3.5 cm wide.

Use: The Guajajara harvest immature fruits and consume the liquid endosperm (Fig. 8). It is a somewhat tart drink that satisfies thirst. Other species in this genus throughout the Amazon Valley are similarly harvested to consume the liquid endosperm. This is a useful fiber plant. The Guajajara process the young inrolled leaves into bowstrings, local crafts (Fig. 9), etc., and the spines are used in weaving fringes on hammocks—to mark the spots where designs are to be fashioned. These fringes are called Kihawmu-piřãg ("that which reddens the hammock").

Voucher specimens: *Balick et al. 1475, 1626.*

Bactris sp.

Portuguese: Marajá do campo.
Guajajara: Marari'ɨw.

This is a small caespitose palm found in the secondary forests of the Caru reserve. The palm has slender stems, ca. 4 cm in diam., covered with rings of flattened black spines 3–6 cm long, and grows to 5 m in height. The leaves are pinnate, ca. 3 m in length.

Use: The fruit is edible, with the mesocarp tasting somewhat sweet-acidic. The Guajajara harvest the stems to weave fish traps.

Voucher specimen: *Balick et al. 1525.*

Desmoncus polyacanthos Mart.

Portuguese: Titara.
Guajajara: Iwɨpo-tsu.
Apinayé: Řoingandí.

This is the only genus of vining palms in the New World. It is common in both the Caru and São José reserves, growing in the secondary forests (capoeira) often in association with babassu. The palm was observed growing to 7 m or more into the forest canopy. The apical pinnae on the leaves are modified into reflexed spines, which attach onto surrounding vegetation. Small panicles of greenish (unripe) fruits were observed on the stem.

Use: The Guajajara use the central portion of the stem, after cutting away the spiny leaf bases, to attach arrow points to arrows. The Apinayé use the fruits of this species as a curative, when a stomachache, caused by consuming too much

FIGS. 6, 7. FIG. 6. Apinayé necklace made from unidentified seeds beaded on *Astrocaryum campestre* thread with fish carved from the seed of the same species. These necklaces are for personal use. FIG. 7. Apinayé necklaces made for trade or sale. Necklace on left is made from seeds of *Oenocarpus distichus* and *Ormosia* sp.

FIGS. 8, 9.   FIG. 8. Guajajara drinking liquid endosperm of *Astrocaryum jauari*. FIG. 9. Traditional feather ornaments worn by the Apinayé; cord on which feathers are strung is made from *Astrocaryum campestre*.

Acrocomia occurs. Eating a few fruits of řoingandí is said to ease the pain.

Voucher specimens: *Balick et al. 1470, 1493, 1588.*

Euterpe oleracea Mart.

Portuguese: Juçara.
Guajajara: Watsa'ɨw.
Apinayé: Kambíre.

This caespitose palm is found in moist areas of Caru and São José, growing to 7 m in height. It grows along streams and in primary forest remnants. It is common throughout much of lowland Amazônia, and the cluster of tall, thin stems bearing gracefully drooping, pinnate leaves is strikingly beautiful in the landscape. Juçara, or açai as it is more widely known, yields heavy panicles of purple, globose fruits ca. 1 cm in diam.

Use: Both the Guajajara and Apinayé collect the fruits of this palm and eat them fresh or make them into a beverage. People claim that juçara fruit is full of vitamins. The dried seeds of this species are also used by the Apinayé to make necklaces, along with seeds from *Ormosia* sp. (Fig. 7). They are pierced with a hot needle and put on strings. The *Euterpe* seeds often are dotted with black color from *Genipa* dye, and animal teeth or feathers are also added to the necklace. These were used traditionally by the people and are now offered for sale along the highway.

Voucher specimens: *Balick et al. 1476, 1621.*

Geonoma pohliana Mart.

Portuguese: Içai.
Apinayé: Teeré.

This is a diminutive understory palm found in the disturbed forests around São José, growing in association with *Orbignya.* The slender stem, 2.2 cm in diam., supports a tuft of pinnate leaves 4 m above the forest floor. The ripe panicles consist of red rachillae and round black fruits 0.5 cm in diam.

Use: The Apinayé use this as a remedy for stomachache caused by drinking too much *Euterpe* beverage. Young developing leaves gathered from the crownshaft (palmito) are used to make an infusion with water. The tea is consumed warm and is said to calm the stomach and lessen the pain.

Voucher specimen: *Balick et al. 1587.*

Mauritia flexuosa L. f.

Portuguese: Buriti.
Guajajara: Miriti'ɨw.
Apinayé. Ngrá.

This is a tall species, to 15 m in height, with palmate leaves. It is common in moist areas such as along the margins of the river and in the moist gallery forests near São José and Caru. The trees bear massive panicles of ovoid, rust-colored fruits. These fruits can be 5 cm in length, and are covered with small scales, under which is a yellow, oleaginous mesocarp.

Use: The Apinayé consume the mesocarp of this fruit as a regular component of their diet. It is common to see people walking around with baskets or bags of these fruits and, after stripping off the scales, sucking on them to remove the pulp (Figs. 10, 11). The Guajajara also eat this fruit. It is very important as a fiber plant. The Apinayé collect the young, inrolled leaves, cut off the segments and place them in the sun to dry. The segments are beaten with a stick and shredded into many fibers. These are rolled between the hands to form a cord and used to make baskets (Fig. 12), belts, head straps for pack baskets commonly constructed from *Orbignya* pinnae, and necklaces. It is common to see bunches of the fiber hanging in people's houses. The artifacts are sold along the Trans-Amazon highway and in Tocantinópolis. In addition, the outer portion of the leaf petiole provides fibers for weaving the baskets that are used to press cassava, known as tipi-tipi or sebucan elsewhere in the Amazon Valley. The petiole fiber is said to be quite durable.

The gurá palm is a part of the traditional folklore of the Apinayé. When a young man wishes to marry, he must first prove his strength by carrying a piece of the trunk of *Mauritia flexuosa* (at least 1 m long) from the forest to the middle of the encampment. Upon his arrival, he is met and surrounded by a circle of singing women from the village. The sister of the bride and her godmother ("madrinha") take the groom by either arm to greet his bride. A meal is shared by the

FIGS. 10, 11.   FIG. 10. Apinayé children collecting fallen fruits of *Mauritia flexuosa* growing along the river. FIG. 11. Apinayé children eating *Mauritia flexuosa* fruits. Note pack basket made from *Orbignya eichleri*.

FIGS. 12, 13. FIG. 12. Basket woven from *Mauritia flexuosa* fiber; this style is often sold along the road by the Apinayé. FIG. 13. Carrying basket used by the Apinayé woven from *Mauritiella armata*. Headstrap (not shown) is woven from *Mauritia flexuosa*.

bride and groom and they are considered to be married.

Voucher specimen: *Balick et al. 1624.*

Mauritiella armata Mart.

Portuguese: Buritirana.
Apinayé: Ǧrařəre.

This is a much smaller palm than the previous species, but it is found in similar environments—moist areas and gallery forests close to the river. Buritirana grows in clusters of 4–6 trunks, to 7.5 m in height, and has stems covered with spines. The leaves are pinnate, with a waxy bloom on their underside. Fruits are borne in panicles ca. 1 m long, are ovoid, and 2.5 cm long × 1.3 cm wide, turning orange when ripe.

Use: The mesocarp is pulpy, although not as thick and oleaginous as the previous species. The fruits are eaten and made into a beverage by soaking in water. The segments of the leaves are woven into baskets (Fig. 13) and other handicrafts, and the stem wood is used to make bows.

Voucher specimen: *Balick et al. 1622.*

Maximiliana maripa (Correa da Serra) Drude.

Portuguese: Inajá.
Guajajara: Inaʑá.
Apinayé: Řigré.

This species is commonly found in association with babassu, in the forests and fields cleared for cultivation. Because it provides a useful product, and because of its massive stem, it is usually left when clearing the forest. The palm grows to 8 m or more in height, and the stem is 25–30 cm in diam. The large pinnate leaves are often 7.5 m in length, with pinnae irregularly spaced along the rachis and inserted at various angles to the plane of the leaf. Heavy panicles of fruit are produced each year.

Use: The Guajajara eat the fruits. These can be boiled or roasted, and the endocarp split to obtain the coconut-like endosperm. The mesocarp is oleaginous, and in some areas is exploited for oil; no mention was ever made of this practice during the present study, however. I have also seen the leaves woven into thatch, but did not notice it used for this purpose at any of the villages visited. It appears to be of lesser impor-tance, as the babassu palm is in such great abundance and provides superior products.

Voucher specimen: *Balick et al. 1555.*

Oenocarpus distichus Mart.

Portuguese: Bacaba.
Guajajara: Pinuwa'ɨw.
Apinayé: Kambérdi.

This distinctive palm is common in the primary forests around São José and Pindaré, where it grows in association with babassu. It can be easily identified by the 2-ranked arrangement of its pinnate leaves. The palm is solitary, growing to 12 m in height, with a massive trunk ca. 26 cm in diam. Another distinctive feature of this species is its hippuriform or horsetail inflorescence, in which over 100 pendulous rachillae hang from a stubby primary axis in the same manner as a horse's tail. The fruits are deep purple, ovoid, ca. 2 cm long × 1.5 cm wide and are borne in great abundance.

Use: The fruits of kamberdí are edible, and the mesocarp rich in oil. In addition to being consumed as a refreshing beverage, the Apinayé use the drink to treat hepatitis. Fruits are macerated in warm water, and the mesocarp removed. This is boiled and the fibers filtered out. It is allowed to cool off and then is consumed once per day for three days of treatment. Balick (1986) discussed the high nutritional quality of the fruits in this complex, and it is likely that this beverage serves to fortify the patient during bouts of hepatitis. The Apinayé were also seen gathering the newly-emerging pinnae for weaving into baskets (Fig. 14), and stringing the dried endocarps into necklaces (Fig. 7).

Voucher specimens: *Balick et al. 1527, 1615.*

Orbignya eichleri Drude.

Portuguese: Piassava.
Apinayé: Řõdiře.

This is a common palm in the chapada vegetation in the area where the Apinayé hunt, Cabeceira do Riberão Serrinha. It is an acaulescent palm, growing to ca. 1 m tall. Small bracts to 60 cm long are produced in the center of the rosette of leaves and bear curled panicles with 7–16 fruits, each about 5 cm long. The leaves are pinnate, with pinnae arranged in irregular groups on the rachis and at various angles to the plane of the leaf.

Use: The fruits contain an oleaginous kernel, and are harvested by some Apinayé for eating and for oil production. However, as the fruits of *Orbignya phalerata* are much more abundant and yield more kernel per fruit than *O. eichleri,* the former species appears to be the preferred palm, especially in this region where it is so predominant in the landscape. The mesocarp of *Orbignya eichleri* is chewed by rodents and the fruits cracked open by larger animals. Because of this, a field of *O. eichleri* is a good location for hunting game. While we were working with a Shavanté Indian who lived in the reserve, he disappeared with his shotgun into the cerrado. We assumed that he had become bored with our laborious examination of palm germplasm, so we kept on working. Shortly thereafter, I sensed that another person had joined us, and turned around to see who it was. There was our Shavanté friend covered with woven leaves of *O. eichleri,* with his shotgun pointed at us (Figs. 16, 17). He had transformed himself into a "walking blind," and blended in completely with the surrounding vegetation. "I wanted to show you how we hunt and stalk game without them knowing," he said proudly, as he lowered his gun. We were amazed at his skill in "stalking" us, without making a sound or attracting our attention during the entire time.

Voucher specimens: *Balick et al. 1578, 1579, 1580, 1597.*

Orbignya phalerata Mart.

Portuguese: Babassu (Babaçu).
Guajajara: Wahú.
Apinayé: Řõřo.

This is a tall, stately palm with a massive, solitary trunk to 15 m tall. The leaves are pinnate, spirally arranged on the stem, and have regularly deposited pinnae. The massive panicles contain up to several hundred ovoid brown fruits, each weighing 250 g or more. When mature, these fall to the ground and germinate within a few months. Because of its characteristic cryptogeal germination, the apical meristem of the seedling is pushed into the ground, where it is protected from predation and fire. The young stems become established underground, and then begin to grow above ground after a few years (Anderson & Anderson, 1983). Babassu is found scattered throughout the primary forest in all three reserves visited, and when the land has been cleared, forms dense monospecific stands.

Use: The subsistence economies of the Apinayé and Guajajara depend heavily on their use of the babassu palm. The subsistence utilization of babassu in general in the northeast of Brazil is discussed in depth in another article (May et al., 1985) and will not be duplicated here. Table 1 is a summary of the uses presented in that paper. However, it is interesting to note some of the more unusual ways in which this palm is employed by the Guajajara and Apinayé.

After making a rather complete collection of *Orbignya* germplasm at the Caru reserve, one of our party cut his hand and it began to bleed. As I unpacked the first aid kit, one of our informants said that he wished to treat the problem. He selected a young plant of babassu and cut off one of the newly-emerging leaves. He stripped off the pinnae and peeled the rachis, exposing its white pithy portion (Fig. 20). After a bit of scraping, he had a mass of fibrous cotton-like material in his hand, and squeezed this on the open wound. The clear juice that came out had styptic properties and the wound stopped bleeding within a few seconds (Fig. 21). According to our informant, this bitter juice stops the flow of blood and allows the wound to heal more quickly. It is used for injuries while working in the field or walking in the forest.

At São José we were able to document the preparation of "farinha" or meal made from babassu (Figs. 23–29). While this is not commonly prepared, having been replaced by cultivated cassava, one of the women agreed to prepare it for us in the traditional manner. People say that the preparation of babassu flour is more common outside of the reserves, such as among the Guajá Indians. Fruits of babassu are selected and tasted to make sure their mesocarp has not spoiled (turned "bitter"). Informants report that the bitterness of the mesocarp varies from tree to tree. When only the bitter variety can be obtained, the mesocarp is removed, put in a basket and soaked in the river for 24 hours; it is subsequently used for processing. The preparation we observed was with non-bitter fruits. The fruits are selected and put out in the sun to dry, until the mesocarp is somewhat powdery. The epicarp is removed with a knife (Fig. 23) and the mesocarp is beaten with a stick until it falls off in

FIGS. 14, 15.   FIG. 14. Apinayé man cutting young emerging leaf of *Oenocarpus distichus* to weave a basket. FIG. 15. Apinayé pack baskets made from *Orbignya* species: left: large basket made from *O. phalerata*; right (upper): medium-sized basket made from *O.* × *teixeirana*, a hybrid palm; right (lower) smaller basket made from *O. eichleri*.

FIGS. 16–19.   FIGS. 16, 17. Camouflage hunting outfit woven from *Orbignya eichleri* leaves. FIG. 18. Bridge in São José constructed from *Orbignya phalerata* stems. FIG. 19. Apinayé hunting traps covered with pinnae of *Orbignya phalerata*.

FIGS. 20, 21.   FIG. 20. Scraping the rachis of *Orbignya phalerata* to make a styptic for wounds. FIG. 21. Guajajara applying a styptic liquid from rachis of *Orbignya phalerata* to stop bleeding.

Table I

Subsistence uses of babassu fruits

Kernels

  Snack nut*

  Milk   stewing meat and fish

                         beverage

  Liquid endosperm   treatment of sties and bleeding

                         beverage

  Oil*   cooking

                         soapmaking

                         burning in lamps

  Residues   animal feed

                         substitute or filler for coffee

                         shrimp bait

  Larvae*   food for people

                         fish bait

Husks

  Charcoal*   primary source of fuel for cooking

  Smoke*   insect repellant

                         smoking rubber

  Anesthetic   condensed gases and tar from burning used to alleviate toothache

  Handicrafts*   pencil holders, keychains, figurines

Mesocarp

  Animal feed

  Flour*   substitute for manioc flour and former staple among Indian tribes

                         chocolate-like beverage

                         medicine for gastrointestinal complaints

  Hunting   attractant for rodents

SUBSISTENCE USES OF BABASSU LEAVES

Fibers*

  Baskets   storage and transport

  Mats   doors, windows, rugs, grain-drying

  Fans   ventilating fires

  Sieves   sifting manioc flour and rice

  Others   twine, torches, whisks, bird cages, hunting blinds, animal traps

Construction materials*

  Thatch   roofing and walls

  Laths   support for clay-packed walls

                         frames for windows

  Rails   fencing to protect agricultural plots from animals and delimit hunting zones

Agricultural uses*

  Leaves   burned in shifting cultivation plots to promote nutrient recycling and pest control

  Rachis   crop stakes and building raised planters

  Living leaves   provide shade in pastures for livestock and feed during dry periods

Medicine*

  Liquid   expressed from rachis and used as antiseptic and styptic

SUBSISTENCE USES OF BABASSU STEMS

Contruction*

  Bridges

  Foundations

  Benches

Palm heart*

  Food for people

  Feed for animals

  Ripening agent for banana

Table I

Continued

Sap (collected from stump of felled palms)
  Fermented drink
  Attraction of beetle larvae that are eaten or used as fish bait
Planting medium (obtained from decayed stems)
Salt (made from ash of burned stems)

From: May et al., 1985. Asterisks (*) indicate major categories of uses observed among the Guajajara and Apinayé.

clots from the fruit (Figs. 24, 30). These pieces are put in a mortar and pounded with a stick until the mesocarp is turned into a powder (Fig. 25). The powder is sifted through a screen; currently a plastic screen is used, but in earlier times the material was sifted through a woven basket (Fig. 27). A bowl of water is added to the powder and the doughy mass put into a pan and heated over a low cooking fire. While it is heating, the preparer stirs the mass with a spoon and breaks it up into small granules (Fig. 28). The final product (Fig. 29) is a darker shade of brown than the original mesocarp. When freshly cooked, the farinha is soft and can be eaten as is, or mixed with cassava flour, meat, beans or other food. With time the babassu farinha hardens a bit. The Apinayé call this substance "tvan-gla."

Charcoal made from babassu is used to dye certain fibers for basket weaving.

Pack baskets are commonly made from the three species of *Orbignya* found at São José (Fig. 15). Small baskets for young children are made from *Orbignya eichleri,* medium-sized baskets for older children are made from *O. × teixeirana* and large packbaskets used by adults to harvest crops and collect firewood are made from *O. phalerata* (Fig. 33).

The Apinayé distinguish various types of babassu, based on the ease of cracking the fruits. Several dozen people go into different areas of the forest on an almost daily basis to crack babassu fruits for the cooperative (Figs. 22, 31). The usual method of cracking babassu fruits is to place them on an upturned axe head and pound them with sticks until they open. Some stands of babassu are considered to yield fruits that are too hard to crack, while others are considered easier. The Apinayé ignore stands of palms where the fruits are known to be difficult to crack, favoring instead to work with stands where production is easier. One special variety was shown

us that could be cracked with a knife instead of the usual way. This type is of great interest and was collected for the germplasm banks in Maranhão and Piauí. Naturally, any fruit that is able to be broken with less energy would be of value for industrial processing with mechanical equipment.

As previously mentioned, the harvest of babassu has been organized into a cooperative by the Indians. In Pindaré the harvest has declined over the past few years. In 1980 ca. 2000 kg of kernels per week was harvested. In 1983, with greater agricultural production, ca. 1000 kg per week was harvested, an average of about 50,000 kg of kernels annually from this reserve. It was estimated that each family cracks enough fruits to obtain ca. 600 kg per year. In Caru there was not an organized babassu harvest, as more people depend on agriculture for their livelihood. In São José, the babassu cooperative recorded the collection of 294 kg of kernels over a two day period, and estimated that 50–100,000 kg of kernels were collected for sale each year. The kernels were sold to a middleman who transports them to a factory for the extraction of oil and animal feed. At the time of this study the Indians received 140 Cruzeiros per kg, which at the official rate of conversion in effect during that time was equivalent to US$0.20.

Other miscellaneous subsistence uses for babassu included employing stems to make bridges across streams (Fig. 18) and leaves for making animal traps (Fig. 19).

Voucher specimen: *Balick et al. 1468.*

Orbignya × teixeirana Bondar (pro sp.).

Portuguese: Piassava.
Apinayé: Rõřé.

This is a hybrid species; the preceding two palms are the parents. It is variable in mor-

FIGS. 22–25. FIG. 22. Apinayé cracking *Orbignya phalerata* fruits in the forest to harvest oil-rich kernels. FIGS. 23–29. Preparation of farinha from mesocarp of *Orbignya phalerata*. FIG. 23. Cutting off epicarp with knife. FIG. 24. Pounding fruits to release mesocarp. FIG. 25. Grinding mesocarp.

FIGS. 26–29.   FIG. 26. Passing mesocarp of *Orbignya phalerata* through a sieve. FIG. 27. Adding water to mesocarp powder after it is passed through sieve. FIG. 28. Cooking mesocarp powder in a pan. FIG. 29. The final product, "farinha do babaçu."

FIGS. 30, 31. FIG. 30. Fruit of *Orbignya phalerata* after pounding with pieces of mesocarp still attached. FIG. 31. Village members of São José assembling for the day's work of collecting *Orbignya phalerata* kernels in the primary forest near their village. Person third from left is a FUNAI representative; sixth from left is a member of our party.

FIGS. 32–34. FIG. 32. Apinayé child's bow made for shooting small animals with stones, produced from *Syagrus cocoides*. FIG. 33. Apinayé children carrying the day's harvest of *Orbignya phalerata* kernels in pack baskets. FIG. 34. Apinayé child fishing with bow made from *Syagrus cocoides*.

phology; some individuals have distinct trunks while others do not. Panicles range in size from slightly larger than *O. eichleri* to smaller than *O. phalerata.* The Apinayé do not distinguish this from *O. eichleri,* and it is given the same name. An in-depth study of this hybrid complex is presented in Balick et al. (1987).

Use: This palm is used in the same way as *Orbignya eichleri.*

Voucher specimens: *Balick et al. 1596, 1603, 1604.*

Syagrus cocoides Mart.

Portuguese: Patí.
Apinayé: Voti.

This is a slender palm, to 7 m in height, with a thin, erect stem ca. 10 cm in diam. The pinnate leaves are 2.5 m long and are spirally arranged on the stem. Pinnae are deposited in groups of 2–4 and inserted at various angles to the plane of the leaf. The panicle is ca. 1.5 m long and has a dozen or more rachillae bearing round green fruits ca. 3 cm long.

Use: The Apinayé use this palm to make bows. Formerly, bows were the chief means of hunting, but with the advent of the shotgun have assumed lesser importance. Bows are now made for sale to travellers along the Trans-Amazon highway. A few are still made for personal use. However, children use bows extensively, both for fishing (Fig. 34) and to propel stones for hunting birds and small mammals (Fig. 32). These bows are made of wood from *Syagrus cocoides* with a bowstring of *Mauritia* or *Astrocaryum* fiber.

Voucher specimen: *Balick et al. 1616.*

V. Conclusion

The use of palms by these two groups of Indians is extensive. On the one hand, as cultivated crops are introduced by outside civilization, the utilization of palm products diminishes in everyday life. On the other hand, when so called "modern" houses are built for these people, their more traditional houses are constructed alongside as the palm huts are felt to be more livable in the local environment. Palm products still have a significant impact on the lives of both tribes of Indians at the three reserves we visited. In some areas the palm resource is declining and people are altering their lifestyles to adjust to this reality.

In other areas the stands of aggressive species such as babassu are increasing and the people will probably continue to depend on the harvest and sale of this resource for the foreseeable future. In fact, Balick (1985) has estimated that over US$100,000,000 of commerical products are obtained annually from wild stands of six genera of native palms in Brazil. If one were to quantitatively assess the levels of utilization of different plant families in the different regions visited, it is clear that the palms would be identified as the most important group, providing food, fuel, shelter, fiber, construction materials, medicine, magic and other basics of life. The present state of knowledge about palm utilization among Neotropical Indians is still quite poor, although studies have been carried out among various groups (Anderson, 1978; Balick, 1979; Beckerman, 1977; Boom, 1986). The present survey, while undertaken over a brief period, has documented several important uses of palms and other items of information new to the literature. The interest in the domestication and utilization of native palm resources in Latin America has blossomed in the last five years, with research initiatives underway in many countries (see for example FAO, 1983, as well as other contributions in this volume). The indigenous people in this region possess the greatest body of knowledge about the rational exploitation of these plants, having depended on them during centuries of existence in a well-managed, stable ecosystem. It is important that modern science, in its quest to develop plants for agriculture, not ignore the knowledge and experience of the Indians in dealing with these species. Ethnobotanical surveys must be recognized as an important way to establish criteria for germplasm collection and plant domestication, not only for palms and other tropical trees but for the many plants utilized in agricultural production systems around the world.

VI. Acknowledgments

The inhabitants of the three reserves we visited (Posto Indígena Caru, P.I. Pindaré and P.I. São José) are gratefully acknowledged for their gracious hospitality, curiosity, and collaboration with this study. This paper is dedicated to the Apinayé and Guajajara people who worked with us, freely sharing their knowledge for the benefit of others. Strong institutional collaboration between the Centro Nacional de Recursos Genéticos (CEN-ARGEN) and The New York Botanical Garden (NYBG) has supported the six year program of babassu domestication. I am particularly grateful to Lidio Coradin (CENARGEN) for his help in making this trip possible. Permission from the Conselho Nacional de Desenvolvimento Científico e Tecnológico (CNPq) and Fundaçao Nacional do Indio (FUNAI) enabled us to carry out the studies reported in this paper. I am very grateful to William Balée for transcribing my field notes on common names into a standard format. The field team consisted of José Mario F. Frazão, José G. A. Vieira, Walber S. da Silva, and myself. I thank these colleagues for their enthusiastic participation in the fieldwork.

Finally, none of this would have been possible without the financial sponsorship of the U.S. Agency for International Development, through a grant for the domestication of babassu from the Office of the Science Advisor (DAN-5542-G-SS-1089-00-ST/FN). Support was also received from CENARGEN, NYBG and the former Instituto Estadual do Babassu (INEB) in São Luis, Maranhão.

VII. Literature Cited

Anderson, A. B. 1978. The names and uses of palms among a tribe of Yanomama Indians. Principes **22(1):** 30–41.
———— **& E. S. Anderson.** 1983. People and the palm forest. Final report to USDA Forest Service, Consortium for the Study of Man's Relationship with the Global Environment. Gainesville, Florida.
Balick, M. J. 1979. Amazonian oil palms of promise: A survey. Econ. Bot. **33(1):** 11–28.
————. 1979. Economic botany of the Guahibo. I. Palmae. Econ. Bot. **33(4):** 361–376.
————. 1985. Current status of Amazonian oil palms. Pages 172–177 in C. Pesce (ed.), Oil palms and other oilseeds of the Amazon. Translated and edited by D. V. Johnson. Reference Publications, Inc., Algonac, Michigan.
————. 1986. Systematics and economic botany of the Oenocarpus–Jessenia (Palmae) complex. Adv. Econ. Bot. **3:** 1–140.
————, **C. U. B. Pinheiro & A. B. Anderson.** 1987. Hybridization in the babassu palm complex. I. Orbignya phalerata Mart. × O. eichleri Drude. Amer. J. Bot. **74:** 1013–1032.
Beckerman, S. 1977. The use of palms by the Barí Indians of the Maracaibo basin. Principes **21(4):** 143–154.

Boom, B. M. 1986. The Chácabo Indians and their palms. Principes **30(2):** 63–70.
Boudin, M. H. 1978. Dicionário de Tupi Moderno. (Dialeto tembé-ténêtéhar do alto do rio Gurupi). Conselho Estadual de Artes e Ciências Humanas, São Paulo.
Da Matta, R. 1973. A reconsideration of Apinayé Social Morphology. Pages 277–291 in D. R. Gross (ed.), Peoples and cultures of native South America. Doubleday/The Natural History Press, Garden City, New York.
Davis, I. 1966. Comparative Jê phonology. Estudos Lingüísticos I, 2. São Paulo.
FAO. 1983. Palmas poco utilizadas de América tropical. Informe de la reunión de consulta sobre palmeras poco utilizadas de América tropical. FAO, San Jose, Costa Rica.
FUNAI. 1975a. Panhĩ kapêr ã 'kagà. Cartilha Apinayé. 1. Fundação Nacional do Índio, Brasília, D.F.
————. 1975b. Panhĩ kapêr ã 'kagà. Cartilha Apinayé 2. Fundação Nacional do Índio, Brasília, D.F.
————. 1975c. Panhĩ kapêr ã 'kagà. Cartilha Apinayé 3. Fundação Nacional do Índio, Brasília, D.F.
————. 1976. Panhĩ kapêr ã 'kagà. Cartilha Apinayé 4. Fundação Nacional do Índio, Brasília, D.F.
Gomes, M. P. 1977. The ethnic survival of the Tenetehara Indians of Maranhão, Brazil. Ph.D. Thesis. University of Florida, Gainesville.
Lowie, R. H. 1946. Part 3. The Indians of Eastern Brazil. Pages 381–400 in J. H. Steward (ed.), Handbook of South American Indians. Vol. 1. Bulletin of American Ethnology. Bulletin 143. U.S. Government Printing Office, Washington, D.C.
Mason, J. A. 1950. The languages of South American Indians. Pages 157–317 in J. H. Steward (ed.), Handbook of South American Indians. Vol. 6. Bulletin of American Ethnology. Bulletin 143. U.S. Government Printing Office, Washington, D.C.
May, P. H., A. B. Anderson, M. J. Balick & J. M. F. Frazão. 1985. Subsistence benefits from the babassu palm (Orbignya martiana). Econ. Bot. **39(2):** 113–129.
Maybury-Lewis, D. 1960. Parallel descent and the Apinayé anomaly. Southw. J. Anthropol. **16:** 191–216.
Nimuendajú, C. 1983. Os Apinayé. Museu Paraense Emílio Goeldi, Belém, Pará (originally published in 1956).
Oliveira, C. E. de. 1930. Os Apinayé do alto Tocantins, costumes, crenças, artes, lendas, contos, vocabulários. Bol. Mus. Nac., Rio de Janeiro **6:** 61–110.
Pereira, E. R. 1982. Informação indígena básica. IIB No. 022/82-AGESP/FUNAI. Fundação Nacional do Indio. Typewritten report.
Wagley, C. & E. Galvão. 1948. The Tenetehara. Pages 137–148 in J. H. Steward (ed.), Handbook of South American Indians. Vol. 3. Bulletin of American Ethnology. Bulletin 143. U.S. Government Printing Office, Washington, D.C.
———— & ————. 1949. The Tenetehara Indians of Brazil. A culture in transition. Colombia University Press, New York.

The Chácobo Indians and Their Palms[1]

Brian M. Boom

Table of Contents

Abstract

An ethnobotanical study of the Chácobo Indians in northeastern Bolivia revealed 12 species of palms recognized by this Amazonian tribe. In a 1 hectare forest inventory 7 of these species were found; ecological importance values were calculated and the ethnological importance of each was assessed.

Key words: Palmae, Chácobo Indians, Amazonian ethnobotany, ecological forest inventory

Resumen

Se realizó un estudio etnobotánico entre los indios Chácobos en el noreste de Bolivia que mostró que los Chácobos conocen 12 especies de palmas. En un inventario de 1 hectárea de selva se encontraron 7 de estas especies; se calcularon los valores de importancia ecológica y se consideró la importancia etnológica de cada especie.

I. Introduction

The Chácobo belong to the southeastern Panoan language group of Amazonian Indians (Métraux, 1948). There are presently only some 400 Chácobo, although the tribe formerly numbered in the thousands. Late in the last century they lived in small groups in the northeastern Bolivian Department of Beni, scattered between Lago Rogoaguado and the Río Mamoré, 13°–14°S, 65°–66°W.

Since then the Chácobo were forced northward by more aggressive Tacanan tribes. Their range and numbers were further diminished this century by "civilized" Bolivians looking for rubber

and "sport" in the form of hunting the Indians like wild animals. The Summer Institute of Linguistics (SIL) claims to have made the first friendly contact with the tribe in 1955 (Prost, 1970). At that time the Chácobo numbered only about 135, and lived in four groups, each with 30–35 individuals. Their villages were located in isolated regions along the Ríos Benicito, Ivón, Geneshuaya, and Yata. They were semi-nomadic and lived by hunting and fishing with bow and arrow, and collecting wild fruits and nuts from the forest. They were also agriculturalists who cultivated principally sweet manioc, maize, and bananas. Both men and women pierced their nasal septum to accommodate an adornment of feathers and earlobes where they wore incisor teeth of the wild pig. The men dressed in barkcloth made from the inner bark of *Ficus* spp. and wore a crown of feathers on their heads. Feathers and

[1] Reprinted with permission from Principes **30(2)**, 1986.

various other adornments were worn around the arms, wrists, and ankles. A collar of beeswax into which they pressed blue-colored seeds completed the outfit. The women wore only a small loin-cloth held in place by a liana belt. Necklaces of different colored seeds were common for both men and women. They cut their hair in bangs in the front, but let it grow long in the back. The men wrapped their long hair into a ponytail, while the women let theirs hang free. They commonly painted their bodies with various red, black, and blue plant dyes. They celebrated the harvests of manioc and maize with festivals. These were the occasions for consuming great quantities of *chicha* (fermented beverage made from manioc or maize flour), and much dancing and singing. Among all the Chácobo, only a couple spoke any Spanish, and they quite effectively lived outside of the Bolivian cash economy. More information on traditional Chácobo culture can be found in Torrico (1971) and Prost (1970).

Today much of this has changed. A number of aspects of their culture, including their ceremonies, traditional mode of dress, and supernatural beliefs have already been lost (Fig. 1). Other aspects, including their botanical knowledge, are to a greater degree intact, although they too are being lost due to the acculturation the tribe is now experiencing. The SIL was responsible for reducing the Indians' nomadism by encouraging them to take up the collection of wild *Hevea* rubber for sale in the town of Riberalta. Also, in the early 1960's they orchestrated several transfers of villages and scattered families to centralized locations. Presently, the SIL has left the region and the Swiss Evangelical Mission has contact with the tribe. With the cash they earn from the sale of rubber and Brazil Nuts, the Chácobo buy clothes, firearms, radios, and various foods (when their agricultural production falls below expectations). Today, the majority of the tribe lives on 43,000 hectares of forested land along the Río Ivón. They own this piece of land, thanks to the SIL, and on it is located their capital village, Alto Ivón. It was here that I centered my study.

Much has been written on the significance of the forest to Amazonian Indians, but the degree of importance has never really been quantified. A primary goal of my study was to attempt such a quantification. In this paper I report on the results obtained for the palms.

II. Methods

During my seven months at Alto Ivón, I employed two basic approaches to study the palms and other plants used by the Chácobo. The first I call the "artifact/interview" technique. It is simply the traditional approach to ethnobotany as generally practiced by anthropologists, and involves asking from what plants a particular artifact is made. For example, what species are employed to make dugout canoes or to thatch house roofs? Once the name is known, a trip is made to the forest to find that specific plant. This approach also involves the outright interviewing of informants, without any particular artifact present, as to the uses of plants as foods, fuels, medicinals, in construction and crafts, ceremonies, or commerce.

The second approach I call the "inventory/interview" technique. This involves the active collection of plants and the subsequent interviewing of informants as to names and uses. In the present study, in addition to making general collections around Alto Ivón, I did an ethno-ecological inventory of 1 hectare of forest about 4 km from the village. This area of forest was far enough from the village so that plants were not collected there by the Indians. Yet, it was typical of areas of the forest closer to the village that were being actively entered and utilized. In this hectare I marked and collected specimens from every tree with a dbh (diameter at breast height) of 10 cm or more. Then I went back and did fifty 2 m square subplots to sample for epiphytes and herbs. For all of these collections I obtained names and use information from Chácobo informants.

III. Palm Occurrence

In the hectare inventoried I found 94 species and 649 individuals of trees. Of this total, seven species and 127 individuals were palms (Table I). In other words, 7.4% of the total species and 19.6% of the individuals in the hectare were palms. The palms accounted for 18,714 sq. cm, or 8.7% of the total of 214,846 sq. cm basal area. By summing these three percentages (relative diversity, relative density, and relative dominance) one obtains the Family Importance Value (FIV), as defined by Mori et al. (1983). For the hectare sampled, the Palmae have a FIV of 35.7. In this

FIGS. 1, 2. FIG. 1. A modern-day Chácobo family posing in front of a mango tree in Alto Ivón, the tribal capital. FIG. 2. Around a Chácobo house, palm uses abound. Seen in the foreground is the spathe of *xëbichoqui, Maximiliana maripa,* which serves as a toy for children. The outer roof and wall thatch on the house is of leaves of *panabi, Euterpe precatoria.* This is underlain by a leaf layer of *mani, Phenakospermum guyanense* (Strelitziaceae).

study only two families had higher FIVs: Moraceae (53.6) and Myristicaceae (41.3). Ecologically, the palms thus appear to be quite significant arboreal components of the forest surrounding Alto Ivón.

Ecological data for each of the seven species are presented in Table II. I have followed the standard definitions and calculations of relative frequency, density, dominance, and importance value as given in Curtis & Cottam (1962). It is

Table I

Occurrence of Palmae in 1 hectare forest inventory

| | All families total | Palmae | |
		No.	% total
Species	94	7	7.4
Trees	649	127	19.6
Basal area, cm sq.	214,846	18,714	8.7
		Family importance value: 35.7	

important not to confuse these species values with the FIVs discussed above. In order to calculate relative frequency, five consecutive 10 m sq. plots were combined to make a single sampling unit (i.e., plots 1–5 = sampling unit 1, plots 6–10 = sampling unit 2, etc.). Thus, my 100 plots yielded 20 sampling units. The presence of each species was then recorded each time it appeared in a sampling unit. It is necessary to aggregate the 10 m sq. plots into larger units because if the plots themselves are used then frequency and density are nearly the same. By counting the total number of occurrences for a particular species, one obtains the relative frequency for that species.

The other two values, relative density and dominance, are easier to understand. Relative density is simply the number of trees of a species divided by the total number of trees recorded (649). Relative dominance is the basal area of a species divided by the total basal area for all trees recorded (214,846 cm sq.). By summing the relative frequency, density, and dominance, one obtains the importance value (I.V.) for each species.

As can be seen from Table II, only two species are really common, *Euterpe precatoria* Mart. (I.V. = 16.01) and *Socratea exorrhiza* (Mart.) H. Wendl. (I.V. = 14.46). It is virtually impossible to stand anywhere in the forest surrounding Alto Ivón and not see both of these species. Both are easy to spot: *E. precatoria* with its crown of leaves with gracefully drooping pinnae and *S. exorrhiza* with its spiny stilt roots. Less common, but certainly not rare, is *Astrocaryum aculeatum* Meyer (I.V. = 6.57), a heavily armed, caulescent species in subgenus *Pleiogynanthus*.

The next two species are about equally important ecologically: *Jessenia bataua* (Mart.) Burret (I.V. = 2.71) and *Oenocarpus mapora* Karst. (I.V. = 2.09). The last two of the seven species in the inventory are quite rare in the forest, each occurring once in the hectare: *Maxi-*miliana maripa* (Correa de Serra) Drude (I.V. = 0.58) and *Scheelea princeps* (Mart.) Karst. (I.V. = 0.56).

Five additional species are found around Alto Ivón, but did not enter into the inventory, so I have no quantitative data for them. Two are semi-cultivated palms (*Astrocaryum huicungo* Damm. ex Burret and *Bactris gasipaes* H.B.K.) which were never found in undisturbed forest, but rather occurred in abandoned fields near the village. The three other palms are small, understory species (*Geonoma juruana* Damm., *Bactris monticola* Barb. Rodr., and *B. humilis* (Wallace) Burret). *Bactris humilis* is quite common in the region, while the other species are much less so.

IV. Palm Utilization

A tabulation of all 12 palms recognized by the Chácobo is presented in Table III. Shown are the vernacular names in Chácobo and Spanish (when known), my collection voucher number, scientific names, uses, and parts of the palm used. Specimens are deposited in the Herbarium of The New York Botanical Garden (NY).

Xëbichoqui (*Maximiliana maripa*) is not a common palm, but its fruits are highly prized so Indians will often travel considerable distances to collect them when ripe. A side bonus of such trips is the collection of the large, woody spathes which are a favorite toy for children (Fig. 2). The leaves are said to be used for thatch, but this cannot be regarded as an important use since the trees of this species are so widely spaced in the forest.

Quëboitsama (*Oenocarpus mapora*) is slightly more frequently encountered than *xëbichoqui*, and it too produces fruits with an edible pulp and has leaves which are employed as roof thatch. A sap extracted from the trunk is drunk as a medicinal to cure high fever.

Table II

Frequency, density, dominance, and importance values for Palmae in 1 hectare forest inventory

Species	No. sampling units of occurrence	No. trees	Basal area (sq. cm)	Rel. freq. (%)	Rel. den. (%)	Rel. dom. (%)	Impor. value
Euterpe precatoria	18	53	6509	4.81	8.17	3.03	16.01
Socratea exorrhiza	17	46	6061	4.55	7.09	2.82	14.46
Astrocaryum aculeatum	10	15	3416	2.67	2.31	1.59	6.57
Jessenia bataua	4	6	1552	1.07	0.92	0.72	2.71
Oenocarpus mapora	4	5	530	1.07	0.77	0.25	2.09
Maximiliana maripa	1	1	346	0.27	0.15	0.16	0.58
Scheelea princeps	1	1	299	0.27	0.15	0.14	0.56

Panabi (*Euterpe precatoria*) is unquestionably the palm most used for roof thatch by the Chácobo (Fig. 2). Generally, the Indians will thatch their roofs with a combination of leaves from *panabi* and *mani, Phenakospermum guyanense* (L. C. Rich.) Endl. ex Miq. (Strelitziaceae). A less important use of the leaves is to employ them as make-shift brooms. The leaves are used medicinally to alleviate chest pains: the pinnae are shredded and boiled in water to produce a decoction which, when cooled, is drunk. The fruits are eaten after being soaked in water to soften them or are made into a drink to which sugar is often added to sweeten it. To my knowledge, the Chácobo do not eat the heart of this palm even though it is palatable.

Itsama (*Jessenia bataua*) has fruits that the Chácobo eat after they are soaked in water or prepared as a drink as with *panabi*. The rather stout petioles of *itsama* are occasionally lashed together to form a door for those houses with walls; some Chácobo houses are open on all four sides.

Xëbini (*Scheelea princeps*) produces a fruit which is highly prized. The Chácobo bite one end of the fruit to enable them to peel back the hard exocarp to get at the thin, edible pulp; this is eaten raw. The leaves are occasionally used as a roof thatch. They are also employed as a medicinal to cure diarrhea (one of the most common medical problems in the tribe), for which a leaf decoction is prepared and drunk as for *panabi*. The most important use for the leaves of *xëbini*, however, is in the weaving of loose, light-duty baskets known in Chácobo as *poropachi*.

Onipa (*Socratea exorrhiza*) is used occasionally to cure fever: a fruit and/or bark decoction is drunk. A much more important use for the species, however, is in construction. The trunks are split to form boards, which are employed as walls, bed slats, or floor platforms for those houses with elevated floors. An interesting use for the palm, now no longer practiced, was the grating of manioc tubers on pieces of the spiny stilt roots to obtain flour. Today, this grating is accomplished on pieces of tin having ragged-edged perforations.

Panima (*Astrocaryum aculeatum*) is a very important species to the Chácobo. The fruits are liked so much that special trips will be made into the forest to collect an infructescence that is just about ripe; if they wait until it falls, most of the fruits will be lost to forest mammals. An interesting, and indirect, use of the fruits is to extract the white-colored grubs that sometimes live inside for use as a fishing bait. The hard, black "wood" from the trunk of *panima* is carved into hunting bows called *canati* in Chácobo. Five varieties of arrowheads are carved from the same wood: *quërëquë, paca, tëpi, tahua quëspini,* and *bicobi*. Each point is designed to hunt a particular type of game or to fish. Today, most hunting is done with firearms, but fishing is still done with bow and arrow, usually with the point *bicobi*. The *bicobi* point has a bent, filed nail affixed into the tip to serve as a gaff. The carved points of most arrows are fitted into a shaft made from the hollow stem of a grass, *Gynerium sagittatum* (Aubl.) Beauv., which is cultivated specifically for this purpose. The leaves of *panima* are the most important materials for basketry. The pinnae are split longitudinally and then tightly woven into different sizes and styles of baskets. An open-topped, low-sided basket, such as would be used for storing rice, is called *shichuma*. A basket with a top for storing valuables is called *chicha-*

Table III

Palms recognized and used by the Chácobo at Alto Ivón. Voucher specimen numbers are on Boom's series and are deposited at NY

Scientific name	Chácobo name	Spanish name	Voucher	Use	Parts used
Astrocaryum aculeatum	*panima*	*chonta*	4159	food, bait	fruits
				bows	"wood"
				baskets	leaves
Astrocaryum huicungo	*pani*	*chonta loro*	4154	food	fruits
Bactris gasipaes	*huanima*	*chima*	4984	food, drink	fruits
				bows	"wood"
Bactris humilis	*canahuanima*	—	4129	medicine	fruits
Bactris monticola	*shinishëoxo*	—	4509	food	fruits
Euterpe precatoria	*panabi*	*assaí*	4151	drink, food	fruits
				medicine	leaves
				thatch	leaves
				brooms	leaves
Geonoma juruana	*tananë*	—	4436	arrows	stems
				thatch	leaves
Jessenia bataua	*itsama*	*mayo*	4538	drink, food	fruits
				doors	petioles
Maximiliana maripa	*xëbichoqui*	*motacusillo*	4573	thatch	leaves
				food	fruits
				toy	spathes
Oenocarpus mapora	*quëboitsama*	*bacaba*	4152	medicine	sap
				food	fruits
				thatch	leaves
Scheelea princeps	*xëbini*	*motacú*	4145	food	fruits
				thatch	leaves
				medicine	leaves
				baskets	leaves
Socratea exorrhiza	*onipa*	*pachuba*	4155	medicine	fruit/bark
				walls, beds	trunks
				grater	roots

bëcasa. A fan woven from *panima* leaves is known as *huana huëquëti*. Given this multitude of uses, I would designate *Astrocaryum aculeatum* as the most important palm to the Chácobo culture.

Pani (*Astrocaryum huicungo*), an acaulescent species in subgenus *Monogynanthus,* is, in comparison to its larger relative, not so important. Yet, it furnishes one of the most prized of all fruits gathered by the Chácobo. They rate it along with the mango in terms of popularity. *Pani* is under semi-cultivation in abandoned agricultural fields and along trails in secondary forest. Also grown in such areas is *huanima* (*Bactris gasipaes*), the Peach Palm. It furnishes a hard, black "wood" which is occasionally carved into hunting bows and arrow points. Of course, the primary utility of *huanima* is the food and drink derived from its fruits.

The remaining species are of comparatively little importance to the tribe. *Canahuanima* (*Bactris humilis*) has medicinal value as a remedy for stomachache: a decoction of the fruits is drunk. *Shinishëoxo* (*Bactris monticola*) produces fruits which are occasionally eaten. *Tananë* (*Geonoma juruana*) has leaves which are sometimes used for thatch on small huts. The stems are reportedly used as arrow shafts when the cultivated *Gynerium sagittatum* is not available.

V. Discussion

As can be seen, a palm's ecological importance is not necessarily proportional to its utilitarian importance. It is precisely this discrepancy that lends support to the view that it is necessary to set aside large tracts of forest as reserves if indigenous Amazonian cultures are to survive. If two of the Chácobo's most useful palm species (*xëbichoqui* and *xëbini*) occur at such a low average density as 1 individual per hectare, then quite a few hectares are needed to accommodate enough trees to meet the cultural needs of the tribe.

Another point that must be remembered is that, while the Chácobo of today make extensive use of their palms, their ancestors of thirty years ago (before they entered into the Bolivian cash economy and began a period of rapid acculturation) must have had an even greater dependancy on the forest in general and palms in particular. It is probable that when the Chácobo were still semi-nomadic they came across a greater variety of palm species. This is certainly the case with the palm known in Bolivia as *Palma Real* (*Mauritia* sp.), a species of the eastern grasslands. The Chácobo know of this species from the time when they lived further south, more on the fringes of the savannas. Today, since they live deep in the forest, they have no more contact with *Palma Real*. Braun (1968) discusses the extensive use made of *Mauritia* palms by various Indians in Venezuela; no doubt they were similarly important to the Chácobo.

More ethnobotanical studies are urgently needed in order to record indigenous palm uses while there are still tribes available to study. The problem of cultural extinction, and consequent information loss, is especially acute in Amazonia. This brief survey of the palms used by the Chácobo serves to illustrate once again the importance of the Palmae to the peoples of this fascinating region.

VI. Acknowledgments

This study was supported by a generous grant from the Edward John Noble Foundation. The assistance of Michael Balick and Andrew Henderson in the identification of specimens is gratefully acknowledged. The cooperation of the government of Bolivia, the Swiss Evangelical Mission in Riberalta, and the Chácobo Indians in and around Alto Ivón made the study possible.

VII. Literature Cited

Braun, A. 1968. Cultivated palms of Venezuela. The Palm Society.

Curtis, J. T. & G. Cottam. 1962. Plant ecology workbook. Burgess Publishing Co., Minneapolis, Minnesota.

Métraux, A. 1948. The southeastern Panoan tribes. Pages 449–452 *in* J. H. Steward (ed.), Handbook of South American Indians. Vol. 3. The tropical forest tribes. Bureau of American Ethnology, Smithsonian Institution, Washington, D.C.

Mori, S. A., B. M. Boom, A. M. de Carvalho & T. S. dos Santos. 1983. Southern Bahian moist forests. Bot. Rev. **49**: 155–232.

Prost, M. D. 1970. Costumbres, habilidades, y cuadro de la vida humana entre los Chácobos. Summer Institute of Linguistics, Riberalta, Bolivia.

Torrico P., B. 1971. Indígenas en el corazón de América. Los Amigos del Libro, La Paz.

Uses of Semi-Wild Palms in Indonesia and Elsewhere in South and Southeast Asia

T. Antony Davis

Table of Contents

Abstract

Indonesia supports about 60 genera and approximately 1000 species of palms, including the vast number of Lepidocaryoid palms collected recently. The most important palms cultivated in Indonesia are *Cocos nucifera* and *Elaeis guineensis* which are being exploited commercially. The rest of the species grow either wild or semi-wild. Some are being exploited for food, alcohol, timber or for ornamental use. The economic importance of 15 semi-wild or wild species is highlighted here: *Areca catechu, A. vestiaria, Arenga microcarpa, A. pinnata, Borassodendron borneense, Borassus flabellifer, Calamus* spp., *Corypha utan, Cyrtostachys renda, Livistona rotundifolia, Metroxylon sagu, Nypa fruticans, Pigafetta filaris, Pinanga* spp. and *Salacca zalacca*. By far the most important species among the semi-wild palms of Indonesia are *Arenga pinnata, Borassus flabellifer* and *Metroxylon sagu* because of their multipurpose utility.

Key words: palms, uses, Indonesia

I. Introduction

The equatorial and insular nature of the Republic of Indonesia, with its expansive volcanic mountain slopes fertilized by frequent eruptions, heavy rainfall with good distribution, extensive swampy areas—especially in Sumatra, Kalimantan and Irian Jaya, the lime hills, the podsolic and the rich alluvial soils in the plains, are all conducive to the successful growth of a multitude of plants, including palms.

Indonesia has members of most major groups of Asiatic palm. The Lepidocaryoideae alone have not less than 500 species under *Calamus, Daemonorops,* and *Korthalsia.* According to Meijer (1962), Indonesia supports 60 genera and about 800 species of palms. The Bogor Botanic Garden held, in about 1960, 195 genera and at least 300

Advances in Economic Botany 6: 98–118, 1988
© 1988 The New York Botanical Garden

98

species of palms. These and subsequent collections have been listed by Sastrapradja and Davis (1983). Surprisingly, there are very few native palms extensively cultivated in Indonesia, the most important being *Cocos nucifera* and *Elaeis guineensis.*

With about 2.9 million ha under cultivation, Indonesia is the second largest grower of coconut in the world. It exports large quantities of African palm oil because of the large area under that crop (265,000 ha). Thus far, only coconut and oil palm have been exploited commercially. The rest of the palms are grown wild or semi-wild. Some of these are also being exploited for food, beverage, timber, thatch, and as ornamentals. According to Johnson (1985), the versatile palms provide edible fruits, oilseeds, sap for beverages or sweeteners, palm hearts, stem starch, leaves for thatching and basketry, leaf midribs for fencing, wax for candles, trunk wood for construction, fuelwood, feed for livestock and traditional medicines. Kitzke and Johnson (1975) considered that only about 30 different palms are commercially useful to man, yet in Indonesia over a hundred species of semi-wild or wild palms are being exploited. The following is an account of the 15 economically most important of the many semi-wild palms used in Indonesia. *Areca vestiaria, Cyrtostachys renda* and *Pigafetta filaris* are valuable ornamentals. *Metroxylon sagu, Arenga microcarpa* and *Corypha utan* yield sago. Endosperms of *Areca catechu* and *Pinanga* spp. are used for chewing and resin from the latter makes good batik paint. *Nypa fruticans, Livistona rotundifolia* and *Corypha utan* supply material for thatch. In addition, *Nypa* supplies beverage, sugar and alcohol. The heart of *Borassodendron* and fruit of *Salacca* are edible. *Calamus* yields the valuable cane. *Borassus flabellifer* and *Arenga pinnata* have multiple utility—food, beverage, alcohol, timber and thatch.

II. Palms Discussed

1. PALMYRA PALM
(*BORASSUS FLABELLIFER*)

Beccari (1913) classified the genus *Borassus* into seven species (*B. flabellifer, B. sundaicus, B. aethiopum, B. deleb, B. sambiranensis, B. madagascariensis* and *B. heineana*). These are distributed over almost half the tropics extending from West Africa to the northern fringe of Australia. Of these, *B. flabellifer* (incl. *sundaicus*) and *B. aethiopum* are the most important. *Borassus flabellifer* covers the entire southern part of India, especially Tamilnadu and Andhra Pradesh, the northern part of Sri Lanka and parts of Burma, Kampuchea, Thailand and West Malaysia, and is native to Indonesia and distributed in South Sulawesi, in dense pockets in East Java (near Surabaya and on Madura Island), the Sunda Islands—covering the East Nusa Tenggara Islands of Flores, Roti, East Timor, etc. *Borassus aethiopum* is confined to Tropical Africa.

Economic importance of palmyra

In Indonesia, thousands of poor families in the Madura and Sunda Island groups make their living from this palm because of its multiple uses. "Tala Vilasam," a famous Tamil poem eulogizes palmyra as the "tree of life," and catalogues 801 uses (Blatter, 1926). Food products from palmyra currently consumed in Indonesia and India are the immature endosperm, mesocarp pulp, tuberous seedling and palm-heart. Especially near Surabaya and Madura Island, about 50% of the palmyra fruits are harvested while still immature for the sweet, jelly-like endosperm. Endosperm from two fruits may be available for Rp 100 (US$0.10). In Java, after carefully extracting the whole endosperm from fruits and wrapping them in palmyra leaves, hawkers sell them to the many tourists tasting the delicacy for the first time. The immature endosperm is about 93% water, and the remainder is mostly glucose (Burkill, 1966)

When the fruit is fully ripe, the fibrous mesocarp encloses a golden colored and sweet pasty mesocarp pulp. It can be eaten fresh, but is more commonly boiled or baked before being consumed. This paste is also mixed with flour and fried in oil to make tasty cookies. According to Kovoor (1983), the mesocarp is about 40% by weight of the whole fruit. Recent studies by Davis (1987) have revealed that the fruits of some palms yield mesocarp pulp which is as much as 60% of the weight of the whole fruit. Not all palms give such a high yield of mesocarp pulp, however. Utilization of the mesocarp pulp has not yet become as popular in Indonesia as the consumption of tender endosperm. Since, during the fruiting season only a very small percentage of the fruits can be consumed either as human or cattle food, small-scale industries could be developed to extract sugar and carbohydrate from ripe fruits.

Another good food source from *Borassus* is the tuberous seedling. After shaving off the mesocarp, the pyrenes are sown in raised beds. The long apocole carries the embryo down to its tip from where the embryo grows vertically, producing the first leaf which becomes tuberous, storing the food transferred from the seed. The tuberous, rudimentary leaves are boiled and eaten for their starch. Production of commercial starch is possible from such tuberous seedlings (Padmanabhan et al., 1978). The tender growing point of palmyra is edible; it is crisp and nutty. However, there is no large-scale gathering and marketing of palmyra hearts prevalent anywhere.

Dransfield (1976a) gave an excellent account of tapping the palmyra in Madura (East Java) and the process of making brown sugar from the spadix sap. The sweet sap obtained by tapping the palmyra inflorescence (Figs. 1, 2) represents its most economically valuable product. Fresh sap from both the male and female palms, popularly known as "neera," is a sweet and nutritious drink. When it is allowed to ferment it becomes toddy, a favorite intoxicating drink. Neera is very popular in Indonesia, especially in the palm-growing provinces. The sweet sap is also bottled and sold in sophisticated restaurants. A company in Singapore is also making brisk money by selling bottled neera. To obtain neera, the tapper has to climb the palm twice daily, which is a strenuous task. Davis (1984) devised an apparatus for easy climbing of palmyra and coconut palms. Arrack and vinegar can be obtained from fermented toddy. When sweet neera is boiled down, brown sugar, treacle, crystallized sugar and sugar candy can be obtained. Brown sugar or jaggery is very popular in Indonesia. Jaggery is made into small cakes using coconut shell, bamboo rings or palmyra leaflet rings as molds. Village women make their living by selling them in streets (Fig. 3).

Although palm leaf writing has become obsolete, at an earlier time palmyra and talipot palm leaves served as an important writing material. Tender leaves are lopped for making hats, bags, baskets and other articles. For this purpose thousands of palms in India are defoliated. Also, because of the increasing demand for fuelwood in

brick kilns, palmyra is being destroyed in South India (Davis, 1985). Fortunately, such large-scale destruction is not felt in Indonesia. Occasionally, the palmyra stem produces branches (Davis, 1969) and some branching stems form artistic decorations in office halls.

Palmyra yields valuable leaf fiber. The leaf base of young palms is cut and the long and strong fiber is extracted by beating it. The petiole margins also yield fiber for tying. But the best fiber for weaving cots and chairs comes from the inner petiole. The outer petiole has another fiber of inferior quality. Brush fiber, cordage, and rough weaving and plaiting fiber are all products of palmyra palm (Davis & Johnson, 1987). Fox (1977) gave more details on the history and culture of the people of Roti and adjoining islands of East Nusa Tenggara Province and their dependance on *Borassus flabellifer*. An account on the botany and utility of the palm is also provided.

2. Sugar Palm
(*Arenga pinnata*)

The Indo-Malaysian sugar palm (*Arenga pinnata*), according to Miller (1964), is the "Prince of Princes." It is one of the wild palms utilized for centuries. For the people of Indonesia, because of its multiple utility, the sugar palm was of immense benefit, especially during the Japanese occupation. *Arenga pinnata,* indigenous to the Indo-Malayan archipelago, with a concentration in Indonesia, is distributed throughout the Malay Peninsula, Thailand, Burma, Kampuchea, Laos, Vietnam, The Philippines and even in northern Australia. Northeastern parts of India and Bangladesh also support a thin population of the sugar palm.

Arenga pinnata is a single-stemmed, pinnate palm, reaching maturity in 8–12 years, when it produces a terminal spadix. Thereafter, flowering continues basipetally during two to five more years, each spadix arising from the axil of older leaves. The leaves are arranged in two spirals moving clockwise or counter-clockwise (Davis, 1971). The terminal as well as the next 2–5 spadices bear only female flowers. In the subsequent 2–5 spadices, male flowers also appear along with the female. In later spadices, female flowers are fully suppressed, the spadices becoming purely male. In many trees, male spadices continue to

FIGS. 1–4. FIG. 1. Palmyra tapper of Surabaya (Indonesia) climbing palm without an ankle ring. Bamboo receptacles are used for gathering sap. FIG. 2. Tapper from East Madura massaging male spike. Palmyra leaf buckets are used for collecting sap. FIG. 3. Woman carrying palmyra brown jaggery for street sale. FIG. 4. Close view of *Arenga pinnata* crown bearing many infructescences.

appear from nodes almost down to ground level. By this time the leaves have lost practically all their leaflets and the palms have acquired a shaggy, dreary appearance, meriting the unenviable state mentioned by Rumphius (1750) as being, "the ugliest shape of all trees."

The many uses of the sugar palm

The sugar palm is primarily a good source of food for man. The shoot apex of the non-flowering individuals is sweet and eaten raw or used as a salad. The endosperm of immature fruit is a hard jelly, edible but insipid. The Javanese and Balinese have the required patience to gather immature fruits, burn them to remove the irritating crystals and extract the endosperm from the fruit wall. The endosperm is soaked in limewater for a few days before it is consumed by mixing it with sugar syrup or coconut milk. Good quality edible sago can also be obtained from the stem of sugar palm as soon as its terminal inflorescence appears. Since the palm is more useful for obtaining neera (or "saguer" or "legen"), *Arenga* is not usually felled for sago extraction.

The female flower-bearing spadices usually are not tapped (Fig. 4); but the male ones are ideal for that purpose. The spadix is elaborately shaped for the collection of sap. When a few male flowers start blooming, the spadix is considered at the proper age to be tapped. After the training, the whole spike-bearing portion of spadix is chopped off, as the peduncle is the source of the sweet sap. After a proper paring of the tip of the peduncle into thin slices, the sap trickles in large quantities and is collected in bamboo receptacles. The most important economic use of the sugar palm is for the inflorescence sap and the brown jaggery ("gula aren") that is obtained by boiling down the fresh juice. When the sweet sap is allowed to ferment into a mild wine, it becomes a more popular drink, "saguer." If the sap is allowed to ferment beyond the drinkable stage, a 3–4% acetic acid vinegar is formed, useable for cooking.

The yield of sap varies with the tree, locality and age of the palms. Even though the volume of sap collected shows variation, the sap concentration remains almost constant (Tammes, 1952). According to Miller (1964), in West Java sap runs for an average period of about five months, the poorest for about two months and the best palms for about nine months. One 20 year old sugar palm was reported to have yielded as much as 10–15 liters of neera per eight hour period. The average yield per day from a single peduncle ranges between 3 and 6 liters. Tammes (1952) recorded a yield of 7.5 liters of juice per day per spadix in North Sulawesi.

An account of preparing sugar from sweet neera in North Sulawesi has been given by Soekarjoto and Mangindaan (1981). The following account is a summary of it.

Sugar from Arenga sap

Fresh sap is clear and straw-colored, gradually becoming milky as fermentation progresses. Fresh sap consists of about 80% water, sucrose, gums, manitol, proteins and inorganic salts. The sucrose content varies from 14% to 16.5%. The process of sugar-making, still a domestic art, varies from region to region. Sap from bamboo collection receptacles attached to palms is poured into bigger bamboo containers and brought to the sugar processing centers, located either close to the tapper's house or in a separate hut erected near the palms. Large metal pans of varying capacity are filled with sap and placed on wide hearths and boiled. Firewood is used for heating. In about three hours, the juice is reduced to a thick syrup. In a syrup-filled pan of average size, three dry fruit capsules of *Ricinus communis* are added and stirred. To prevent the juice from frothing and overflowing the vessel, certain herbs, coconut kernels or coconut oil are also added. At a particular stage, the pan containing the thickening syrup is removed from the fire, continually stirred and allowed to cool a bit. Before it completely cools, small quantities of the thick syrup are poured into coconut shell cups (Fig. 5), usually the half having the eyes. The soft eye is opened but temporarily closed with a small leaf. The syrup hardens into cakes within 15 minutes of pouring. Two such cakes are usually placed face to face and tied together with blades of grass of a palm leaf and sent to the market. The boiling vessel varies in capacity, from as little as 5 liters to in some regions as large as 30 liters. Sometimes, instead of coconut shell molds, bamboo rings are used, which produce more uniform cakes.

Arrack is distilled from fermented toddy. In North Sulawesi, making arrack is not as profit-

FIGS. 5–7. FIG. 5. Thickened *Arenga* sugar syrup being poured into coconut shell mold. FIG. 6. Leaf-base fiber of *Arenga* elegantly used on the multi-tier roof of a family temple in Bali. FIG. 7. Massive terminal spadix of *Metroxylon sagu*.

able as selling fresh juice for drinking. Nevertheless, during rainy days and at other times when there is not much demand for toddy, the surplus quantities of saguer are distilled into arrack. The alcohol content of the distilled arrack can reach 90% and at that point it becomes dangerous to drink. Usually the alcohol content is tested by burning a known quantity of the arrack inside a bottle. Distilleries usually are of a makeshift type consisting of a metal boiler which is heated over a slow fire and the vapor condensed through a long pipeline of narrow bamboo poles joined tightly together.

The sugar palm, while one of the most useful of palms, is unfortunately not exploited fully. Large-scale cultivation and improvements in the tapping techniques and in the manufacture of products are urgently needed to bring more income from this palm.

Leaf-base fiber or "gomuti"

The fiber from the leaf-base is another important product of the sugar palm. The black, tough, horsehair-like fiber, known as "gomuti," is obtained from the broad leaf base of the palm. This fiber has great commercial value and domestic importance. Since the fiber is very durable, strong and resistant to saltwater, it has served as a good material for covering submarine cables and subterranean parts of utility poles. Fish nets and fish lines are also made of this fiber. Gomuti fiber is elegantly used by the Balinese as a lasting and special thatch for their village temples and community tombs (Fig. 6). Brushes and brooms made of *Arenga* leaf fiber are very popular throughout Indonesia. The leaf midribs are used as brooms or made into baskets and fishing implements. Tender leaflets of *Arenga pinnata* are used as cigarette wrappers. The mature stem is turned into bases for drums.

3. SAGO PALM
(*METROXYLON SAGU*)

Sago palm (*Metroxylon sagu*), the source of sago starch, a staple food for millions of islanders in the region between Malaysia and Papua New Guinea, remains mostly a wild species. However, the spineless form is being cultivated in Indonesia. Johnson (1977) mentions many species under five genera that yield sago: *Syagrus* (*Are-*

castrum) *romanzoffianum, Arenga microcarpa, A. pinnata, Caryota urens, C. mitis, C. maxima, Corypha utan, C. umbraculifera, Eugeissona utilis, Mauritia flexuosa, Metroxylon sagu,* and *Roystonea* are sago yielders. Three of them are from the New World. *Metroxylon* and *Arenga* are the most common ones exploited for sago. Extraction of sago from *Arenga microcarpa* is restricted to a small area of North Sulawesi, in the islands of Sangihe and Talaud.

Metroxylon sagu possibly originated from the Maluku (Indonesia). Beccari classified the sago palms thus: *Eumetroxylon* (fruit covered with scales set out in 18 vertical series): and *Coelococcus* (fruits covered with scales set out in 24–28 vertical series). Eight to fifteen years are required for the suckers to flower, from the time they start bearing the aerial stem. The flower bunch is a massive, terminal, racemose inflorescence (Fig. 7). Just before flowering, the stem stores the maximum amount of starch. From a single stem, up to about 410 kg of crude sago can be obtained, but the average seems to be between 110 and 160 kg. In a normal swamp forest grove, about ten palms per ha per year will be suitable for felling. They may yield 2840–3977 kg of crude starch (Barrau, 1960). Sago is not a balanced food for man by any standard. It is almost entirely starch and water, commercial sago paste being about 40% water. Protein content is very low (0.2 g per 100 g), fats are completely absent, and mineral salts are available only in very small quantities (ash 0.35 mg; calcium 10 mg, phosphorus 12.5 mg and iron 1.5 mg per 100 g). Sago does not have an appreciable vitamin content. The islanders for whom sago is staple food (Fig. 8), supplement their diet with fish and greens, an important plant being *Ipomoea aquatica.*

Ruddle et al. (1978) mentioned some industrial uses of sago starch (Fig. 9). Similar to other starches, sago starch is important in the production of adhesives, particularly those for the laminated paper board industry. Custard powder, confections, glucose, gravy powders, sauce mixtures and monosodium glutamate are some products of the food industry where sago is used. The pharmaceutical industry uses sago as a bland, odorless and easily digested filler for drugs and medication. Sago also has uses in the petroleum and textile industries.

Sago is eaten in various ways. A porridge is prepared in a pot and condiments, greens, fish,

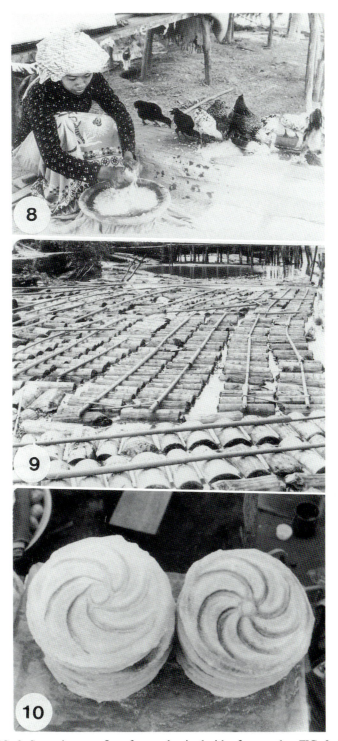

FIGS. 8–10.   FIG. 8. Squeezing sago flour from pulverized pith of sago palm. FIG. 9. Cut pieces of sago stem, transported by river, wait at a processing center in Riau Province. FIG. 10. Pancakes prepared from sago extracted from *Arenga microcarpa*.

cuttle fish, other mollusks, or wild meat are added. Otherwise, a kind of cake is made by cooking sago paste mixed with grated coconut, greens, fish or meat in an oven of hot stones. Small-scale industries may be encouraged to make substantial improvements in the processing of sago under hygienic conditions, fortifying the sago paste with vitamins, minerals and protein to make it a wholesome food. The vast potential of sago in Irian Jaya, Sumatra and Kalimantan could generate revenue for the nation if practical research were to be conducted for better utilization of the immeasureable reserve of sago. In connection with food diversification, sago is potentially important, according to Sastrapradja and Mogea (1977). Several areas in Indonesia have employed it as a staple. However, new technology should be developed to process and preserve it to enable its introduction to other areas.

4. SAGU BARUK
(ARENGA MICROCARPA)

Fairchild (1943) appears to have been the first to record *Arenga microcarpa* as another good source of starch. It is known that in Indonesia, in an emergency, *A. pinnata* has been used for the extraction of sago even though this species is more valuable for sugar, beverage, and alcohol. Dransfield (1977) mentions one hapaxanthic species, *A. ambong,* confined to the Philippines and *A. undulatifolia,* of the Philippines, Borneo and Sulawesi as additional sources for stem sago.

A. microcarpa, originally from New Guinea, grows wild and is also cultivated on the slopes of volcanic hills of the Sangihe Talaud island group of North Sulawesi Province. Two impressive clumps of this hapaxanthic palm grow luxuriantly in the Bogor Botanic Garden. *Arenga microcarpa* flourishes on drained volcanic soil at altitudes between 200 and 500 m, but it cannot grow in waterlogged conditions. Along the winding and steep road from the Sangihe airport to Taruna, the headquarters for Sangihe Talaud District, one passes through patches of elegant *A. microcarpa* with their erect and somewhat distichous leaves, as well as many traditional sago processing centers. Each mature clump has 3–5 tall shoots ready for starch extraction. Being a terminal flowering species, the shoot is usually felled when a spadix just emerges at the zenith. Subsequently, 5–8 spadices are produced basipetally from the axils of older leaves.

The stem is more slender than that of *Arenga pinnata*. One very striking characteristic of this palm is its multiple buds in each node. Up to eight buds were counted from one node, with a minimum of three buds present. Occasionally, one comes across clumps where the shoots bear only one bud in each node. This could be a different cultivar or race. The mature stem is cut into 3 m long pieces and brought to the processing center, located where there is running water available. Though the processing for sago in this species is essentially similar to that for *Metroxylon sagu,* for *A. microcarpa* the choppers and the pounding implements are narrower, to cope with the narrower stem. The pulverized pith is washed and the sago starch obtained by washing and squeezing it in water, followed by decantation.

Sago paste from *Arenga microcarpa* is regarded as superior to that of *Metroxylon sagu,* but I could not detect any differences. Whether raw or baked, the stem starch tasted flat. Different kinds of pancakes (Fig. 10) with or without sugar and coconut are prepared with sago paste. Local people like to eat sago preparations with sugar, honey or coconut milk. They combine this food with seafood and wild meat to obtain the required fat and protein.

5. SALAK PALM
(SALACCA ZALACCA)

Mogea (1982) resolved the confusion over the species name of the Salak palm (*Salacca zalacca*) which produces an edible, spiny fruit. Whatever the significance of the revised name, the fruit is quite delicious, which accounts for it formerly being known as *Salacca edulis.* The numerous tourists as well as the residents of enchanting Bali agree that the salak from Bali is the finest available in Indonesia or the neighboring ASEAN countries. Even though *S. zalacca* is cultivated in Bali and some other parts of Indonesia, it is still a wild palm in Southwest Java and South Sumatra. In some cases, farmers may plant a clump, but neglect to thin the clumps or look after the plant. Such deserted clumps virtually turn wild, producing fruits occasionally.

Salak is very popular in Indonesia, and in the markets of most big towns one can see old women selling the spiny fruits displayed in cane baskets (Fig. 11). This lepidocaryoid palm, like the sago palm and the rattans, produces spherical or

FIGS. 11–14. FIG. 11. Fruits of *Salacca zalacca* dominate a village market in West Java. FIG. 12. Portion of nipa inflorescence, with two male spikes and a female spike. FIG. 13. Leaf mats made from nypa leaflets at Maros, South Sulawesi. FIG. 14. Transverse section through mature fruit of *Borassodendron borneense*.

conical fruits covered with spirally arranged scales. Salak fruits are 5–7 cm long by 3–5 cm in diameter. When the brittle cover is peeled off, a white, creamy (sometimes light pink) pulp becomes visible. This edible part is formed from the outer integument of the seed. The inner integument is distinguishable as a very thin tissue which surrounds the hard seed (1–3 per fruit).

To some the fruit tastes like pineapple; to Allen (1965), it tasted more like an unripe but edible pear—hard, crisp, juicy and very refreshing. Some compare the taste of salak to jack fruit.

Salak Bali, the tastiest of all salaks, is female (Mogea, 1978) and it is not known how the flowers are fertilized. In other places, many pollinating insects carry pollen from the staminate to the pistillate flowers. Where the pollinating insects are not available or are inadequate, the farmers resort to assisted pollination to get good yields from their palms.

6. NYPA PALM
(*NYPA FRUTICANS*)

Status of nypa in Indonesia

Indonesia contains enormous stretches of swampy areas, especially in the larger islands of Sumatra, Kalimantan and Irian Jaya. Also in the thousands of smaller islands like Java, the Nusa Tenggara group, Sulawesi, Bali and Maluku Islands, there are small to large pockets of swamps. Feasibility studies conducted by the Government have revealed that the total swampy areas reach roughly 35 million ha or approximately 17% of the total exposed land surface. Also, it was estimated that about 7 million ha of the swamps are subjected to ocean tides, and such areas could be reclaimed for agricultural purpose (Davis & Corputty, 1983). The primary vegetation of the tidal swamps comprises many species of mangroves and tidal mud palms, the most prominent ones being *Nypa fruticans* and *Metroxylon sagu*. Practically the entire borders of the reclaimed areas are dominated by original nypa forests which add strength to the dikes and offer protection to the crops raised within the reclaimed areas. Even if the nypa area is reckoned to occupy only 10% of the tidal swamps, the area under this palm will reach over 700,000 ha, thus having a very great potential for sugar and alcohol, provided the needed manpower to tap the palms is available. At present, Indonesia makes little effort to exploit the palm for human use. As demonstrated by Duke (1977) with data from the Philippines, the 700,000 ha of nypa has the potential to yield 2,100,000 mt of sugar annually. The 30,000 liters of toddy normally available from 1 ha of nypa is equivalent to 4000 liters of alcohol. According to Gibbs (1911), sap yield can go up to 78,500 liters per ha per year for palms growing under ideal conditions.

Economic importance of nypa

In Sri Lanka, the only use for *Nypa fruticans* is the juice of the young shoot, used medicinally for treatment of herpes. In the Sunderbans area of West Bengal only the leaves, locally known as "gol-patha," are used to thatch rural houses. In Bangladesh, in addition to utilizing the leaves, the palm is tapped for sweet "neera" in isolated villages of the Khulna, Barisal and Patuakhali districts where the palm is cultivated in rice fields. These areas are not traditionally swampy. The heart of nypa and the jelly-like endosperm of its immature fruits are edible (Fig. 12). In parts of Indonesia, tender leaflets of nypa, as well as of sago palm, are sun-dried and used as country-made cigarette wrappers (Meijer, 1962). Among other minor products of utility, bags, brooms, fibers, pith-helmets, palm leaf rain coats and mats are the important items (Guzman-Rivas, 1984). Utilization of leaf and spadix sap are in an early stage of exploitation in Malaysia, Indonesia and Papua New Guinea. However, in the Philippines, nypa is tapped extensively for the sweet sap, which is allowed to ferment into an intoxicating drink ("tuba"). From toddy, alcohol and vinegar are manufactured and sugar is obtained from the sweet sap. Once a nypa palm is five years old, it may be tapped for the next 50 years according to Duke (1977). The toddy yield from 1 ha may be estimated to be 3 mt of sugar or 4000 liters of alcohol, which in terms of energy, equals 1000 liters of gasoline. Brief accounts of the leaf trade in Indonesia and the toddy/sugar industry elsewhere are given below.

Trade of nypa leaf

Even though tapping the nypa palm for toddy is yet to become popular in Indonesia, many villages, especially in South Sulawesi and Riau Provinces, are engaged in selling nypa leaves. Around Maros (South Sulawesi), plentiful colonies of nypa flourish along the mouths of the several streams that divide the land into strips. Here, nypa is even cultivated in new areas on account of a flourishing trade of leaves for homes. The local farmers cut one to three mature leaves per shoot at a time and strip off leaflets from the long, brown, cylindrical petiole and rachis. The petiole-rachises are used as rafters for country houses to hold the leaf mats. The stripped leaflets are retted in swampy lagoons for seven to ten days and woven into mats for roofing (Fig. 13). Leaf mats are sold at Rp 100 (US$0.10) per mat. A capable woman can stitch about 30 mats per day and earn a wage of Rp 750. About ten mats can be prepared from one large leaf, bringing the owner Rp 1000. In South Sulawesi alone, about half a million U.S. dollars worth of nypa leaf mats are made and traded each year.

Method of tapping the nypa for sap

As in *Arenga pinnata,* the stalk of the nypa inflorescence (when cut at the proper stage) exudes a sweet sap. Selection of a spadix of suitable maturity for tapping is important to guarantee a good supply of sap over a long duration. A robust spadix between two and three months prior to anthesis is considered most appropriate for tapping. As a first step, the spathes and bracts at the base of the fruit head are cleaned off. The tapper then gently presses the selected fruit head with his leg on a convenient side. He does it slowly by repeated rubbing of the spadix stalk (peduncle) without breaking or crushing it. He continues this process of massaging for about an hour and leaves the spadix to rest for a day. The second day, the tapper continues massaging the peduncle and bends it further. When the tip of the peduncle (just below the head of the fruits) is bent down to about 60°, the fruit head is cut off at a slant with a sharp chopper. The tapper has already prepared a special bamboo receptacle for the collection of sap. Sweet sap will start to trickle into the bamboo receptacle. The quantity of sap collected from one stalk over one night is between 500 and 750 ml, which is less than the flow from an *Arenga* peduncle.

Yield of sugar

Fresh nypa juice is very sweet. According to Gibbs (1911), the juice has 18% total solids, while *Cocos* and *Arenga* have 17.5% and *Corypha* 17% total solids.

Paivoke (1984) has given statistics on the yield of nypa sap. Under Papua New Guinea conditions, 30% of nypa palms will produce flowers, and one flowering palm brings forth one or two inflorescences per year (Amio et al., 1979). The length of the tappable organ in nypa varies from 0.6 m to 2.2 m. The yield of sap varies between sources. According to Gibbs (1911), about 1.25 liters of sap per palm can be extracted each day. Thus, an average plant (shoot) will yield about 50 liters of sap during the tapping season, amounting to about 440 liters of sap per day per ha. That works out to be about 78,500 liters per ha annually (for a tapping period of about six months). The sugar content of fresh nypa sap is between 14% and 17% depending on the locality (Pratt et al., 1913). An alcohol content of about 6–7% may be taken as the average for the fully fermented sap.

7. Bendang Palm (*Borassodendron borneense*)

Dransfield (1972) described *Borassodendron borneense* as a new species occurring in the lowland Dipterocarp forest in Borneo, Sarawak, Brunei, Sabah and East Kalimantan. In Indonesia, it occurs only in East Kalimantan on low lateritic hills and slopes. This solitary, erect, dioecious and hardy palm resembles *Borassus* in several respects including utility. But, as it is still confined to a small remote forest area, people have not yet exploited the palm for their benefit. Locally the palm is known as "bidang" or "bendang."

The erect stem, especially the mature lower portion, is sawn into rafters and reepers (strips) for the construction of village homes. The apex of the crown is tasty and edible. According to Dransfield (1972), the Ibans collect the palm-cabbage for sale in Bintulu market at about one Malaysian dollar each. The crispy nature and sweetness of the heart make it popular. As more of the *Borassodendron* areas become accessible, there is a great threat to the survival of this species, as the exploitation of palm heart is bound to increase. The populations in the Kutei Nature Reserve of East Kalimantan Province are reported (Dransfield, 1972) to show damage caused by the depredations of orangutans. Orangutans pull out developing tender leaves and eat the soft, sweet, meristematic tissue at the leaf bases. Such repeated damage results in the death of the palm.

When some forest-dwellers of East Kalimantan were consulted, it became clear that no one knew how to tap *Borassodendron* to collect the sweet spadix sap. But local people gather the ripe fallen fruits, roast them on an open fire and eat the golden pulp that fills the mesocarp (Davis, in press). They are also unaware of the importance of the tuberous seedlings as a source of starch. Moreover, no one uses the palmate leaves as thatch or for extracting the petiole fiber. A cross-sectional view of this fruit is shown in Figure 14.

8. RATTAN PALMS
(*CALAMUS* SPP., ETC.)

Our knowledge of the rattans has increased, thanks to Dransfield's monograph on the rattans of the Malay Peninsula (1979). There are 12 genera of rattans comprising about 600 species, most of them native to Southeast Asia. Contrary to common belief, not all species are climbing. The climbing species in particular yield the commercially important rattan sticks, core, cane, and split cane used in the manufacture of light and elegant cane-furniture. World trade of rattan is a multimillion dollar business. Indonesia has a good share in this growing trade since cane, until recently a wild crop, is being cultivated (at least three species) on some islands, notably Kalimantan.

The Biological Institute at Bogor collected, up to 1980, 118 species of rattans, including 58 from Kalimantan alone. More varieties were added to the list during subsequent plant collecting expeditions. In Sumatra there are about 14 species of wild *Calamus* according to Meijer (1962). Some of them are thin-stemmed rattans good for binding material, others are heavy spiny ones, like *Calamus ornatus* used for making sticks. The monocarpic species *Plectocomia elongata* is the most elegant. Apart from being used as sticks and binding material, rattans are woven into fine baskets, fish traps, trays, etc.

In Kalimantan there are several useable species, including two cultivated ones. Sulawesi and most other forest areas also have many wild species from which cane is harvested, mostly for domestic use. *Calamus minanassae* is cultivated on a small scale in North Sulawesi. Kuswara and Samsoedin (1983) gave an account of the canes regularly cultivated in Central Kalimantan province which contribute largely to the cane exported to Japan, Taiwan, Singapore and the Philippines. Small quantities of cane and cane products are exported to Europe and America. Between 1977 and 1979, an average of 33,578 mt of dry rattans in the form of raw canes and as articles of utility was exported and earned a significant quantity of foreign exchange for Indonesia. There are several cane processing factories established along the banks of large rivers of Central Kalimantan, such as the Arut, Barito, Kapuas and Rongon.

The fruits of some rattans are edible, although most of them are sour and astringent. In country markets adjoining forest areas, it is possible to see elderly women selling such fruits, mainly to children, who enjoy sour fruits. The fleshy layer in rattan fruit is the outer seed coat and not the fruit wall. Dransfield (1979) mentions that in *Calamus exilis* the meat is sour, astringent and disgustingly foetid. But *Calamus lobbianus* produces edible fruits with thick sweet flesh. *Calamus manan* is planted in South Borneo for its fruits. Dragon's blood (a dye or varnish) is obtained from the fruit scales of a few species of *Daemonorops*.

In Central Kalimantan, regular cultivation of rattans has been going on for several decades. Other areas, like North Sulawesi and South-East Sulawesi Provinces, also have started cultivating canes. The bulk of the cultivated canes in Indonesia comes from Central Kalimantan. The two important species cultivated here are *Calamus caesius,* locally known as "rattan irit," and *C. trachycoleus,* locally known as "rattan taman," "rattan sigi" or "rattan sega." Rattan areas are ditched to drain off excess water into the nearby rivers. Many dicot trees (dead or alive) are maintained in cane areas for the rattans to climb on. New plantations are established with seedlings either raised from seeds or transplanted from the wild. Rattan irit is ready for harvest in 7–10 years and rattan taman in 10–15 years after transplanting in a regular plantation. About 100 clumps are accommodated per ha. At first harvest, two to six shoots are cut from each clump. Subsequent harvests are done every two to five years. The canes are cut into lengths of about 7 m and the tender parts of the stem and leaves discarded. Each shoot will produce about three or four such lengths. One ha will yield about 6–7 mt of wet rattan canes. A quantity of 100 kg of wet cane will give about 40 kg of dry rattan. Quality control measures are adopted while cleaning and grading the canes. Such activities are done at the many factories (Fig. 15), most of which are owned by Chinese businessmen.

9. WANGA PALM
(*PIGAFETTA FILARIS*)

Pigafetta filaris, the single-stemmed, pinnate palm, native to Sulawesi Island, Indonesia, is the most elegant of palms according to David Fairchild, the famous palm explorer. Those who have

FIGS. 15–18. FIG. 15. Rattan canes being cleaned and graded at a factory in South Kalimantan. FIG. 16. Impressive infructescences at *Pigafetta filaris* crown. FIG. 17. Toraja houses raised on pillars carved from *Pigafetta filaris* trunk. FIG. 18. Defoliated crowns of *Corypha utan* in Flores Is.

admired this dioecious species in its wild state, which grows at elevations between 460–1200 m above sea level on slopes of well-drained volcanic hills studded with lush equatorial vegetation, can only agree with Fairchild's esteem of *Pigafetta*. Dransfield (1976c) reported that *Pigafetta* in North Sulawesi is restricted to volcanic mountains between 300 m and 1500 m. This palm demands high light intensity at the seedling stage. In open areas, seedlings develop well, but in primary forest they do not progress beyond the one-leaf stage. Sneed (1981) observed in Central Sulawesi numerous mature *Pigafetta* of ca. 25 m and higher, with their unique gray rings distinctive on shiny green trunks. By his estimate, he saw at least 500,000 *Pigafetta* palms in the area.

Pigafetta is fast growing with, according to Darian (1973), three year old palms (from seed) attaining a height of ca. 7 m. Dransfield (1973) mentions that *Pigafetta* is also native to New Guinea (including Irian Jaya). It was introduced to the Botanical Garden at Sibolangi, Sumatra and from there Dransfield established many palms at the Bogor Botanical Garden. The trunk is about the size of coconut, but differs markedly in the beautiful, shiny greenish-brown surface, almost as if the trunk had been wax-polished. Because of this, climbing the palm unaided is extremely difficult.

Davis and Kuswara (1987) made observations on the germination of seeds and early growth of seedlings, growth rate and size of stem, production and shedding sequence of leaves and their size, numbers of spikes and fruits per spadix (Fig. 16).

Economic importance of Pigafetta

Apart from using the palm as an elegant ornamental in homestead gardens and in parks, the polished, colorful, erect and hardy stem has other uses. The periphery of the mature trunk is very hard, but the pithy core is soft. The stem is sawn into convenient lengths and the pithy core scooped out. The resultant palm tube is used as an effective and relatively cheap conduit in rice fields. Since the diameter of the tube is much wider than most bamboos, *Pigafetta* pipes are used where large quantities of water must be moved. Over time, the shiny outer layer of stem disappears and the nodes and internodes look distinct from each other, giving a characteristic look to the *Pigafetta* stem.

Another important purpose for which the stem of *Pigafetta* finds use is the following. In a deep-forest area of South Sulawesi, the Torajans (an ethnic group) have lived for generations. The Torajans are good agriculturalists and buffalo breeders who have adopted their lifestyle to suit the conditions of their mountainous territory. *Pigafetta filaris* also exists in large numbers on

these hills, handy for constructing their strange-looking granaries and even houses. These buildings are raised on long pillars, perhaps to offer more security from unfriendly tribes, wild animals and unexpected floods. The only wood used as pillars for these buildings is that of *Pigafetta*. For security, many granaries and traditional houses are built close to each other forming an avenue. The stout legs of these buildings appearing in rows or arches reveal the importance of the *Pigafetta* stem. Even in old buildings, the palm pillars remain in good condition. Usually fully mature stems of very stout palms are used for this purpose (Fig. 17).

10. GEBANG PALM
(*CORYPHA UTAN*)

In many islands of Indonesia, especially in Sulawesi, Java, East Nusa, Tenggara, West Nusa Tenggara, the drier regions of Sumatra and Kalimantan, there is a single-stemmed, palmate palm, *Corypha utan* (Fig. 18). It also occurs in the Philippines and grows wild in dense colonies or as scattered individuals. This species is much different from the Indian talipot palm (*C. umbraculifera*). Formerly, one of the Indonesian species of *Corypha* was known under a different name, *C. gebanga* (Moore, 1963), which is now considered to be a synonym of *C. utan*.

In North Sulawesi, as one proceeds to Lolak from Bolaank Mongandow, one can see several hundred of these palms, many displaying a single massive spadix (Fig. 19). After the fruit is ripe, the spadix snaps at the base and hangs awkwardly from the terminus of the stem. The stem is not strong and thus not used for any important purpose. With time, it decays and falls to the ground. The massive spadix should yield plentiful quantities of sap if it is trained and pared, following special tapping methods. The related talipot palm is tapped for neera in India and Burma.

The main use of this wild palm is for its large palmate leaves in the construction of country homes, especially for the roof and interior walls. In Nusa Tenggara Province, where more valuable thatch such as nypa leaves and *Metroxylon* fronds are not common, the young palms are severely harvested for house construction. The leaves of *C. utan* are arranged in three striking spirals (running clockwise in one palm and counter-clockwise in another). Hence, lopping

FIGS. 19–22.   FIG. 19. Terminal flowering in *Corypha utan*. Two palms on right have already died after fruiting. FIG. 20. Palm jaggery wrapped with lamina of *Livistona rotundifolia*. FIG. 21. *Areca catechu* in Bali bearing semi-ripe and fully ripe fruits. FIG. 22. Portion of clump of *Cyrtostachys renda*.

green leaves from the crown is convenient if one follows the spirals. Local people report that the cost of 100 leaves is about US$5.00. Over-harvesting of tender leaves sometimes causes the death of palms. Its tender leaves are not used for making "janur" (decorative material) even though the tender leaves of *Livistona rotundifolia* and *Cocos nucifera* are extensively used for that purpose.

Sago is also obtained from *C. utan,* although it is not very popular. Apart from the use for thatching, leaves are employed for making raincoats and a fine matting which has use also in foreign countries as a wall covering (Dransfield, 1976b).

11. WOKA PALM
(*LIVISTONA ROTUNDIFOLIA*)

Livistona rotundifolia is native to extensive areas in many provinces of Indonesia. My experience with this species is restricted mostly to Sulawesi Island. On practically all volcanic forest mountain slopes and even on the lower plains, this single-stemmed, stately palm is to be found. It is a thin-stemmed, hardy, tall, pleonanthic palm with roundish palmate laminae from which its name is derived. The fruits, red to dark-red, are seen in profusion on long, spreading spadices, adding beauty to the crown. Because of the elegant crown shape, the fan-shaped leaves and the attractive fruiting panicles, this palm is grown in parks and near homes and public buildings. *Livistona rotundifolia* is also ideal for keeping in tubs or pots. Barry (1961) praised this species as an indoor plant. "One of the most delightful palms for interior use if *Livistona rotundifolia.* It is a tall tropical tree. When young and in small containers, it will remain small. The numerous fan leaves look like fringed dinner plates. The effect is charming. Its more hardy relative, *L. chinensis,* a fairly common plant in Florida, is not as suitable for interiors as *L. rotundifolia.*"

The most important use of this palm is for its leaves. Leaves that are just about to unfold their leaflets are cut and sold in markets where they are used for wrapping vegetables, fish or meat. Jaggery cakes prepared from *Arenga pinnata* juice ("gula aren") are wrapped with this leaf before sending to market (Fig. 20). At this tender stage, the entire leaf occupies a small area, and so is convenient for transportation and storage in markets. The vendors have a special way of cutting portions of the lamina according to the quantity of material to be wrapped. They spread out a portion of the lamina where the leaflets are united at the lower ⅔ of their length, wrap the material and tie the bundle with one leaflet singled out from the lamina. From forest areas around Manado, truck-loads of *L. rotundifolia* leaves are harvested and transported to the markets in Manado. The supply is greatest on Sundays. Scaling the mature palms is difficult because the stem is thin, smooth and very tall. Therefore, the numerous young palms that regenerate through fallen fruits are harvested in the forests. Many young palms are killed due to over pruning. The leaves of *L. rotundifolia* remain pliable even when they are semi-dry or fully withered. Very exquisite leaf decorations ("janur") are made with tender immature leaves of *L. rotundifolia* before they turn green. In North Sulawesi, such janur are further decorated with rose flowers and ribbons, while in Bali and Java, where janur is more popular, only immature leaves of coconut are used. The tall, sturdy stems of *Livistona* are used as pillars and rafters.

12. BETELNUT PALM
(*ARECA CATECHU*)

The areca palm (*Areca catechu*) is the source of the masticatory known as betelnut, which is very popular in India, Sri Lanka, Bangladesh and Burma, but only sparingly used in Thailand, Malaysia, South China, the Philippines, Africa, Arabia and Pakistan. However, nowadays it is much less popular than formerly in Indonesia. Chewing "pan" (slices of areca kernel are chewed with a leaf of *Piper betle* together with a dash of slaked lime) is popular among the elderly people in areas of Sumatra, Java and in Bali. Around the several cock-fighting areas in Bali, one can see many stalls selling pan. That there was early international trade of arecanut in the Moluku is clear from a letter written by the king of Cochin in 1500 to one Alfonso de Albuquerque recommending that he send ships to Coromandel and the Moluccas to transport arecanut (Furtado, 1960). According to Watt (1889), the earliest historic reference by a European to the habit of chewing betelnut occurs in the writings of Marco Polo in 1298 A.D. Thomas Green (quoted by

Gode, 1961) considered the areca palm to be native to Indonesia and Cochin China.

Unlike India, where arecanut palm is regularly cultivated on small or large estates, in Indonesia this palm is seldom cultivated (Fig. 21). But in several homesteads one or two palms can be seen which provide arecanuts for the elderly members of the house. Bats and squirrels carry ripe fruits for the pericarp juice, and after sucking, they are dropped in nearby areas. Villagers collect resultant seedlings and raise them into mature palms near their homes.

Bavappa et al. (1982) mention medicinal uses for arecanut, such as treatment for leucoderma, leprosy, cough, fits, worms, anaemia and obesity. It is also used as a purgative and in an ointment, along with several other ingredients, for the treatment of nasal ulcers. Arecanut also has properties as a stimulant and appetizer. Because arecanut is pungent, spicy, bitter as well as sweet, it has the properties to expel gas, to remove phlegm and bad odor. It kills worms. Powdered nuts are held in repute as an antihelminthic for dogs, efficacious in the expulsion of tapeworms (Watt, 1889). The value of the nut as an antihelminthic is due to the presence of the alkaloid arecoline, which occurs along with tannin and gallic acid. Jayaweera (1961) gave additional uses for arecanut apart from its masticatory properties. The dried young nut is a stimulant, astringent, and taeniafuge. The young shoot is an abortifacient in early pregnancy. The expressed juice of the pericarp is applied to tarantula bites. In Java, where the batik industry is a flourishing business, the endosperm of *Areca* and *Pinanga* is used as a source of dye for batik paint.

13. SEALING WAX PALM
(*CYRTOSTACHYS RENDA*)

According to Corner (1966), the finest coloration among palms occurs in the Malaysian sealing wax palm, *Cyrtostachys renda* which has scarlet leaf sheaths and leaf stalks, with color extending almost up to the tip of the rachis (Fig. 22). The bright color is in the epidermis and determines this as the most ornamental palm. However, the spathe and fruits are less colorful than those of *Areca vestiaria*. The fruits turn black at maturity. The seedlings and even young palms of *C. renda* are green prior to flowering and their leaf sheath is least impressive at this stage.

The sealing wax palm is primarily an ornamental palm. However, the long, slender and strong stems are used as pillars and rafters for buildings. The color of the leaf sheath or crown shaft of adults resembles red sealing wax, hense its popular name. When one alights at the airport of Pontianak, West Kalimantan, a few majestic clumps of *Cyrtostachys renda* in front of the terminal building appear to greet the visitor. Just along the approach road to the airport, several nurserymen display rows of *C. renda* clumps, nicely packed in bags for the convenience of air travellers flying to other islands, especially to Jakarta. Each bundle of this clustering palm is priced according to the size of the main shoots. Where the tall shoot is 1.5–2 m tall, it may cost about US$5.00. The smallest ones cost about a dollar. The smaller clumps are least impressive as their leaf sheath has not yet developed the typical red color. Also near the airport are nurseries selling mostly *C. renda*. It was at one such nursery that I saw a bed of young seedlings (sprouted from fruits) which at first sight did not impress me as *C. renda* seedlings. They bore no sign of red color anywhere. But the owner took me to other beds of seedlings of different ages which displayed the scarlet color. Even though *C. renda* is propagated from seeds, it is more customary for people to hunt young clumps from peat forests in the interior of Kalimantan. Suckers establish easily, and hence there is greater demand for clumps packed for air transport rather than seedlings. At Jakarta, a good clump with larger shoots displaying the bright red color can command up to US$50.00. Because of the demand, many clumps transplanted in front of homes Jakarta are pilfered by thieves who have links to the nurserymen. It will be interesting to watch the performance of *C. renda* at higher altitudes since the native habitat in Kalimantan is within 200 m of sea level.

14. PINANG MERA
(*ARECA VESTIARIA*)

By whatever name *Areca vestiaria* has been known until recently, this palm, native to North Sulawesi and North Maluku, is one of the most beautiful ornamental pinnate palms, comparable to *Cyrtostachys renda*. Dransfield (1974a), on the basis of an elaborate literature search on the name for this palm, reports that *Areca langloisiana* and

Areca vestiaria are synonyms. Other names for *A. vestiaria* are: *A. leptopeltata, A. heinrici, A. paniculata, Ptychosperma paniculatum, P. vestiarius, Mischophloeus paniculatus, Pinanga sylvestris* and *Seaforthia vestiaria.* The wide morphological variation observed in this palm ranges from a profusely stilt-rooted condition to having no aerial root at all, and clustered, to a single-stemmed nature. The color of the leaf sheath ranges from red to a bright orange, light orange or brown color; this variation as well as the variation in the fruit color have all contributed to the confusion of its name. I had the opportunity to admire this indigenous palm on several volcanic mountains of North Sulawesi, especially in Gunung Soputan and around Lake Tondano. There is confusion even in the local name for the species. "Pinang mera" (red pinanga) is a more common name, but it is also known as "pinang yaki" (monkey pinanga).

Areca vestiaria is very colorful at altitudes between 600 and 1200 m (Fig. 23). At lower elevations, as one can see in front of houses along the mountain slopes and valleys as well as the clumps maintained at the Bogor Botanical Garden, the color is less spectacular. The clustering stems are slender, tall and smooth with distinctive leaf scars. The crownshaft/leaf sheath is deep orange and attractive even at a distance. As the leaf sheath splits open, exposing the inflorescence, the large spathe is deeper in its reddish orange hue. But the peduncle, spikes and flowers are all cream-colored. After fertilization, the female flowers, including the perianth cap, first turn green and then gradually become dirty brown and as the fruits develop and mature, the color changes to light brown, light orange, deep orange and crimson red. The spikes and peduncles also turn orange. A ripe bunch bearing 25–300 fruits is extremely pretty, much more attractive than the infructescence of *Cyrtostachys renda.* The freshly emerged spadix with cream-colored spikes and flowers is a pleasant contrast to the background of the orange crownshaft. The stiltroot is another striking feature of *A. vestiaria* that enhances the ornamental value of the plant. Moore (1962) published a picture (by E. P. Beckwith) of a very impressive stilt-rooted *A. vestiaria.*

A good clump of pinang yaki could cost as much as Rp 11,000 (US$10.00). However, trade of this attractive palm is not popular. The palm becomes less attractive at Jakarta, and, in ad-

FIG. 23. Suckering clump of *Areca vestiaria* in North Sulawesi.

dition, it has competition from the more hardy and colorful *Cyrtostachys renda.* Hence *A. vestiaria* is not a popular ornamental in Jakarta.

15. PINANG
(*PINANGA* SPP.)

There are at least 100 species of *Pinanga* according to Dransfield (1974b). The Bogor Botanic Garden has ten species in its collection (Sastrapradja & Davis, 1983). Local people do not make a distinction between *Pinanga* and *Areca.* For them all palms that yield nuts suitable for chewing along with the leaf of *Piper betle* and lime are known as "pohon pinang." The red-, and orange-crown shafted palms like *Cyrtostachys renda* and *Areca vestiaria* are, without distinction, called "pinang mera" (red *pinanga*). Although most *Pinanga* species grow on slopes of low hills and plains, at least one species grows at an altitude of 2000 m on Mt. Kornichi in Sumatra.

The kernel of *Pinanga* fruit is the main economic product. It is primarily used for chewing as with the kernel of *Areca catechu*. The dark tan dye extracted from the kernel is also used extensively in the batik industry. The mature stem of *Pinanga* is very strong and can serve in house-construction as with the stem of *Oncosperma tigillarium*. Since many species of *Pinanga* produce larger and more numerous fruits than *Areca catechu*, in India, areca kernels are "adulterated" with pinang endosperm.

Some species of *Pinanga* are good ornamentals in parks, in homesteads and in homes. Dransfield (1974b) recorded *Pinanga* with variegated leaves. They showed 'subtle marbling of light green, dark green, chocolate, and in young leaves, pink.' These palms showing variegation in leaf color belong to *Pinanga densiflora* and make impressive ornamentals.

III. Conclusion

Semi-wild palms play an important role in the economy and lifestyle of people in Indonesia. There are many uses for subsistence purposes, such as for food and drink, construction, fiber and other categories of use. A contribution to the cash economy is also made by semi-wild palms, such as the significant export trade of rattan palms. Finally, the ornamental value of this family must also be recognized; this involves a significant nursery trade as well as the harvest of young plants from native forest areas.

IV. Literature Cited

Allen, D. O. 1965. Balinese salak. Principes **9(2):** 72.

Amio, E. C., D. S. Alonzo & B. A. Lomibao. 1979. Nipa palm tapping, collection and distilling practices of nipa sap in Cogayan. Forest Prod. Industr. Developm. Techn. Publ. No. FPIDD-2, Laguna, Philippines.

Barrau, J. 1960. The sago palms. Principes **4(2):** 44–53.

Barry, D., Jr. 1961. Palms for home and greenhouse. Principes **5(1):** 13–20.

Bavappa, K. V. A., M. K. Nair & T. Premkumar (eds.). 1982. The arecanut palm (*Areca catechu* Linn.). Central Plantation Crops Res. Inst., Kasaragob, Kerala, India.

Beccari, O. 1913. Studio sui *Borassus* e descrizione di un genera nuovo Asiatico di Borassoideae. Webbia **4:** 293–385.

Blatter, E. 1926. The palms of British India and Ceylon. Oxford University Press, London.

Burkill, I. H. 1966. A dictionary of the economic products of the Malay Peninsula. 2 vols. Ministry of Agriculture and Co-operatives, Kuala Lumpur.

Corner, E. J. H. 1966. The natural history of palms. Weidenfeld and Nicolson, London.

Darian, M. E. 1973. *Pigafetta filaris*. Principes **17(1):** 32–33.

Davis, T. A. 1969. Ramifying and twisting stems of palmyra (*Borassus flabellifer*). Principes **13(2):** 47–66.

———. 1971. Right-handed, left-handed and neutral palms. Principes **15(2):** 63–68.

———. 1984. A climbing device to reach to palmyra's valuable toddy. Pages 63–65 *in* Michi Nagi (ed.), The spirit of enterprise: The 1984 Rolex Awards. Aurum Press, London.

———. 1985. Palmyra palm, the state tree of Tamilnadu, is on the verge of extinction: Protect this very useful tree. Environ. Awareness **8(4):** 95–106.

———. 1987. The components of palmyra fruit and tuberous seedling. IBPGR Newsletter, Regional Commission Southeast Asia, Bangkok 10.

———. (In press). *Borassodendron* of North Kalimantan, Indonesia. Principes.

——— & C. P. Corputty. 1983. The tidal swamps of Indonesia: Problems and promises of establishing coconut gardens. 1983 Yearbook, Malay Penin. Agric. Assoc., pages 39–46.

——— & D. V. Johnson. 1987. Current utilization and further development of the palmyra palm (*Borassus flabellifer*) in Tamilnadu, India. Econ. Bot. **41(2):** 247–266.

——— & T. Kuswara. 1987. Observations on *Pigafetta filaris*. Principes **31(3):** 127–137.

Dransfield, J. 1972. The genus *Borassodendron* (Palmae) in Malesia. Reinwardtia **8:** 351–363.

———. 1973. *Pigafetta filaris* in Sibolangi. Principes **17(3):** 105–107.

———. 1974a. New light on *Areca langloisiana*. Principes **18(2):** 51–57.

———. 1974b. Variegated pinangas. Principes **18(1):** 22–24.

———. 1976a. Palm sugar in East Madura. Principes **20(3):** 83–90.

———. 1976b. Palms in the everyday life of West Indonesia. Principes **20(2):** 39–47.

———. 1976c. A note on the habitat of *Pigafetta filaris* in North Celebes. Principes **20(2):** 48.

———. 1977. Dryland sago palm. Pages 76–83 *in* K. Tan (ed.), Sago 76, Sarawak. 1st Internat. Sago Symp., Kermajuan Kanji Sdn Bhd., Kuala Lumpur.

———. 1979. A manual of the rattans of the Malay Peninsula. Forest Department, Ministry of Primary Industries, Kuala Lumpur.

Duke, J. A. 1977. Palms as energy sources: A solicitation. Principes **21(2):** 60–62.

Fairchild, D. 1943. Garden Islands of the Great East. Charles Scribner's Sons, New York.

Fox, J. J. 1977. Harvest of the palm. Harvard University Press, Cambridge.

Furtado, C. X. 1960. The philological origin of *Areca* and *catechu.* Principes **4(1):** 26–31.

Gibbs, H. D. 1911. The alcohol industry of the Philippine Islands. Part I. A study of some palms of commercial importance with special reference to the saps and their uses. Philipp. J. Sci. **6A:** 99–143.

Gode, P. K. 1961. Studies in Indian cultural history. Vol. I. Vishveshvarananda Vedic Research Institute, Hoshiarpur.

Guzman-Rivas, P. 1984. Coconut and other palm use in Mexico and the Philippines. Principes **28(1):** 20–30.

Jayaweera, D. M. A. 1961. Palms in the Royal Botanic Gardens, Peradeniya, Ceylon. Principes **5(2):** 53–59.

Johnson, D. V. 1977. Distribution of sago-making in the old world. Pages 65–75 *in* K. Tan (ed.), Sago 76, Sarawak. 1st Internat. Sago Symp., Kermajuan Kanji Sdn Bhd., Kuala Lumpur.

———. 1985. The versatile palms: The case of multipurpose development. Ceres **106(4):** 27–31.

Kitzke, E. D. & D. V. Johnson. 1975. Commercial palm products other than oils. Principes **19(1):** 3–26.

Kovoor, A. 1983. The palmyra palm: Potential and perspectives. FAO Plant Production and Protection Paper 52, Rome.

Kuswara, T. & I. Samsoedin. 1983. Cultivation of rattan cane in Indonesia. Sci. Reporter **20(8):** 458–461.

Meijer, W. 1962. Palms of Indonesia. Principes **6(1):** 15–26.

Miller, R. H. 1964. The versatile sugar palm. Principes **8(4):** 115–147.

Mogea, J. P. 1978. Pollination in *Salacca edulis.* Principes **22(2):** 56–63.

———. 1982. *Salacca zalacca,* the correct name for the salak palm. Principes **26(2):** 70–72.

Moore, H. E., Jr. 1962. Exotic palms in the Western world. II. *Areca langloisiana.* Principes **6(3):** 90–96.

———. 1963. An annotated checklist of cultivated palms. Principes **7(4):** 119–182.

Padmanabhan, D., S. Pushpa Veni, M. Gunamani & D. Regupathy. 1978. Tuberous seedlings of *Borassus flabellifer.* Principes **22(4):** 119–126.

Paivoke, A. E. A. 1984. Tapping patterns in the nipa palm (*Nypa frutican* Wurmb.). Principes **28(3):** 132–137.

Pratt, D. S., L. W. Thurlow, R. R. Williams & H. D. Gibbs. 1913. The nipa palm as a commercial source of sugar. Philipp. J. Sci. **8A:** 377–398.

Ruddle, K., D. V. Johnson, P. K. Townsend & J. D. Rees. 1978. Palm Sago, a tropical starch from marginal lands. University Press of Hawaii, Honolulu.

Rumphius, G. E. 1750. Herbarium Amboinense. Vol. I. M. Uytwerf & S. Schouten, Amstelaedami.

Sastrapradja, D. & T. A. Davis. 1983. The Bogor Botanic Garden and its rich collection of palms. Principes **27(1):** 18–30.

——— **& J. P. Mogea.** 1977. Present uses and future development of *Metroxylon sagu* in Indonesia. Pages 112–117 *in* K. Tan (ed.), Sago 76, Sarawak. 1st Internat. Sago Symp., Kermajuan Kanji Sdn Bhd., Kuala Lumpur.

Sneed, M. W. 1981. *Pigafetta* and other palms in Sulawesi (Celebes). Principes **25(3):** 106–119.

Soekarjoto, N. & H. Mangindaan. 1981. Sugar from an Indonesian palm. Sci. Reporter **18(6):** 328–332.

Tammes, P. M. L. 1952. On the rate of translocation of bleeding sap in the fruit stalk of *Arenga.* Proc. Nederl. Akad. Wetenschappen. Ser. C. **55(2):** 141–143.

Watt, G. 1889. A dictionary of economic products of India. Vol. I. Periodicals Experts, Delhi.

The Use of Palms and Other Native Plants in Non-Conventional, Low Cost Rural Housing in the Peruvian Amazon

Jose López Parodi

Table of Contents

Abstract

The local technology for building construction in the lowlands of the Peruvian Amazon, including the use of palms and other native plants, is discussed. Problems in species identification and research orientation are considered in terms of cultural patterns and biases. A non-conventional, low cost construction system for use in rural areas is presented, and recommendations for further research and development outlined.

Key words: native plants, local technology, construction system, palms, Peruvian Amazon

Resumen

Se explica el uso de plantas nativas y de la technologia local para la construcción de viviendas y otras edificaciones. Se discuten problemas de identificación de especies y de orientación de la investigación basados en patrones y prejuicios culturales. Se explica un sistema no convencional y de bajo costo para construcción de edificaciones en areas rurales de la selva baja Peruana. Se dan recomendaciones para investigación y desarrollo.

I. Introduction

The technology used to construct houses and other buildings in rural areas is controlled by the availability of local materials. Thus, in hot, dry tropical regions, adobe is usually the main component for the construction of dwellings, storage structures and ceremonial buildings. In humid tropical areas, however, buildings are made using different types of plant materials such as trees, palms and lianas. Indigenous peoples obtain these materials from nearby forests, selecting different species for each part of the house.

Based on their social and economic status or cultural characteristics, native peoples have different types of houses, although ecological restrictions and security measures play an important role in defining house models (Charernsupkul & Temiyabandha, n.d.; San Ramon, 1977). Introduction of foreign technology from urban areas has brought changes in the use of materials, i.e., bricks, cement, tin roofs, plywood, wooden boards, nails, wire and paint, which have all changed the design and size of the houses. The perception of higher social status associated with the use of these materials has often led to the rejection of native technology and materials. Although not every family can have a house of "noble" materials, as they are called in Amazonia (due primarily to economic reasons), the tendency is to "nobilize" the house as much as possible. In rural villages of the Peruvian Amazon one can see in the houses gradations of design and materials that are living examples of this phenomenon.

II. Local Technology for House Building

In most of the tropics, rural housing is traditional housing. The traditional building forms of the rural tropics often incorporate sound solutions to climatic problems. Given technological limitations and the always overriding consideration of safety, some of these solutions must be considered ingenious, and there can be no doubt that they deserve careful study (Koenigsberger et al., 1974).

The present paper considers local technology as "mestizo" technology, due to the characteristics of the population where this study was conducted. "Mestizo" in the Peruvian Amazon refers to people who are of mixed European and native American heritage, or are acculturated natives. This mestizo technology, however, has a heavy native or indigenous technology component. The main difference is that the house is built and used by an individual family, instead of by several related families as often occurs with native people.

Indigenous houses are predominantly of the communal type (multifamilial use), and four basic models are defined for the Peruvian Amazon: elliptical in shape or rectangular in shape, with differentiated roof and walls or with the roof going down to the ground serving also as a wall. Nowadays, however, most tribes are developing individual houses as a consequence of acculturation. A detailed description of a Jivaro communal house can be found in Harner (1973). The usual mestizo riverine house is ordinarily built according to the following standard scheme. It is rectangular, 7 by 5 m, and the structure is made of hardwood posts and beams. The roof structure is made of round softwood poles, and the floor constructed of split palm trunks elevated about 1.5 m above the ground. The house is usually divided into two areas, a private section or dormitory closed by walls made of palm staves, and the open area that serves as a living and meeting room. The roof is pitched and covered with palm leaves (San Ramon, 1977). The unions and joints between the structural elements and the palm leaves are tied together using thin lianas. As a result, the house is made entirely of plant materials.

One important thing to keep in mind is that the transformation of the raw material, which is done by local people using simple tools such as axes and machetes, does not require high technology, such as sawmills. Because the entire process is accomplished by the villager, final cost of materials is much less than it would be for sawn timber, plywood, bricks or tin roof sheets.

III. Use of Native Plants

The following list is by no means complete, but gives an idea of the numerous species of plants used for house construction. These can be grouped according to physical characteristics: hardwoods (H), softwoods (S), palms (P) and lianas (L). These can also be grouped based on their uses as columns or posts, beams and elements of roof structures, walls and floors, ceilings, roof coverings and cordage.

A. Columns (H)

Caryocaraceae
"Almendro"   *Caryocar glabrum* (Aubl.) Pers.
              C. microcarpum Ducke

Olacaceae
"Huacapú"   *Minquartia guianensis* Aubl.

Flacourtiaceae
Lindackeria paludosa (Benth.)
Gilg

Leguminosae
Voucapoua americana Aubl.

Lecythidaceae
Eschweilera mexicana (Knuth.)
Macbr.

Lauraceae
"Itauba"   *Mezilaurus itauba* (Meis.)
Taub. ex Mez
M. synandra (Mez) Kosterm.
"Moena ne-   *Aniba perutilis* Hemsl.
gra"   *Ocotea aciphylla* (Nees) Mez
O. marmellensis Mez

Moraceae
"Palisangre"   *Brosimum guianense* (Aubl.)
Huber
B. rubescens Taub.

Leguminosae: Caesalpinioideae
Dialium guianense (Aubl.)
Sandw. ex A. C. Smith

Humiriaceae
"Quinilla co-   *Humiriastrum excelsum*
lorada"   (Ducke) Cuatr.

Sapotaceae
Manilkara surinamensis (Miq.)
Dubard
Mastichodendron williamsii
(Baehni) Baehni ex Bernardi
Pouteria aubrevillei Bernardi
P. torta (Mart.) Radlk.
P. ulei (K. Krause) Baehni
P. venulosa (Mart. et Eichl.)
Baehni

Annonaceae
"Carahuasca"   *Guatteria elata* R. E. Fries
G. hyposericea Diels
G. modesta Diels
G. pteropus Benth.

Guttiferae
"Charichuelo"   *Rheedia acuminata* (R. et P.)
Planch. et Triana
R. gardneriana Planch. et
Triana
R. macrohylla Planch et Triana

Annonaceae
"Espintana"   *Anaxagorea brachycarpa* R. E.
Fries
Guatteria citriodora Ducke
G. melosma Diels
Unonopsis stipitata Diels
Oxandra xylopioides Diels
"Espintana de   *Xylopia benthami* R. E. Fries
varillal"   *X. neglecta* (O. Ktze.) R. E.
Fries
"Icoja"   *Unonopsis floribunda* Diels
U. spectabilis Diels

Apocynaceae
"Remo caspi"   *Aspidosperma excelsum* Benth.

Leguminosae: Mimosoideae
Pithecellobium laetum (Poepp.
et Endl.) Benth.

Leguminosae: Caesalpinioideae
Swartzia brachyrachis Harms
S. polyphylla A. P. DC.

Annonaceae
"Tortuga cas-   *Duguetia tessmannii* R. E. Fries
pi"

Olacaceae
"Yutabanco"   *Heisteria duckei* Sleumer

Leguminosae: Caesalpinioideae
Hymenaea oblongifolia Huber
var. *oblongifolia*

B. BEAMS AND ROOF STRUCTURES (S)

Moraceae
"Capinurí"   *Maguira coriacea* (Karsten)
C. C. Berg
Clarisia biflora Ruiz et Pavon
C. racemosa Ruiz et Pavon

C. WALLS AND FLOORS (P)

Palmae
"Huasaí"   *Euterpe precatoria* Mart.
"Cashapona"   *Iriartea exorrhiza* Mart.
"Huacrapona"   *I. deltoidea* R. et P.

D. Ceilings

	Gramineae
"Caña brava"	*Gynerium sagittatum* (Aubl.) P. Beauv.

	Palmae
"Aguaje"	*Mauritia flexuosa* L.f.

E. Roofing Materials (P)

	Palmae
"Irapay"	*Lepidocaryum tessmannii* Burret
"Palmiche"	*Geonoma* sp.
"Yarina"	*Phytelephas microcarpa* R. et P.
"Palmichillo"	*Hyospathe* sp.
"Ponilla"	*Wettinia augusta* Poepp. et Endl.
	Catoblastus drudei Cook et Doyle
"Catirina"	*Orbignya polysticha* Burret
"Shapaja"	*Scheelea cephalotes* (Poepp. ex Mart.) Karst.

F. Cordage (L)

	Cyclanthaceae
"Tamshi"	*Eviodanthus funifer* (Poit.) Lindm.
	Torococarpus bissectus (Vell.) Hawl.
	Asplundia peruviana Harl.

	Araceae
	Heteropsis jenmani Oliv.
	Philodendron sp.

G. Data Sources

In making the above list, several different procedures have been followed. The taxonomic literature covering the country and locality where the study was conducted was consulted (e.g., Beguin et al., 1985; Bernardi & Spichiger, 1981; Bernardi et al., 1981; Encarnación, 1983; Encarnación & Spichiger, 1981, 1982; Mejia, 1983; Soukup, 1970; Spichiger et al., 1985). In these publications references were obtained on vernacular names, scientific names and uses, although this last item was very general. Herbarium specimens were consulted and the

descriptions given by specialists concerning the use, vernacular name, and scientific name were noted. The locality (Jenaro Herrera) was studied, and an inventory made of the species in actual use, either in the field or in houses under construction. In addition, I consulted with local people about names and habitats of origin of the plants being used.

As can be seen, for a single vernacular name there are often several scientific binomials, some of which belong to different families. Very few of the names correspond to a single species. There is also a lack of knowledge of indigenous languages, which contributes to the confusion in writing and pronouncing aboriginal and foreign languages (Soukup, 1970).

IV. Species Identification Problems

The purpose of presenting the above species list using both vernacular and scientific names is to comment further upon the well known discussion about the validity and equivalence of such names. But another point that comes out is the very nature of taxonomic work in the field when scientific knowledge and methodology are confronted with popular and local knowledge. For example:

1. A botanist is interested in studying the genus *Minquartia*. He will go to the field and make collections of the species belonging to that genus. If he does not know the plants in the wild, he will probably seek the help of the local people, but *Minquartia guianensis* or *M. punctata* will not mean much to a native. But if the botanist knows the local name, i.e., "Huacapú," and he also knows that it is used as posts for houses, he will do better.

2. A native man wants to build his house. He knows that the best kind of posts are "Huacapú." He also knows that the small leaved "Huacapú" which grows in well drained soils in highland terraces is the one he is looking for, and not the big leaved "Huacapú" which grows in the lowlands.

The problem is how to reconcile these two approaches. I suggest that an ethnobotanical approach will improve the quality and usefulness of both the scientific work and local knowledge. For instance, native secondary school students

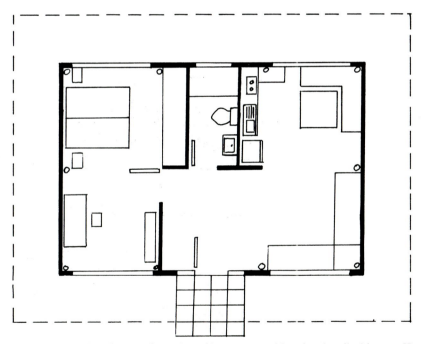

FIG. 1. General outside view and floor plan of low cost, rural housing described in text. House illustrated is 6 × 9 m; scale is 1:100.

could learn that small leaved "Huacapú" is *Minquartia guianensis* belonging to the family Olacaceae.

Encarnación (1983) mentions that there are tendencies to over-emphasize vernacular names registered in catalogs and forestry species lists. In these, one can observe great phonetic and orthographic variability, arising from the localities of origin and culture of the person who registers the name. Ethnobotanical and linguistic studies as well as floristic inventories can define the variability or invariability of such names in order to find an easier way of communication among native peoples and interested specialists. In many cases, vernacular names express true characters that can define species. However, these values are not being interpreted or exploited for scientific knowledge.

V. Research Orientation

The development of a construction technology based on local native materials has shown how research studies and forest inventories are influenced by cultural, economic and social biases. In fact, most of the taxonomic studies on native Peruvian plants reflect either academic attitudes or the commercial requirements of private sawmills or public projects. This is not to say that the taxonomy is not important, but it often fails to take into consideration popular knowledge and uses, and if it does, the references are mostly generalities. I feel that taxonomy is not only useful for taxonomists, but it must be usable and used by all who need it.

Publications concerning forest inventories, plant propagation research, ecological and phenological studies, plantation trials, and studies of physical and mechanical properties are mostly concerned with species that are used in the wood industry, i.e., processed wood (sawn boards, plywood, veneer and particle board). Almost nothing has been published concerning round wood and other plant products used by local populations, especially in house construction.

VI. Construction System

A. Criteria and Materials Used

Based on the guidelines proposed by the United Nations (1973), the goal of this project was to develop an improved construction system based on local technology and materials. The construction system explained below was developed on the basis of the following criteria:

a) *Low cost.* Budgetary allocations for the Centro de Investigaciones—Jenaro Herrera (CIJH) were insufficient to cover costs of a more expensive system.

b) *Availability of materials.* The most abundant were local materials such as round wood, palm leaves, palm staves, cane, clay and sand.

c) *Skilled labor.* Most men in Jenaro Herrera know how to build houses with local materials.

d) *Comfort.* According to design norms for warm, humid tropical areas, an acceptable degree of comfort can be obtained with local materials.

e) *Durability.* With proper maintenance and cleaning, the materials used in this type of construction system will last many years. Worn materials are easy to replace.

B. Building Procedures

The basic procedures used to construct a standard house such as shown in Figure 1 are outlined in detail below:

1. Site selection, orientation and clearing (see Stulz, 1980). In this case, the site is a flat, well drained upland terrace.
2. Lay-out and marking of distances.
3. Digging holes for hardwood posts for foundation and columns. They are usually from "Huacapú" (*Minquartia guianensis*) or "Palisangre" (*Brosimum guianense*) which are termite proof and resistant to decay. The posts are not treated, but sometimes local people will superficially carbonize the bottom end.
4. Beam installation. These are softwood species (see species list), very light but resistant and used to construct the frame for the roof as well as provide support for walls and ceilings. Long beams ("soleras") are nailed and tied to notches carved on the posts. Short beams ("vigas") go on the soleras (Fig. 2), and are also nailed and tied with "tamshi."
5. Construction of roof structure. This has two models:
   a) "Scissor." Here the height and weight of the roof are defined and supported by two structures composed of four inclined posts resting in each of the external long beams. These two units are tied at the apex forming a tetrahedral structure (see Fig. 2a). The space inside the roof is free from poles and can be used as an attic.
   b) "Chicken foot." The height and weight of the roof are determined and supported

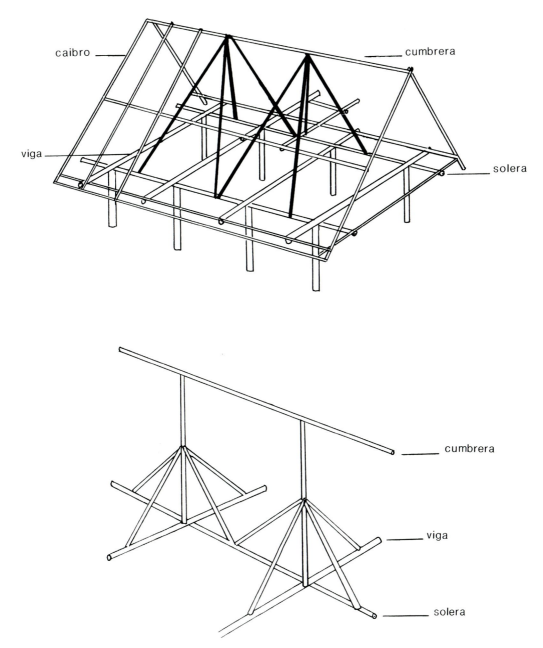

FIG. 2. Schematic drawing of different types of roof construction used for rural houses in the Peruvian Amazon. A. Scissor construction; B. chicken foot construction. See text for explanation of structural components.

by two central, vertical posts which rest on small beams (vigas). From each of these central posts, four diagonal supports go to the beams giving strength to the structure (see Fig. 2b). This type of construction does not allow the use of the space inside the roof.

On top of either of these structures goes the "cumbrera" beam which runs longitudinally and parallel to the soleras. Down from the

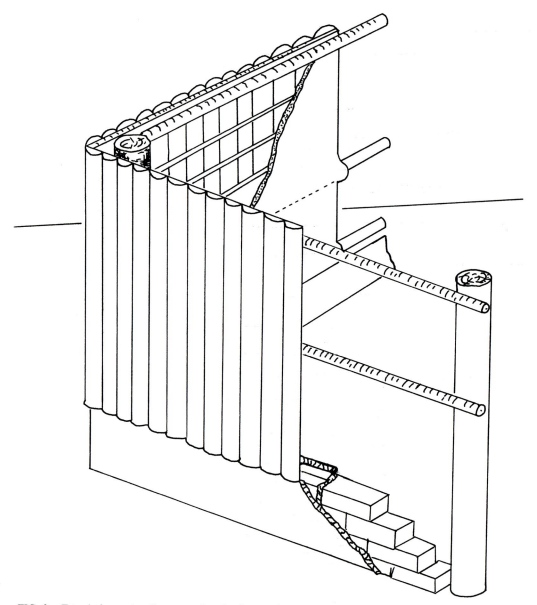

FIG. 3.   Foundation and wall construction details used in low cost, rural housing in the Peruvian Amazon.

cumbrera come the "caibros" which are the thinnest structural elements on top. The eaves of the roof extend out 1.5 to 2 m to provide shading and protection from the rain for the walls and windows.

6. Covering the roof structure. In this house model, palm leaves have been used. These are woven along a single axis made of "po-

nilla" (*Wettinia augusta*). These units are called "crisnejas" and each has about 130 "irapay" (*Lepidocaryum tessmannii*) leaves (Kahn & Mejía, 1987). The crisnejas are placed on top of the caibros to form the roof.

Although most authors consider palm thatch to be very prone to fire (e.g., Koenigsberger & Lynn, 1965; Stulz, 1983), the occurrence of fire in rural areas is very rare. One way to reduce fire hazard is to install all the electrical wire inside plastic tubes to avoid short circuits. Another measure is to construct the houses widely spaced from each other. There is also a fire retardant treatment (Stulz, 1983) which is simple and inexpensive if additional measures must be adopted.

The peak of the roof is covered by cumbas, or three palm leaves woven together longitudinally. These units are usually made from *Orbignya* or *Phytelephas* leaves.

The durability of a palm roof depends on the steep angle of the roof (usually 45° or more), which permits the rapid drainage of rain, the number of crisnejas per meter of roof on the inclined side (usually 5 to 7), and the number of irapay leaves per crisneja (around 130).

7. Constructing a small foundation (15 × 15 cm) with cement and sand (1:6) around the house. On top of the foundation a low base wall is erected, using adobe bricks (7 × 11 × 24 cm); mortar is simply clay, sand and water. The base wall is covered with cement mortar (1:5) to give strength and protection from the rain. The palm staves go on top of this wall (Fig. 3).

8. Walls. They are made by nailing four round wood poles (caibros) on the columns. Palm staves of *Euterpe* are nailed on the caibros, the smooth part facing out, the rough part inside. The staves are laid perpendicular to the caibros and on top of the base wall (Fig. 3). On the inside of the palm staves, perpendicular slats of cane are nailed 10–15 cm from each other, their function being to add strength to the wall and to prevent the mortar from sliding down. At this time, the electrical tubing is installed. Finally, the wall is covered by a mixture of cement and sand (1:6) on the inside. Coverings of mud, a mixture of cement, wood ash and clay (1:3:6) and cement mortar have all been tested, but the best covering was determined to be cement and sand mortar (1:6) because it is fast drying and hard. Although the mixture of cement, ash and clay has not been discarded, it needs more testing and modification of the proportions of ingredients.

9. Ceiling. It is made using "caña brava" (*Gynerium*) split longitudinally in half, the smooth part facing down. The cane is nailed to the lower half of beams. The junctions are covered by a *Euterpe* stave. Canes are covered on the upper surface by "mud cake," a mixture of cement, ashes and clay (1:3:6) in order to seal the spaces between canes and give additional insulation. The electrical tubing is laid on top of this.

10. Floor. In this case, the floor is made on the ground. A rough floor is made using cement and sand (1:6) applied to a depth of 4 cm. On top, a smooth, thin layer of cement and sand (1:1) is applied, and then a final coat of pure cement is used to make the surface lustrous and somewhat waterproof. In cases where the floor has to be raised, split palm trunks (*Iriartea*) are used and the cement and sand mixture is applied on top.

11. Windows and doors. The window frames and doors are the only components of the house made from sawn boards. Windows have wire screen as protection against mosquitoes. There is no glass used. The windows are located on opposite sides of the house to facilitate cross ventilation. When installed, windows make up 50–60% of the entire wall area.

12. Painting. All wood and palm surfaces are given two coats of varnish, especially the ones exposed to rain and sun. Cemented surfaces such as walls are painted with latex which adheres very well. Since these materials have to be bought in a city and then transported they have a high cost. There are two local solutions which will be tested:

a) The use of "copal" resin instead of varnish. Copal resin is obtained from *Protium carana* March., *P. llewelynii* Macbr., *P. puncticulatum* Macbr., and *Tetragastris panamensis* (Engl.) Kuntze of the Burseraceae. However, I have no information about the chemical and physical characteristics of these resins, or the yield per tree and collection. Copal resin is used locally for ceramics and for sealing boats.

b) The use of a latex from *Couma macrocarpa* Barb. Rodr. (Apocynaceae) mixed with white clay to produce a locally obtainable paint. Again, no written information is available.

13. Insect protection. Although the characteristics of the species used provide protection

against insects, additional treatment may be given by spraying a long-lasting insecticide.

C. Costs

An 8 × 9 m house like that of Figure 1 has a total cost of US$2440.00. This includes costs of materials plus labor. It does not consider the cost of the terrain. If a rural family gets its own plant materials and provides the labor, costs will drop to about US$500.00. The same house built in an urban area with cement, brick, asbestos sheet roof, plywood ceiling, and other conventional materials will cost about three times more.

VII. Availability of Plant Resources for Construction

It is interesting to note that no studies on the availability of plant resources for rural construction have been made, except that of Kahn and Mejía (1987). Malleux (1973) made an evaluation of natural populations of *Euterpe,* but the study was conducted for a palmito canning paint, and no estimate of "Huasaí" wood volume was made. In a 6 × 9 m house, about 500 *Euterpe* staves are needed, or approximately 50–60 palm trees. The average density of usable palms (*Euterpe*) in an homogeneous palm forest (see Encarnación, 1985) varies from 68 to 88 per hectare. This is about 1 ha per house. In the Jenaro Herrera region there exists about 15,000 ha of palm forest according to López Parodi and Freitas (1986). The population of the area is about 1000 families, so there is more than an adequate quantity of palm staves for house building. It is important to know that the canning factory in Iquitos uses about 2000 palm hearts per month, but that no use is made of the wood. Material for 33 houses is left in the forest every month.

In terms of "irapay" (*Lepidocaryum tessmannii*), in a 6 × 9 m house about 300 crisnejas are used, each having 130 leaves. A total of 39,000 leaves are needed. Kahn and Mejia (1987) report finding 40,000 leaves per hectare. Based on this estimate, one house requires 1 ha of "irapay." The 125,000 ha of highland, well drained terraces around Jenaro Herrera should produce enough leaves to thatch 50,000 standard houses.

The system described here can be used in public buildings such as schools or medical posts in rural areas in lowland Amazonia. Silos constructed using this system together with solar driers will be tested at the CIJH for grain storage. The main advantages are the availability of materials and the possibility of the participation of local population in making their own public buildings. At the CIJH there are five experimental houses in use; three are 6 × 9 m, one is 6 × 12 m and one is 6 × 15 m. New buildings will be constructed with slight modifications.

VIII. Recommendations for Research and Development

In the United Nations document (1973), a list of possible study topics is provided. Also, Koenigsberger and Lynn (1965) give some pointers for research and development on roofs in tropical areas. However, I would like to emphasize some needs for research about round wood, palms and lianas:

1. Ethnobotanical studies concerning species used in construction.
2. Evaluation of local availability of plant material resources for construction.
3. Physical and mechanical properties.
4. Ecological and biological studies.
5. Propagation studies and plantation trials.
6. Economic and social studies on costs, design and acceptability of new systems.
7. Construction of experimental buildings.

IX. Acknowledgments

The author wishes to thank Don Manuel Chota for his assistance in identifying many plant species, and Don Francisco Suarez and Don José Alvarado for turning the ideas and drafts into reality. Special thanks are owed the work crew at CIJH for their enthusiasm and cooperation. This research was funded by the Instituto de Investigaciones de la Amazonía Peruana.

X. Literature Cited

Beguin, D., R. Spichiger & J. Miége. 1985. Las Lauráceas del Arboretum Jenaro Herrera (provincia de Requena, departamento de Loreto, Perú). Contribución al estudio de la flora y de la vegetación de la Amazonía Peruana. VIII. Candollea 40: 253–304.

Bernardi, L., F. Encarnación & R. Spichiger. 1981. Las Mimosoideas del Arboretum Jenaro Herrera (provincia de Requena, departamento de Loreto, Perú). Candollea 36: 301–333.

——— & R. Spichiger. 1981. Las Anonaceas del Arboretum Jenaro Herrera (provincia de Requena, departamento de Loreto, Perú). Candollea 35: 341–383.

Charernsupkul, A. & V. Temiyabandha. (n.d.). Northern Thai domestic architecture and rituals in house-building. The Fine Arts Commission of the Association of Siamese Architects Under Royal Patronage, Thailand.

Encarnación, F. 1983. Nomenclatura de las especies forestales comunes en el Perú. Documento de Trabajo No. 7. Proyecto PNUD/FAO/PER/81/002. Ministerio de Agricultura, PNUD, FAO. Lima, Perú.

———. 1985. Introducción a la flora y vegetación de la Amazonía Peruana: Estado actual de los estudios, medio natural y ensayo de una clave de determinación de las formaciones vegetales en la llanura amazónica. Candollea 40: 237–252.

——— & R. Spichiger. 1981. Las Cariocaráceas del Arboretum Jenaro Herrera (provincia de Requena, departamento de Loreto, Perú). Candollea 36: 335–347.

——— & ———. 1982. Las Dicapetaláceas del Arboretum Jenaro Herrera (provincia de Requena, departamento de Loreto, Perú). Candollea 37: 327–338.

Harner, J. J. 1973. The Jivaro. People of the sacred waterfalls. Anchor Press/Doubleday, Garden City, New York.

Kahn, F. & K. Mejía. 1987. Notas sobre la biología, ecología y utilización de una pequeña palmera de la Amazonía Peruana: *Lepidocaryum tessmannii* Burret. Informe Técnico No. 2. IIAP-CIJH, Iquitos, Perú.

Koenigsberger, O., T. G. Ingersoll, A. Mayhew & S. V. Szokolay. 1974. Manual of tropical housing and building. Part one: Climatic design. Longman, London. 320 pp.

——— & R. Lynn. 1965. Roofs in the warm humid tropics. Architectural Association, Paper No. 1. Lund Humphries, London. 56 pp.

López Parodi, J. & D. Freitas. 1986. Mapa de uso de tierras en Jenaro Herrera. Instituto de Investigaciones de la Amazonía Peruana, Centro de Investigaciones Jenaro Herrera. Iquitos, Perú.

Malleux, J. 1973. Informe de avance del estudio de factibilidad de aprovechamiento del huasaí en la zona de Tamishiyacu, Río Itaya (Iquitos). Universidad Nacional Agraria, Departamento de Manejo Forestal. La Molina, Lima. 61 pp.

Mejía, K. 1983. Las Palmeras de Jenaro Herrera (departamento de Loreto, provincia de Requena). Unpublished report. Universidad Nacional Mayor de Sand Marcos, Departamento de Biología. Lima, Perú.

San Ramon, J. 1977. Pautas de asentamiento en la selva. Amazonía Peruana 1(2): 29–52.

Soukup, J. 1970. Vocabulario de los nombres vulgares de la flora Peruana. Colegio Salesiano, Lima. 380 pp.

Spichiger, R., F. Encarnación & M. Chota. 1985. Catálogo de los nombres vernaculares de los árboles del Arboretum Jenaro Herrera y alrededores (provincia de Requena, departamento de Loreto, Perú). Contribución al estudio de la flora y de la vegetación de la Amazonía Peruana. IX. Candollea 40: 595–629.

Stulz, R. 1980. Elements of solar architecture for tropical regions. Publication no. 10. SKAT. St. Gallen, Switzerland.

———. 1983. Appropriate building materials, 2nd ed. Swiss Center for Appropriate Technology & Intermediate Technology Publications Ltd., St. Gallen, Switzerland.

United Nations. 1973. El clima y el diseño de casas. Diseño de viviendas económicas y servicios de la comunidad. Vol. 1. Departamento de Asuntos Económicos y Sociales, Doc. ST/SOA/93. United Nations, New York. 90 pp.

Utilization of Palms in Eleven Mestizo Villages of the Peruvian Amazon (Ucayali River, Department of Loreto)

Kember Mejia C.

Table of Contents

Abstract

The utilization of palms in eleven mestizo communities of the lower Ucayali River, Department of Loreto, Perú is described. A total of 27 different palm species are used for various purposes. The fruits of 13 species are eaten, palm heart are extracted from 5 species, and construction materials are obtained from 15 species. Domestic articles and handicrafts are made from 8 palm species. Acculturation and forest destruction are modifying the traditional use of palms in the Peruvian Amazon.

Key words: palms, palm products, mestizo, Peru

Resumen

Se describe la utilización de palmeras en 11 caserios mestizos del bajo Rio Ucayali, Departamento de Loreto, Perú. Un total de 27 diferentes especies de palmeras se utilizan para varios propositos. Se consumen los frutas de 13 especies, se extrae el palmito de 5 especies, y de 15 especies se obtienen materiales diversos para la construcción de viviendas. Artículos domesticos y artesanías se confeccionan de 8 especies de palmeras. Procesos de aculturación y la destrucción del bosque estan modificando el uso tradicional de las palmeras en la Amazonia Peruana.

I. Introduction

Studies dealing with the use of palms have been conducted in several areas of the Amazon basin over the last century (e.g., Balick, 1984; Barbosa Rodrigues, 1903; Cavalcante, 1977; Schultes, 1974; Spruce, 1908; and Wallace, 1853 among others). Ethnobotanical studies dealing specifically with the palms of the Peruvian Amazon, however, are very few (Bodley & Benson, 1979; Mejia, 1983). The little information which has been collected in Perú shows that palms are an extremely important forest resource in this region. Indigenous groups extract edible products from various palm species, including fruits, palm hearts, edible insect larvae that burrow into the trunks, juices, and alcoholic beverages. Wood and leaves are used to construct and thatch houses. Various palm products are used to fabricate equipment for hunting, fishing and other domestic uses. Palm fibers are also important for weaving clothing, bags, hammocks, nets and other products.

In this article, I review the uses that accultur-

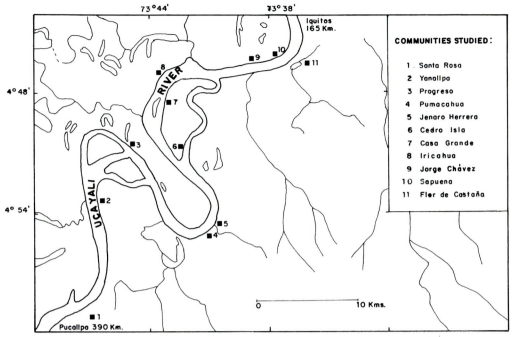

FIG. 1. Map of lower Ucayali River, Department of Loreto, Perú, showing location of 11 mestizo communities studied.

ated natives ("mestizos") and recent immigrants to the Peruvian Amazon have for many of the local palm species. The results presented are based on three years of study and personal observation. Voucher specimens for all of the species discussed are deposited in the herbaria of Geneva, Switzerland (G), and University of San Marcos, Lima (USM). Specific voucher numbers are indicated in the text where appropriate.

II. Study Area

Observations on the use of palms were made in 11 rural settlements located along the Ucayali River in the Department of Loreto, Perú (Fig. 1). The elevation of the study area averages 125 m, the mean temperature is 27°C, and the average annual precipitation is 2542 mm (unpublished climatological data of the Instituto de Investigaciones de la Amazonia Peruana). Both the lowest temperatures (20.5°C) and the lowest precipitation (162 mm) tend to occur during the months of June, July and August. The native vegetation is classified as wet tropical forest (Holdridge, 1978).

The majority of the inhabitants of the villages studied are descendants of the Cocama, a native group of the Tupi ethnolinguistic family. This native heritage is quite evident in two of the settlements, the residents admitting their Cocama roots and still retaining some of their traditional culture. An appreciable percentage of the local people have immigrated from other cities along the Ucayali River, while a smaller number have come from the neighboring department of San Martin in the foothills of the Andes, or from the city of Iquitos.

III. Palm Uses

A. Food and Drink

The most important species yielding edible products are *Bactris gasipaes* HBK, *Mauritia flexuosa* L.f., and *Jessenia bataua* (Mart.) Burret. *Bactris gasipaes* (*Mejia 0129*), known locally as "pijuayo," is the only palm species that has been cultivated since ancient times in the Peruvian Amazon. It is most frequently encountered in agricultural fields, but it is also planted in house gardens. The species does not grow wild in undisturbed forest, presumably having been introduced to the Amazon in pre-Columbian times (Patiño, 1963). Pijuayo fruits are harvested from February to March and from August to October. Fruits are boiled prior to consumption. To preserve the fruits for a longer period, they are boiled and then roasted. Fruits prepared in this manner are frequently ground into a coarse meal ("farina") prior to storage. A fermented beverage known as "masato de pijuayo" is made from fruits which have been boiled, peeled, mashed and mixed with sugar.

Local people distinguish two varieties of pijuayo based on the color and texture of the fruit. One type has a yellow or greenish-orange fruit with a high starch content, while the other has a smaller, bright red fruit that contains more oil and which is called "huira pijuayo."

The fruits of several other species of *Bactris* [e.g., *B. maraja* Mart., (*Mejia 0111*); *B. concinna* Mart., (*Mejia 0058*); and *B. amoena,* Burret, (*Mejia 0067*)] are eaten in the Ucayali region, although to a much lesser extent than pijuayo. These species, known collectively as "ñejilla," produce fruit in the months of April and June.

Mauritia flexuosa (*Mejia 0021*) or "aguaje" occurs naturally in dense stands known as "aguajales" (see Kahn, present volume), and also grows spontaneously around houses where seeds have been discarded. The fruits, which are highly valued, are harvested all year long, although they are found in greatest abundance during July and August. The edible portion of the aguaje fruit is the thin, oily mesocarp. To facilitate the removal of the scaly epicarp, the fruits are usually soaked in a pan of water for several hours in the sun. Most of the fruits which have been "ripened" by soaking are eaten directly, yet some are also mashed to prepare a very tasty beverage called "aguajina."

Two types of aguaje are known from the Ucayali region. One type has an orange mesocarp, the other has a reddish mesocarp and is more oily. The latter variety, which is preferred, is known locally as "aguaje shambo." The fruit of *Mauritiella peruviana* (Becc.) Burrett (*Mejia 0054*), known locally as "aguajillo" because it resembles a miniature aguaje, is also edible and used to prepare a type of aguajina.

The fruits of *Jessenia bataua* (Mart.) Burret (*Mejia 0033*), known locally as "ungurahui," are also consumed after being left to soak for several hours in warm water. The most important use of the fruits, however, is to prepare a thick, oily

beverage or "chapo." Although of lesser importance, the fruits of *Oenocarpus mapora* Karsten (*Mejia 0109*) and *Euterpe precatoria* Mart. (*Mejia 0119*) are also made into chapo.

The immature endosperm of a number of palm fruits is eaten. Among these are: *Astrocaryum chambira* Burret (*Mejia 0097*) or "chambira"; *A. jauari* Mart. (*Mejia 0095*) or "huiririma"; *A. huicungo* Damm. ex Burret (*Mejia 0096*) or "huicungo," and *Phytelephas microcarpa* R. and P. (*Mejia 0069*) or "yarina." The fruits of this last species are considered locally to be effective in the control of diabetes.

The young growing tip or "heart" of *Euterpe precatoria* ("hausai") is a well-liked vegetable. Known as "palmito" or "chonta," palm hearts are eaten raw in salads, or cooked and mashed for use in soups. The delicacy is most frequently consumed during the week before Easter. The palmito of several other palms are also eaten, although they are considered to be of inferior quality. Examples include *Bactris gasipaes, Iriartea deltoidea* R. and P. (*Mejia 0060*) or "huacrapona," *Astrocaryum chambira,* and *A. huicungo.*

A final use of palms as a source of food is somewhat indirect. Beetles of the species *Rynchophorus palmarum* lay their eggs within the pith of fallen aguaje trunks. These develop into edible larvae or "suri," which are extracted and eaten by local residents. Fallen fruits of *Scheelea cephalotes* (Poepp.) Karst (*Mejia 0169*) or "shapaja" also harbor edible suri of a smaller size.

B. Construction Materials

The most important use of palms in the 11 mestizo communities is as a source of materials for the construction of houses. The trunk of *Oenocarpus mapora* is sometimes used as a house post. In the construction of secondary or temporary buildings, the use of the trunks of *Jessenia bataua* has also been observed. The floors of village houses are commonly made from the beaten trunk of *Iriartea deltoidea, Dictyocaryum* sp. (*Mejia 0065*), known locally as "pona colorada" and *Socratea exorrhiza* (Mart.) Wendl. (*Mejia 0121*) or "cashapona." To make the flat floor sections, the palm trunks are beaten until they split. They are then opened and the soft material in the center is removed. Sections up to 95 cm in width can be obtained using this method. Flooring made of palm trunks is referred to as "emponado." To lay the flooring for a house measuring 7 × 5 m, five to eight palms must be felled. An emponado usually lasts for about ten years.

The inner and outer walls of houses can also be made from the flattened trunk sections of these species. However, the preferred material for this purpose is the trunk of *Euterpe precatoria* which has been cut into boards or "ripas." In several of the larger villages along the Ucayali, palm products are gradually being replaced by sawn boards in the construction of both floors and walls.

The most common use of palms in construction is as a roofing material. Given their abundance and durability, the leaves of *Lepidocaryum tessmannii* Burret (*Mejia 0010*) or "irapay" are generally favored for this purpose. Inventories conducted within the study area indicate that natural densities of irapay may exceed 2500 stems/ha (Kahn & Mejia, 1987). The leaves of several species of "palmiche" (*Geonoma* spp., *Mejia 0003, 0101* and *0104*) are occasionally used for roofing, and in one village, the use of *Hyospathe* sp. (*Mejia 0088*) or "palmichillo" was also observed.

The leaves of these species are elegantly woven into roof sections ("crisnejas") attached to a 3.2 m long pole. This pole is made from the trunk of either *Wettinia augusta* Spruce (*Mejia 0089*) or *Socratea* cf. *salazarii* Moore (*Mejia 0065*), both plants known locally as "ponilla." Each crisneja uses approximately 100–130 leaves of "irapay" or "palmiche," or 150 leaves of "palmichillo." Depending on the number and spacing of leaves, a roof made of irapay normally lasts four to six years, while a roof made from palmiche may last up to eight years.

The peak of the roof is covered by a woven section known as a "cumba," commonly made from the leaves of "catirina," *Orbignya polysticha* Burret (*Mejia 0133*) or *Phytelephas microcarpa*. Each cumba consists of 18–21 leaves and lasts for about three years.

Secondary buildings and temporary shelters are sometimes covered with the leaves of *Maximiliana maripa* (Correa) Drude (*Mejia 0077*) or "inayuga," and *Jessenia bataua*.

In the majority of the villages located on periodically flooded terrain, roofs are made from the leaves of *Scheelea cephalotes* (Shapaja) or *Phytelephas microcarpa* (yarina). Roofs made from these species involve a different technique.

The leaves are folded double and then tied to the rafters in groups of three. The observed preference for *S. cephalotes* and *P. microcarpa* is a direct result of the local abundance of these two species in flooded habitats.

C. Domestic Articles and Handicrafts

The leaves of several palm species are utilized in the manufacture of articles for daily use in the home as well as for handicrafts. For example, many of the residents of the villages studied weave baskets and sieves using the outer layer of the rachis of the leaves of *Oenocarpus mapora* and *Astrocaryum jauari,* or the petioles of *Mauritia flexuosa.* The latter species also serves for making large screens which are used as floor mats or temporary dividers in the home. The unopened young leaves of three *Astrocaryum* species, i.e., *A. chambira, A. huicungo,* and *A. jauari,* are employed in weaving hats and fans; three leaves are normally required to make a hat.

The young leaves of chambira also offer a flexible and strong fiber. Prior to weaving, these fibers are first soaked in water with soap or detergent for about ten hours until they are bleached. They are then dried in the sun and dyed various colors. After drying, the chambira fibers are twisted together to form a cord and this material is then woven into multi-purpose bags ("shicras") and hammocks. To weave a shicra measuring 35 × 25 cm, three young chambira leaves are used.

The leaves of *Jessenia bataua, Orbignya polysticha* and *Phytelephas microcarpa* are commonly employed to make temporary baskets known as "capillejos." These disposable, quickly made artifacts are used to carry wild game and other products from the forest.

D. Miscellaneous

In shaping a dugout canoe—i.e., to open it up and make it wider—the leaves of *Mauritia flexuosa* are burned to heat up the unfinished hull while it is being hollowed out. Stiff poles are then placed crosswise like thwarts in the canoe so that the desired form will be maintained when it cools.

In the two villages with the most pronounced Cocama roots, I observed the construction of bows and arrow points using the trunk of *Bactris gasipaes.* I also noted that the shaft of fishing

Table I

Palm species, with their common names and uses by mestizo villagers in the Peruvian Amazon

| Scientific name | Common name | Fruit | | Termi-nal bud | Thatch-ing | Wood for con-struction | Floors & walls | Domes-tic arti-facts & handi-crafts | Other uses |
		Meso-carp	Endo-sperm						
Astrocaryum chambira	chambira		X	X				X	
Astrocaryum spp. (2)	huicungo		X	X		X		X	
A. jauari	huirirma		X			X		X	
Bactris spp. (3)	nejilla	X							
B. gasipaes	pijuayo	X		X				X	
Catoblastus drudei	ponilla				X				
Euterpe precatoria	huasai	X		X			X		X
Geonoma spp. (2)	palmiche				X				
Hyospathe sp.	palmichillo				X				
Iriartea deltoidea	huacrapona			X			X		X
Dictyocaryum sp.	pona colorada								
Iriartella setigera	ponilla							X	
Jessenia bataua	ungurahui	X			X	X	X		
Lepidocaryum tessmannii	irapay				X				
Mauritia flexuosa	aguaje	X						X	
Mauritiella peruviana	aguajillo	X							X
Orbignya polysticha	catirina				X			X	
Oenocarpus mapora	sinamillo	X				X		X	
Phytelephas macrocarpa	yarina		X		X				
Scheelea cephalotes	shapaja		X		X				
Socratea exorrhiza	casha pona						X		
S. salazarii	ponilla					X			X
Wettinia augusta	ponilla					X			

arrows is occasionally made from *Iriartella se-tigera* (Mart.) Wendland (*Mejia 0017*).

Finally, during the carnival before lent, villagers celebrate by holding a traditional dance known as "humsha," and, here too palms are used. For this dance, a trunk of *Socratea exorrhiza* or *Euterpe precatoria,* its leaves woven into arcs and decorated with colored ribbons and small gifts, is planted upright. As the dancers circle the palm, they strike the trunk with an axe. The palm is eventually felled and the gifts are collected by all the dancers.

IV. Conclusion

As is summarized in Table I, a large number of palm species are used by mestizo villagers of the lower Ucayali River to satisfy a multitude of daily needs. Fifteen different species of palms are used for food. In nine of these palms, the edible part is the mesocarp of the fruit, in four other species, the immature endosperm is consumed. Palm hearts are extracted from five different species. A total of 17 palm species are used in the construction of dwellings, and eight species provide materials for the manufacture of domestic articles and handicrafts.

Although mestizo populations continue to use palm products, the patterns of use are changing. Processes of acculturation, migration, and the formation of multi-ethnic villages are modifying traditional uses of palms in the Peruvian Amazon. For example, the use of sawn boards and sheet metal are gradually replacing the traditional use of palm products in house construction. Some forms of palm use have disappeared completely in the last few years. Among the villages included in this study, the technique of extracting oil from the fruit or ungurahui is known, but hardly ever practiced. The commercial harvest of palm fruits, leaves and trunks which are often sold with a minimum of processing and, therefore, with almost no value added, is another source of change. Commercial harvests are exerting a significant pressure on natural palm populations in the Peruvian Amazon. Concurrent with the change in palm resource availability, patterns of use have also changed.

This brief outline of the use of palms by the mestizo populations of the Peruvian Amazon

suggests that further study should be undertaken in this region. Mestizos, until now almost forgotten by ethnobotanists, are the inheritors and developers of regional native traditions. Ethnobotanical studies of mestizo communities and research comparing mestizo to native use of plant resources in the Amazon would be most valuable.

V. Acknowledgments

This study forms part of the overall research program of the Instituto de Investigaciones de la Amazonia Peruana (I.I.A.P.). Fieldwork was carried out at the I.I.A.P. field station at Jenaro Herrera, and the continual support of the resident scientists and staff is gratefully acknowledged. Special thanks are due to the Director of the field station, Dr. J. Lopez-Parodi, for his help in all phases of the investigation, and to Dr. F. Kahn (ORSTOM) for taxonomic advice and helpful discussions. I would especially thank Drs. Christine Padoch and Charles Peters (Institute of Economic Botany of the New York Botanical Garden) for translating the original manuscript, and for making innumerable constructive suggestions. The comments provided by the anonymous reviewers were also extremely beneficial. Finally, I would like to thank all of the local people in the 11 communities studied for sharing their knowledge and time.

VI. Literature Cited

Balick, M. J. 1984. Ethnobotany of palms in the neotropics. Adv. Econ. Bot. **1:** 9–23.

Barbosa Rodrigues, J. 1903. Sertum palmarum Brasiliensium. 2 vols. Bruxelles.

Bodley, J. & C. Benson. 1979. Cultural ecology of Amazonian palms. Laboratory of Anthropology, Bulletin No. 56, Washington State University, Pullman.

Cavalcante, P. B. 1977. Edible palm fruits of the Brazilian Amazon. Principes **21:** 91–102.

Holdridge, L. 1978. Ecologia basada en zonas de vida. Inst. Amer. Ciencias Agric., San Jose, Costa Rica.

Kahn, F. & K. Mejia. 1987. Notes on the biology, ecology and utilization of a small Amazonian palm: *Lepidocaryum tessmannii* Burret. Principes **31:** 14–19.

Mejia, K. 1983. Las palmeras de Jenaro Herrera. Informe, Universidad Nacional Mayor de San Marcos, Lima, Peru.

Patiño, V. M. 1963. Plantas cultivadas y animales domesticos de America Equinoccial. Tomo 1: Frutales. Cali, Colombia.

Schultes, R. E. 1974. Palms and religion in the northwest Amazon. Principes **18**: 3–21.

Spruce, R. 1908. Notes of a botanist on the Amazon and Andes (A. R. Wallace, ed.). Macmillan, London.

Wallace, A. R. 1853. Palm trees of the Amazon and their uses. John van Voorst, London.

Utilization of Indigenous Palms in the Caribbean
(In Relation to Their Abundance)

Robert W. Read

Table of Contents

Abstract

Wherever palms are found growing naturally, a use will have been found for some or all of their vegetative or fruiting parts. However, the introduction of the coconut has without doubt provided an alternative and more readily available supply of useful products, thereby relieving pressure on indigenous species. The most frequently used indigenous palms of the Caribbean region are those that produce construction materials such as thatch or lumber in regions lacking the coconut, and palms whose leaves provide attractive weaving materials for crafts sold in the tourist markets. The most important economic palms are frequently common species that are not now endangered by exploitation. In fact, only two species may be said to be in danger of over-exploitation, *Scheelea urbaniana* of Tobago for thatch, and *Attalea crassispatha* of Haiti, because the seeds produced by the only known plants are all eaten by children as soon as they fall. Heart of palm is not a commercial industry and does not appear to be a serious threat to indigenous palm populations, since such harvesting is not a common practice in the Caribbean.

Key words: palms, palm products, Caribbean

I. Discussion

The palm flora of the Caribbean is perhaps the best known, floristically, of any region in the Americas outside the U.S. Nonetheless, new taxa are still being discovered, old species—long thought to be extinct or very rare—are being rediscovered, and there will still be some reconsideration of taxonomic affinities as monographic treatments are undertaken. Some taxa are exceedingly common, others are of greatly restricted local distribution. At the same time, further study will elucidate the occurrence of localized subspecies or variants within the range of the more extensive distribution of certain species (i.e., *Prestoea montana, Thrinax morrisii*). Most palms are used in the local economy of the various regions. Their importance depends primarily on the economic situation of the area and secondarily on the relative abundance of a particular species; making them more frequently used simply because of their presence. Palms may provide many products, such as food, either as a vegetable or for oil or fodder; fiber for weaving baskets, hats, bags, etc.; material for construction or utensils; a source of energy in the form of charcoal or firewood; assumed medicinal uses; or products having ritualistic or religious significance. You can be certain that wherever palms are growing someone will find a use for some part of the plant. In only two cases, however, can I suggest an immediate threat to any species resulting from overexploitation: *Scheelea urbaniana* (Tobago), for thatch, and *Attalea crassispatha* (Haiti), where the seeds of the only three known extant plants are eaten by children as soon as they fall to the ground.

None of the indigenous palm species in the Caribbean are of primary economic importance, except perhaps the royal palms of Cuba and Hispaniola for construction and fodder. The introduced coconut (*Cocos nucifera*) and African oil palm (*Elaeis guineensis*) are highly commercialized species developed as crop plants, but they

Advances in Economic Botany 6: 137–143, 1988
© 1988 The New York Botanical Garden

FIGS. 1–3. *Sabal causiarum* in Puerto Rico. Photographs taken by O. F. Cook or associates around the turn of the century. FIG. 1. *Sabal causiarum,* the Puerto Rican hat palm, full grown as it would look without cropping, on the road to Las Marias. FIG. 2. *S. causiarum,* cropped extensively, to the detriment of the plants. FIG. 3. A young woman, near Joyuda, carefully weaving a hat from the split and shredded pliable young leaves.

also have the effect of relieving pressure on in-digenous species. I believe the greatest and most conspicuous use of indigenous palms is for thatching shelters, be they homes, cattle or work shelters, or for the thatched beach shelters of resort hotels. Thatch-roofed houses were a common sight in Jamaica in the 1950's, although they now are rare. Today, thatch is used mainly for barns or work shelters. Wherever the genus occurs, *Sabal* is the major palm for thatching, with *Thrinax* and *Coccothrinax* next in importance (to say nothing of the coconut). *Thrinax morrisii* is commonly used by hotels in the Bahamas as a durable, very decorative thatch on hotel structures such as cabanas and outdoor refreshment areas. Elsewhere, *Roystonea* or *Prestoea* are commonly the leaves of choice, providing the next best source apart from the coconut. On Tobago the rare *Scheelea urbaniana* is probably overly collected for thatch. Other genera providing

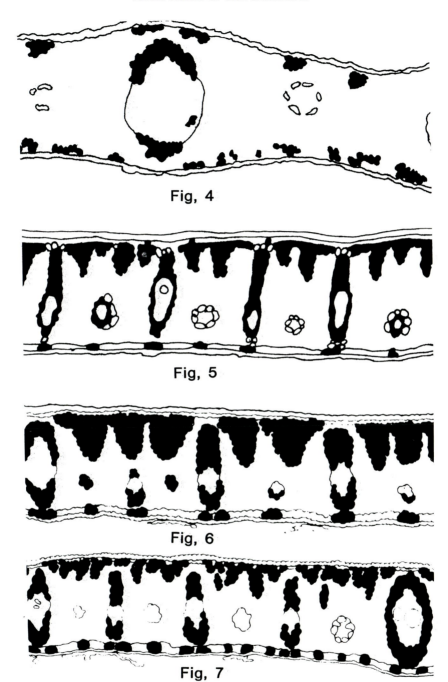

FIGS. 4–7.   Anatomical sections of the lamina of *Coccothrinax* species illustrating the distribution of clusters of fibers, the different species being used in different crafts. FIG. 4. *Coccothrinax barbadensis* from Barbados, used only for thatch or brooms as a rule. FIG. 5. *C. argentata,* from the Bahamas, used extensively in weaving mats, hats, bags and baskets. FIG. 6. *C. proctorii,* from the Cayman Islands, used primarily in rope making. FIG. 7. *C. jamaicensis,* from Jamaica, used extensively in weaving mats, hats, bags and baskets.

FIGS. 8–10. Broom making (Escobas de palma) from the leaves of a species of *Coccothrinax* near Jarabacoa, Republica Dominicana. Photographs by Thomas A. Zanoni. FIG. 8. Lacking the broom handle, escobas are displayed at a roadside stand. FIG. 9. Closeup of the broom's construction. FIG. 10. Preparation of the leaves of *Coccothrinax* sp. for broom or brush making, in a shelter constructed from the flattened leaf sheaths of *Roystonea hispaniolana.*

Survey of the Economic Use of Palms relative to Abundance

GENUS & SPECIES	PRODUCT OR UTILITY	COUNTRY	PRESENT UTILIZATION	ABUNDANCE
A. INTRODUCED SPECIES				
Cocos nucifera	Coconut: water, milk, meat (copra), oil, soap, lotion, thatch, utensils	All tropical lowland coastal areas	Extensive	Common dooryard & commercial cultivation
Elaeis guineensis	African oil palm, vegetable oils, soap, lotions, margarine etc.	Many tropical areas	Extensive	Commonly cultivated commercially
B. INDIGENOUS SPECIES				
1. HANDICRAFTS OR UTENSILS				
Acrocomia spp.	Seeds carved as rings, beads, pipe bowls etc. stems as canes	All areas esp. St. Vincent	Slight	Common
Coccothrinax argentata	Baskets, bags, hats, or mats	Bahamas	Extensive straw market	Common
Coccothrinax jamaicensis	Baskets, bags, mats, etc.	Jamaica	Extensive	Common
Coccothrinax proctorii	Rope, baskets, bags, mats, etc.	Cayman Islands	Dying out	Common ?
Coccothrinax barbadensis	Brooms	Tobago	Slight	Common
Copernicia berteroana	Brooms	Hispaniola	Common	Common
Sabal sp.	Hats	Bermuda & Puerto Rico	Dying out ?	Common ?
Thrinax morrisii ssp. morrisii	Brooms	Brit. Virgin Islands	Common	Common
Thrinax parviflora	Basket-stakes	Jamaica	Common	Very common
2. CONSTRUCTION				
Acrocomia spp.	Planks, boards	Wherever available	Rare	Common
Coccothrinax barbadensis	Thatch	Caribbean, Lesser Antilles	Slight	Common on Tobago
Coccothrinax jamaicensis	Thatch	Jamaica	Common	Very common
Copernicia berteroana	Thatch	Hispaniola	Common	Common
Maximiliana caribaea	Thatch & framing	Trinidad	Common	Common
Manicaria saccifera	Thatch	Trinidad	Common	Common
Mauritia flexuosa	Thatch	Trinidad	Common	Common
Prestoea montana	Thatch, lumber	Caribbean	Common	Common
Roystonea spp.	Thatch, planks	Caribbean	Slight	Common
Sabal spp.	Thatch, pilings	Wherever available	Common	Common
Scheelea urbaniana	Thatch & framing	Tobago	Common	Rare
Thrinax excelsa	Thatch, poles	Jamaica	Slight	Common
Thrinax morrisii	Thatch, poles	Bahamas & Puerto Rico	Common	Very common
Thrinax parviflora	Thatch, poles	Jamaica	Common	Very common
Thrinax radiata	Thatch, poles	Wherever available	Common	Common
3. FOOD & BEVERAGE				
Euterpe & Prestoea	Heart of Palm	Wherever available	Uncommon	Common
Pseudophoenix sargentii	Fodder from bud	Bahamas	Rare	Uncommon
Pseudophoenix spp.	Beverage	Hispaniola	Uncommon	Common
Roystonea spp.	Heart of Palm, Fodder from fruits	Wherever available	Common	Common

thatch that are less frequently used are *Mauritia, Manicaria* and *Maximiliana* in Trinidad/Tobago. Certain palms (whatever's handy) provide various construction materials in addition to thatch. The trunks of slender palms are often used for rafters, fencing, etc. The trunks of some palms are used occasionally for pilings, especially *Sabal* because of its resistance to marine borers and durability in salt water. The large leathery leaf sheaths of *Roystonea* provide clapboard or shingle type roofing or wall boards in Puerto Rico and Hispaniola. The thick rind of the royal palm trunk may also be sawn into boards for flooring or wall coverings. The trunk of *Acrocomia,* while very dense and hard, is nevertheless occasionally sawn into planks for construction, or, on St. Vincent, shaped into walking sticks. The dark hard fibers provide an attractive contrast against a lighter background material. But, I must add, one has to search out such relatively uncommon practices.

Perhaps the next most common use of palm leaves is in the manufacture of baskets, containers, hats (Fig. 3), and rope. Rope was once an important palm product peculiar to the Cayman Islands, for use by local boatmen or even exported to Jamaica. It is made from the leaves of the local endemic *Coccothrinax proctorii* (Fig. 6), which are especially well suited to twisting and bending because of their unique anatomical traits, in contrast to other closely related species (Figs. 4, 5, 7). Rope manufacture has all but died out, however, probably both because of a stronger economy (and importation of sisal rope therefore) and because, as the Cayman Island News Bureau says, the country's main industry is now banking and tourism and the craft is no longer practiced by anyone except a few elderly people. They tell me that the last shop for such things recently closed, as the owner died. Young people are not interested in "straw" (palm) or rope crafts, and such crafts are demonstrated at annual District Fairs only by a few elderly craftspeople who would gladly make things to order, the Bureau said. Straw markets (palm fiber material) have been very popular with tourists over the years. I am informed by the Embassy staff of Jamaica that the annual sales of native handicrafts, which I believe to include a large proportion of palm products (mainly *Coccothrinax* leaf products), is reported to have risen from 14,720 Jamaica dollars in 1983 to 38,724 Jamaican dollars in 1984. This is no doubt due to increased tourism following an improved political climate. The Embassy said there is presently a determined effort to train 12,500 persons in crafts development. The long, slender, but very tough flexible petioles of *Thrinax parviflora* are used in Jamaica as the basic structure (stakes) upon which large baskets are woven. These are primarily for local use, but

the weaving of *Coccothrinax* leaves is an extensive cottage industry, supplying the large crafts markets in Montego Bay, Ochos Rios and hotels around the island.

In Puerto Rico, use of *Sabal causiarum,* the famous hat palm (Fig. 1), was said to have resulted in overcollecting to the extent that native stands are no longer able to flower and fruit adequately (Fig. 2). Correspondents in Puerto Rico have disproven this, based on personal observation and surveys of the existing populations. Luis Martorell, Botanical Associate at the University of Puerto Rico reports that, ". . . the cutting of the leaves is of not much influence on the extermination of the species. The important factor in this sense is when the land is cleared. . . ." The palm is fairly common in cultivation and had even been introduced to the Windward Islands, but a hat-making industry was never established there. On the British Virgin Islands, Anegada and Anguilla at least, *Thrinax morrisii,* of exposed limestone areas, is a diminutive palm near the extreme eastern part of its natural range. Entire leaves are cut, bunched together and used as brooms, giving it the local name of broompalm. Brooms are also made from such palms as *Copernicia berteroana* and *Coccothrinax* species in the Dominican Republic (Figs. 8–10).

Apart from the coconut, palms provide minimal sources of food or beverage in the Caribbean Islands. The fruits of *Roystonea* may, where commonly available, be used as fodder for livestock, especially hogs. Palm cabbage is not commonly collected, partly, I suspect, because many locals either do not care for it or are not aware of its desirability. An abundance of other fresh vegetables may relieve pressure for the use of palms, which are probably considered to be more difficult of access or require special techniques to harvest. Of palms indigenous to the region none of the fruits are really very desirable as sustenance. The seeds or nuts of some *Acrocomia* species (and *Attalea crassispatha*) are commonly eaten by children, or are rarely used as an oil source. *Pseudophoenix* species are destroyed occasionally for wine making in Haiti and the Dominican Republic, but it is not yet a serious threat to the species. Wherever the coconut is available such minimal sources are usually overlooked, or avoided. Table I represents a survey of the economic uses of palms in relation to their abundance.

II. Acknowledgments

I would like to extend my sincere appreciation to the Cayman Island News Bureau, and the Staff of the Embassy of Jamaica, for information graciously extended regarding the use of palms in the economy of their countries; and to Vincente Quevado Bonilla, Botanist of the Department of Natural Resources, Puerto Rico, Luis F. Martorell, Botanico Asociado, Jardin Botánico, U. of Puerto Rico, and Thomas A. Zanoni of the Jardin Botánico Nacional, Santo Domingo, for valuable information and photographs generously supplied regarding palms in their respective countries. My greatest appreciation is extended to the World Wildlife–U.S. for support during 1985 toward studies of the Economic Botany and Threatened Species of the Palm Family in Latin America and the Caribbean, a report by Dennis Johnson and collaborators to the World Wildlife–U.S.

Use and Management of Native Forests Dominated by Açaí Palm (*Euterpe oleracea* Mart.) in the Amazon Estuary

ANTHONY B. ANDERSON

Table of Contents

Abstract

Native forests dominated by economically important palms occur over wide areas of the tropics. Such forests represent a concentrated resource that is potentially simple to manage. This paper examines a forest-dominant palm that is exceptionally abundant in floodplain forests of the Amazon River estuary: *Euterpe oleracea* Mart. ("açaí"). Sites where this palm abound are subject to frequent, tide-driven flooding, which imposes serious constraints on conventional forms of agriculture. As a result, local inhabitants are highly dependent on use and management of forest resources. Açaí provides a diverse array of market and subsistence products and indirectly supports a variety of other economic activities. Forests dominated by this palm are subject to various types and intensities of management, which invariably require relatively few inputs and yet appear to significantly increase yields of native forest products. This case study illustrates the tight integration that can exist between native palm forests and rural communities. Comparison with other case studies in the literature suggests that palm forests are most viable as a resource when they occur on agriculturally marginal sites, which are less subject to competitive and potentially disruptive forms of land use.

Key words: palms, açaí, *Euterpe oleracea,* extractivism, forest management, floodplain forests, Amazon

Resumo

Florestas nativas dominadas por palmeiras economicamente importantes ocorrem em amplas áreas tropicais. Tais florestas representam um recurso concentrado e potencialmente simples de manejar. Este trabalho examina uma dessas palmeiras, a qual é excepcionalmente abundante em florestas de várzea do estuário do rio Amazonas: *Euterpe oleracea* Mart. ("açaí"). Os locais onde essa palmeria ocorre estão sujeitos a inundações frequentes dirigidas, pelos marés, fato que impõe sérios obstáculos às formas convencionais de agricultura. Como resultado, os moradores locais são altamente dependentes do uso e manejo dos recursos florestais. O açaí fornece diversos produtos de subsistência e de mercado, além de apoiar indiretamente várias atividades econômicas. As florestas onde essa palmeira é dominante são submetidas a vários tipos e intensidades de manejo, os quais invariavelmente requerem pouco investimento e, no entanto, parecem provocar um aumento significativo da produção florestal. O presente estudo de caso ilustra a íntima integração que pode existir entre palmeirais nativos e comunidades rurais. A comparação com outros estudos de caso citados na literatura sugere que as florestas de palmeiras são um recurso mais viável quando ocorrem em locais impracticáveis para a agricultura, os quais estão menos sujeitos a formas competitivas de uso da terra.

I. Introduction

From an ecological perspective, management of native forests is often cited as the most preferable form of land use in the humid tropics (e.g., Goodland, 1980). From an economic perspective, however, the high biological diversity characteristic of humid tropical forests represents a serious obstacle to their long-term management and utilization. Although high biological diversity is the rule, native forests that are low in diversity are surprisingly common in the lowland tropics. These forests are often dominated by economically important species of palms. The "lontar" palm (*Borassus sundaicus* Beccari), which dominates derived savannas in Indonesia (Fox, 1977), and the "nipa" palm (*Nypa fruticans* Wurmb.), which occurs in pure stands in coastal swamps from Southeast Asia to Australia (Moore, 1973; Paivoke, 1984), produce edible sap that is marketed and consumed by local inhabitants. The "sago" palm (*Metroxylon sagu* Rottb.), which abounds in freshwater swamps of Southeast Asia and the Pacific, is an important source of edible starch (Ruddle et al., 1978). A counterpart to the sago palm in the Americas is the "buriti" or "moriche" palm (*Mauritia flexuosa* L. f.), which dominates in freshwater swamps throughout northern South America (Heinen & Ruddle, 1974). In addition to plantations established throughout the humid tropics, the oil palm (*Elaeis guineensis* Jacq.) forms extensive, high-density stands on secondary forest sites in West Africa (Zeven, 1967). One of the oil palm's principal counterparts in the Americas is the "babaçu" palm (*Orbignya phalerata* Mart.), which flourishes on secondary forest sites in Brazil, Bolivia, and the Guianas (Anderson & Balick, in press). The preceding is only a small sampling of economically important palms that are ecologically dominant. In the Brazilian portions of the Amazon Basin, for example, the list could be expanded to include at least 22 species in 12 genera (Anderson, 1986).

Because of their local abundance, forest-dominant palms often play a crucial role in both market and subsistence economies. These palms provide commercial products such as fibers, waxes, vegetable oils, edible fruits, beverages, palm hearts, and flavorings. Products from native palm forests make a substantial contribution to national economies. For example, in 1979 Brazil reported over US$100,000,000 of commerce from the sale of products from six native palm genera (all represented by forest-dominant species): *Astrocaryum, Attalea, Copernicia, Euterpe, Mauritia,* and *Orbignya* (IBGE, 1981). In addition to market products, palm forests provide an astonishing array of subsistence products, including shelter, clothing, foods, beverages, oils, protein from palm-feeding larvae, charcoal, kitchen utensils, tools, weapons, bait, hammocks, baskets, fishing nets, brooms, ornaments, cosmetics, toys, medicine, and magic (Moore, 1973). As shown in the case study described below, the combination of market and subsistence products obtained from these forests often makes a crucial difference in rural economies.

Forest-dominant palm species usually occur on marginal sites that are not suitable for agriculture. For example, most forest-dominant palms in the Amazon Basin occur on temporarily or permanently inundated sites where agricultural activities are minimal or nonexistent; other genera flourish on sites that have been degraded due to agricultural activities (Anderson, 1986). Evidence suggests that palms may provide an important and possibly unique contribution to site restoration through their role in the recovery of deep soil nutrients (Anderson, 1986; Furley, 1975). Palm forests also provide important sources of food for animal communities (Bradford & Smith, 1977; Costa Lima, 1967–1968; Janzen, 1971, 1972). Many animals that are hunted for game appear to thrive in palm forests (e.g., Kiltie, 1981; Smith, 1974; but see Myers, 1981) and products harvested from these sites represent important nutritional supplements for domesticated animals such as chickens and pigs. Palm forests also appear to play an important role in the maintenance of aquatic communities, as evident from the nutritional dependence of the economically important "tambaquí" (*Colossoma macropomum,* Characidae) and other fishes on the fruits of the "jauarí" palm (*Astrocaryum jauari* Mart.) in Amazonian Brazil (Goulding, 1980).

Palms attain high-density populations that are generally self-maintaining and apparently pest-free. The long-term management of palm forests is consequently simple, in contrast to more heterogeneous forests in the tropics. The relatively open crowns of palms permit underplanting of crops and formation of multi-levelled agroforestry systems (Johnson, 1983). In addition to native palm forests, underplanting of crops and pasture is successfully carried out in plantations of coconut (Plucknett, 1979) and oil palm (Hartley, 1977).

Despite the present and potential importance of native palm forests, surprisingly little is known about them. I am not aware of any published reviews concerning these forests on even a regional level. Information on the species involved and the sites they dominate is only available in widely scattered sources. Maps showing the distribution of palm forests are limited to a few species (e.g., Anonymous, 1981) and are confined to a few individual countries. Ethnobotanical studies are fairly detailed (e.g., Barrau, 1959; Putz, 1979; Wilbert, 1976) but rarely contain quantitative economic data (but see Martin, 1956; Ruddle et al., 1978). Government sources of data on the economic production of native palms are few and often suspect. Ecological studies of forest-dominant palms are rare (e.g., Anderson, 1983; Myers, 1981), and almost nothing has been published concerning their management (but see Anderson, 1986; Calzavara, 1972; Zeven, 1967).

Why are these economically and ecologically important resources so neglected? In my opinion, one of the chief reasons is that the study of native palm forests lies outside traditional research domains. Many foresters have traditionally focused their attention on wood production, whereas agronomists are trained to work with cultivated crops. The substantial contribution of native palm forests to subsistence economies is extremely difficult to quantify, which has probably contributed to the neglect of these resources by economists. As a result, the study of native palm forests has largely been left to economic botanists, whose publications have apparently been ignored by scientists in other fields.

The potential for exploitation of palms and other native forest resources also frequently suffers from the stigma of extractivism. In Amazonia extractivism has been historically associated with resource depletion, environmental degradation, socio-economic disruption, and cultural decimation (Anderson & Gély, in press). This grim precedent has fostered a conviction among regional development agencies that land can only be properly exploited after the original forests have been removed, thus ignoring the potential for exploiting these forests in their intact state.

In this paper I provide a case study of the use and management of floodplain forests dominated by the "açaí" palm (*Euterpe oleracea* Mart.) in the Amazon estuary. The case of açaí illustrates the potential contribution of palm forests toward the ecological and economic well-being of rural communities. By comparing this case study with other published studies currently available, I shall attempt to provide an overview of the use and management of native palm forests.

II. The Amazon Estuary

Throughout the Amazon floodplain, flooding provides both opportunities and risks for agriculture. The principal opportunity lies in the regular input of nutrient-rich sediments; the principal risk is due to the unpredictable scale and duration of flooding. In the Amazon estuary, floods are primarily controlled by tides and thus occur diurnally rather than seasonally; salinization due to mixing with sea water represents a further hazard for agriculture.

Aboriginal populations appear to have circumvented the limitations of the floodplain by developing complex food production systems, characterized by intensive seed crop cultivation on sites subjected to flooding, manioc cultivation on the terra firme, and animal capture in both zones (Roosevelt, 1980). Nearly four centuries of colonization effectively destroyed these societies by turning a predominantly subsistence economy based on sustainable forms of food production into a market economy geared toward extraction of forest and riverine products (Ross, 1978). In the Amazon floodplain, contemporary society—characterized by a widely scattered settlement pattern and non-intensive agriculture—is well adapted to the economic demands imposed within Amazonia since the outset of the colonial era. A scattered population permits more efficient extraction of natural resources while effectively impeding agricultural production in the floodplain. Much of the indigenous knowledge of natural resources inherited by the contemporary residents of the floodplain has likewise contributed toward maintaining an essentially extractive economy.

In the Amazon estuary, not only the nature of

the local inhabitants but their very environment seems to be eminently suited to the demands of extractivism. The intricate network of rivers and canals ("furos") that characterizes this landscape has facilitated wood extraction for centuries (Huber, 1943). The flooding cycle also contributes toward extraction of forest products such as timber. Insufficient drainage imposes severe limitations on plant growth, primarily by restricting the availability of oxygen to roots. Many of the tree species that grow under these conditions exhibit structures that are probably adaptations to oxygen-poor soils: the aerial roots and lenticels of the açaí palm are classic examples of such structures. Few species appear to thrive under such conditions, and as a result the floodplain forests are characterized by relatively low biological diversity and pronounced dominance by a few tree species, many of which are of economic importance. In addition to açaí, examples of native tree species that are abundant and economically important include rubber (*Hevea brasiliensis* (A. Juss.) M. Arg.); cocoa (*Theobroma cacao* L.); "andiroba" (*Carapa guianensis* Aubl.), a source of timber and medicinal oil; "ucuuba" (*Virola* spp., especially *V. surinamensis* (Rol.) Warb.), used primarily for timber; the "miriti" or "buriti" palm (*Mauritia flexuosa* L. f.), which provides edible fruits and excellent fibers, along with numerous other products; and the "jupati" (*Raphia taedigera* Mart.) and "ubuçu" (*Manicaria saccifera* Gaertn.) palms, additional sources of fibers. At least 34 tree species are currently exploited for timber in the Amazon floodplain (Pandolfo, 1978), many of which are abundant in the estuary.

Forest resources in the Amazon estuary are not only concentrated but appear to be highly productive. Many of the dominant, economic tree species are extremely fast growing, possibly due to high soil fertility. The forests as a whole are extremely dynamic. Shallow root systems due to impeded drainage—combined with constant soil movement associated with flooding—apparently result in a high frequency of tree falls in these ecosystems, and abundant light gaps provide ample opportunities for forest regeneration. As a result, floodplain forests regenerate quickly and appear to have the potential to support short-cycle timber extraction on a sustained basis.

Although the floodplain of the Amazon estuary is frequently cited for its agricultural potential, its suitability for extraction of forest products is frequently overlooked. The ecology of this landscape and the characteristics of its inhabitants suggest that such extraction can be sustainable when integrated with long-term forest management. The case of the açaí palm described below illustrates an example of such integration.

III. Açaí

The following description of use and management of açaí is largely derived from an in-depth study (Anderson et al., 1985) on Ilha das Onças (Fig. 1), adjacent to the city of Belém. Additional field research at other locales (Fig. 1)—as well as reconnaissance trips throughout the estuary—complements the data from Ilha das Onças and enables me to offer a tentative overview of use and management of açaí-dominated forests in the Amazon estuary as a whole.

Euterpe oleracea, known as "açaí" in Brazil, ranges over widespread areas of northern South America but attains its greatest coverage and economic importance in the estuary of the Amazon River. The floodplain forests of the Amazon estuary cover an estimated 25,000 km² (Lima, 1956). Much of this area (ca. 88% according to Lima, 1956) is subjected to frequent inundation, and on such sites açaí is often the most ecologically important tree species. Calzavara (1972) conservatively estimated the coverage of açaí-dominated forests in the Amazon estuary at 10,000 km².

Açaí produces a wide variety of market and subsistence products (Fig. 2). The foremost of these—in both market and subsistence economies in the Amazon estuary—is a beverage obtained from the pulp of the fruits. This beverage is consumed on an almost daily basis throughout the region, especially among poorer segments of the population; details on the preparation of this beverage are provided by Strudwick and Sobel (this volume). Contrary to popular opinion, it is not particularly nutritious: protein content ranges from 1.25 to 4.34%; fatty acids range from 7.6 to 11.0%; Ca, P, and Fe average 0.050%, 0.033% and 0.0009%, respectively; and traces of vitamins B_1 and A occur (Altman, 1956; Campos, 1951; Mota, 1946). Yet the beverage is extremely filling, especially when mixed with manioc flour.

In the 1960's, commercial extraction of açaí palm heart began in the Amazon estuary. Re-

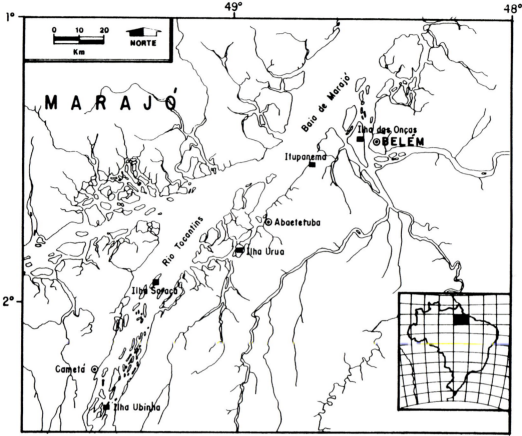

FIG. 1. Map of the southeastern portion of the Amazon estuary. Squares indicate sites where author has conducted studies of forest management.

gional consumption of palm heart is minimal, and most of the production is destined for markets elsewhere in Brazil or abroad. Extraction of açaí palm heart began following exhaustion of other sources, especially native stands of the "juçara" palm (*Euterpe edulis* Mart.) in southeastern Brazil. Although "Juçara" palm produces a more massive palm heart, it typically requires eight to ten years to attain maturity (Macedo et al., 1975), compared with only three to four years for açaí (Calzavara, 1972). Furthermore, juçara is a single-stemmed species, and harvesting of its palm hearts thus eliminates individual palms. By contrast, açaí is a multi-stemmed species that can potentially regenerate indefinitely when subjected to palm heart extraction.

Despite their obvious potential for rational management, açaí stands were initially subjected to widespread clearcutting when palm heart extraction began in the Amazon estuary. Uncontrolled extraction continues in certain areas of the estuary today, with negative consequences for large segments of the rural population that depend on the harvest of açaí fruits for subsistence and sale (Anonymous, 1985).

Alternative management practices that permit both fruit harvest and palm heart extraction appear to be increasingly implemented by rural inhabitants in the Amazon estuary. Inhabitants commonly introduce seeds or seedlings of açaí onto shifting cultivation plots, thus promoting establishment of high-density stands that can be utilized during subsequent fallow periods. In already existing stands (established either spontaneously or through human intervention), management practices include selective pruning of

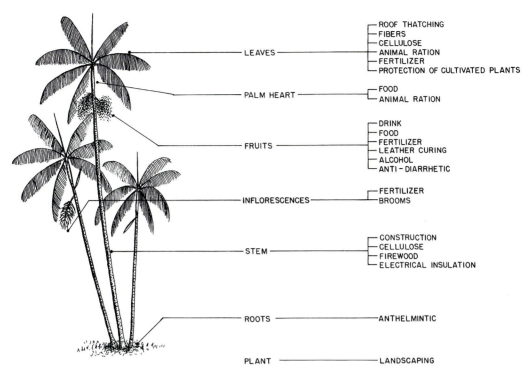

FIG. 2.   Market and subsistence uses of the açaí palm.

açaí stems combined with selective thinning of forest competitors. An individual açaí palm may consist of over a dozen stems, and local inhabitants report that selective pruning not only provides palm heart but enhances fruit production in the remaining stems. On Ilha das Onças, Anderson et al. (1985) found that the mean number of stems per açaí clumped declined from 9.5 in unmanaged floodplain forest to 6.5 on a managed site. Although the density of açaí stems declined, its relative importance actually increased on the managed site due to selective thinning of competitors. When pruning, local inhabitants tend to eliminate young juvenile and old adult stems,

Table I

Relative importance of species and resources in areas of managed and unmanaged floodplain forest on Ilha das Onças

Item	Importance (%)	
	Managed forest	Unmanaged forest
Species (20)	96.4	84.9
Food	64.0	40.1
Drink	48.4	33.8
Medicine	59.2	55.1
Wood	36.8	52.5
Game attractant	46.0	36.2
Energy	29.3	47.0
Fertilizer	29.3	27.1
Utensils	30.1	38.1
Fibers	29.2	27.1
Other uses	21.4	10.3

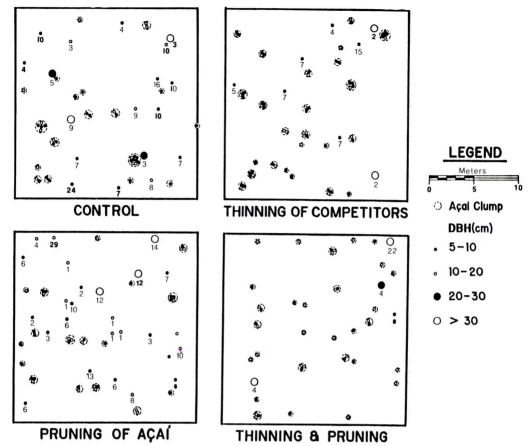

FIG. 3. Basal map of experimental plots on Ilha das Onças. The plots are representative of four treatments designed to test effects of local management practices on açaí. All stems have DBH ≥ 5 cm. *Euterpe oleracea* Mart. is not numbered, 1 = *Astrocaryum murumuru* Mart., 2 = *Carapa guianensis* Aubl., 3 = *Inga edulis* Mart., 4 = *Hevea brasiliensis* (A. Juss.) M. Arg., 5 = *Pentaclethra macroloba* (Willd.) Kuntze, 6 = *Pithecellobium glomeratum* (DC.) Benth., 7 = *Virola surinamensis* (Rol.) Warb., 8 = *Theobroma cacau* L., 9 = *Pterocarpus officinalis* Jacq., 10 = *Matisia paraense* Huber, 11 = *Hura crepitans* L., 12 = *Licania macrophylla* Benth., 13 = *Symphonia globulifera* L. f., 14 = *Allantoma* cf. *lineata* (Mart. ex Berg) Miers, 15 = *Cytharexylum* sp., 16 = *Socratea exorrhiza* (Mart.) H. Wendl., 17 = *Macrolobium angustifolium* (Benth.) Cowan, 18 = *Mora paraensis* Ducke, 19 = *Quararibea guianensis* Aubl., 20 = *Bombax* sp., 21 = *Cecropia* sp., 22 = *Ceiba pentandra* Gaertn., 23 = *Ficus* sp., 24 = *Genipa americana* L., 25 = *Licania* cf. *heteromorpha* Benth., 26 = *Mauritia flexuosa* L. f., 27 = *Theobroma speciosum* Willd. ex Spreng., 28 = *Vismia guianensis* (Aubl.) Choisy, and 29 = unidentified tree.

sparing old juvenile and young adult stems. This practice appears to favor life stages in which current or imminent fruit production is maximal.

Likewise, selective thinning of forest competitors preserves a wide variety of forest resources. Selective thinning tends to concentrate on vines and trees that are used primarily for timber or firewood. Trees that branch at a height of 10–15 m and consequently interfere directly with the crowns of mature açaí stems are especially prone to thinning. Examples of such trees indicated by

informants on Ilha das Onças include *Pithecellobium glomeratum* (DC.) Benth., *Pentaclethra macroloba* (Willd.) Kuntze, *Matisia paraensis* Huber, *Quararibea guianensis* Aubl., and *Protium* cf. *polybotrium* (Turcz.) Engl.

The effects of these practices can be observed in a comparison of the relative importance of species and resources in 0.25 ha areas of managed and unmanaged floodplain forest on Ilha das Onças (Table I). The number of species (DBH ≥ 5 cm) declined from 52 on the unmanaged

Table II

Commercial products sold in local markets during Jan–Dec 1986 by a family on Ilha das Onças

Product	Quantity	Unit	Weight (kg)	US$[1]	%
Fruits of açaí	5259	can (15 kg)	78,885	15,532.86	63.1
Timber	180	m³	—	3142.86	12.8
Palm hearts of açaí	35,026	individual	—	2916.79	11.8
Shrimp	1037	kg	1037	1371.43	5.6
Rubber latex	1812	kg	1812	1294.29	5.3
Pigs	7	individual	—	300.00	1.2
Cocoa seeds	50	kg	—	57.14	0.2
Bananas	3	bunch	—	3.21	—
Total	—	—	—	24,618.58	100.0

[1] Average exchange rate: US$1.00 = Cz$14,00.

site to 28 on the managed site. Resources were more concentrated in the managed forest. For example, the five most important species had a combined importance value (expressed as %) of 52.1% on the unmanaged site, compared with 71.7% on the managed site; for the 20 most important species, the figures were 84.9% and 96.4%, respectively (Table I). Comparing the relative importance of specific resources in the forest types, sources of food and drink had a considerably higher (>10%) relative importance on the managed site, whereas sources of wood (principally as timber) and energy (principally as firewood or charcoal) had a considerably higher relative importance on the unmanaged site (Table I).

I am currently investigating the effects of floodplain forest management in an experiment on Ilha das Onças involving four treatment combinations (each replicated four times): control, thinning of competitors, pruning of açaí, and thinning and pruning (Fig. 3). The principal response variables being measured are growth, fruit production, and regeneration of açaí. Preliminary results indicate that the combined treatment—which duplicates local inhabitants' management of floodplain forests—produces significant increases in fruit production with minimal investment of labor.

Although palm heart extraction has become an important economic activity in recent years, local informants report that increasing fruit production is the major motive behind the forest management practices described above. This is evident from data on commercialization of forests and riverine products by a family on Ilha das Onças (Table II): sale of fruits contributed 63.1% of total family income during a one year period (Jan–Dec 1986), compared with 11.8% from sale of palm hearts. The combined contribution of fruits and palm hearts to total family income (74.9%) indicates the crucial role that açaí can play in the household economy of rural inhabitants in the Amazon estuary.

The management practices described above appear to be most frequently encountered near major market centers such as Belém and Abaetetuba (Fig. 1). These centers provide the only large-scale commercial outlets for both açaí palm heart and fruits. Because the latter can only be stored at ambient temperatures for a maximum of 48 hours, their commercialization is limited to areas near market centers. It is consequently in these areas that the strongest incentives exist for integrating fruit harvesting with palm heart extraction.

Local inhabitants derive additional benefits by increasing the ecological importance and productivity of açaí in native floodplain forests. Açaí is an extremely versatile species that provides

Table III

Mineral analysis of a sample of organic mulch obtained at açaí palm heart factory

pH	5.0
C (%)	10.29
P (ppm)	995
Ca + Mg (meq/100 g)	4.0
K (meq/100 g)	0.33

Table IV

Comparison of two forest-dominant palm species

	Açaí (*Euterpe oleracea*)	Babaçu (*Orbignya phalerata*)
Site characteristics		
Soil fertility	high	high
Drainage	poor	good
Principal land uses	—extractive activities —shifting/permanent cultivation	—grazing —shifting cultivation
Economic characteristics		
Principal subsistence uses	—staple beverage —shelter & construction —fertilizer —implements	—snack foods —shelter & construction —fuel —implements
Principal market products	—beverage & fertilizer from fruits —palm heart	—oil, soap & animal feed from seeds —charcoal from fruit husks
Relative value of market products	high	low
Prospects for in-situ management	promising	dubious

numerous subsistence benefits. In addition to thatch, the leaves of the palm are used as mulch and shading for planted and/or favored species on managed sites. Residues from palm heart extraction and açaí beverage production represent important sources of feed for domesticated animals such as pigs and chickens, and the sites where these animals feed subsequently provide compost. The extraordinarily high fertility of this compost is evident from the mineral analysis presented in Table III. Finally, açaí provides additional subsistence products such as medicines, utensils, construction materials, and firewood (Fig. 2).

IV. Discussion

The case study of açaí just described illustrates the important role of forest-dominant palms in rural economies, and how this role can be enhanced by simple and inexpensive management practices. These practices appear to represent a viable land-use alternative to the social and economic disruption produced by uncontrolled palm heart extraction. By subjecting the açaí palm to in-situ management, rural inhabitants appear to be minimizing economic risks while maximizing ecological sustainability. Such management requires minimal risks because investments are low and economic returns are virtually guaranteed. As shown in Table II, income generated by açaí is substantial in both absolute and relative terms,

which indicates that its products command high market value. In addition to cash income, the palm provides numerous subsistence benefits that contribute to household well-being, especially in rural areas. Conservation of numerous other forest resources likewise minimizes risks by multiplying economic opportunities. Finally, conservation of native forest cover assures the long-term sustainability of this form of land use.

These considerations suggest that the prospects for in-situ management of açaí-dominated forests are bright. Other forest-dominant palms likewise appear to have excellent potential for such management. One of the best documented cases in the literature is the "lontar" palm (*Borassus sundaicus* Beccari), which occurs over widespread areas of Eastern Indonesia (Fox, 1977). Like açaí, lontar occurs in high-density stands and provides a wide variety of market and subsistence products. Both palms provide important sources of nutrition: in the case of lontar, tapping of the inflorescences produces a sweet juice that constitutes the principal food for local inhabitants. Both açaí and lontar stands provide substantial sources of income: the juice of lontar is used to make gin for export, and the stands are preferred sites for beekeeping. Finally, both palms occur on sites where conflicting land uses are strictly limited: in the case of lontar, stands of the palm occur on deeply weathered soils in a region of low and unpredictable rainfall.

A contrasting case of in-situ management is

represented by the so-called "babaçu" palm (*Orbignya phalerata* Mart.), which forms nearly pure stands on secondary sites in Brazil, Bolivia, and the Guianas (Anderson, 1983; Anderson & Balick, in press). Like açaí and lontar, babaçu provides a wide variety of market and subsistence products; but except under unusual circumstances, it does not produce a staple food. Although babaçu can contribute significantly to rural incomes (May et al., 1985), in general its products are of relatively low absolute value. Finally, babaçu stands occur on sites with generally high soil fertility, sufficient drainage, and ample rainfall. As a result, conflicting forms of land use such as shifting cultivation and grazing are resulting in the eradication of the stands over increasing areas (Anderson & May, 1985). In comparison to species such as açaí, the prospects for in-situ management of babaçu are consequently dubious (Table IV).

These case studies indicate that in-situ management of native palm forests may be a more viable enterprise when product value is high and the potential for conflicting land uses is minimal. The latter requirement is generally true for agroforestry systems throughout the world, which seem to be best suited to sites where more capital-intensive land uses are not competitive. Given these conditions, in-situ management of palm forests may prove to be a promising land use alternative over considerable areas of the tropics.

V. Acknowledgments

The research for this paper was supported by grants from the Ford Foundation, the Conselho Nacional de Desenvolvimento Científico e Tecnológico (CNPq), and the World Wildlife Fund. I wish to express my gratitude to Mário Jardim, Socorro Padilha, and Marinaldo da Silva for assistance in the field, to Sandoval Martins for the illustrations, to Lylianne Theodoro for typing the manuscript, and to Suely Anderson for translating the abstract.

VI. Literature Cited

Altman, R. F. A. 1956. O caroço de açaí (*Euterpe oleracea*, Mart.). Bol. Técn. Inst. Agron. N. (IAN) **31:** 109–111.
Anderson, A. B. 1983. The biology of *Orbignya martiana* (Palmae), a tropical dry forest dominant in Brazil. Ph.D. Dissertation. University of Florida, Gainesville.
———. 1986. Use and management of native palm forests. Anais do I Simpósio do Trópico Úmido, Vol. 2: 253–261. EMBRAPA, Belém.
——— & M. J. Balick. 1988. Taxonomy of the babassu complex (*Orbignya* spp.: Palmae). Syst. Bot. **13(1):** 32–50.
——— & A. Gély. (In press). Extractivism and forest management by rural inhabitants in the Amazon estuary. Adv. Econ. Bot. 7.
———, A. Gély, J. Strudwick, G. L. Sobel & M. G. C. Pinto. 1985. Um sistema agroflorestal na várzea do estuário amazônico (Ilha das Onças, Município de Barcarena, Estado do Pará). Acta Amazonica, Supl., **15(1–2):** 195–224.
——— & P. H. May. 1985. A palmeira de muitas vidas. Ciência Hoje **4(20):** 58–64.
Anonymous. 1981. Mapeamento das ocorrências e prospecção atual do babaçu no estado do Maranhão. Companhia de Pesquisa e Aproveitamento de Recursos Naturais (COPENAT) & Fundação Instituto Estadual do Babaçu (INEB), São Luis, Brazil.
Anonymous. 1985. Açaí some da Vigia devido à extração descontrolada. Jornal "O Liberal," 29 Nov., page 5.
Barrau, J. 1959. The sago palm and other food plants of marsh dwellers in the South Pacific islands. Econ. Bot. **13:** 151–162.
Bradford, D. F. & C. C. Smith. 1977. Seed predation and seed number in *Scheelea* palm fruits. Ecology **58:** 667–673.
Calzavara, B. B. G. 1972. As possibilidades do açaizeiro no estuário amazônico. Bol. Fund. Ci. Agrár. Pará (FCAP), no. 5, 103 pp.
Campos, F. A. M. 1951. Valor nutritivo de frutos brasileiros. Inst. Nutr., Trab. Pesq. **6:** 72–75.
Costa Lima, A. M. 1967–1968. Quarto catálogo dos insetos que vivem nas plantas do Brasil, seus parasitos e predadores. Parts 1 & 2. Ministério da Agricultura, Rio de Janeiro.
Fox, J. J. 1977. Harvest of the palm. Harvard University Press, Cambridge. 290 pp.
Furley, P. A. 1975. The significance of the cohune palm, *Orbignya cohune* (Mart.) Dahlgren, on the nature and development of the soil profile. Biotropica **7(1):** 32–36.
Goodland, R. 1980. Environmental ranking of Amazonian development projects in Brazil. Environ. Conserv. **7(1):** 9–26.
Goulding, M. 1980. The fishes and the forest. University of California Press, Berkeley.
Hartley, C. W. S. 1977. The oil palm. Longman, London.
Heinen, H. D. & K. Ruddle. 1974. Ecology, ritual, and economic organization in the distribution of palm starch among the Warao of the Orinoco Delta. J. Anthropol. Res. **30:** 116–138.
Huber, J. 1943. Contribuição à geografia física da região dos furos de Breves e da parte ocidental da Ilha do Marajó. Revista Brasil. Geogr. **5(3):** 449–474.

IBGE. 1981. Produção extrativa vegetal—1979. Vol. 7. Fundação Instituto Brasileiro de Geografiaa e Estatística, Rio de Janeiro, Brazil.

Janzen, D. H. 1971. The fate of *Scheelea rostrata* fruits beneath the parent tree: Predispersal attack by bruchids. Principes **15**: 89–101.

———. 1972. Association of a rain forest palm and seed-eating beetles in Puerto Rico. Ecology **53**: 258–261.

Johnson, D. 1983. Multi-purpose palms in agroforestry: A classification and assessment. Int. Tree Crops J. **2**: 217–244.

Kiltie, R. A. 1981. Distribution of palm fruits on a rain forest floor: Why white-lipped peccaries forage near objects. Biotropica **13**: 141–145.

Lima, R. R. 1956. A agricultura nas várzeas do estuário do Amazonas. Bol. Técn. Inst. Agron. N. **33**: 1–164.

Macedo, J. H. P., F. O. Rittershofer & A. Dessewefy. 1975. A silvicultura e a indústria do palmito. Instituto de Pesquisa de Recursos Renováveis, Porto Alegre, Brazil. 61 pp.

Martin, A. 1956. The oil palm economy of the Ibidio farmer. Ibadan University Press, Nigeria.

May, P. H., A. B. Anderson, M. J. Balick & J. M. F. Frazão. 1985. Subsistence benefits from the babassu palm (*Orbignya martiana*). Econ. Bot. **39**: 113–129.

Moore, H. E. 1973. Palms in the tropical forest ecosystems of Africa and South America. Pages 63–88 *in* B. J. Meggers, E. S. Ayensu & W. D. Duckworth (eds.), Tropical forest ecosystems in Africa and South America: A comparative review. Smithsonian Institution Press, Washington, D.C.

Mota, S. 1946. Pesquisas sobre o valor alimentar do assaí. Anais da Assoc. Quím. Brasil **5(2)**: 35–38.

Myers, R. L. 1981. The ecology of low diversity palm swamps near Tortuguero, Costa Rica. Ph.D. Dissertation. University of Florida, Gainesville.

Paivoke, A. E. A. 1984. Tapping patterns in the nipa palm (*Nypa fruticans* Wurmb.). Principes **28(3)**: 132–137.

Pandolfo, C. 1978. A floresta amazônica brasileira: Enfoque econômico-ecológico. Superintendência do Desenvolvimento da Amazônia (SUDAM), Belém, Brazil.

Plucknett, D. L. 1979. Managing pastures and cattle under coconuts. Westview Press, Boulder.

Putz, F. E. 1979. Biology and human use of *Leopoldinia piassaba*. Principes **23**: 149–156.

Roosevelt, A. C. 1980. Parmana: Prehistoric maize and manioc subsistence along the Amazon and Orinoco. Academic Press, New York.

Ross, E. B. 1978. The evolution of the Amazon peasantry. J. Latin Amer. Stud. **10(2)**: 193–218.

Ruddle, K., D. Johnson, P. K. Townsend & J. D. Rees. 1978. Palm sago: A tropical starch from marginal lands. The University Press of Hawai'i, Honolulu. 207 pp.

Smith, N. 1974. Agouti and babassu. Oryx **12**: 581–582.

Strudwick, J. & G. L. Sobel. 1988. Uses of *Euterpe oleracea* Mart. in the Amazon estuary, Brazil. Adv. Econ. Bot. **7**.

Wilbert, J. 1976. *Manicaria saccifera* and its significance among the Warao Indians of Venezuela. Bot. Mus. Leafl. Harvard Univ. **24(10)**: 275–335.

Zeven, A. C. 1967. The semi-wild oil palm and its industry in Africa. Ph.D. Dissertation. University of Wageningen, Wageningen, The Netherlands.

Domestication of the Pejibaye Palm (*Bactris gasipaes*): Past and Present

CHARLES R. CLEMENT

Table of Contents

Abstract

The *Guilielma* taxon (here considered a sub-genus of *Bactris*) probably originated in northwestern South America. By the Pleistocene species of this taxon were distributed along the Andes foothills from Bolivia to Panama. One of these species, or hybrids between several of them, gave rise to the pejibaye, which was then domesticated by the Amerindians. During the course of centuries, the pejibaye has become the most domesticated palm in the Americas, as attested by the great diversity of names, uses and fruit sizes. The principal use was of the starchy fruit, cooked for direct human consumption, fermented to make chicha, or ground and dried to make flour. Considerable genetic diversity and different Amerinidan preferences have given rise to many distinct pejibaye races, varying in fruit size, shape and composition. A summary of what is known about the Amazonian races is presented. Potential modern uses are directed at further exploitation of some Amerindian uses and refinements of these: (1) heart of palm or palmito and fruit (2) for direct human consumption, (3) for animal ration, (4) for flour and meal, and (5) for oil. The economic potential of each of these is mentioned. The breeding programs in Costa Rica and Brazil are outlined and preliminary plant ideotypes for each breeding objective are presented. The pejibaye has high immediate potential and will be even more useful once the breeding programs now underway are producing selected planting material. International support for these research programs is required however.

Key words: pejibaye, taxonomy, origin, domestication, potential, ideotype

Resumo

A taxon *Guilielma* (aqui considerado um sub-gênero de *Bactris*) provavelmente originou no noroeste da America do Sul. Até o Pleistoceno, espécies desta taxon foram distribuidas ao longo do sopé dos Andes de Bolivia a Panama. Uma destas espécies, ou híbridos entre varias delas, deu origem à pupunha, que foi domesticada pelos Amerindios. Durante o decorrer dos séculos a pupunha se tornou a palmeira mais domesticada nas Américas, como testemunha a grande diversidade de nomes, usos e tamanhos dos frutos. Seu uso principal foi como fruto amidoso, cozido para consumo direto, fermentado para fazer chicha, ou moido e secado para fazer farinha. Uma grande diversidade genética e variadas preferencias indígenas deram origem a muitas raças distintas de pupunha, que variam no tamanho, forma e composição do fruto. Um resumo do que se sabe sobre as raças Amazonicas é apresentado. Os usos potenciais modernos são dirigidos à exploração mais ampla dos usos indígenas: (1) palmito e fruto (2) para consumo humano direto, (3) para ração animal, (4) para farinha, e (5) para óleo. O potencial econômico de cada um destes è mencionado. Os programas de melhoramento de Costa Rica e Brasil são delineados e ideotipos preliminares para cada objetivo são apresentados. A pupunha tem um alto potencial imediato e isto será maior quando os programas de melhoramento estarão produzindo material seleccionado. Porém, se requer ajuda financeira internacional para estes programas.

I. Introduction

The pejibaye palm (*Bactris gasipaes* H.B.K.) was domesticated by the Amerindians in the lowland humid neotropics. Patiño (1963) traced early European contact with this palm, noting many reports of its usefulness and importance both to Amerindians and to early explorers. He lists dozens of common names; there may have been as many as one per tribe in areas where it was most important. After the arrival of the Europeans, however, the use of and knowledge about pejibaye faded, with only the peasants still aware of its great usefulness and nutritional potential.

The widely cited article of Popenoe and Jimenez (1921) was responsible for awakening modern interest in the pejibaye. There was little research activity, however, until sporadic efforts began in the fifties and sixties in Costa Rica, Colombia and Brazil. The current surge in research started in the early seventies and received international stimulus from the NAS (1975) booklet on underexploited tropical plants. This research effort has since become more international in scope, attracting researchers from the above mentioned countries and Bolivia, Ecuador, Panama, Peru and the United States as well.

Current pejibaye research is concerned with accumulating genetic resources, genetic improvement and industrialization possibilities. The first two topics have led to considerable interest in the origin and domestication of the species, since an enormous amount of genetic improvement was achieved by the people who originally domesticated the pejibaye. The search for origins is complicated by the vague taxonomic status of the pejibaye, so that the definition of its origin is dependent upon clarification of its taxonomic status. For these reasons the first section of this paper summarizes the taxonomic status of the species and its close relatives. The second section presents the little information available upon which a center of origin may be hypothesized.

The Andean foothills and adjacent hylea, where mild pejibaye and its close relatives are concentrated, have the ecological conditions that favor the development of genetic diversity. This genetic diversity formed the basis for the domestication of the pejibaye, but this required an appropriate cultural system as well. Upon examination, the major agricultural system in the Amazon basin is found to contain the spatial, genetic and cultural elements necessary to account for the extensive domestication of the pejibaye. Genetic diversity in modern times is arrayed in the region as a large number of landraces, many of which are described in the third section of this paper.

This species may be used in various ways to contribute to the long-term sustained development of the humid tropics: (1) as heart of palm or palmito and as fruit (2) for direct human consumption, (3) for animal ration, (4) for flour and meal, and (5) for oil (Clement & Mora-Urpí, 1984). The economic potential of each of these potential uses is discussed in section V. The modern domestication effort, generally known as plant breeding, is just starting with pejibaye, and a review of the preliminary plant ideotypes for each potential use is presented in the final section.

The need for research in all areas discussed becomes evident with the reading of this paper and many of the points raised still cannot be resolved conclusively. Further advances are needed in all the areas discussed in this paper and will require the dedicated attention of a group of researchers and the support of national and international organizations.

II. Taxonomy of *Guilielma*

The pejibaye is a caespitose, monoecious palm. The 2–15 stems are 10–30 cm in diameter, densely armed with black spines (rarely unarmed), and may attain heights of 20–25 m. There are 15–25 pinnate fronds in the crown, which vary from 3 to 4 m in length, of which 1–1.5 m is spiny petiole, with 200–300 pinnae arranged in groups of 2–13 and inserted at diverse angles along the rachis. The inflorescence is axillar, 50–80 cm in length, with 20–60 rachillae (each 20–30 cm long) which support the 50–1000 pistillate and 10,000–30,000 staminate flowers. The fruit is a drupe, variable in shape (obovoid to cordiform is most common), in size (2–7 cm in length by 1.5–7 cm in diameter), weight (4–200+ g), skin color (red, yellow, orange), and mesocarp composition. The seed is 1–2 cm long, with a three-pored woody endocarp.

The genus *Bactris* contains between 197 (Glassman, 1972) and 239 (Moore, 1973) described species. There are several sub-generic taxa within the genus, most of which were originally described as separate genera. The status of the *Guilielma* taxon, which has had pejibaye and a varying number of other species attributed to it, has been controversial for some time. In this paper I shall consider *Guilielma* as a sub-genus, following MacBride (1960).

Humboldt, Bonpland and Kunth (1816, cited by Glassman, 1972) described the pejibaye for the first time as *Bactris gasipaes*, based on plants found along the Magdalena River, Colombia. A few years later Martius (1824) described *Guilielma*, using as a type species a sample of pejibaye, which he named *G. speciosa*, found in what is today Maranhão, Brazil. For Martius there were enough differences between his type species and other *Bactris* species to warrant a new genus.

D'Orbigny (1847) collected *Guilielma insignis* in the Bolivian Amazon, which Martius included in the new genus. According to Mora Urpí (1984), who has observed both *B. gasipaes* in eastern Amazonia and *G. insignis* in Bolivia, there are great similarities between these taxa. He implies that *G. insignis* may have contributed a large part of the genome of the eastern Amazonian *B. gasipaes*. Martius (d'Orbigny, 1847) also included in *Guilielma, G. macana,* from the region of Maracaibo, Venezuela, which is vegetatively smaller than *G. insignis* and *B. gasipaes.*

Triana (1854, cited by Glassman, 1972) described *G. chontaduro* in Colombia, and Oersted (1858, ibid.) described *G. utilis* in Costa Rica. Karsten (1857, ibid.) added several new, small-statured species to the taxon: *G. granatensis* from northern Colombia; *G. piritu* from northern Colombia and Venezuela; and *G. tenera* from the Magdalena River, Colombia.

The nineteenth century also saw several species transferred from *Bactris* to *Guilielma* by Wendland (1878, cited by Glassman, 1972): *G. caribaea* (Karsten) Wendl. from northern Colombia and Venezuela, and *G. ciliata* (Ruiz & Pavon) Wendl. from Peru. Wendland also transferred Karsten's *G. granatensis* out of *Guilielma* into *Bactris.*

Barbosa Rodrigues (1898, 1903) described *G. mattogrossensis,* from northern Mato Grosso, Brazil, and hypothesized that the new species might be a parent of *B. gasipaes,* although he stated that it was different from both *B. gasipaes* and *G. insignis.* In a later publication, based on material growing in the Botanical Gardens at Rio de Janeiro, Barbosa Rodrigues (1907) transferred *G. mattogrossensis* to *B. coccinea* (in *Bactris* sensu stricto).

Huber (1904) described *G. microcarpa* from the head waters of the Purus and Acre Rivers in Brazil and the Ucayali River in Peru. The species is clearly a *Guilielma.* Huber suggested, however, that *G. microcarpa* might be merely a distinct population of Barbosa Rodrigues' *G. mattogrossensis,* rather than a new species, although Barbosa Rodrigues' changes of name later invalidated this, since *B. coccinea* would not be closely enough related to be considered parental. Huber modified Barbosa Rodrigues' origin hypothesis by suggesting that *B. gasipaes* was of hybrid origin, with *G. microcarpa* and *G. insignis* as possible parental species.

At the beginning of the twentieth century the *Guilielma* taxon contained 12 species, several of which were synonymous. Burret (1934) questioned the validity of some of these species. He supported Wendland's transfer of *G. granatensis* and *G. piritu* to *Bactris,* and he transferred *G. tenera* to *Pyrenoglyphis.* Burret recognized seven species, *G. gasipaes, G. utilis, G. microcarpa, G. insignis, G. ciliata, G. macana* and *G. caribaea,* as valid members of this taxon.

MacBride (1960) placed *Guilielma* within *Bactris* but suggested that it be maintained as a subgenus. He also reduced the number of species in the taxon by suggesting that *G. microcarpa* is actually the primitive form of *B. gasipaes.*

Glassman (1972) further reduced the taxon. Following Bailey (1930), Glassman recognized *G. speciosa* and *G. utilis* as synonymous with *B. gasipaes* and followed Burret (1934) by recognizing the synonymy of these with *G. chontaduro.* These four names are widely recognized today as being synonymous with *B. gasipaes,* the generally recognized name. Some botanists, however, continue to use *G. speciosa* (e.g.,

Table I

Probably valid species of the *Guilielma* taxon (genus *Bactris*), with probable synonyms. Those thought to be synonyms are indented under the valid species; those thought to be invalid are separated by a line

---

B. gasipaes Humboldt, Bonpland & Kunth
    G. speciosa Martius
    G. utilis Oersted
    G. chontaduro Triana
    G. microcarpa Huber = *B. dahlgreniana* Glassman
B. insignis (Martius) Baillon
B. ciliata (Ruiz & Pavon) Martius

B. macana (Martius) Pitter
B. caribaea Karsten

    G. tenera Karsten = *B. maraja* Martius
    G. piritu Karsten to *Bactris* sensu stricto
    G. granatensis Karsten to *Bactris* sensu stricto

Schultes, 1984) or *G. gasipaes* (H.B.K.) Bailey (e.g., Prance, 1984). Glassman (1972) suggested the synonymy of *G. tenera* with *B. maraja* Martius. He changed the name of *G. microcarpa* to *B. dahlgreniana*.

Dugand (1976), arguing from geographical distribution, suggested that *B. caribaea* is synonymous with *B. macana*. However, sympatry is known to exist for palm species (e.g., Lleras et al., 1984), even in those which hybridize readily, so that synonymy based on geographic distribution alone is of questionable value.

Table I summarizes the probably valid species and their probable synonyms. Huber's (1904) hypothesis and MacBride's (1960) position support the notion that *G. microcarpa* and *B. gasipaes* are synonymous, although Prance (1984) did not agree. Clement (1985) used discriminant analysis, with 40 morphological characters, to study these two taxa. He found continuous variation between them, suggesting that they are not separate species, although neither the number nor botanical usefulness of these characters are sufficient to make a categorical statement. It may be useful to maintain *microcarpa* as a sub-species of *B. gasipaes*.

While Martius did not recognize *B. ciliata* as a member of the taxon, possibly because he never had first hand experience with it, Wendland (1878, cited by Glassman, 1972), Burret (1934) and Prance (1984) have recognized it as valid. Dugand's (1976) position on the synonymy of *B. macana* and *B. caribaea* is unconvincing and they are kept apart in accordance with Burret

(1934) and Glassman (1972). However, a detailed study of *Bactris* in northern Colombia and Venezuela is urgently needed to clarify these and other points.

In recent years several new taxa have been observed. Unfortunately, none of these have been intensively studied nor described by botanists. I will follow Mora-Urpí (1984) and Mora-Urpí and Clement (1985) in designating these new taxa as races.

V. Patiño (Mora-Urpí & Clement, 1981) has long known of an Andean race that he equates with *B. gasipaes*. This may be Karsten's *G. chontaduro* Triana, variety *chichagui* (1857, cited by Burret, 1934; Glassman, 1972). Called Chinamato in Colombia, it occurs along the western flank of the Andes from northern Ecuador to northern Colombia, as well as in the Cauca and Magdalena valleys, and has quite small fruit. Both the Colombian and Costa Rican germplasm banks have samples for study.

Patiño and Mora-Urpí (Mora-Urpí & Clement, 1981) found a race in the eastern Andean foothills of Ecuador, above 1500 m. The race shows many characteristics of *Guilielma* but is clearly different from *B. gasipaes,* being smaller in all vegetative characteristics, similar in stature to *B. macana*.

In 1984, the US AID-sponsored *B. gasipaes* germplasm expeditions found a race along the Río Tigre, in Loreto, Peru. This Tigre race appears to be *Guilielma* in both vegetative and fruit characteristics (Mora-Urpí & Clement, 1985), though of smaller stature and different seed shape.

The same expeditions found a race along the upper Río Putumayo, in Colombia. This Nariño race is apparently *Guilielma* (Mora-Urpí & Clement, 1985), but smaller in stature. J. Mora Urpí (pers. comm.) reports that there were indications of introgression between this race and the local landrace of *B. gasipaes*. V. Patiño has suggested to J. Mora-Urpí (pers. comm.) that this race may extend up the eastern flanks of the Andes in Colombia and possibly Ecuador.

J. Mora-Urpí (pers. comm.) has also found a race in the Darién region of Panama with some characteristics of Chinamato but smaller. There are also rumors of wild pejibayes in the Talamanca foothills of southeastern Costa Rica, and in Nicaragua.

Given the great area occupied by *Guilielma* and the number of recent possible additions to the taxon, it is probable that more taxa remain to be discovered. Some of these appear to introgress with *B. gasipaes* (e.g., the Nariño race) and/ or with other species of the taxon. This increases both variability and the difficulty of specific classification. Further definition of species and synonyms in *Guilielma* will require much more study, especially of variability within each taxon. Most of the species named, generally with only one or a few examples from one local population having provided the basis for the specific description, have received very little study. *Bactris gasipaes* is extremely variable (Mora-Urpí, 1984; Mora-Urpí & Clement, 1985), as is evident from the number of specific descriptions of it. It is therefore obvious that an understanding of phylogenetic relationships within this taxon must rest upon extensive collections and genetic experimentation, neither of which are available for most of the species. A detailed revision of *Guilielma,* and of *Bactris* in general, is urgently needed, not only to resolve taxonomic controversy, but to better orient the geneticists and biologists currently working with the group.

III. Origin and Evolution of Pejibaye

Moore and Uhl (1973, 1982) discuss evolutionary trends in Palmae. A few of their conclusions may be applied to the *Guilielma* taxon as a unit within *Bactris* and to the position of *B. gasipaes* within *Guilielma*. Only *B. gasipaes* has received critical attention, so that the following comments can not be used to resolve the questions raised in the discussion of *Guilielma* taxonomy.

Moore and Uhl (1973) point out a trend in chromosome number within the Palmae, from 18 to 13, stating that $n = 15$ is characteristic of the advanced Bactridae. Mora-Urpí and Solis (1980) have shown that the Costa Rican pejibaye karyotype has $n = 14$, suggesting that pejibaye, and possibly *Guilielma* as a whole, is more advanced than the other bactrids. A karyotypic survey of *Guilielma* and *Bactris* would allow firmer conclusions to be drawn.

Moore and Uhl (1982) suggested many evolutionary trends in the Palmae. Whether or not these may be extrapolated to the generic level is not clear. Assuming that this extrapolation is valid for plant and inflorescence size (with intermediate sizes as primitive and large and small as derived), *Bactris* shows clear evidence of following both a trend towards large size, i.e., *Guilielma,* and towards dwarfism, i.e., *Yuyba* (Bailey, 1947). This extrapolation assumes that a species like *B. maraja* (Martius) is the ancestral type. Even within *Guilielma* there is a clear size differential between *B. gasipaes, B. insignis, B. ciliata* and *B. macana, B. caribaea,* with the first three consistently larger.

If this extrapolation is permissible we may also hypothesize that the *macana* types are more primitive and that their present distribution may indicate the center of origin of *Guilielma*. Examination of Figure 1 shows that both *B. macana* and *B. caribaea* occur in the extreme northnorthwest of South America. However, if we add the undescribed Nariño, Tigre and Ecuadorian races to this list of more primitive *Guilielma,* the possible center of origin becomes much larger and more diffuse, and simply corresponds with Moore's (1973) suggestion that northwestern South America may be the center of origin of Palmae.

If *Guilielma* originated in northwestern South America, it then spread southward along what are today the Andes. The larger species of the taxon occur along both sides of the Andes, although principally on the east, in the foothills and adjacent hylea. The only taxon besides *B. gasipaes* that extends significantly into the hylea is *G. microcarpa*. The Chinamato race occurs within the area hypothesized as the center of origin of the taxon and may indicate that this is the more primitive type within *B. gasipaes*.

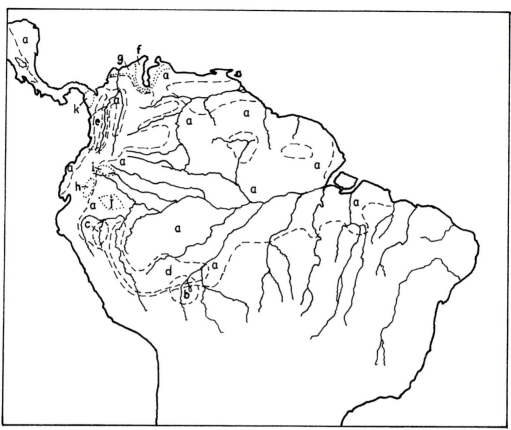

FIG. 1.   Modern distribution of the members of the *Guilielma* taxon (genus *Bactris*) in the neotropics. Dashed lines represent the taxa with large stature: a. *B. gasipaes*; b. *B. insignis*; c. *B. ciliata*; d. the *microcarpa* taxon (*B. dahlgreniana*); and e. Chinamato (? *B. gasipaes,* var. *chichagui*). Dotted lines represent the taxa with smaller stature: f. *B. macana*; g. *B. caribaea*; h. Ecuadorian race; i. Nariño race; j. Tigre race; and k. Darien race.

However, all other taxa suggested as possible parents of pejibaye, either monophyletically or polyphyletically, are found south of this area.

Mora-Urpí (1984) wrote about speciation in *Guilielma*; he suspects that floral biology is an important determinant of population isolation. Mora-Urpí and Solis (1980) have shown that very small curculionid beetles are the principal pollinators in Costa Rica, and Mora-Urpí (1982) has shown that similar curculionid beetles are pollinating pejibaye in Bolivia and around Manaus, Brazil. These beetles may have a flight autonomy of only 100–200 m when leaving any tree (Mora-Urpí & Solis, 1980). Combined with a short pollen viability period, effective pollen flux within populations is limited, unless other minor pollinators (e.g., bees) play a significant role, which is thought unlikely. Seed dispersal has not been

studied in detail but is thought to be quite limited also. If these data and hypotheses are correct then effective population size, sensu Wright (1978), is limited and each sub-population is easily isolated.

Mora-Urpí (1984) states that geographic barriers between populations can be as small as a major river, and that *Guilielma* populations separated by even small mountain ranges and savanna areas in northwestern South America are clearly distinct, which suggests that the floral biology, pollen and seed dispersal hypotheses are essentially valid. Once isolated, small populations are subject to random genetic drift and inbreeding, that may rapidly change gene frequencies (Grant, 1981; Wright, 1978). This may be illustrated by the differences in fruit size in *G. microcarpa,* where the Acre race has much smaller fruit than the Ucayali race (Mora-Urpí & Clement, 1985). Allopatric speciation does not always create genetic isolation (Grant, 1981), so that hybridization, and especially introgression, between populations is not necessarily inhibited.

If isolation of populations in *Guilielma* occurs by restricted pollen and seed dispersal, it is more probable that single pollen grains or seeds would migrate from one population to the next, rather than large quantities of either. The former case would lead to introgressive hybridization, while the latter could lead to much more extensive population hybridization. Mora-Urpí (1984) implies that introgressive hybridization may be quite common in *Guilielma,* which would explain much of the diversity found in primitive and advanced species, and in landraces of pejibaye itself.

The origin of pejibaye has been alluded to several times in the previous section, with some authors suggesting its origin in *G. microcarpa* (e.g., MacBride, 1960) and others suggesting a hybrid origin (Huber, 1904; Mora-Urpí, 1979, 1984). As mentioned above, Clement (1985) observed continuous variation from the smallest *G. microcarpa* to largest *B. gasipaes* in a discriminant analysis, apparently supporting the monophyletic origin hypothesis implied by MacBride (1960). If the *G. microcarpa* hypothesis proves to be correct (and the Chinamato race is merely another primitive landrace), or if Huber's hybrid origin is correct, the center of origin of the species can be located rather precisely: southeastern Peru and northeastern Bolivia. This corresponds rather well with Vavilov's (1951) South American center of origin, in which he includes pejibaye. Others who support this area as a center of origin include Seibert (1950), Lathrap (1970) and Prance (1984).

Mora-Urpí (1979) supported Huber's hypothesis, without specifically accepting *G. microcarpa* as one of the parents. In a later study, Mora-Urpí (1984) suggests that pejibaye may have originated more than once, at different places, through different hybridizations. This hypothesis takes into account the existence of the Chinamato race, *G. microcarpa* and other species and races that are similar to *B. gasipaes,* and the differences between the Amazonian and Occidental racial groups of pejibaye, which will be discussed below. Mora-Urpí (1984) also cites the presence of primitive segregants in otherwise advanced land-

races of pejibaye, specifically Chinamato type fruit in the Costa Rican pejibaye populations. Introgression between species could also explain the presence of these segregants, however, especially if the rumors of primitive, wild races are eventually proved to be correct.

Confirmation of one of these positions will come as a result of further exploration of *Guilielma* in South America and study of the variability already present in the three main pejibaye germplasm collections. Cytogenetic studies in Costa Rica and isoenzyme studies in Brazil will play a major role in resolving this controversy. Whichever hypothesis is finally proved correct, it is certain that the Amerindians found a variable and useful palm when they arrived in South America. The continued evolution of pejibaye then becomes intimately intertwined with its progressive domestication.

IV. Domestication of Pejibaye

By the end of the last glaciation *Guilielma* was amply distributed along the Andes foothills and adjacent lowland areas. It is probable that several taxa had been restricted to some of the refuges suggested by Prance (1973, 1977) and Simpson and Haffer (1978). As seed dispersal is probably limited, the taxa were probably in geographic expansion when the Amerindians found them. Where this first happened will probably never be known, but three likely areas are the Ucayali River valley of Peru (where *G. microcarpa* occurs), the Bolivian Amazon (where *B. insignis* occurs) and the Pacific coast and Cauca River valley of Colombia (where the Chinamato race occurs). I am suggesting these areas because of the variability observed in those modern populations, parts of which would surely be attractive to hunter-gatherers and the first farmers.

Sauer (1958) has suggested that pejibaye was domesticated for its starch. However, although the more primitive pejibayes contain reasonable amounts of starch, they are also relatively rich in oils and carotene. The oilier, higher carotene fruit would make a more energy rich food than the starchier types, which suggests that pejibaye may have first attracted attention for these qualities and only later become an important source of starch. Patiño (1963) reports that all parts of the plant were used in various ways. Table II presents many of these uses.

Table II

Pre-Colombian uses of pejibaye (*Bactris gasipaes*) as reported by Patiño (1963)

Roots: medicine (vermicide)
Stem: bows, arrows, fishing poles, harpoons, flooring and paneling for habitations
Spines: needles
Leaves: thatch, basketry
Heart of palm: vegetable
Flowers (male): ingredient in flavorings
Fruits (cooked): direct consumption, fermented to make chicha (a nutritious, slightly alcoholic gruel),
     ground and dried to make flour, cooked with meat or fish, etc.
Seed: direct consumption as nut

Whatever the reasons for its domestication, this must have happened early in the occupation of the tropical lowlands, because the difference between the primitive pejibayes (e.g., *G. microcarpa,* fruit size 4.4 g) and the most advanced landraces (e.g., Putumayo, 100.8 g) is enormous. In this discussion I define primitive forms as being small-fruited, with an oilier mesocarp and generally spiny stems, and advanced forms as being large-fruited, with starchier mesocarp and frequently less spiny stems. For fruit size the difference between primitive and advanced is about 2000%. A change of this magnitude takes considerable time and requires specific breeding conditions, since pejibaye is allogamous.

The domestication process may have started with the hunter-gatherers planting a few seeds around the areas that they visited most frequently and along their hunting trails. This stage of the domestication process still occurs among the Indians of the Xingú River, for example (Posey, 1984). Lathrap (1977) suggests that the next step in domestication is the inclusion of the species in the house gardens maintained around the first fixed habitation sites, and specifically includes pejibaye as a component of these house gardens. As agriculture developed in different areas, the pejibaye was introduced into the swidden crop mix, where it remained productive for many years as the swidden reverted to fallow. The swidden agricultural system appears to have the specific characteristics necessary for a relatively rapid advance under selection, and Table III notes the importance of its special qualities for the improvement process.

Kerr and Clement (1980) showed that the Ticuna Indians (Leticia, Colombia) have a tribal policy which may be paraphrased as follows: all fruit, or other edible product, that is especially large or flavorful, should be distributed among tribal members and the seed planted. In modern terms, this is mass selection, a basic, powerful breeding method (Simmonds, 1979).

The swidden breeding process appears to work as follows: a few seed from two or three selected plants are planted in a new swidden, and random genetic drift will determine the alleles present; cross and self-pollination will occur within the clearing, isolated from other plants [remember that pejibaye pollen flux is probably limited to

Table III

Characteristics of swidden agriculture that make it especially efficient as a plant breeding system for allogamous perennial species, like pejibaye (*Bactris gasipaes*)

1. Small plots, 1 to 3 hectares
   1.a. Limits population size
2. Small population size, 5 to 20 individuals
   2.a. Favors genetic drift
3. Individuals selected from limited number of parents
   3.a. Favors inbreeding
4. Plot isolation
   4.a. Limits immigration of foreign genes
5. Short duration, 3–10 years
   5.a. Each swidden is a generation
   5.b. No generation overlap within the swidden

Table IV

Provisional classification of pejibaye (*Bactris gasipaes*) landraces in the Amazon basin, following
Mora Urpí & Clement (1985)

Racial group	Landrace	Location	Approximate weight (g)
Microcarpa			10–20
	Juruá	Amazonas, Brazil	20
	Pará	Pará, Brazil	20
Mesocarpa			25–65
	Pastaza	Ecuador	25
	Pampa Hermosa	Loreto, Peru	35
	Solimões	Amazonas, Brazil	45
	Inirida	Inirida, Colombia	60
Macrocarpa			70–120
	Putumayo	Putumayo, Colombia	100
		Amazonas, Brazil	
		Loreto, Peru	
		Ecuador	
	Vaupés	Vaupés, Colombia	115
		Amazonas, Brazil	

about 200 m (Mora Urpí & Solis, 1980)]; inbreeding, combined with drift, may fix favorable alleles; and, finally, the best plants in the swidden will be selected to start a new generation in a new swidden. If there are 20 plants in each swidden and two are selected to form the next generation (selection intensity of 10%), it will take about 1000 years to achieve the 2000% change in fruit size noted above. This rough calculation assumes that fruit size has a narrow-sense heritability of 0.25 [as in the oil palm, *Elaeis guineensis* Jacq. (Ooi, 1975)], that there is sufficient variability present to start with, that there is no generational overlap caused by using the same parent trees (e.g., from the village) in successive swiddens, and that there is no migration from less advanced populations. Since the last three assumptions are surely not valid, the time necessary to achieve the mentioned improvement would be much greater. The example does show, however, that the system could work relatively rapidly.

The domestication and selection process outlined above, combined with ample genetic variability due to introgression with related species, allowed the selection of numerous landraces of pejibaye. Genetic variability was probably also enhanced by trade, tribal migration and even warfare. Additionally, different tribes certainly had differing agricultural abilities and differing preferences with respect to fruit quality, all of which have determined the landraces found to-

day. In the following discussion I will use the word selection, without qualification, to signify the change in pejibaye fruit and other characters brought about by the processes outlined above, including random drift, and natural and artificial selection.

Mora-Urpí and Clement (1985) summarized the information on the distribution of the landraces of pejibaye left by the Amerindians in the Amazon basin, some of which are still being improved by the tribes that live with them. They proposed a classification based on fruit size, since, of the 40 characters measured, this was the one most affected by selection. Table IV lists these landraces and their respective fruit sizes.

The small-fruited or "microcarpa" landraces are the most primitive, being little modified from wild populations such as *G. microcarpa*, the Chinamato race or the closely related *B. insignis*.

The Juruá landrace, found in the vicinity of Cruzeiro do Sul, Acre, Brazil, is characterized by small fruit, with frequently high oil and carotene levels. The tree produces medium sized bunches and has very spiny stems. It has some characteristics of the "mesocarpa" Solimões landrace, and may contain parts of this genome by way of migration along the Juruá River, which connects these two landraces and had Amerindian populations along the entire distance.

The Pará landrace is found along the lower Amazon River, from near Manaus to the mouth of the Amazon. The extent to which it occurs, both north and south of the main river and along the tributaries, is unknown, but is assumed to extend to the southern limits of pejibaye distribution (Figs. 1, 3). The fruit are small, frequently oily, and mostly very fibrous. The tree produces medium size bunches, and has spiny to very spiny stems. This landrace appears to contain parts of the *B. insignis* genome and may have reached its present distribution by spreading along the Madeira River, which connects Bolivia to the Amazon. This is the landrace that Martius described as *G. speciosa.*

The "mesocarpa" landraces have all been completely domesticated and many show the results of intensive selection. There is a gradation from more primitive to more advanced within the group, suggesting the transitional nature of these "mesocarpa" landraces.

The most primitive of the "mesocarpa" landraces is the Pastaza race, occurring in the central-eastern Ecuadorian Andean foothills and adjacent hylea. The fruits are small (averaging about 25 g), frequently oily, and somewhat fibrous. The tree produces small to medium size bunches, and has very spiny stems.

The Pampa Hermosa landrace is found in the area of Yurimaguas, Alto Amazonas, Peru. It has medium size fruit (averaging 35 g), moderate amounts of oil, moderate to high levels of starches and moderate to low levels of fiber. The tree produces medium to large bunches and frequently has spineless stems. The Yurimaguas area appears to be the site of extensive cultivation and moderate to intensive selection. There are indications of several races in the region and Yurimaguas itself appears to be an ancient hybrid population. The whole region is characterized by selection against spines on the stem, with some almost completely spineless sub-populations.

The Solimões landrace occurs along the Solimões (middle Amazon) River in Brazil, extending from east of Leticia, Colombia, to west of Manaus, Brazil. It has medium to large size fruit (averaging 45 g), moderate amounts of oil, high starch and low fiber levels. The tree produces medium to large bunches, and has moderately spiny stems with occasional spineless plants. The distribution of this landrace appears to coincide precisely with the presence of the Omagua Indians (Lathrap, 1970) who may have selected for its specific qualities. It is also the landrace that Bates (1962) described at Ega (now Tefé) as being

much superior to the pejibaye at Belém (of the Pará landrace). There appears to be introgression with neighboring landraces, with larger, starchier fruit in the western part of the landrace (introgression with "macrocarpa" Putumayo landrace?) and smaller, oilier, more fibrous fruit in the east (introgression with "microcarpa" Pará landrace?).

The final "mesocarpa" landrace is the Inirida, which occurs along the Inirida River in the Colombian Amazon and may extend into Venezuela. It is characterized by medium to large fruit (averaging 65 g), low oil and fiber levels, and high to very high starch levels. The tree produces medium to large bunches, and has spiny stems, with occasional plants showing reduced spininess. The most important diagnostic character, however, is fruit shape. Most pejibayes have obovoid to cordiform fruit shape, generally longer than wide; the Inirida fruit has a clearly truncated base and greatly widened maximum diameter, making it always wider than long. Figure 2a–d contrasts the "mesocarpa" fruit outlines.

The "macrocarpa" landraces are the pinnacle of pejibaye domestication and selection. These are the very starchy, very large fruit that must have influenced Sauer's (1958) suggestion that pejibaye was domesticated for starch. Fruit size ranges from 50 to 200 g, with occasional even larger fruit on very small bunches.

The Putumayo landrace occurs along the Putumayo and Caquetá Rivers and around Leticia, Colombia, and adjacent areas of Brazil and Peru, along part of the middle Napo River in Peru and into the Ecuadorian Amazon. The very largest fruit are found around Leticia, Colombia. This landrace is characterized by large fruit (averaging 100 g), with typical pejibaye fruit shape. The fruit is very high in starch, very low in oil and fiber. The tree produces medium to large bunches and frequently has spineless stems. Some Amerindian tribes are still actively selecting for fruit size and spinelessness, e.g., the Hitoto on the Putumayo (Mora Urpí, pers. comm.).

The Vaupés landrace is found along the Vaupés River and its tributaries in the Colombian Amazon and extends east of San Gabriel da Cachoeira, Brazil. It is characterized by large fruit (averaging 115 g), very high starch levels, and very low oil and fiber levels. The tree produces medium size bunches and occasionally has spineless stems. Its most distinctive identifying characteristic is a severely truncated fruit base and apex, which gives the fruit a very deformed appearance. Figure 2e, f contrasts the fruit shapes of the Putumayo and Vaupés landraces. Although the distribution of this landrace appears to coincide with that of the Arawak inhabitants of the region, tribal myths suggest that this pejibaye came from the west (J. Chernela, pers. comm.), as was also observed by Wallace (1853) and Spruce (1908).

From this short description of the Amazonian landraces it is clear that the Amerindians of the region extensively domesticated and selected pejibaye there. Figure 3 shows the distribution of the landraces discussed. The most extensively selected landraces occur in the northwest Amazon, precisely the region that Schultes (1979, 1984) has identified as a center of potential "new" crops. I suggest that this region may be a center of plant domestication, distinct from Vavilov's (1951) South American center of diversity, which is more to the southwest and mostly in the Andes. Pejibaye is only one of the many fruit tree species domesticated there; the number of cassava cultivars is enormous and but little studied (Kerr & Clement, 1980). Other food, medicinal, fiber and ornamental plants are also found in great diversity in this area (Schultes, 1979, 1984).

Mora-Urpí (1984) reports that the pejibaye populations of Central America and the Pacific coast of Colombia show significant differences from the populations already discussed. He proposes two supra-racial groups: the Amazonian or Oriental group and the Occidental group. The Occidental group differs in vegetative characters, such as a longer leaf rachis, larger leaf area, thicker and tougher stems, and tougher and more diverse spines. The fruit, ranging from 25 to 70 g, with an average between 35 and 45 g, are generally starchy, with low fiber and oil levels—all characteristics of "mesocarpa" races. Bunch weights average slightly less than the Amazonian average. Variation in Central America does not appear to be as great as that in Amazonia, with similar fruit types in Costa Rica, Panama and the Colombian Pacific.

Valverde (1986) and Valle (1986) recently studied flower and inflorescence characters using discriminant analysis. They were unable to completely separate the Costa Rican and Panamanian populations of pejibaye, and these showed only a slightly less close relationship with the western Colombian population studied. The Costa Rican and Panamanian populations were shown to be completely distinct from the Brazilian plants studied (mostly collected from the Solimões and Putumayo landraces), but the western Colombian and Brazilian populations showed a closer relationship. One possible explanation for the relationships observed is that there is some genetic migration between the Amazon and the Colombian Pacific, which would support Prance's (1984) and Schultes' (1984) suggestion that pejibaye was taken to Central America via the lower passes in the Andes of northern Ecuador and southern Colombia.

As a final point, Johnson (1983) mentions that there are four extensively domesticated palms: coconut (*Cocos nucifera* L.), date (*Phoenix dactylifera* L.), arecanut (*Areca catechu* L.) and African oil palm (*Elaeis guineensis*). From the extent of domestication and resultant change due to selection shown to exist in the Amazon basin and the number and diversity of the landraces present in only that region, it must be concluded that there are five extensively domesticated palms and that pejibaye may be the most extensively domesticated of them all!

V. Modern Potential

The domestication of pejibaye has resulted in many different types, which have now been defined as landraces. Each landrace appears to differ in fruit composition, as well as macromorphologic characteristics. Fruit composition defines four potential uses of pejibaye. The caespitose growth habit, with numerous lateral stems arising from the bole, defines the fifth potential. These major potential uses are: (1) heart of palm or palmito and fruit (2) for direct human consumption, (3) for animal ration, (4) for flour and meal, and (5) for oil.

Before examining each potential use, fruit mesocarp composition must be mentioned. The major study of fruit chemical composition was done by Arkcoll and Aguiar (1984), using fruit from the Pará, Solimões and Putumayo landraces, although without specifying which, because these had not been identified at that time. The following comments are based on their results and on a summary prepared by Clement and Arkcoll (1985).

Moisture content ranges from 25 to 82%, with

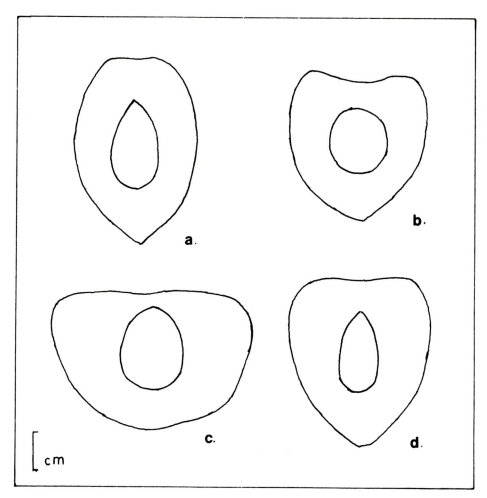

FIG. 2. Fruit shapes of the four "mesocarpa" (a–d) and two "macrocarpa" (e, f) landraces of pejibaye (*Bactris gasipaes*) found in Amazonia by the US AID expeditions (numbers in parentheses are the weights of the fruit shown, in grams): a. Pampa Hermosa (29.3); b. Pastaza (21.3); c. Inirida (60.2); d. Solimões (41.0); e. Vaupés (203.3); and f. Putumayo (148.7).

an average of 55% in Amazonia and 51% in Central America. This is a major problem for most industrial uses of pejibaye, as its removal is expensive. Tracy (1985) has pointed out that most of the analyses were done on market quality fruit, except for Arkcoll and Aguiar (1984), which may mean lower than true averages for most areas. Tracy, for example, found an average of 60% in second-quality fruit processed for animal ration, which is considerably higher than the figures previously reported for Central America.

Protein ranges from 3 to 18% of dry weight, with averages of 6.5% in Amazonia and 6% in Central America. Zapata (1972) determined that most amino acids are present. C. Piedrahita (pers. comm.) found tryptophane, the only essential amino acid previously undetected. Although all essential amino acids are not present in recommended quantities, pejibaye protein is of excellent quality (NAS, 1975).

Oil ranges from 2 to 62% of dry weight, with an average of 23% in the Amazon (principally the Pará landrace) and 9.5% in Central America. Zapata (1972) and Hammond et al. (1982) analyzed the fatty acid composition of several oil samples. They found them rich in oleic acid, averaging nearly 50% of total fatty acids, with an overall insaturation percentage of 63%.

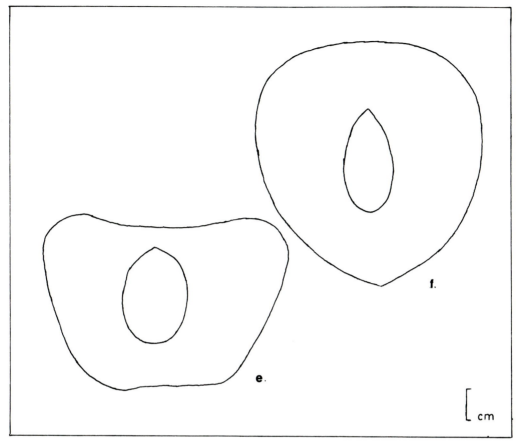

FIG. 2.   Continued.

Carbohydrates range from 14 to 85% of dry weight, with an average of 46% in Amazonia and 78% in Central America. The low average for Amazonia is due to the Pará landrace, with the maximum from the Putumayo landrace.

Fiber ranges from 2 to 18.5% of dry weight, with an average of 13.5% in Amazonia (again the Pará landrace) and 4.5% in Central America.

Carotene, responsible for the yellow to deep orange color of the mesocarp, is the major vitamin present in pejibaye. It ranges from 0 to 70 mg/100 g fresh mesocarp, averaging higher in Amazonia than in Central America. In general, the more primitive landraces have higher carotene levels than the more advanced.

The qualities mentioned in the preceding paragraphs have helped make the pejibaye an important crop in the American tropics. Different combinations of these qualitites lend themselves to different uses. The order of their presentation is determined more by the time and research necessary to attain full potential than by economic returns, which are still very hypothetical.

1. Heart of palm or palmito

This is the major modern agrobusiness based on pejibaye. Camacho and Soria (1970) demonstrated pejibaye's potential for producing this luxury vegetable. Shortly thereafter, Costa Rican agrobusinesses started planting pejibaye and now have more than 2000 ha planted for export. Mora-Urpí et al. (1984) give full agrotechnical details and report that it should be possible to obtain 3 t/ha/year of palmito when the plantation is in full production, generally in the third year after planting. These yield projections are based on improved varieties, good soils and adequate agronomic techniques, especially fertilization (which will be true for all yield figures presented

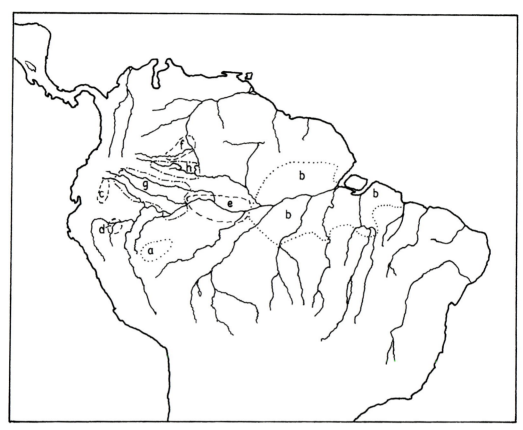

FIG. 3.   Approximate distributions of the pejibaye (*Bactris gasipaes*) landraces found in Amazonia by the US AID expeditions. Dotted lines represent the "microcarpa" landraces: a. Juruá; and b. Pará. Dashed lines represent the "mesocarpa" landraces: c. Pastaza; d. Pampa Hermosa; e. Solimões; and f. Inirida. Dashed and dotted lines represent the "macrocarpa" landraces: g. Putumayo; and h. Vaupés.

in this paper). Experimental results in Brazil have been less encouraging, with yields of 1.2 t/ha/ year in Manaus (Gomes, 1983).

The expansion of the pejibaye palmito industry is limited by competition from *Euterpe oleracea* Martius and *E. edulis* Martius, which are currently harvested in Brazil. *E. oleracea* is especially competitive because it comes from enormous wild populations, is harvested without infrastructure or overhead and is caespitose. The canning factory is taken to the population and local peasants are paid for the palmito delivered at the factory door. The technically managed pejibaye plantations in Costa Rica have full infrastructure, overhead, labor, social and management costs, which raise the price of the final product. Costa Rican quality control permits a better product, but the international market is

not yet sophisticated enough to pay for the difference. This makes marketing difficult and less lucrative than if pejibaye had to compete with another plantation crop.

2. Fruit for direct human consumption

This is the major traditional use of pejibaye. The fruit is separated from the bunch, boiled in salted water for an hour, skinned and pitted and consumed directly. It must be boiled to remove a proteolytic enzyme inhibitor (Murillo et al., 1983) which reduces digestion efficiency, and because of the possible occurrence of oxalic acid (Arkcoll & Aguiar, 1984).

Recently, whole cooked fruit have been canned (peeled and pitted or otherwise) in Costa Rica. Out of season these show a reasonable turnover on supermarket shelves, even though they are generally of inferior quality. The whole fruit may also be thin-sliced or cut into sticks, which are deep fried and salted. In this form they make an excellent snack. The whole fruit may also be used in many meat, poultry and fish recipes (Calvo, 1981).

In Costa Rica the market for fresh fruit is strong, with first quality fruit commanding US$0.50 to US$1.50 per kg at the market and US$0.15 to US$0.25 at the farm gate. In Manaus, Brazil, first quality fruit may sell for slightly more than in Costa Rica because it is rarer, due to the high proportion of Pará landrace fruit, which do not command the price of Solimões fruit.

Clement and Mora-Urpí (1984) have hypothesized that fresh fruit yields may reach 30 t/ha/year in Amazonia and as much as 50 t/ha/year in Costa Rica. About 85% of a bunch is fresh fruit, thus economic yield may range from 25 to 42 t/ha/year. At the lowest farm gate price, this means a possible income of US$3750 to US$6300/ha. Mora-Urpí et al. (1984) give agrotechnical specifications and costs and suggest that fruit plantations reach full production by the fifth year after field planting.

3. Fruit for animal ration

Pejibaye protein quantity and quality, oil and carbohydrate combine to form an excellent base for animal rations. Zumbado and Murillo (1984) and their students have studied many aspects of small-animal nutrition, with pejibaye as the major carbohydrate and energy source. While any fruit can be used to make meal, Tracy (1985) showed that high moisture content significantly raises the cost of drying the fruit. This suggests that only improved (i.e., drier) pejibaye will economically produce animal ration. If dry (30% humidity) fruit could be produced at the same level as fresh market fruit (i.e., 30–50 t/ha/year), yields of 17–30 t/ha of dry meal might be obtained. Zumbado and Murillo (1984) show that animal ration may be made from whole fruit, without peeling or pitting, although it must be heated sufficiently to de-activate the proteolytic enzyme inhibitor.

The use of pejibaye for animal rations may be an attractive economic proposition for many countries in the humid tropics because of low native production of cereals. Although Costa Rica produces adequate maize for human consumption, it imports maize for animal rations. If dry pejibaye fruit could be produced and processed economically it could substitute for some imports, while saving hard currency and providing needed jobs in rural areas (Tracy, 1985).

4. Fruit for flour and meal

This is a traditional use in parts of the Brazilian and Colombian Amazon, supplementing or substituting for cassava meal. The preparation of flour and meal for human consumption is basically similar to the preparation of meal for animal ration, except that the fruit must be pitted. For human consumption high protein levels would be just as important as for animal consumption, while oil levels could be lower and fiber levels need not be changed. Carotene would also be important, especially as it is frequently deficient in tropical diets. Based on fresh market fruit yields, it should be possible to obtain 16–27 t/ha/year of pejibaye flour.

Tracy (1985) studied different baking uses of pejibaye flour. His recent studies (M. Tracy, pers. comm.) showed that 10% pejibaye flour can be used in bread without changing baking characteristics, although it lowered protein levels slightly and raised oil and carotene levels significantly. The light yellow color was very attractive and the taste very agreeable, while not being very different from wheat breads. He also tried cakes and other pastries with excellent results, and tried deep-fried batter chips (similar to batter potato chips) with moderate results. The economic significance of substituting even 10% of wheat importations in moist tropical countries justifies intensive research on this potential use.

5. Fruit for oil

Although oil may have been a quality that attracted the earliest Amerindian pejibaye users, it does not seem to have been selected for in any of the landraces studied to date. In fact, higher oil levels are found in the more primitive landraces and related taxa, always in relatively low frequency. Arkcoll and Aguiar (1984) analyzed more than 300 bunches to find about a dozen with more than 40% oil levels.

The relatively high insaturation levels mentioned make the pejibaye a potential oil crop. In

Table V

Preliminary pejibaye (*Bactris gasipaes*) ideotype for heart of palm

1. Trunk diameter >18 cm	7. Rapid growth, first cut at 1.5 year
2. Leaf rachis length >2.5 m	8. Rapid regrowth, second cut at 1 year
3. Leaf area >3.0 m	9. Resistant to leaf mite
4. High Net Assimilation Rate	10. Good flavor
5. High basal shoot production	11. Yield >3 t/ha/year
6. Spineless petioles	

the humid tropics the African oil palm is rapidly becoming extremely important. Its introduction into the Americas has been hindered by disease (Hartley, 1977), however. One way of insuring against a disease-caused production disaster is to have more than one major oil crop in the humid tropics. Lleras et al. (1984) point out that the palm flora of South and Central America is especially rich in potential oil palms. The best studied indigenous American "oil" palm is the pejibaye, so that it seems reasonable to concentrate research attention on this species.

Clement and Arkcoll (1985) examined pejibaye's oil potential and research needs. They calculate that clonal monoculture of the current best plants could produce slightly more than 2 t/ha/year of oil and 2–3 t/ha/year of protein and carbohydrate rich residue. It is expected that 5 t/ha/year of oil (the current average yield of *Elaeis guineensis*) can be produced within a decade, if adequate resources are allocated to the breeding effort.

For the pejibaye to actually become an important crop, rather than a potentially important crop, the selection efforts of the Amerindians must be continued and modern breeding methods must be used to accelerate the production of varieties that will be high yielding, with high quality fruit or palmito. A first step in these breeding programs is the preparation of a varietal ideotype.

VI. Pejibaye Ideotypes

Clement and Mora-Urpí (1984) discussed Brazilian and Costa Rican breeding plans. Costa Rica is more advanced, since floral biology has been studied (Mora-Urpí & Solis, 1980), some hybridizations have been made and it has the most extensive germplasm collections. Brazil is starting and has done some work on pollen manipulation (Miranda, 1987) and self-compatibility

(Clement & Arkcoll, 1984), and there is a large germplasm collection. Colombia has a large germplasm collection but has not yet organized a breeding effort.

Clement (1986) has outlined many research necessities that will permit early success of the breeding efforts. These include full characterization and evaluation of the major germplasm banks, further prospection of landraces and exploration of unvisited areas, chemical characterization of fruit from promising germplasm, adaptation of methodology to determine growth and physiological parameters, and an increase in phytosanitary research. Financial support is lacking, however, in all countries that consider pejibaye to be a priority.

Planning in these research areas is already underway, and in some cases research has already started. Breeding methodology is currently being studied and crop ideotypes are being drawn up. Ideotypes are the ideal plant types that the breeder has in mind when selecting material for hybridization. Reciprocal recurrent selection (Simmonds, 1979) has many advantages for pejibaye breeding, since the different landraces could function as the base populations in this methodology. A wide selection of landraces as the basis would insure against an excessively narrow genetic base. A short outline of the ideotypes follows.

The palmito ideotype is the simplest, because only vegetative characters are considered important. Growth, in all its dimensions, is most basic (see Table V). Gomes (1983) reports that seedling growth is extremely variable, as expected from an allogamous species. Some plants are ready for first cutting at one year, while others are not ready at two. First generation selection will favor uniform cutting at less than 1.5 years, with regrowth cutting one year later. High Net Assimilation Rate and large vegetative dimensions should allow yields of 3 t/ha/year.

Table VI

Preliminary vegetative pejibaye (*Bactris gasipaes*) ideotype for fruit production

1. Narrow trunk <16 cm	7. Resistant to leaf mite
2. Annual trunk increment <1 m	8. Resistant to Phytophtera
3. Leaf rachis length <2.5 m	9. Tolerant of infraspecific competition
4. Leaf area >3.0 m	10. High Bunch Index
5. Leaf production >25/year	11. High Net Assimilation Rate
6. Spineless stem and petiole	

Ideotypes of fruit production may be divided into two parts: vegetative and reproductive. Table VI lists the most important elements of the vegetative ideotype. Selection for dwarf vegetative characteristics should mean low vegetative growth rates and should allow rapid advances in selection for Bunch Index (percent dry bunch production to total dry biomass), which measures both yield and tolerance to competition (Breure & Corley, 1983). Dwarfed plants, with competition tolerance, may be planted at higher densities and thus raise yields.

Table VII lists the most important elements of the reproductive ideotypes for each major use. Only slight differences exist in bunch characters. Fruit size is important, as starchy fruit will be larger than oily fruit for the same energetic investment by the plant (Arkcoll & Aguiar, 1984). Whole fruit for direct consumption will be intermediate, as they are expected to have medium oil levels.

Mesocarp composition is what differentiates most between the major uses, with the exception of animal ration and flour and meal fruit types. For direct human consumption, taste and palatability must be considered by each breeding program and are not listed in the table.

The oil ideotype is the most distinctive, as it requires low carbohydrate, fiber, water and carotene with high oil and protein. The high protein is to ensure a strong market for the residue, which should make an excellent base for animal ration or may even serve as a human nutritional supplement. Not listed in Table VII is the ease of oil/starch separation, which will be one of the major research questions when studying fruit composition. Arkcoll and Aguiar (1984) mention that oil separates readily in some pejibayes, but that oil/starch emulsions are the most frequent result of simple hot pressure extraction. If favorably separating germplasm is not available for the oil breeding programs this will raise the

Table VII

Preliminary reproductive pejibaye (*Bactris gasipaes*) ideotypes for whole fruit, animal ration, flour and meal, and oil production

Character	Whole fruit	Animal ration	Flour meal	Oil
Bunch rachis	long	long	long	long
Rachillae #/bunch	>40	>40	>40	>50
Fruit #/bunch	100–200	>100	>100	>200
% fruit/bunch wt.	>85	>90	>90	>85
Fruit size (g)	40–70	>60	>60	>25
% mesocarp	85–95	>95	>95	>90
Mesocarp composition				
% water	35–45	<30	<30	<30
% d.w. protein	>12	>12	>12	>12
% d.w. oil	15–25	10–15	<10	>45
% d.w. carboh.	60–70	>70	>75	<40
% d.w. fiber	3–7	5–10	<5	<10
Carotene[1]	20–70	20–70	20–70	0
Harvest Index	high	high	high	high
Yield (t/ha/year)	>30	>35	>35	>20

[1] Mg/100 g fresh mesocarp.

costs of extraction, since solvent extraction will be necessary. High residue value could offset this extra cost.

First generation fresh bunch yields must be on the order of 30–35 t/ha/year, except for oil (20 t/ha/year), if pejibaye breeding is to be considered successful. This means that growth and physiological parameters must receive careful consideration from the very start of the program, as less than careful selection for these parameters may not produce the desired result.

Perennial crop breeding is a long-term, expensive proposition and great care must be taken in selection of material and the execution of experiments. Hybridization is easy in pejibaye, as floral biology assists the experimenter (Mora-Urpí, 1980). Progeny testing, however, requires large areas, with generally high maintenance costs that are raised even further by the long generation span (five to seven years) of the species. At the moment, long-term financing is not available, either nationally or internationally, so that the pejibaye breeding programs planned in Brazil and Costa Rica are proceeding very slowly. Thus, this species has yet to be tailored to the needs of farmers and agrobusinesses, who will decide whether the pejibaye will become an important tropical crop.

VII. Acknowledgments

The author gratefully acknowledges the help of Dr. Jorge Mora-Urpí (Univ. Costa Rica) for information on related races, discussions of breeding and general criticism of the paper, Dr. William Eberhard (Univ. Costa Rica) for critical reading, numerous helpful suggestions and discussions that greatly improved the first three sections of the manuscript, Dr. Jorge Leon for critical reading of the manuscript, and the editor and anonymous reviewers of *Advances in Economic Botany* for their many helpful suggestions for improving the manuscript.

VIII. Literature Cited

Arkcoll, D. B. & J. P. L. Aguiar. 1984. Peach palm (*Bactris gasipaes* H.B.K.), a new source of vegetative oil from the wet tropics. J. Sci. Food Agric. 35: 520–526.

Bailey, L. H. 1930. Binomials of certain palms. Gentes Herb. 2: 182–199.

———. 1947. Palmae indigenae Trinitenses et Tobagenses. Gentes Herb. 7: 353–445.

Barbosa Rodrigues, J. 1898. Palmae Mattogrossenses, novae vel minus cognitae. Typo. Leuzinger, Rio de Janeiro.

———. 1903. Sertum Palmarum Brasiliensium. Vol. II. Typo. Veuve Monnom, Bruxelles.

———. 1907. Supplementum ad Sertum Palmarum Brasiliensium. Contrib. Jard. Bot. Rio de Janeiro 4: 105–123.

Bates, H. W. 1962. A naturalist on the river Amazon. University of California Press, Berkeley.

Breure, C. J. & R. H. V. Corley. 1983. Selection of oil palms for high density planting. Euphytica 32: 177–186.

Burret, M. 1934. Bactris und verwandte Palmengattungen. Feddes Repert. Spec. Nov. Regni Veg. 34: 167–253.

Calvo, I. M. 1981. Usos culinarios del chontaduro. INCIVA/FES, Cali, Colombia.

Camacho, E. & J. Soria. 1970. Palmito de Pejibaye. Proc. Amer. Soc. Hort. Sci.-Trop. Reg. 14: 122–132.

Clement, C. R. 1985. Analysis of the descriptor lists and a proposal for a new minimum field descriptor list. Pages 34–81 in C. R. Clement & L. Coradin (eds.), Final report, Peach palm (*Bactris gasipaes* H.B.K.) germplasm bank. US AID, project report.

———. 1986. El pejibaye (*Bactris gasipaes* H.B.K.), resultados y necesidades de investigación. Noticiario de Palmeras Utiles de América Tropical (FAO/CENARGEN, Brasília).

——— & D. B. Arkcoll. 1984. Observações sobre autocompatibilidade em pupunha (*Bactris gasipaes* H.B.K., Palmae). Acta Amazonica 14(3/4): 337–342.

——— & ———. 1985. El *Bactris gasipaes* ((H.B.K.) Palmae) como cultivo oleaginoso—potencial y prioridades de investigación. Seminario-Taller sobre Oleaginosas Promisorias, PIRB/INTERCIENCIA, Bogotá.

——— & J. Mora-Urpí. 1984. Pejibaye palm (*Bactris gasipaes*): Multi-use potential for the lowland humid tropics. 23rd Annual Meeting, Society for Economic Botany, College Station, Texas.

Dugand, A. 1976. Palmas de Colombia. Cespedesia 5: 238–273.

Glassman, S. F. 1972. A revision of B. E. Dahlgren's index of American palms. Phanerogamarum monographiae, Tomus VI. J. Cramer, Germany.

Gomes, J. B. M. 1983. Avaliação de caracteristicas agronômicas da pupunheira para produção de palmito. Thesis, Agronomist. Univ. Amazonas, Manaus.

Grant, V. 1981. Plant speciation, 2nd ed. Columbia University Press, New York.

Hammond, E. G., W. P. Pan & J. Mora-Urpí. 1982. Fatty acid composition and glyceride structure of the mesocarp and kernel oils of the pejibaye palm (*Bactris gasipaes* H.B.K.). Rev. Biol. Trop. 30: 90–93.

Hartley, C. W. S. 1977. The oil palm (*Elaeis guineensis* Jacq.), 2nd ed. Longman, London.

Huber, J. 1904. A origem da pupunha. Bol. Mus. Paraense Hist. Nat. **4**: 474–476.

Johnson, D. V. 1983. Multi-purpose palms in agroforestry: A classification and assessment. Int. Tree Crops J. **2**: 217–244.

Kerr, W. E. & C. R. Clement. 1980. Práticas agrícolas com consequências genéticas que possibilitaram aos Indios da Amazônia uma melhor adaptação as condições da região. Acta Amazonica **10**: 251–261.

Lathrap, D. W. 1970. The Upper Amazon. Ancient peoples and places. Vol. 70. Praeger, New York.

——. 1977. Our father the cayman, our mother the gourd: Spinden revisited, or a unitary model for the emergence of agriculture in the New World. Pages 713–751 *in* C. Reed (ed.), Origins of agriculture. Aldine, Chicago.

Lleras, E., D. C. Giacometti & L. Coradin. 1984. Areas críticas de distribución de palmas en las Américas para colecta, evaluación y conservación. Pages 67–101 *in* Palmeras poco utilizados de América Tropical. FAO/CATIE, Turrialba, Costa Rica.

MacBride, J. F. 1960. Flora of Peru, 27. *Bactris.* Pub. Field Mus. Nat. Hist., Bot. Series **13(1)** no. **2**: 403–412.

Martius, C. F. P. 1824. Historia naturalis palmarum. Vol. 2: 81–83. Leipzig, Germany.

Miranda, I. P. A. 1987. Morfologia e aspectos práticos da germinação e do armazenamento do pólen de "pupunha" *Bactris gasipaes* H.B.K. (Arecaceae). M.Sc. Thesis. Inst. Nac. Pesquisas da Amazônia/Fund., Universidade do Amazonas, Manaus, Brazil.

Moore, Jr., H. E. 1973. The major groups of palms and their distribution. Gentes Herb. **11**: 27–141.

—— & N. W. Uhl. 1973. The monocotyledons: Their evolution and comparative biology. VI. Palms and the origin and evolution of monocotyledons. Quart. Rev. Biol. **48**: 414–438.

—— & ——. 1982. Major trends of evolution in palms. Bot. Rev. **48**: 1–69.

Mora-Urpi, J. 1979. Consideraciones sobre el posible origen del pejibaye cultivado. ASBANA (Costa Rica), año 3, **9**: 5, 14–15.

——. 1980. Consideraciones sobre el desarrollo de una técnica de polinización controlada en pejibaye. Agron. Costarr. **4**: 119–121.

——. 1982. Polinización en *Bactris gasipaes* H.B.K. (Palmae): Nota adicional. Rev. Biol. Trop. **30**: 174–176.

——. 1984. El pejibaye (*Bactris gasipaes* H.B.K.): Origen, biología floral y manejo agronómico. Pages 118–160 *in* Palmeras poco utilizados de América Tropical. FAO/CATIE, Turrialba, Costa Rica.

—— & C. R. Clement. 1981. Aspectos taxonómicos relativos al pejibaye (*Bactris gasipaes* H.B.K.). Rev. Biol. Trop. **29**: 139–142.

—— & ——. 1985. Races and populations of peach palm found in the Amazon basin. Pages 107–141 *in* C. R. Clement & L. Coradin (eds.), Final report, Peach palm (*Bactris gasipaes* H.B.K.) germplasm bank. US AID, project report.

—— & E. M. Solis. 1980. Polinización en *Bactris gasipaes* H.B.K. Rev. Biol. Trop. **28**: 153–174.

——, E. Vargas, C. A. Lopez, M. Villaplana, G. Allon & C. Blanco. 1984. The pejibaye palm (*Bactris gasipaes* H.B.K.). FAO, San José, Costa Rica.

Murillo, M., A. Kronenberg, J. Mata, J. Calzada & V. Castro. 1983. Estudio preliminar sobre factores inhibidores de enzimas proteolíticas presentes en la harina del pejibaye. Rev. Biol. Trop. **31**: 227–231.

NAS. 1975. Underexploited tropical plants with promising economic value. National Academy of Sciences, Washington, D.C.

Ooi, S. C. 1975. Variability in the Deli Dura breeding population of the oil palm. II. Within bunch components of oil yield. Malayan Agric. J. **50**: 20–30.

d'Orbigny, C. A. 1847. Voyage dans l'Amerique Meridionale. Vol. 7(3): Botanique, Palmetum Orbignianum. (Descriptions by C. F. P. Martius.) Paris.

Patiño, V. M. 1963. Plantas cultivadas y animales domesticos en América equinoccial. **I**: 97–184. Imp. Dept., Cali, Colombia.

Popenoe, W. & O. Jimenez. 1921. The pejibaye: A neglected food plant of tropical America. J. Hered. **12**: 154–166.

Posey, D. A. 1984. A preliminary report on diversified management of tropical forest by the Kayapó Indians of the Brazilian Amazon. Adv. Econ. Bot. **1**: 112–126.

Prance, G. T. 1973. Phytogeographic support for the theory of Pleistocene forest refuges in the Amazon basin, based on evidence from distribution patterns in Caryocaraceae, Chrysobalanaceae, Dichapetalaceae and Lecythidaceae. Acta Amazonica **3**: 5–18.

——. 1977. The phytogeographic subdivisions of Amazonia and their influence on the selection of biological reserves. Pages 195–213 *in* G. T. Prance & T. S. Elias (eds.), Extinction is forever. New York Botanical Garden, New York.

——. 1984. The pejibaye, *Guilielma gasipaes* (H.B.K.) Bailey, and the papaya, *Carica papaya* L. Pages 85–104 *in* Stone, D. (ed.), Pre-Colombian plant migration. Peabody Mus. Arch. Ethnonol. 76, Harvard University Press, Cambridge.

Sauer, C. O. 1958. Age and area of American cultivated plants. 33rd Congresso Intern'l Americanistas, Vol. **I**: 215–229. San José, Costa Rica.

Schultes, R. E. 1979. The Amazonia as a source of new economic plants. Econ. Bot. **33**: 258–266.

——. 1984. Amazonian cultigens and their northward and westward migration in pre-Colombian times. Pages 19–38 *in* Stone, D. (ed.), Pre-Colombian plant migration. Peabody Mus. Arch. Ethnonol. 76, Harvard University Press, Cambridge.

Seibert, R. J. 1950. The importance of palms to Latin America, pejibaye a notable example. CEIBA **1**: 63–74.

Simmonds, N. W. 1979. Principles of crop improvement. Longman, London.

Simpson, B. B. & J. Haffer. 1978. Speciation patterns in the Amazonian forest biota. Annual Rev. Ecol. Syst. **9**: 497–518.

Spruce, R. 1908. Notes of a botanist on the Amazon and Andes. Vols. 1 and 2. Macmillan, London.

Tracy, M. D. 1985. The pejibaye fruit: Problems and prospects for its development in Costa Rica. M. Sc. Thesis. Univ. Texas at Austin, Austin, Texas.

Valle B., L. M. 1986. Descriptores de la inflorescencia de pejibaye (*Bactris gasipaes* H.B.K.) de cuatro poblaciones y sus implicaciones filogenéticas. Thesis (Licenciatura). Univ. Costa Rica, San Jose, Costa Rica.

Valverde G., M. E. 1986. Descriptores de la flor de pejibaye (*Bactris gasipaes* H.B.K.) en cuatro poblaciones y sus posibles implicaciones filogenéticas. Thesis (Licenciatura). Univ. Costa Rica, San Jose, Costa Rica.

Vavilov, N. I. 1951. The origin, variation, immunity and breeding of cultivated plants (trans. K. S. Chester). Ronald Press, New York.

Wallace, A. R. 1853. Palm trees of the Amazon and their uses. van Voorst, London.

Wright, S. 1978. Evolution and the genetics of populations. Vol. 4. Variability within and among natural populations. University of Chicago Press, Chicago. 580 pp.

Zapata, A. 1972. Pejibaye palm from the Pacific coast of Colombia (a detailed chemical analysis). Econ. Bot. 21: 371–378.

Zumbado, M. & M. Murillo. 1984. Composition and nutritive value of pejibaye in animal feeds. Rev. Biol. Trop. 32: 51–56.

Overview of Palm Domestication in Latin America

LIDIO CORADIN AND EDUARDO LLERAS

Table of Contents

Abstract

A brief review of research being carried out towards domestication of neotropical palms with economic potential is presented. Summaries of the state of the art and current research activities, at a generic level, are given for some of the most important groups: *Acrocomia, Astrocaryum, Bactris* (*Guilielma* complex), *Elaeis, Euterpe,* the *Jessenia/Oenocarpus* complex, *Mauritia,* the *Orbignya/Attalea* complex, *Scheelea, Syagrus* and *Ynesa.* Experience accumulated during the past decade on domestication of palms in Latin America is discussed in light of the conclusions and recommendations arrived at during the recent FAO and PIRB meetings held on neotropical palms and native oil crops. The need to establish data banks and an effective network for the exchange of information is emphasized. It is also concluded that scattered research activities must be encompassed within unified, coherent domestication programs if significant results are expected. Another significant conclusion is that as probably no one country or institution has the resources or manpower to mount and carry out complete programs of this kind on its own, national and international cooperative schemes are essential to the domestication of neotropical palms.

Key words: neotropics, palms, domestication, agricultural research, perennial crops, Latin America

Resumo

Fez-se uma revisão da situação atual das pesquisas presentemente sendo conduzidas no sentido de domesticação das palmeiras neotropicais com potencial econômico. Apresenta-se um resumo das atividades de pesquisa conduzidas atualmente, a nível genérico, para alguns dos grupos de palmeiras mais importantes: *Acrocomia, Astrocaryum, Bactris* (complexo *Guilielma*), *Elaeis, Euterpe,* complexo *Oenocarpus/Jessenia, Mauritia,* complexo *Orbignya/Attalea, Scheelea, Syagrus* e *Ynesa.* Com base nas conclusões e recomendações alcançadas nas recentes reuniões sobre palmeiras neotropicais e oleaginosas nativas promovidas pela FAO e PIRB, discute-se a experiência acumulada durante a última década

sobre a domesticação de palmeiras na América Latina. Enfatiza-se a necessidade do esta-
belecimento de um banco de dados e uma rede efetiva de intercâmbio de informação.
Conclui-se que atividades de pesquisa isoladas devem ser agrupadas em programas de
domesticação unificados e coerentes se resultados significantes são esperados. Conclui-se
também que em virtude de, provavelmente, nenhum país ou instituição possuir os recursos
ou pessoal suficiente para implantar e executar um programa completo, esquemas coope-
rativos a nível nacional e internacional são essenciais para a domesticação de palmeiras
neotropicais.

I. Introduction

Although as far back as the middle of the 19th
century explorers such as Wallace (1853) and
Spruce (1871, 1908) were reporting the potential
of neotropical palms for a variety of uses, interest
in economic exploitation of these resources only
came into its own well into the present century.
Until a little more than ten years ago, palms were
seen only as resources to be exploited, not renewed or cultivated, and practically all attention
was directed to making extractivism more efficient. Furthermore, the sheer bulk of some of the
resources, such as the standing potentials of babassu (*Orbignya phalerata*), moriche (*Mauritia*
spp.) and even macaúba (*Acrocomia* spp.), allied
to the then fairly unaggressive agricultural practices, led to a false sense of security in that these
resources would be available forever, and that
their untapped potential would be a continuous
source of untold wealth. In this context, as recently as 1980, Brazilian newspapers were reporting that babassu could meet 50% of the
world's oil demands!

For all practical purposes, however, the rude
awakening was somewhat earlier. With the oil
crunch of the 1970's, many countries started to
look for renewable sources of energy, and as palms
had been touted as one of the most attractive
alternatives since the 1920's, they looked in that
direction. The situation was alarming. Apart from
some very subjective, overly enthusiastic estimates on yields and standing potentials, and a
few very superficial papers on a handful of species,
practically nothing was known. Surveys, such as
the one carried out for babassu in Maranhão
(INEB, 1981), showed that real potentials were
several orders of magnitude lower than previously postulated. Also, due to a series of complex
factors, traditional extractive exploitation was
stagnating, and, most critical, the massive de-

struction of native vegetation due mainly to the
expansion of a more aggressive mechanized agriculture was rapidly eroding and seriously men-
acing the survival of the palms themselves (i.e.,
Anderson & Anderson, 1983; Lleras & Coradin,
1988; Pick, 1985).

Thus, from the late 1970's to the present, the
issue has not been how to best utilize palm resources, but whether there will be any of these
resources left to utilize at all. With the realization
of this radical change in the situation, it was
obvious that a new approach was mandatory. It
was not enough to look for ways to maximize
efficiency of extractive exploitation, which was
on its way out anyhow, nor was it feasible to plan
exclusively on postulated potentials of native
stands. Alternatives had to be found to establish
well-founded management schemes that would
protect the remaining populations from the encroachment of modern agricultural practices, or
to work towards domestication of the species
involved.

The present paper gives an overview of efforts
towards palm domestication in Latin America
with the purpose of trying to define research needs
and priorities for the future. Two principal aspects have been considered. The first is an assessment of the state of the art for the different
groups of palms, while the second is a description
of coherent efforts at overall domestication of
some of these groups, outlining the basic approaches underlying the same.

II. Status of Research on Some Neotropical Palms

The present section will briefly summarize the
state of the art on research of some of the most
economically important taxa of neotropical
palms. Neither systematics nor biogeography will

be discussed in detail, as these topics have been extensively covered by Lleras et al. (1984).

A. *ACROCOMIA*

Although during the past 50 years sporadic research was directed toward evaluation of the extractive potential of various species of *Acrocomia* (Cunha-Bayma, 1947; Markley, 1956; Novaes, 1952; Pinto, 1932; Poliakoff, 1961; Rocha, 1946), it has been only in the last three years that an overall research program has been established. In 1983, with support from the Energy Mobilization Program of the Brazilian Ministry of Agriculture, and within the National Program for Energy Research of the Empresa Brasileira de Pesquisa Agropecuária (EMBRAPA), the Centro Nacional de Recursos Genéticos (CENARGEN) established an ambitious program for the domestication of this group of palms, in cooperation with the Centro Nacional de Pesquisa de Tecnologia Agroindustrial de Alimentos (CTAA/EMBRAPA), the Empresa de Pesquisa Agropecuária de Minas Gerais (EPAMIG) and the Universidade de Brasília. This genus is valued primarily for the production of oil.

In 1984 the project was expanded to include other countries where *Acrocomia* is important, due to the need to define adequate strategies for germplasm sampling and collection. With support from the United States Agency for International Development (AID), research activities are being carried out in cooperation with the Corporación Araracuara and the Instituto Vallecaucano de Investigaciones Científicas (INCIVA) in Colombia, the Centro de Investigaciones Fitotécnicas y Ecogenéticas de Paimaruni and Universidad Gabriel René Moreno in Bolivia, the Instituto Agropecuário Nacional (IAN) in Paraguay, and the New York Botanical Garden in the United States. In spite of the short time of effective research, significant advances have been made, due in great part to the existence of a coherent domestication program.

Thus, at CENARGEN, in a little over a year it was possible to adjust the methodology for isoenzyme characterization within and between populations, with eight isoenzyme systems giving excellent results. Embryo culture in vitro is routine at CENARGEN, and embryogenesis has been induced from embryo callus tissue. Research on somatic embryogenesis is also ad-

vancing. Kernel protein characterization has shown promising results not only in the assays for essential amino acids, but also as a valuable tool for genotypic characterization of parental plants. At CTAA, qualitative and quantitative analysis of oils from the different populations sampled is routinely carried out.

However, progress has been most noticeable in the areas of field characterization of native populations, definitizing germplasm sampling strategies and germplasm collection. Up to the present, ca. 40 populations from the Brazilian states of Pará, Goiás, Minas Gerais and Paraná have been characterized in the field and sampled (Fig. 1). Several populations in the Distrito Federal are being studied in great detail by the Universidade de Brasília, and almost two years of data are now available on ecology and reproductive biology. Similar research is being initiated in Minas Gerais by the Universidade Federal de Minas Gerais, and in Bolivia by the Universidad Gabriel René Moreno.

The active gene bank, established in 1984 at EPAMIG, is currently studying germination and carrying out a characterization and preliminary evaluation of the palm germplasm of macaúba from the state of Minas Gerais.

B. *ASTROCARYUM*

This genus has several species that have been cited as economically viable sources of edible and industrial oil. However, it is very difficult to discern the true importance of many species due to the widespread usage of the same, or very similar, common names for totally different taxa.

With the exception of some isolated data on oil analysis (i.e., Pesce, 1941) and estimates of extractive production for a few species, very little is known of the potential for this genus. Madeira-Neto (1981) gives estimates on the extractive potential of *Astrocaryum aculeatum* for the state of Piauí (Brazil) and Patiño (1977) gives some data for the genus in Colombia. With the exception of Pesce's (1941) data on oils, practically nothing is known in respect to murumuru (*A. murumuru* and other species with the same common name), the basis for an oil industry in Belém 50 years ago. In spite of the excellent paper (Piedade, 1985) on the ecology of *A. jauari* (jauari or guara), a species which sustained an oil factory at Barcellos on the Rio Negro, data on yields are

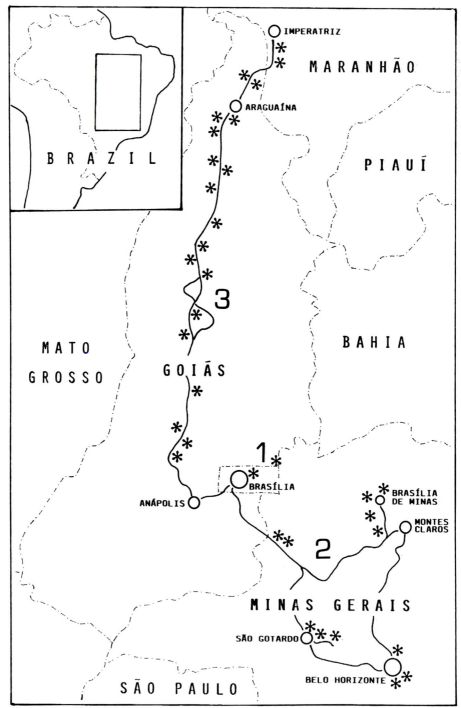

FIG. 1. Areas covered for research and collection of *Acrocomia* germplasm. 1, Nuclear research area in the Distrito Federal; 2, research and collections, 1984 campaign; 3, research and collections, 1985 campaign. Asterisks indicate areas of high concentrations of *Acrocomia*.

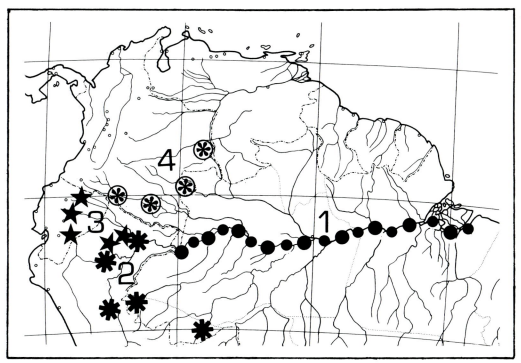

FIG. 2.   Areas covered for collection of *Bactris* (*Guilielma* alliance) germplasm in the Amazon basin. 1983 campaign: 1, First expedition (Brazil); 2, second expedition (Peru, Brazil). 1984 campaign: 3, third expedition (Peru, Ecuador); 4, fourth expedition (Colombia).

mere inferences. Presently, Francis Kahn from ORSTOM is initiating a taxonomic revision of the genus which is basic to any work on domestication.

C. *ATTALEA*

This genus is closely allied with *Orbignya,* and with the exception of the so-called "piassavas," important for their fibers, other economically important species have been traditionally considered within the babassu complex. Since current babassu research also covers *Attalea,* this genus will be treated together with *Orbignya.*

D. *BACTRIS*

In spite of being the largest genus of neotropical palms with ca. 280 names published (Costa, in press; Glassman, 1972), economically important species are basically restricted to about ten taxa which constitute the *Guilielma* complex. This group, which includes *Bactris gasipaes* and related species, is undoubtedly the most econom-

ically important group of neotropical palms. It is an important source of food, and has great potential as an oilseed crop. At the time of preparation of this paper we received an excellent review on the state of the art of domestication in pejibaye written by Charles Clement (1986). Due to the existence of this survey, we will limit ourselves to pointing out some of the most significant highlights in pejibaye research.

Although research on pejibaye is well over 50 years old, unified efforts at domestication only date from the last two decades. Credit must be given to the pioneer efforts of Victor Manuel Patiño in Colombia and Jorge Mora-Urpí in Costa Rica who, from the beginning, have led domestication efforts of these palms. At present, the institutions that lead pejibaye research are the Universidad de Costa Rica, the Instituto Nacional de Pesquisa da Amazônia—INPA/CNPq (Brazil), the Instituto Vallecaucano de Investigaciones Científicas—INCIVA (Colombia) and the Centro de Agricultura Tropical para la Investigación y Enseñanza—CATIE (Costa Rica).

Regarding genetic resources, there are three active germplasm banks (Univ. Costa Rica, INPA, INCIVA) as well as three other important collections (CATIE, INIPA—Yurimaguas, Peru and INIAP—Río Napo, Ecuador). During 1983 and 1984, with US-AID support and coordinated by CENARGEN and INPA, four multinational expeditions for germplasm collection in the Amazon Basin [Brasil, Colombia, Ecuador and Peru (Fig. 2)] were carried out (Clement & Coradin, 1986). The germplasm collected, together with existing materials in the collections, guarantees an ample genetic base for selection and breeding, and the institutions responsible for these collections are presently carrying out research on characterization and preliminary evaluation.

Practically all aspects germane to domestication of pejibaye are being adequately covered with diverse research projects, and certainly the number of researchers involved is larger than for all other neotropical palms put together. Thus, in terms of vegetative reproduction and tissue culture, somatic embryogenesis with plantlet regeneration has been achieved (Arias & Huete, 1983), with work continuing on the subject at CATIE, the Universidad de Costa Rica and the Universidade de São Paulo; research on morphology and definition of phenotypic traits is actively pursued at the University of Costa Rica and at INPA, and preliminary studies on reproductive biology are also being carried out at these two institutions.

The agronomy of the group is being researched by several institutions in Brazil (INPA, CPATU/EMBRAPA and CEPLAC), Colombia (Secretaria de Agricultura del Valle and INCIVA), Costa Rica (Associación Bananera Nacional—ASBANA) and Peru (INIPA—Yurimaguas), while several teams are working on fruit component analysis and isoenzyme characterization of select populations (CTAA and CENARGEN, Brasil; Univ. Costa Rica). Food technology is the only area where research is deficient, although some work is being done by the Universidad Nacional and the Universidad del Valle in Colombia.

E. ELAEIS

Work on the American representative of this genus, *Elaeis oleifera,* cannot be separated from research on the African oil palm. Many institutions throughout the world have incorporated *E.*

oleifera into their breeding and research programs, and for all practical purposes it can be considered that the state of the art for this species is equivalent to the African oil palm.

F. EUTERPE

Of the ca. 40 species of this genus, only two groups have been noted for their economic potential: *Euterpe edulis,* the palmito, found in northern Argentina, Paraguay and, in Brazil, as far north as the state of Bahia, and assaí or huasai constituted by two species, *E. oleracea* and *E. precatoria,* which have their centers of distribution in the Amazon basin. Extractive exploitation of *E. edulis* was the mainstay of the palmito industry. Over 96% of the palmito is now being obtained from *E. oleracea. Euterpe oleracea* and, to a lesser extent, *E. precatoria,* are extractive sources of assai wine.

In the past ten years it has been realized that unless these species are domesticated, extractive practices will probably lead to their extinction. Thus, the bulk of the populations in the southernmost range of *E. edulis* have disappeared, with the resulting loss of genotypes adapted to colder, more temperate conditions.

At present, research on *E. edulis* is being carried out at the Instituto Agronómico de Campinas—IAC where a small germplasm collection exists, and by the Universidade de Santa Catarina which is actively involved in management and recuperation of remnant native populations. Regarding assai, initial research is being carried out by the Centro de Pesquisa Agropecuária dos Trópico Úmido—CPATU/EMBRAPA and the Museu Paraense Emilio Goeldi/CNPq in Belém and by INIPA in Iquitos, Peru.

G. JESSENIA/OENOCARPUS

This complex has received quite a bit of attention in the past five years regarding its extractive potential as a source of fine oleic oils for food use, as well as its importance for aboriginal communities. The most detailed research has been carried out by M. J. Balick of the New York Botanical Garden (Balick, 1986). Technical aspects on oil extraction in rural micro-industries have been researched by G. Blaak of the Netherlands Royal Tropical Institute in collaboration with the Centro de Desarrollo "Las Gaviotas" in Colombia. The food value of the oil and protein-rich pulp has been researched by M. J. Balick, and S. N. Gershoff of the Tufts University School of Nutrition (Balick & Gershoff, 1981). In 1984, with domestication as an ultimate objective, CENARGEN, together with CPATU established an active gene bank at Belém and began germplasm collections. Currently, there is a US-AID supported study of the importance of mycorrhizae in early nursery growth of this complex, with the collaboration of the New York Botanical Garden, the Instituto Nacional de Investigación y Promoción Agropecuaria (INIPA) in Yurimaguas, Peru, and the Commissão Executiva do Plano da Lavoura Cacaueira (CE-PLAC) in Itabuna, Bahia, Brazil.

H. MAURITIA

In spite of being the palm genus that occupies the largest effective area in the neotropics, and being Humboldt's "tree of life", little concrete information is available for the genus *Mauritia*. Taxonomy is undefined, and data on yields and fruit analysis are ambiguous. Undoubtedly, extractive potential is gigantic, and *Mauritia* spp. may also be excellent alternatives under cultivation. The palms are valuable sources of fruit, fiber and thatch. In Brazil the mesocarp is concentrated to make a sweet confection; in Peru, sherbets are made from the same mesocarp. Some research has been carried out at the Estación Experimental de San Roque/INIPA, Iquítos (Bohórques, 1976), but the lack of a critical mass of researchers, as well as financial limitations, have seriously hampered work on this important group. Presently, INPA is beginning research on the ecology and reproductive biology of populations of *M. flexuosa* near Manaus.

I. ORBIGNYA/ATTALEA

Due to its great social importance and to the large effective area covered (over 12 million hectares) the extractive potential of the babassu complex has been the object of many publications throughout this century. Babassu is a source of oil, charcoal, flour and presscake for animal feed, among other uses. However, as in the case of pejibaye, integrated research activities are only fairly recently begun.

In effect, 1980 may be considered as the starting point of this new phase. That year, the Instituto Estadual do Babaçu—INEB, finished a survey of the "babaçuais" for the state of Maranhão (INEB, 1981) and Anthony Anderson started work on the biology and ecology of these palms. In 1981, the New York Botanical Garden, together with CENARGEN and INEB, initiated with AID support an ambitious project for the domestication of babassu, which included activities in systematics, sampling and collection of genetic resources, and the establishment of an active gene bank at Bacabal, Maranhão. In 1982, EMBRAPA created the National Program for Babassu Research under the coordination of the Unidade de Execução de Pesquisa de Ambito Estadual (UEPAE)–Teresina/EMBRAPA, where, in 1984, CENARGEN established a second gene bank.

From 1981 to present seven germplasm collection expeditions have been carried out: three in Brazil, two in Bolivia, one in Mexico and one in Colombia (Fig. 3). The gene banks are currently working on the characterization and preliminary evaluation of the materials collected, and special techniques have been developed for kernel germination. CENARGEN is working on isoenzyme characterization within and between populations, as well as on tissue culture. The confusing taxonomy of *Orbignya/Attalea* complex is being tackled in collaboration between NYBG and UEPAE–Teresina. These two institutions are also cooperating on research on management of natural population and the effects of fertilizers. The socio-economics of extractivism have been reviewed by Anderson and Anderson (1983) and more recently by Pick (1985) and Peter May (1986).

In March of 1986, UEPAE–Teresina hosted a meeting co-sponsored by EMBRAPA and NYBG with AID support, to discuss accomplishments of the previous five years and to establish research priorities for future cooperation.

J. SCHEELEA

As in other genera, what little data is available for *Scheelea* basically addresses extractive potential, as may be evidenced by Hernández-Xolocotzi's (1947) paper on coyol real (*S. liebmannii*) for Mexico. However, some species, such as *S. butyracea*, which according to Pérez-Arbeláez (1956) is the most important palm in Colombia,

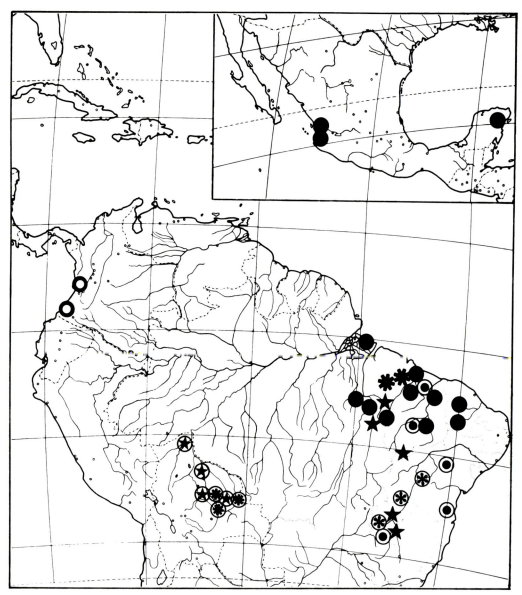

FIG. 3.   Areas covered for collection of *Orbignya/Attalea*. Bolivia: ✪, 1982; ✸, 1983. Brazil: ●, 1981; ✱, 1983; ★, 1984; ◉, 1985/86; ✳, 1986. Colombia: O, 1984. In-set: Mexico, 1982.

probably merit domestication. The major use of current interest is as an oilseed.

K. *Syagrus*

The situation for this genus is practically identical to that of *Scheelea*. Extractivism was re-

viewed by Bondar (1938, 1942) for licurí (*Syagrus coronata*) and little more has been done.

L. *Ynesa*

One of the most intriguing palms in terms of its potential as a source of lauric oils (useful in soaps, for example) occurs under the common names of shapaja or palm real. *Ynesa* was originally published by Cook (1942) on material and data from Ynes Mexia. The name may, in fact, be superfluous. Victor M. Patiño (pers. comm.) considers it a species of *Maximiliana,* while H. Balslev and A. Henderson (pers. comm.) believe it to be an *Attalea.* Apart from some data on yields and other parameters of wild populations observed by Acosta-Solís (1971), that suggest that the low densities (ca. seven plants/ha) preclude extractive exploitation, and a few observations on the fruits presented by Patiño (1977), practically nothing is known on this species.

From the above, it can be seen that, excepting *Acrocomia,* the *Guilielma* complex of *Bactris* and the *Orbignya/Attalea* alliance, for which fairly adequate research programs are being carried out, little is being done. It should be acknowledged here that AID support has been one of the decisive factors for the success of the research with the above-cited groups.

III. Domestication

It is estimated that man has used over 3000 plant species over the last 20,000 years (Lleras, 1985a; Mangelsdorf, 1966), including many palms. However, the bulk of all species have simply been exploited without any pretense at domestication. Although palms have always been important resources in the tropics, at present only four can be considered as domesticated: the date palm (*Phoenix dactylifera*), the coconut (*Cocos nucifera*), the African oil palm (*Elaeis guineensis*) and the pejibaye (*Bactris gasipaes*).

Domestication has generally been a gradual process involving hundreds or even thousands of years. Furthermore, Heiser (1981), citing De Candolle in this context, noted that little or nothing was brought into domestication in the past 100 or 200 years, so that no experience is available on rapid domestication schemes. This is generally true, and in fact, both the date palm and coconut have been domesticated from time immemorial, while it seems that pejibaye was brought into domestication ca. 1500 years ago or more, somewhere near the western edge of the Amazon Basin.

However, good examples of what can be achieved in a short time when concrete efforts are directed towards domestication can be seen by the successes with rubber (*Hevea brasiliensis*) and the African oil palm, both of which are among the very few cases of recent, rapid domestication. Domestication for these species dates from the latter part of the 19th century, and in the 80–100 years since, yields have increased many fold, and highly advanced genetic material has been obtained for use under a variety of conditions.

As noted before, throughout Latin America—until very recently—extractive exploitation was emphasized. But, while there were always isolated efforts at introducing a few species into cultivation, these were usually limited to very narrow research activities without a global view of domestication. Research was, and to a large extent still is, repetitious, with several institutions working on the same problems, making the same mistakes, and with exchange of information largely non-existent.

The latter half of the 1970's saw a surge of interest in introducing new alternatives into cultivation in Latin America. By the beginning of this decade, international cooperation was already underway for pejibaye, and a domestication program had been instituted for babassu. By 1983, CENARGEN was well advanced towards the design of a unified model for the domestication of tropical perennials, with macaúba as a test case, mainly for oil production.

In August of the same year, FAO and CATIE sponsored a consultation on lesser known palms of tropical America, with participation of scientists from several countries. The state of the art was analyzed for several important groups of palms, and research priorities were defined for the same. Among the conclusions was that emphasis be given to the need for international cooperation. The need for an effective system for exchange of information was considered essential, and the Newsletter "Useful Palms of Tropical America", edited by CENARGEN with FAO support, was created for this purpose. It was also proposed that data banks, accessible to all palm researchers, be established, with CENARGEN, CATIE and NYBG being asked to do so.

The above meeting was undoubtedly an important catalyst in conveying the need to establish coherent research programs in palm domestication. With the newsletter as a vehicle for

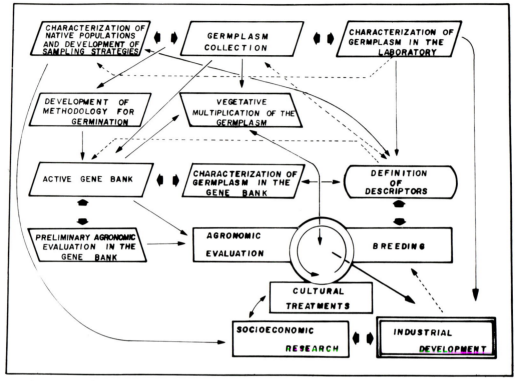

FIG. 4. Flow of research activities proposed by CENARGEN as basic to domestication of tropical perennials. Model is self-explanatory.

communication, contact has been made possible between researchers working on related topics.

The model developed for tropical perennials at CENARGEN was presented in a proposal for the domestication of native fruit species (Lleras, 1985b) at meetings held in 1985 by the Instituto Nacional de Investigación y Promoción Agraria—INIPA, Peru, where it was adopted as the basic guideline for future research programs. The same year, the Programa Interciencia de Recursos Biológicos—PIRB hosted a workshop in Bogotá, Colombia, to discuss international cooperation for the domestication of promising oil species. Once again, the CENARGEN scheme, modified to attend to specific situations, was adopted for the establishment of international cooperative programs for *Bactris gasipaes,* the *Jessenia/Oenocarpus* complex, and *Caryodendron orinocense* (Euphorbiaceae).

Recent information (Carl Gallegos, pers. comm.) is that the CENARGEN proposal, which will be presented below, is very close to the ideas for domestication that have been arrived at by

various international institutions. This, together with the ready acceptance of models of this kind, as evidenced above, suggests that coherent unified domestication programs have finally come into their own.

A. THE MODEL

Figure 4 presents the flow of activities considered basic to the domestication of tropical perennials. As indicated, these range from the assessment of genetic resources in the wild to possible industrialization, while always considering socio-economic issues, which must underlie any decisions on priorities for agricultural practices and modes of utilization in a continent with so many rural poor.

It may seem that a bias is shown towards genetic resources and their manipulation. However, considering that for most of the target species information is so deficient, research on basic parameters is unavoidable. Furthermore, the mod-

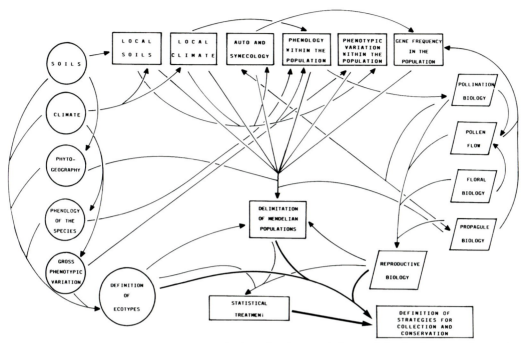

FIG. 5. Research involved in the characterization of native populations and the development of strategies for sampling of germplasm or in situ conservation of tropical perennials. For a detailed discussion see Lleras & Coradin (1988).

el is a reduction of many research activities under a few convenient headings. For example, the first item—characterization of native populations and development of sampling strategies—involves all basic research on phytogeography, ecology and reproductive biology, all of which are essential for successful domestication or management of native populations (Fig. 5).

For many palms, work on germination and vegetative reproduction is essential; first, unless adequate methods for breaking dormancy are found, the time involved in germination may become the major bottleneck for research and agriculture. Under these circumstances, somatic embryogenesis is the only alternative if cloning is desired for many important species. It must be kept in mind that, if in the future palms are to become major components in the agriculture of tropical perennials, and if they are to replace annual oilseeds, adequate methods for the production of huge numbers of seedlings must be developed.

The establishment of an active gene bank is one of the first priorities, and must involve germplasm characterization and preliminary evalua-

tion. These last two activities, together with the definition of descriptors, are described in Lleras (1985b).

Promising germplasm from the gene bank, or exceptionally, subsamples of materials directly from the field collections, is channeled, together with data on field and laboratory characterization, to agronomic research. The latter involves advanced agronomic evaluation, testing of cultural treatments, (spacing, irrigation, fertilizers, consociates, etc.) and breeding.

Studies on its industrial development and socio-economics must be concomitant with the other activities described above: the first defines the characteristics for specific purposes desired from the crop, while the second considers the social and economic implications of bringing the species into domestication.

From the above, it is evident that domestication is not a simple process, and that few, if any, institutions or even countries, can tackle programs of this magnitude on their own. Cooperation at the national and international level is thus necessary, if domestication of any neotropical palm is to be achieved.

Table I

Institutions involved with different aspects of existing domestication programs. For *Elaeis oleifera* coordination is not formalized, and names refer to coordination within the individual research institutions. *Bactris gasipaes* includes all of the *Guilielma* complex, while under *Orbignya phalerata* are all species of the *Orbignya/Attalea* alliance known as babassu

Activities	Bactris gasipaes	Jessenia/ Oenocarpus	Orbignya phalerata	Acrocomia spp.	Elaeis oleifera
			Species		
General coordination	J. Mora-Urpí V. M. Patiño C. R. Clement	R. E. Schultes M. J. Balick L. Coradin	J. M. Frazão M. J. Balick	L. Coradin E. Lleras	E. B. da Silva J. Meunier A. Carmona N. Rajanaidu
Phytogeography and systematics	INPA/UCR/INCIVA/ARARACUARA/INIPA	NYBG	NYBG/UEPAE-TERESINA/CENARGEN	CENARGEN/EPAMIG/UGRM/IAN/INCIVA/ARARACUARA	CNPSD/CENARGEN/IRHO
Germplasm sampling, collection, characterization and evaluation	INPA/INCIVA/ARARACUARA/INIPA/CENARGEN	CENARGEN/CPATU/NYBG	NYBG/CENARGEN/UEPAE-TERESINA/EMAPA	CENARGEN/UnB/EPAMIG/CTAA	CNPSD/CENARGEN/IRHO/UNITED BRANDS/UNIFIELD
Chemical characterization	INPA/CIPTRONA/U.VALLE/CTAA/U. ALBERTA	IIT/CTAA/U. SASKATCHEWAN		CENARGEN/CTAA	CTAA/IRHO/UNITED BRANDS/UNIFIELD
Vegetative reproduction and tissue culture	UCR/CATIE/USP/INPA	NYBG/U. JAVERIANA	UEPAE-TERESINA/CENARGEN	CENARGEN/EPAMIG/ESALQ	CNPSD/CENARGEN/IRHO/UNIFIELD/UNITED BRANDS/PORIM
Breeding and agricultural practices	INPA/UCR/CEPLAC/CPATU/INIPA-YURIMAGUAS	CPATU/ARARACUARA/INIPA/NYBG/CONIF	UEPAE-TERESINA/NYBG	EPAMIG/GRUPO ULTRA	CNPSD/UEPAE-BELÉM/CEPLAC/IRHO/UNITED BRANDS/UNIFIELD/PORIM
Marketing industrialization and socioeconomics	CIPRONA/U.VALLE/CTAA	ITT/U. SASKATCHEWAN	UEPAE-TERESINA/NYBG	EPAMIG/GRUPO ULTRA/NYBG	CNPSD/IRHO/UNITED BRANDS/UNIFIELD
Utilization systems		NYBG	NYBG/UEPAE-TERESINA	CENARGEN/EPAMIG	
Data bank	PIRB/CATIE	PIRB/CENARGEN	NYBG/UEPAE-TERESINA	CENARGEN	CNPSD/IRHO/UNIFIELD

B. EXISTING PROGRAMS

As can be expected, the five existing domestication programs do not follow exactly the same models nor did they originate in the same way. Table I presents research activities within these programs, grouped for convenience along the lines adopted at the PIRB conference held in Colombia in 1985.

For *Elaeis oleifera,* it would be incorrect to speak of a unified domestication program. What exists is a network of institutions which cooperate on research without an outright commitment towards domestication. However, domestication is advancing very rapidly due to the importance of the species, not only for its own potential, but especially as a valuable source of genetic variation and crossing with the African oil palm.

Babassu was the first group for which a formal commitment was made towards domestication (1980/81), without, however, following a unified model, which was first proposed for macaúba (1983) and adopted by PIRB in 1985 for the initial domestication of the *Jessenia/Oenocarpus* complex. Although domestication is fairly advanced for pejibaye (*Guilielma* complex of *Bactris*), it was agreed to fit existing research within the framework of activities approved at the PIRB meeting cited above.

As shown in Table I, ca. 30 institutions throughout the Americas have formally committed themselves to domestication of neotropical palms in the past five years, and this number is increasing day by day. However, when comparing what is being done with what needs to be done, just for the groups cited earlier in this paper, and considering that these only represent a small sampling of neotropical palms, it is obvious that the process of palm domestication is still an incipient one.

IV. Future Priorities

Although the past five years have completely altered the situation for neotropical palm research, serious problems and limitations still exist. Foremost among these is the lack of trained researchers, with financial limitations running a close second. Priorities for the future must therefore give maximum attention to training and to fund-raising.

During the PIRB meeting in late 1985, participants agreed that isolated research projects have less chance of obtaining financial support than overall domestication programs, in spite of the significantly larger sums involved. This is because such overall programs have well defined objectives and represent a consensus and commitment by the scientific community. They also address problems with major social impacts throughout the continent and thus would benefit a larger segment of the population.

For the purposes of the particular meeting (domestication of *Bactris gasipaes,* the *Jessenia/Oenocarpus* complex and *Caryodendron orinocense*) it was also agreed that the scientific community would be responsible for technical aspects while the Programa Interciencias would take it upon itself to make the necessary contacts and to coordinate fund-raising and financial management. Although we are not implying that PIRB should take upon itself the responsibility for all domestication programs in neotropical palms, scientific organizations with similar wide international participation (i.e., Society for Economic Botany, FAO) should certainly follow their example.

All projects should plan to include training not only in their budgets but also "on the job" within programmed research. Short and middle term training programs, such as those offered by NYBG (palms and economic botany) and CENARGEN (palms and genetic resources) should certainly be encouraged, and financial support found for them. Financial support should also be given to graduate research, as it is highly reliable and fairly inexpensive, while also introducing new blood into palm research.

The taxa presented here may be considered as front-line priorities for domestication; after all, their potential has been known for some time. No doubt, however, other, maybe even better, alternatives will appear as we increase our knowledge on neotropical palms.

V. Acknowledgments

The authors wish to thank all of the many persons with whom they have had the opportunity to discuss domestications. In terms of palms, thanks are due to Drs. M. J. Balick (NYBG), G. Blaak (FAO), V. M. Patiño (IN-

CIVA), J. D. Hay (UNB), Jorge León (CATIE) and especially to Dr. D. C. Giacometti (CEN-ARGEN) who not only gave much of his time for many discussions and suggestions, but also reviewed this manuscript. Thanks are also due to Sra. Vania Lima de Almeida, who patiently typed many versions of this paper.

VI. Literature Cited

Acosta-Solís, M. 1971. Palmas económicas del noroccidente Ecuatoriano. Naturaleza Ecuatoriana **1(2)**.

Anderson, A. B. & S. E. Anderson. 1983. People and the palm forest. Final report to USDA Forest Service. Washington, D.C. 157 pp.

Arias, O. & F. Huete. 1983. Propagación vegetativa de pejibaye (*Bactris gasipaes* H.B.K.) in vitro. Turrialba **33(2)**: 103–107.

Balick, M. J. 1986. Systematics and economic botany of the *Oenocarpus–Jessenia* (Palmae) complex. Adv. Econ. Bot. **3**: 1–140.

——— **& S. N. Gershoff.** 1981. Nutritional evaluation of the *Jessenia bataua* palm: Source of high quality protein and oil from Tropical America. Econ. Bot. **35(3)**: 261–271.

Bohórques, J. A. 1976. Monografía sobre *Mauritia flexuosa* L. et F. *In* Simpósio internacional sobre plantas de interés económico da flora Amazónica. Instituto Interamericano de Cooperación para la Agricultura. Informes de Conferencias, Cursos y Reuniones **93**: 223–248.

Bondar, G. 1938. O licuriseiro (*Cocos coronata* Mart.) e suas possibidades na econômia Brasileira. Bol. Inst. Centr. Fomento Econ. Bahia **2**: 1–18.

———. 1942. As cêras no Brasil e o licurí (*Cocos coronata* Mart.) na Bahia. Bol. Inst. Centr. Fomento Econ. Bahia **11**: 1–86.

Clement, C. R. 1986. El pejibaye (*Bactris gasipaes* H.B.K.), resultados y necesidades de investigación. Useful Palms Trop. Amer. Newsl. **2**: 2–4.

——— **& L. Coradin.** 1986. Peach palm (*Bactris gasipaes* H.B.K.), germplasm bank. Final report submitted to the Agency for International Development. 174 pp. (typescript).

Cook, O. F. 1942. A new commercial oil palm in Ecuador. Nat. Hort. Mag. **21**: 70–85.

Costa, J. T. M. 1985. Sistemática das palmeiras neotropicais—Situação atual. *In* Anais do 36° Congresso Nacional de Botânica. Brasil. (Abst.).

Cunha-Bayma, A. 1947. Babaçu, dendê e macaúba perante a falta de gorduras. Revista Agric. **22(1–3)**: 67–69.

Glassman, S. F. 1972. A revision of B. E. Dahlgren's index of American palms. Phanerogamarum monographiae, Tomus VI. J. Cramer, Germany. 294 pp.

Heiser, C. B. 1981. Seed to civilization. The story of food. W. H. Freeman & Co., San Francisco. 254 pp.

Hernández-Xolocotzi, E. 1947. La *Scheelea liebmannii* Becc. (coyol real o corozo): Su distribución y produción. Anal. Inst. Biol. **18**: 43–70.

Instituto Estadual do Babaçu (INEB). 1981. Mapeamento das occorências e prospecção do potencial atual do Babaçu no estado do Maranhão. Companhia de pesquisa e Aproveitamento de Recursos Naturais/Fundação Instituto estadual do Babaçu, São Luís. 67 pp. + appendixes.

Lleras, E. 1985a. Domesticación, agricultura y recursos genéticos: Pasado, presente y futuro? Instituto Interamericano de Cooperación para la Agricultura, Serie Ponencias, Resultados y Recomendaciones de Eventos Técnicos **349**: 31–42.

———. 1985b. Estrategias para la domesticación de frutales nativos de la Amazonía. Presented at the annual program meetings, Instituto Nacional de Investigación y Promoción Agropecuaria (INIPA), Chanchamayo, Peru 16–24 November, 1985. 28 pp. (typescript).

——— **& L. Coradin.** 1988. Neotropical oil palms: State of the art and perspectives for Latin America. Adv. Econ. Bot. **6**: 201–213.

———, **D. C. Giacometti & L. Coradin.** 1984. Areas críticas de distribución de palmas en las Américas para colecta, evaluación y conservación. Pages 67–101 *in* Palmeras poco utilizadas de Américas tropical. Food and Agriculture Organization of the United Nations/Centro de Agricultura Tropical para la Investigación y la Enseñanza, Imprenta Lil, San José.

Madeira-Neto, A. 1981. Estudo sócio-económico dos principais produtos do estrativismo vegetal do Piauí–Tucúm. Fund. CEPRO, Teresina, 64 pp.

Mangelsdorff, P. C. 1966. Genetic potentials for increasing yields of food crops and animals. Proc. Nat. Acad. Sci. **56**: 370–375.

Markley, K. S. 1956. Mbocayá or Paraguay coco palm: An important source of oil. Econ. Bot. **10(1)**: 3–32.

May, P. H. 1986. A modern tragedy of the non-commons: Agro industrial change and equity in Brazil's babassu palm zone. Doctoral Thesis. Cornell University, Ithaca. 432 pp.

Novaes, R. F. 1952. Contribuição para o estudo do coco macaúba. Escola Superior de Agricultura Luiz de Queiroz, Piracicaba, Brasil, 86 pp.

Patiño, V. M. 1977. Palmas oleaginosas del Pacífico. Cespedesia **6(23/24)**: 131–254.

Perez-Arbelaez, E. 1956. Plantas utiles de Colombia. Camacho Roldán, Bogotá, 832 pp.

Pesce, C. 1941. Oleaginosas da Amazônia. Rev. Veterinária **2**: 1–128.

Pick, P. J. 1985. Babassu (*Orbignya species*): Gradual disappearance vs. slow metamorphosis to integrated agrobusiness. Report prepared for the New York Botanical Garden Institute of Economic Botany. 56 pp.

Piedade, M. T. F. 1985. Ecologia e biologia reprodutiva de *Astrocaryum jauari* Mart. (Palmae) como exemplo de população adaptada à áreas inundaveis do Rio Negro (igapós). M.Sc. Thesis. Instituto Nacional de Pesquisa da Amazônia/Fundação Universidad do Amazonas, Manaus. 184 pp. + appendixes.

Pinto, C. A. S. 1932. Côco macaúba. Bol. Agric. Zoo-tecn. Vet. **5(2):** 60–69.

Poliakoff, J. 1961. Le macauba, *Acrocomia sclerocarpa*. Son intérêt dans l'economie sul-américaine des corps gras. Oleagineux **16(1):** 37–40.

Rocha, O. 1946. O côco macaúba. Rev. Agric. **21(9–10):** 249–358.

Spruce, R. 1871. Palmae Amazonicae. Jour. Linn. Soc. Bot. **11:** 65–183.

———. 1908. Notes of a botanist on the Amazon and Andes. Vol. 1 (A. R. Wallace, ed.). Macmillan, London. 518 pp.

Wallace, A. R. 1853. Palm trees of the Amazon and their uses. J. van Voorst, London.

Prospects for Rattan Cultivation

John Dransfield

Table of Contents

Abstract

Rattans, climbing Calamoid palms occurring in greatest abundance in Southeast Asia and Malesia, the source of cane entering world trade as the basis of a furniture industry, are also intensively utilized locally for a wide range of purposes. Of the ca. 600 species, about 25 are highly sought after. Most cane is collected from the wild but with current shortages, efforts to cultivate rattan on a commercial scale have been intensified. Cultivation of the small diameter canes, *Calamus caesius* and *C. trachycoleus* is now feasible but sylvicultural techniques need refinement, particularly in the manipulation of light regimes by opening of the canopy of support trees, and the problems of efficient harvesting need to be addressed. Unfortunately, large diameter canes have proved to be less promising as sylvicultural subjects, while, at the same time, demand is high and wild stocks are seriously depleted. The potential of small diameter cane as a crop for marginal lands in the humid tropics is great, particularly as a smallholder's crop, but the prospects for cultivation of larger canes are less certain.

Key words: palms, rattan, cane, Southeast Asia, sylviculture

I. Introduction: What are Rattans?

Rattans (Fig. 1A) are climbing palms belonging to the subfamily Calamoideae, the scaly-fruited palms (Dransfield & Uhl, 1986). There are about 600 species in 13 genera confined to the Palaeotropics. Three genera, *Laccosperma, Eremospatha* and *Oncocalamus* are restricted to the perhumid areas of Africa. One (or a few) species of the large genus *Calamus* is also found in Africa. The remaining rattans are all found in Asia, Malesia and the western Pacific, where they form a conspicuous and important component of many forest types and are partly responsible for the unique character of these forests. Modern taxonomic inventories of rattans are available for the Malay Peninsula (Dransfield, 1979) and

for Sabah (Dransfield, 1984) and are planned for other areas. Rattans are the source of cane entering world trade as the basis of a furniture industry, but are also used very intensively for a wide range of local purposes such as cordage, raw material for baskets and mats, thatch and many other purposes. It is hard to conceive of village life in the southeast Asian region without rattans. Most cane is harvested from wild rattans growing in primary tropical rain forest, and is regarded as the most important minor forest product in many areas. It is the most important product in government statistics after timber. Yet to the villager, rattan can often be of much greater significance than timber, providing a source of income in times of agricultural scarcity or financial hardships. The great social importance of rattan

Advances in Economic Botany 6: 190–200, 1988
© 1988 The New York Botanical Garden

FIG. 1. A. *Calamus manan* in primary forest. Pahang, West Malaysia. B. Leaf sheaths of *Calamus trachycoleus* (left) and *C. caesius* (right), to show differences in armature. Sabah. C. *Calamus trachycoleus* seedling at 11 months old, ready for planting. Sabah. D. Within a plantation of *Calamus trachycoleus,* six years from planting, copious development of stolons. Sabah.

has tended to be overlooked by governments or forest departments, but has been nicely quantified by Siebert and Belsky (1985) for one area of the Philippines.

II. Rattan Size Classes

It is convenient to divide rattans into two broad categories based on their size and end use. Small diameter canes have a diameter less than about 18 mm; they are used whole, in some furniture designs, for smaller struts, but their main use is in the split state, as "chair cane" used for woven backs of chairs, for matting, and fine handicrafts, and as "core" (a by-product of splitting rattan to produce chair cane), used for woven chairs and baskets. There will always be a demand for chair cane, if for no other purpose than the repair of cane-backed chairs. Large diameter canes are the large canes with diameters exceeding 18 mm, usually 25–40 mm, which are used for the construction of the framework of cane furniture. Without them traditional cane furniture designs would have to change dramatically and wood would have to be substituted for cane.

III. The Development of Research Projects

As the demand for cane remains but the habitat of rattan decreases through logging and forest clearance, shortages have developed. Such scarcity of rattans is by no means a new phenomenon; from time to time in the past, forest departments in several southeast Asian countries have received reports of difficulties experienced by the rattan trade in satisfying the demand for raw material, and have responded by investigating the possibilities of developing methods of cultivating rattan. Most of these investigations have proved unsuccessful, largely because shortages of canes have been temporary and changes of management of research have led to changes in emphasis and subsequent loss of interest. By the early 1970's real and long term shortages of the best quality canes were being experienced in Peninsular Malaysia, one of the very richest areas for rattan in the region, and the Forest Research Institute Malaysia (FRIM), Kepong, started yet again to investigate possibilities of cultivation.

Unlike previous rattan projects, the FRIM project had a firm base and long term commitment. It can be fairly stated that the Kepong project was largely responsible for stimulating interest in the region and, however indirectly, for the initiation of research projects in other southeast Asian nations, together with the support of aid agencies such as the British Overseas Development Administration, FAO and, in particular, the International Development Research Center of Canada (IDRC).

The International Development Research Center approached the Forest Research Institute Malaysia in 1977 to try to identify forestry projects which might directly benefit rural people, and rattan was one of the suggested areas in need of further research. IDRC employed K. D. Menon, the then newly retired Director General of Forestry in Malaysia to write a "state of the art" report on rattan. This report served as a paper for discussion at a workshop held in Singapore in 1979, attended by delegates from forestry departments and rattan industries throughout southeast Asia and elsewhere. The report was eventually published (IDRC, 1980) and did much to stimulate interest in rattans. At the Singapore meeting proposals were made for the creation of a clearing house for information on rattan. This was set up as the Rattan Information Centre at the Forest Research Institute Malaysia at Kepong with partial funding from IDRC. The Rattan Information Centre publishes a quarterly bulletin which includes a wide range of information on rattans and rattan research. In October 1984, IDRC and the Rattan Information Centre jointly sponsored an international seminar on rattan held in Kuala Lumpur. The proceedings of this meeting (Wong & Manokaran, 1985) include 23 papers and numerous country reports representing a most valuable source for further research on rattan. The Rattan Information Centre has also published a very extensive bibliography on rattan (Kong-Ong & Manokaran, 1984). This extraordinary change in interest has developed over the last ten years. I know of active rattan projects now in the People's Republic of China, Taiwan, the Philippines, Thailand, India, Bangladesh, Sri Lanka, Malaysia, and Indonesia, with interest at a preliminary stage in Papua New Guinea and Vanuatu. I have also received requests for information concerning the cultivation of rattan from Jamaica, Trinidad, Colombia, Argentina, Zimbabwe and Senegambia.

IV. Early Rattan Cultivation

Before the renewed efforts of the mid 1970's, rattan was cultivated on a large scale only in a relatively small area of Kalimantan, Indonesian Borneo. Elsewhere small areas of rattan are cultivated on the margins of villages, in orchards and beside longhouses, most particularly in Borneo. Such small scale cultivation would help supplement wild stocks for domestic purposes, but would not be used for international trade. In a few areas such as parts of the First Division of Sarawak where much of the primary forest has been cleared by shifting cultivation and where there is a very poor supply of wild rattan, several species of rattan are cultivated by longhouses in quantity sufficient to satisfy most of the domestic demands for cordage, basketry and matting. Such small scale cultivation is clearly successful and it is remarkable that the scale of cultivation has not been increased to meet the shortfall between supply from the wild and demand.

The rattan plantations in Central Kalimantan appear to have originated over one hundred years ago, at the suggestion of Dutch missionaries. Two species, *Calamus caesius* Bl., "rotan sega" or "rotan taman," and *Calamus trachycoleus* Becc. (Fig. 1B) are planted on a very wide scale in areas of low-lying secondary alluvial forest on the banks of the Barito River and its tributaries (Dransfield, 1977, 1979; Heyne, 1949; Tuil, 1929). These areas are subject to periodic severe and prolonged flooding making them unsuitable for the planting of crops such as coconut, oilpalm or cocoa, and the soils are liable to become extremely acidic if too disturbed, thus making rice cultivation difficult. Rattan has proved to be an extremely successful and important crop in these areas, with whole villages depending for much of their livelihood on the products of the plantations. In 1974 when I visited the area, villagers from the rattan growing areas seemed to enjoy a much better standard of living and a greater income than villagers elsewhere in Kalimantan. It seems strange that this obviously successful plantation system has not spread to other areas of

Borneo. The rattan plantations of the Barito watershed are almost all permanent features. Weinstock (1983) has reported an extremely interesting modification of this system which occurs on the boundary of Central and East Kalimantan, where the cultivation of *Calamus caesius* is fitted into the cycle of shifting cultivation. In this system rattan seedlings are planted in the regrowth developing after the dry paddy fields are abandoned after two year's cultivation. The seedlings grow with the developing secondary forest and, after a period of about 10–15 years, are ready for harvest prior to the cutting and burning of the forest to reestablish dry paddy. There are many advantages to this unique system. It is one of the few instances where a cash crop is obtained from the fallow period of the shifting cultivation cycle. There is a strong incentive to wait before cutting down the forest again so that a reasonable rattan harvest can be obtained, thus incidentally giving greater opportunity for the recovery of soil fertility.

It was obvious that if rattan was to be developed as a plantation crop elsewhere, the system of cultivation in Central Kalimantan should be used, at least initially, as a model. The success of the Central Kalimantan rattan plantations in part is due to the use of *Calamus trachycoleus.* This species is only known from the area of the Barito and Central Kalimantan Kapuas (not West Kalimantan Kapuas) Rivers and their tributaries. Reports of its occurrence elsewhere have not been substantiated or have proved to be based on mistaken identification. *Calamus trachycoleus* was described by Beccari based on material collected during the preparation of Heyne's "De nuttige planten van Nederlandsch-Indie" (Heyne, 1917) of cultivated plants. The species is obviously closely related to *C. caesius* and might even be regarded as a selection from the great variability of this species in Borneo. Its cane is of a quality similar to that of the best quality *C. caesius,* though perhaps not quite so durable nor with such a lustrous skin. However, for some purposes, for instance the weaving of the very finest mats, it is preferred to *C. caesius* because it is easier to work. The most important quality of *C. trachycoleus,* which makes it unparalleled as a plantation subject, is its growth form. I have discussed at length and illustrated elsewhere (Dransfield, 1977) the growth forms of *C. caesius* and *C. trachycoleus,* and will only summarize the differences here. In *C. caesius* the first seedling stem produces basal suckers, each of which has a short (rarely exceeding about 5 cm long) rhizomatous portion before becoming apogeotropic and developing into an aerial stem. The rhizomes have very short, rather wide internodes, while the aerial stems have slender and long internodes (Fig. 2A). At the point where the rhizome metamorphoses into an aerial stem, one or two axillary buds develop which may grow into new short rhizomes or remain dormant. In *C. trachycoleus* the growth pattern is the same but the short rhizomes are replaced by long stolons which can be as much as 3 m long (Fig. 2B). The consequence of this difference is that *C. trachycoleus* is much more invasive than *C. caesius,* and because the clump is not crowded or congested there is little competition between aerial stems within the clump and the stolons do not become dormant (Fig. 1D). From every aerial stem produced, two more stolons are produced; thus the clump has the potential for producing an exponential increase in the number of aerial stems. Although the branching pattern of *C. caesius* is basically similar, many of the branch buds remain dormant. Recently it has been observed that individuals of *C. trachycoleus* do not always produce two stolon buds at the point of metamorphosis; Shim & Muhammad (1985) record stolons as long as 5.8 m, producing along their length 3–4 aerial stems. I have observed in the Batu Putih Estate that other stolons may branch only once at the point of metamorphosis. Shim and Muhammad (1985) confirmed the exponential increase in the number of aerial stems in *C. trachycoleus* but observed that *C. caesius,* at least when young, also produced an exponential increase—in other words, competition between aerial stems and dormancy does not appear to occur until the plants are over three years old.

A further great advantage of *C. trachycoleus* is its ability to withstand prolonged and severe flooding. With these remarkable qualities, and the preexistence of sylvicultural techniques, it seemed obvious that every effort should be made to obtain planting material of *C. trachycoleus* for trials elsewhere.

Only one major new planting program has been carried out in the Southeast Asian region. In an evaluation of rural development projects which might have direct benefit to the Murut people of

the Interior Residency of Sabah, the Sabah Forest Development Authority (SAFODA) identified rattan as an indigenous minor forest product of importance in the local cash economy, and that restructuring of the market and, possibly, cultivation could have great potential. A meeting was held in Kota Kinabalu, Sabah in 1977 to discuss potential problems in the cultivation of rattan and aspects of processing and marketing. On the basis of this meeting and further discussions between the state government of Sabah, SAFODA and Markiras Associates, an independent group of economic and management consultants, SAFODA committed itself to the establishment of commercial sized rattan plantations. A new company, Sabah Rotan Corporation, was formed jointly with the Sabah Government to market rattan from the wild.

SAFODA started to obtain large quantities of rattan seed in late 1977. They purchased seed of *Calamus caesius* and *C. subinermis* H. A. Wendl. ex Becc. locally in Sabah. Seed of *C. manan* Miq. was imported from the Forest Research Institute Malaysia, Kepong and members of a consultancy firm were able to purchase the first batch of 5000 seeds of *C. trachycoleus* within the rattan plantations in Central Kalimantan in November 1978. I had advised SAFODA that the acquisition of *C. trachycoleus* should be their highest priority. Seed was cleaned and sown immediately. Knowledge of palm seed germination and rattan plantation practices in Central Kalimantan resulted in good germination rates. By April 1979, SAFODA had begun to establish trial plots in different parts of the State. Attempts were also made to establish plots using vegetative material (suckers or stolons) rather than from seed, but mortality rates were too high and insufficient quantities of planting material were obtained.

V. The Batu Putih Estate Rattan Plantation

SAFODA selected a site in the lower reaches of the Kinabatangan River on the east coast of Sabah for the establishment of a large scale rattan project. The Batu Putih Estate is low-lying, exceeding about 20 m elevation only on a small steep-sided hill. The estate was originally developed before the Second World War as a tobacco plantation, but the frequent and severe floods of

FIG. 2. A. The base of a clump of *Calamus caesius,* to show the short rhizomes and somewhat congested aerial stems. Sabah. B. The branching behavior of *Calamus trachycoleus*: In the center an axis developing into an aerial stem; above and below, two branches developing into new stolons. Sabah.

the Kinabatangan made the area unsuitable for agriculture and it had remained derelict for many years. Before rattan planting began much of the estate was covered by secondary forest of various ages. Along the levees of the Kinabatangan and its tributaries occurs a relatively high forest dominated by the characteristic riverside tree, *Octomeles sumatrana* Miq. (Datiscaceae). In the lower areas behind the levees occurs secondary forest with a lower and uneven canopy. The Kinabatangan floods at least twice a year and the high water level usually reaches at least 1.5 m above the levees. During some of the worst flooding in 1981, most of the estate was under 2.5 m of muddy water. Flooding lasts from two weeks to two months. Although I have not seen soil analyses, there is little doubt that the topsoil is very fertile, and with the constant flooding of the river and the consequent deposition of silt, high fertility is maintained.

SAFODA first established a nursery to handle large quantities of seed. The practices followed are those developed at Kepong and recommended by Darus and Aminah (1985), but applied on a very large scale. Techniques were developed for the rapid removal of pericarp and sarcotesta in very large quantities of fruit. Seedlings (Fig. 1C) were potted in black polythene tube "pots" and shaded with black netting or palm thatch.

Planting was begun by SAFODA in late 1979, with an area of 404 hectares devoted to *Calamus caesius* and *C. trachycoleus*. In July 1980, a private company was formed to take on the responsibility of additional planting on behalf of SAFODA. Rattan Management Services (RMS) planted a further approximately 4000 hectares during the period July 1980 to September 1984.

During 1981 flooding was very severe and there was considerable mortality of rattan seedlings throughout the estate. However, *Calamus trachycoleus* survived much better than *C. caesius*, of which most of the seedlings died. This happened in spite of the fact that *C. caesius* occurs naturally in abundance along the banks of the Kinabatangan. It appears that at the seedling stage *C. caesius* is much less tolerant of flooding than is *C. trachycoleus*. Subsequently emphasis was placed on obtaining large quantities of *C. trachycoleus* seed from Indonesia. Not only did the species respond differently to flooding, but within *C. trachycoleus* there was much greater mortality during the 1981 floods in the lowest-lying

areas than on the levees of the river; indeed, mortality was as high as 90 percent in the lowest areas. Overall, the mortality rate was about 15 percent. Using this experience, RMS revised their plans for planting, concentrating on the levees and avoiding the lowest areas. By September 1984 planting was completed. The estate now has 4068.73 hectares under rattan, consisting of 2834.63 hectares under "rotan irit" (*C. trachycoleus*) and 1234.10 hectares under "rotan sega."

Planting was carried out on lines running East to West, about 10 m apart, the plants spaced at intervals of about 6 m along the lines. In all 1,449,919 seedlings of "rotan irit" and 662,301 seedlings of "rotan sega" were planted. Lines were cut in the secondary forest and weeded to keep the undergrowth clear, with some trees along the lines poison-girdled to open up the canopy. *Dillenia* appears to be the worst support tree as it sheds too much shade. Initially planting was carried out down the center of each line. However, it was soon found that the abundant feral elephants (descendants of tribute elephants given to the Sultan of Sulu in the late 18th Century by the East India Company, and released in Sabah) were wont to wander down the lines and pull up the young rattans. If planting occurred at or about 50 cm from the edge of the lines, hidden in the undergrowth, the elephants seemed to miss the rattans at their most vulnerable stage. Wild pigs also have proved to be troublesome, but again hiding the rattans at the edge of the lines seems to be very effective against grazing. During 1983 Borneo and Sabah in particular, suffered severe drought related to the El Niño effect. During this period, fire from neighboring land under shifting cultivation spread from time to time into the rattan plantations, with subsequent loss of seedlings. The first individuals of *Calamus trachycoleus* to flower outside Indonesia produced inflorescences during the drought, but fruit did not develop. The first mature viable seeds were produced in 1984. In February 1986 many of the earliest planted individuals of this species showed signs of flowering or fruiting, so Batu Putih Estate now is capable of producing relatively large quantities of seed.

Estimates of growth are very difficult to make within the rattan plantations because the rattan entanglements make even the counting of stems difficult, let alone the measurement of canes more than about 3 m long, without actually cutting them. There also has been a shortage of skilled observers to keep records. This is most unfortunate as valuable information for the future management of rattan plantations is being lost. Firm data will not be obtained until the first harvest. However, first impressions are most encouraging. Seedlings of *Calamus trachycoleus* are planted at an age of about 9–12 months, when they have aerial stems about 1 m tall. If planting is delayed for any reason (such as dry weather or lack of labor) there is a tendency for the aerial stems to become too long for easy handling and the longest stems have to be pruned back. After two and a half years it is estimated the most rapidly growing individuals have already produced about ten aerial stems, some of which may be as long as 6 m. Stolons are just beginning to form. Once the stolons are produced, further development of the rattans seems to be very rapid. At four years old, well grown individuals may consist of over forty aerial stems and some plants begin to produce inflorescences. The most exciting area within the estate is at Tanjung Bulat which was planted in late 1979. In February 1986 the levees of the Kinabatangan strongly resembled the rattan plantations of Central Kalimantan, being filled with an entanglement of *Calamus trachycoleus* (Fig. 1D). RMS staff estimate that some of the clumps now consist of about 80 aerial stems, of which some are about 25 m tall and have reached the canopy; some stolons have grown to about 10 m from the original planting point. This area is without doubt the best part of the estate and has become something of a showpiece.

The main concern in managing the plantation has not been with weeds, but with the control of light reaching the rattans. It is clear that in heavily shaded areas, such as under the canopy of *Dillenia* spp., the rattans have not performed well. Canopy opening was originally carried out by poison-girdling, but eventually it was found to be satisfactory to use a chain saw to remove offending trees without destroying all support for the canes. The control of the canopy has been a rather "hit or miss" affair and is obviously in need of refinement. There is another problem related to the light regime of the plantation. In deep shade rattan internodes are usually long; with increased light they become shorter. Cane with short internodes (i.e., less than 23 cm) has a lower market value than cane with long inter-

nodes (i.e., greater than 23 cm). Little is known of the internal qualities of the canes in relation to the light regimes. Many of these factors may only be investigated when the first harvest takes place.

At the moment it seems likely that the first harvest can take place when the plants are eight years old or in 1988 in some parts of the plantation. The estimate of the timing of the first harvest is based on the experience of the rattan planters in Central Kalimantan and on the growth rates of SAFODA's own rattan. One of the most intriguing questions is what is production likely to be? Average growth rates of 3 m per year per aerial stem have been recorded for *C. trachycoleus* in Sabah by Shim and Tan (1984). Although the Central Kalimantan rattan plantations have been in existence for over a century, and despite several recent pleas for further research, there are still no reliable data on the productivity of *Calamus trachycoleus*. That it is economically viable as a plantation crop is obvious from the fact that whole communities depend for their livelihood on rattan cultivation. RMS have made an estimate, based on what they have been told by villagers in Central Kalimantan, and based on random sampling of growth rates in the rattan plantations in Sabah (Shim & Tan, 1984), that after about 11 years, harvests of about 2.5 metric tonnes per hectare per year of raw rattan can be expected. This does not conflict greatly with estimates made by a smallholder in the Lower Labuk, Sabah based on two acres of cultivated *Calamus caesius*. At present the value of untreated cane is Malaysian $1600 per metric tonne, and that of treated cane Malaysian $3000 per metric tonne (treatment here means cleaned and smoked with sulphur).

If such estimates prove to be accurate, then the prospects for the Batu Putih Estate are excellent. The plantation appears to require relatively little cultivation, no fertilizer application seems to be necessary and harvesting probably requires much less manpower than crops such as rubber or oilpalm. Furthermore, land which was derelict and unsuitable for other crops has been utilized.

Most of the growth data and estimates of productivity are based on the performance of *Calamus trachycoleus*. As mentioned earlier, *C. caesius* has been very susceptible to damage caused by flooding, yet strangely enough there are scattered throughout the low-lying parts of the Batu Putih Estate very vigorous old clumps of this species. This suggests either there may be differences in behavior between individuals from different provenances or that adult plants are resistant to flooding. Certainly in *C. trachycoleus,* individuals do show flood damage. It appears that stolons are tolerant of flooding but that newly developing aerial stems are likely to die if severely flooded. Once an aerial stem reaches a certain height it is no longer susceptible to flooding. This needs further research.

As mentioned earlier, the Batu Putih Estate includes a small steep-sided hill which rises well above the levels of maximum flooding. This hill carries a beautiful fragment of primary hill dipterocarp forest. RMS have carried out small scale experimental planting of different species of rattan on the lower slopes of the hill and of *C. caesius* towards the top of the hill. *Calamus caesius* on the upper slopes has performed very poorly with very high mortality rates probably due to severe droughting. On the lower slopes, however, it has produced dense clumps of many stems in the damper sites. Other species tried include the large diameter canes *C. manan* and *C. subinermis.* The best grown individuals of the former have reached a height of about 6 m in three years while growth of the latter is slightly slower. *Calamus subinermis* is a clustered species which should make it more attractive as a plantation crop than the solitary *C. manan,* but the three year old plants of *C. subinermis* have yet to show any sign of suckering.

VI. Problems of the Cultivation of Small Diameter Canes

All in all, the Batu Putih Estate displays some of the great potential of rattan as a plantation crop. There are obviously many problems to be overcome, in particular the balancing of light and shade to give maximum growth rates of good quality canes, and the devising of efficient methods of harvesting canes from the great entanglements of rattans which are developing. As an experimental ground the estate could be put to very much greater use, but under present circumstances of manpower and cash shortages in Sabah this seems not to be possible. We do know enough about the cultivation of *C. caesius* and *C. tra-*

chycoleus to go ahead and establish plantations in perhumid areas. It seems unlikely that these species will perform well outside the tropical rain forest belt. In monsoon areas there is a completely different rattan flora and it would seem sensible to screen indigenous species in these areas for suitable sylvicultural subjects before embarking on large scale projects involving *C. caesius* and *C. trachycoleus.*

VII. Prospects for Large Diameter Canes

The prospects for the cultivation of large diameter canes are much less encouraging. Within Sumatra and the Malay Peninsula, and the one very small area of Kalimantan where it is also native, *Calamus manan,* "rotan manau" (Fig. 1A), is without doubt the most sought after and the best quality rattan. Through overexploitation, mature, harvestable canes are very rare and the demand for large diameter canes has now resulted in the harvesting of canes of poorer quality. Species such as *C. ornatus* Bl., *C. scipionum* Lour., *C. peregrinus* Furt. and *C. subinermis* have been used as "manau" substitutes until they themselves have become rare and overexploited. In the Philippines, "palasan," *Calamus merrillii* Becc. (*C. maximus* of some authors but not of Blanco) is the most important of the large diameter rattans, but it too has been overexploited. Most serious is the destructive exploitation of large species from Sulawesi before they are botanically known and their potential assessed (Dransfield, 1985). Without the cultivation of large diameter canes the long term prospects for the trade in such canes are bleak, yet it is these species which have proven to be most difficult to cultivate.

Observations on *C. manan* in the wild and in abandoned trial plots near Kepong suggested to Manokaran and me in 1977 that rapid growth of seedlings of this species required rather precise light conditions. Seedlings in small light gaps appear to respond well and can grow at rates of about 3 m per year. In the absence of light gaps seedlings remain as rosette plants on the forest floor for as long as 11 years without any appreciable aerial growth, yet full sunlight is detrimental to growth. Plantations of this species will require very precise manipulation of the canopy to produce optimal light conditions. Furthermore, *C. manan* is a very massive rattan, with stems capable of reaching about 180 m or more in length (Burkill, 1935), with sheaths to about 11 cm in diameter (Dransfield, 1979). The leaves, together with their terminal cirri, may reach 7 m or more in length, thus giving a crown diameter of about 14 m. Such a massive climber will probably require massive support, and it is not at all certain that large densities of mature *C. manan* plants can be supported by secondary forest. The trial plots of this species established by Manokaran near Kepong in logged-over forest may provide valuable data for cultivation. In 1984, after about seven years the trial plots of *C. manan* presented a spectacular sight, but already many of the canes had reached the canopy and the limit of support. The main disadvantage of this species as a sylvicultural subject is its solitary habit. Replanting would have to be carried out after each harvest. Clustering forms of *C. manan* have been reported from time to time (Dransfield, 1979; Manokaran, 1981) and these may have potential in the future. I believe priority should be given to the selection of good quality, large diameter species which cluster freely (Dransfield, 1985). One such is *C. merrillii*, widespread in the Philippines. Though not of such good quality as *C. manan*, this species is nevertheless the mainstay of the rattan industry in the Philippines. Trial plantings of *C. merrillii* have been established in the Philippines (Madulid, 1985) but have yet to give encouraging results. I have already made the plea for taxonomic inventories to identify large clustering canes of sylvicultural potential (Dransfield, 1985). One most promising species is *C. zollingeri* Becc. of Sulawesi; it belongs to the same section of the genus as *C. merrillii*. *Calamus merrillii* itself is very variable and canes from different provenances may possess different qualities. Variation in this species and the systematics of Section *Podocephalus* to which it belongs are currently being studied by E. Fernando in Los Banos, Philippines.

In summary, we know too little about the performance of large-diameter rattans to start large scale plantations. As I have stressed elsewhere (Dransfield, 1981, 1985), there is an urgent need for the setting up of more trial plots and for further taxonomic field work to identify species with sylvicultural potential.

VIII. The Future of Rattan Cultivation

The large scale cultivation of rattan in Central Kalimantan and the small scale cultivation near longhouses and in village orchards should be sufficient to indicate that rattan cultivation is economically viable. Observations from a smallholding of rattan in the Lower Labuk District of Sabah (Dransfield & Hepburn, unpubl.) indicate cash returns considerably in excess of a similar acreage of smallholding rubber, and as the rattan on this particular smallholding is planted in an orchard, there is also a financial return from durians, rambutans, and other fruit trees on the land. Small diameter canes such as *Calamus caesius* and *C. trachycoleus* are ideal crops for smallholders on marginal lands. The long period before the first harvest should present little problem when rattan is planted amongst a pre-existing tree crop such as fruit trees or rubber, or on marginal lands such as river banks and swamp margins. Village people in Southeast Asia are familiar with rattans as plants and as the source of cane, if not as a plantation crop, so introduction of planting methods may not be too difficult. Active extension through social forestry projects and, perhaps, making available planting material of *C. caesius* and, if possible, *C. trachycoleus* should be priorities for forest departments in the region. Although the plantation at Batu Putih promises so well, such large scale projects are prone to management problems and can be adversely affected by changes in the economic climate, whereas small scale plantations which act as a supplementary source of income to villagers are more likely to weather economic vicissitudes. The extraordinary shifting cultivation cycle with rattan cultivation during the fallow period recorded by Weinstock (1983) has great potential for areas where shifting cultivation is the most satisfactory method of rice cultivation, but there are few areas now where population pressure would allow a fallow period as long as 10–15 years.

The future for the cultivation of large diameter canes is much less certain. I believe cultivation will present problems in relation to the control of light regimes and the provision of support. Without some form of planting of large rattans or very strict control of exploitation, the trade in large canes will collapse. One exciting possibility for the future is the enrichment planting of forest with large canes. Protection forest such as water catchments or buffer zones to national parks and nature reserves would be ideal for the development of forest crops such as rattan which can be harvested without destruction of forest structure (Dransfield, 1981). The social importance of rattan can be great and governmental aid in the establishment of small scale rattan plantations could have far-reaching effects.

IX. Acknowledgments

I should like to thank the staff of Rattan Management Services Sdn. Bhd, Sandakan, in particular Mr. Tan Ching Feaw, and the staff of SAFODA at Batu Putih, in particular Mr. Shim Phyau Soon for their hospitality, their enthusiasm for rattans and for their willingness to share the research results of the Batu Putih Plantation.

X. Literature Cited

Burkill, I. H. 1935. A dictionary of the economic products of the Malay Peninsula. Crown Agents for the Colonies, London.

Darus, Haji Ahmad & Aminah Hamzah. 1985. Nursery techniques for *Calamus manan* and *C. caesius* at the Forest Research Institute nursery, Kepong, Malaysia. Pages 33–40 *in* K. M. Wong & N. Manokaran (eds.), Proceedings of the rattan seminar, 2nd–4th October, 1984, Kuala Lumpur, Malaysia. The Rattan Information Centre, Kepong, Malaysia.

Dransfield, J. 1977. *Calamus caesius* and *Calamus trachycoleus* compared. Gard. Bull., Singapore **30**: 75–78.

————. 1979. A manual of the rattans of the Malay Peninsula. Malaysian Forest Records No. 29. Forest Department, Malaysia.

————. 1981. The biology of Asiatic rattans in relation to the rattan trade and conservation. Pages 179–186 *in* H. Synge (ed.), The biological aspects of rare plant conservation. J. Wiley & Sons, London.

————. 1984. The rattans of Sabah. Sabah Forest Records No 13. Forest Department, Sabah.

————. 1985. Prospects for lesser known canes. Pages 107–114 *in* K. M. Wong & N. Manokaran (eds.), Proceedings of the rattan seminar, 2nd–4th October, 1984, Kuala Lumpur, Malaysia. The Rattan Information Centre, Kepong, Malaysia.

———— & N. W. Uhl. 1986. An outline of a classification of palms. Principes **30**: 3–11.

Heyne, K. 1917. De nuttige planten van Nederlandsche Indie, 1st ed. Weltevreden, Netherlands.

————. 1949. De nuttige planten van Indonesie, 3rd ed. n.v. Uitgeverijw van Hoeve, s'Gravenhage/Bandung, Indonesia.

IDRC. 1980. Rattan: A report of a workshop held in Singapore, 4–6 June, 1979. IDRC, Ottawa, Canada.

Kong-Ong, H. K. & N. Manokaran. 1984. Rattan: A bibliography. Forest Research Institute, Kepong, Malaysia.

Madulid, D. A. 1985. Cultivation trials of rattans in the Philippines. Pages 57–61 *in* K. M. Wong & N. Manokaran (eds.), Proceedings of the rattan seminar, 2nd–4th October, 1984, Kuala Lumpur, Malaysia. The Rattan Information Centre, Kepong, Malaysia.

Manokaran, N. 1981. Clustering in Rotan manau (*Calamus manan*). Malaysian Forest. **44**: 557–560.

Shim, P. S. & Muhammad A. Momen. 1985. A preliminary report on the growth forms of *Calamus caesius* and *C. trachycoleus* in SAFODA's Kinabatangan rattan plantation. Pages 63–71 *in* K. M. Wong & N. Manokaran (eds.), Proceedings of the rattan seminar, 2nd–4th October, 1984, Kuala Lumpur, Malaysia. Rattan Information Centre, Kepong, Malaysia.

———— & C. F. Tan. 1984. Development of rotan plantation in Sabah. A case study of rotan plantations in seasonally flooded areas. Paper presented at the Seminar on Forest Plantation Development in Malaysia, 9–14 July, 1984, Sabah. 15 pp.

Siebert, S. F. & J. M. Belsky. 1985. Forest product trade in a Filipino village. Econ. Bot. **39**: 522–533.

Tuil, J. H. van. 1929. Handel en cultuur van rotan in de Zuideren Oosterafdeeling van Borneo. Tectona **22**: 695–717.

Weinstock, J. A. 1983. Rattan: Ecological balance in a Borneo rainforest swidden. Econ. Bot. **37**: 58–68.

Wong, K. M. & N. Manokaran. 1985. Proceedings of the rattan seminar, 2nd–4th October, 1984, Kuala Lumpur, Malaysia. Rattan Information Centre, Kepong, Malaysia.

Native Neotropical Oil Palms: State of the Art and Perspectives for Latin America

EDUARDO LLERAS AND LIDIO CORADIN

Table of Contents

Abstract

A survey was made of the potential of neotropical palms as sources of oils and fats. Two distinct groups of oils, oleics and laurics, are found in palm fruits. Palm oleics, present in the mesocarp, are equivalent in their fatty acid composition and properties to oils from traditional oilseeds such as soybeans, groundnuts, maize, cotton, and olives, while laurics are exclusive to palm kernels. The sparse data on the productivity of neotropical palms suggests that many species have considerably higher potential yields than traditional oilseeds. In spite of the millions of hectares annually planted with oilseeds, the continent as a whole faces a shortage of vegetable oils and fats. The diversion of arable lands to oilseeds has led to a steady decline in per capita food production in Latin America, and palms may offer attractive alternatives. Most species are amenable to association with other crops, and areas planted with palms would not only be highly productive in terms of oils, but would also be available for growing foodstuffs. The decline of traditional extractive systems is discussed, and a domestication scheme is proposed. The need for international cooperation on palm research is emphasized. It is proposed that as a first priority, a survey of neotropical palms with potential as oil sources is necessary.

Key words: neotropics, oilpalms, yields, potential, extractive exploitation, domestication, palm oils

Resumo

Realizou-se um levantamento das palmeiras neotropicais a fim de se verificar o potencial destas espécies como fontes de óleos e gorduras. Basicamente são encontrados dois tipos de óleos em palmeiras. Os oleicos, que estão localizados na polpa dos frutos e são equivalentes, em têrmos de composição de ácidos graxos aos óleos das sementes de oleaginosas tradicionais, tais como: soja, milho, amendoim, algodão, e azeitona, e os láuricos que são exclusivos das amêndoas de palmeiras. Os dados existentes sobre a produtividade de diferentes espécies de palmeiras neotropicais indicam que estas apresentam potenciais significativamente superiores à das oleaginosas tradicionais. Apesar de que milhões de hectares são plantados anualmente com oleaginosas, a América Latina enfrenta uma falta crônica de óleos e gorduras. A utilização extensiva de terras agrícolas para a produção de oleaginosas anuais tem contribuído para uma queda crescente na produção de alimentos *per capita* na América Latina. Dado ao seu elevado potencial de produção e adaptabilidade às diferentes condições edafoclimáticas, as palmeiras constituem uma excelente alternativa agrícola. Enfatiza-se a possiblidade de consorciação com muitas culturas o que permite a utilização simultânea da terra para a produção de óleos e gorduras e a alimentação humana, com grãos e folhosas. Discute-se o declínio dos sistemas extrativos tradicionais e propõe-se um esquema para domesticação. Dá-se ênfase à necessidade de maior cooperação internacional e recomenda-se como primeira prioridade, o levantamento das espécies de palmeiras neotropicais que apresentam real potencial para exploração como oleaginosas.

I. Introduction

In the past two decades it has become evident that there is a world-wide shortage of vegetable oils and fats. This deficit, which not only affects products for direct human consumption, but is also reflected at an industrial level, is increasing at an alarming rate.

In-depth discussions on the causes and possible consequences of this situation are not relevant to the objectives of this paper. However, a few pertinent examples for the Americas may be cited. Balick (1982) notes that Colombia presently imports 35% of its needs for vegetable oils and fats, while having one of the lowest per capita consumptions of oil in the world. A similar, or perhaps even more critical situation can be observed in Peru, where some estimate that most vegetable oils and fats are imported. Brazil, the second largest soybean producer in the world, annually imports 10,000 metric tons of lauric derivates (Rogerio Igel, pers. comm.). The United States, while independent in terms of oleics, will never be autonomous regarding other types of oils such as laurics.

Throughout this century a great deal of literature on palms has been produced, exalting their potential as one of the most attractive sources of vegetable oils and fats. But, except for the coconut (*Cocos nucifera*), the African oil palm (*Elaeis guineensis*) and, most recently, the pejibaye (*Bactris gasipaes*), little has been done to follow up this postulated potential, or to modify extractive use of the species considered as most promising.

This paper is an effort to assess what is currently known concerning the potential of neotropical palms and to propose some lines of action for the future.

II. State of the Art

Of the possible 1600 species of palms for the Americas (Costa, in press; Glassman, 1971) perhaps 200 have been reported as sources of oils.

However, data are available for at most 20 or 25 species.

Most publications up to the present time, such as Pesce's (1941) classic, or those of Acosta-Solís (1971); Patiño (1977); Balick (1979, 1982); Martin & Guichard (1979), Moses (1982), Lleras et al. (1984) and Wandeck (1985) are limited to brief reviews of several species with a very general approach. Others (i.e., Anderson & Anderson, 1983; Blaak, 1983, 1984; Bondar, 1938; Hernandez-Xolocotzi, 1947; Lleras & Coradin, 1984; Markley, 1956, 1971, 1984; Mora-Urpí, 1984; Wandeck & Justo, 1983) treat individual species in more detail. Thus, research on production systems under cultivation has been carried out only for pejibaye (*Bactris gasipaes*—see Mora-Urpí, 1984), while complete studies on extractive exploitation are known only for babassu (*Orbignya phalerata*; i.e., Anderson & Anderson, 1983; Pick, 1985). For a few other species, such as macaúba (*Acrocomia aculeata*) and totai (*A. totai*), reasonable estimates exist of yields in native populations (Lleras & Coradin, 1984; Markley, 1956; Wandeck, 1985; Wandeck & Justo, 1983).

For practically all other species, data are at best fragmentary. Thus, although great emphasis is given to physical and chemical properties of the oils (e.g., Pesce 1941), usually no data are cited for productivity; when fruit yields are cited, little importance is given to percentages of oils or their characteristics. Therefore, inferences can only be made from a complex mosaic of references, and many important items are lacking.

In the following sections an attempt has been made to give a composite picture of what we know of the oils, yields, and other parameters of interest for neotropical oil palms. As will become evident, consistent estimates are only possible for a handful of species.

A. THE OILS

Several references to neotropical palm oils can be found in the literature. Some deal mainly with

Table I

Percentages of fatty acids in oleic oils in the pulps of some neotropical palms and in some important oil seeds. Data from various sources

Species	Myris-tic	Palmitic	Palmit-oleic	Stearic	Oleic	Linoleic	Lin-olenic	Arachid-ic
Acrocomia aculeata	—	17.5	2.3	2.7	65.9	11.6	—	—
Bactris gasipaes	—	4.6–33.2	1.6–9.0	0–2.7	35.8–68.2	13.3–24.0	—	—
Elaeis oleifera	0.1–2.5	18.8–47.0	1.2–1.5	0.6–9.0	40.0–67.0	2.0–15.9	0.5–0.6	—
Jessenia bataua	—	9.2	—	5.9	81.4	3.5	0.2–4.6	—
Oenocarpus spp.	—	11.8–14.6	—	7.8–9.6	54.3–64.8	13.8–23.3	—	—
Anacardium occiden-tale	—	11.7	—	—	74.6	6.9	—	—
Bertholletia excelsa	—	14.1	—	6.2	—	58.9	21.7	—
Arachis hypogaea	—	8.0	—	4.0	55.0	25.0	—	3.0
Zea mays	—	6.0	—	2.0	37.0	54.0	—	1.0
Glycine max	—	9.0	—	2.0	32.0	53.0	3.0	1.0
Helianthus annuus	—	5.0	—	2.0	35.0	57.0	—	1.0
Olea europaea	1.0	9.0–11.2	1.0–1.5	2.0	76.0–80.0	8.0–8.5	—	1.0
Gossypium hirsutum	1.0	21.0	—	2.0	25.0	50.0	—	1.0
Caryocar spp.	0.3–1.4	32.0–50.0	0.4–1.7	0.7–3.0	44.0–54.0	2.0–19.0	0.3–1.2	0.5–0.8

their suitability for industrial use (e.g., Pesce, 1941), and thus focus on defining physical and chemical properties of the oils such as melting points, acidity, and iodine and refraction values. Others (i.e., Balick, 1982; Mora-Urpí, 1984; Novaes, 1952; Wandeck & Justo, 1983) also give fatty acid compositions. However, data are limited to a very few species, and even for these, are incomplete.

In spite of the fact that many different types of fatty acids are known in nature, the great majority of vegetable oils and fats produced and consumed presently belong to the two main categories commonly referred to as oleics and laurics.

Oleic oils have in their basic composition fairly high percentages of oleic and linoleic acids, and are found in the mesocarp (pulp) of many palms as well as in the seeds of many other species such as soybeans, groundnuts, sunflowers, maize, cotton, olives, linseed, Brazil nuts, cashews, and sesame. These oils account for over 90% of world production of vegetable oils.

Laurics have high percentages of lauric and myristic acids, with varying percentages of other fatty acids. For all practical purposes, lauric type oils are only present in palm kernels, and the bulk of world production is centered on two species: the coconut (*Cocos nucifera*) and the African oil palm (*Elaeis guineensis*), in the latter

as a by-product of oleic production from the pulp. Laurics are considered as more noble than oleics and although perfectly appropriate for direct human consumption, their great demand for industrial use has made their price prohibitive for the former purpose.

Table I shows the fatty acid composition of pulp oils from various neotropical palms, compared to some other important oilseeds. As can be observed, there are no significant differences in fatty acid composition between palms and other oilseeds, and some palm oils are very similar to some of the finer grade oleics from other sources: for example *Jessenia bataua* and *Oenocarpus* spp. pulp oils are practically identical to olive (*Olea europaea*) oil. In this respect, Spruce (1908) noted that in the Amazon, olive oil was consistently adulterated with oils from these species, and it was impossible to tell the difference.

Table II shows that there are no significant differences in fatty acid composition when comparing some neotropical palm kernel oils with coconut and the African oil palm. Considering that data for most species are limited to one or two samples, it is likely that intraspecific variation will prove to be equal to variations observed between taxa in distant genera. Note, for example, the high variation in fatty acid composition cited by Mora-Urpí (1984) for *Bactris ga-*

Table II

Percentages of fatty acids in lauric type oils from kernels of some palms. Data from various sources

Species	% fatty acids							
	Myristic	Palmitic	Stearic	Lauric	Oleic	Linoleic	Capric	Ca-prylic
Acrocomia aculeata	8.5–15.4	6.2–15.4	1.6–2.6	43.7–44.9	16.5–24.6	1.6–24.6	5.3–2.8	7.4–7.8
Astrocaryum muru-								
muru	36.8	4.6	2.2	47.5	10.2	0.4	1.6	1.1
A. vulgare	21.6	6.4	1.7	48.9	13.2	2.5	4.4	1.3
Attalea oleifera	13.1	8.9	2.9	41.8	19.4	3.1	5.9	4.9
Bactris gasipaes	19.0–38.0	1.8–14.4	0.6–4.2	27.0–46.4	13.0–24.4	1.4–8.0	0.3–0.9	0.2–0.8
Cocos nucifera	13.1–18.5	7.5–10.5	1.0–3.2	44.1–51.3	5.0–8.2	1.0–2.6	4.5–9.7	7.8–9.5
Elaeis guineensis	14.1–17.1	6.5–8.8	1.3–2.5	46.9–52.0	10.5–18.5	0.7–1.3	3.0–7.0	2.7–4.3
Manicaria saccifera	18.9	8.2	2.4	47.5	9.7	1.4	6.6	5.3
Orbignya cohune	16.0	9.5	3.0	46.5	10.0	1.0	6.5	7.5
O. phalerata	15.4–16.5	5.8–8.5	2.7–5.5	44.1–45.1	11.9–16.1	1.4–2.8	6.6–7.6	4.1–4.8
Scheelea phalerata	14.6	11.5	4.2	28.5	26.8	4.7	4.2	5.1

sipaes, and by Wandeck (1985) for *Acrocomia aculeata* (Table II).

Therefore, no technical limitation exist for the use of palm oleics in substitution for oils from annual oilseeds, and as noted before, palms are the only sources of laurics.

B. YIELDS AND POTENTIAL

An objective evaluation of palm yields required an extensive review of available information. The idea was to address two basic questions: at what level do yields of neotropical palms under cultivation or rational management of native stands become economically viable and do reliable data exist to make inferences on this matter?

Information on yields of individual plants, or per hectare, or as estimates for existing natural stands are practically non-existent for most neotropical palms. Moreover, as is evident when examining the literature, estimates tend to be highly subjective and, often, wildly speculative.

Babassu (*Orbignya phalerata*) is an excellent example of this situation. Estimates on standing potential of native populations have varied between 4.2 billion (Gonsalves, 1938) and 45 million (Braga & Dias, 1968) metric tons of fruit per year. Likewise, great divergence is found in purported yields per hectare: Gonsalves (1938) gives figures of ca. 320 metric tons, Abreu (1940) estimates yields at 26 metric tons, while the Instituto do Babaçu—INEB (1981) has reached the more realistic figure of ca. 1800 kg of fruit/ha

based on a detailed survey of native babassu stands in Maranhão and Piauí.

Table III presents estimated yields for those neotropical oil palms for which information was available. However, since for many species the data presented are a composite from several sources, estimates cited here must be accepted with caution. Some important traditional oil palms, such as *Astrocaryum murumuru* and *Scheelea butyracea* (according to Pérez-Arbelaez, 1956, the most important oil palm in Colombia) were not listed, as available data were insufficient. As evident in the table, data are lacking for many items among those species listed; as more detailed, reliable data become available, many of these estimates may suffer profound modifications.

Furthermore, for the only species where genetic variability has been amply documented, *Bactris gasipaes*, it has been possible to detect a large degree of variation for all items listed. Thus, material obtained during recent collections in the Amazon basin (see Clement & Coradin, 1983) show variations in pulp to fruit ratios of between 98/100 to 40/100, with kernels varying from between 1–60% of total fruit weight. Concentrations of pulp and kernel oils have also been shown to be highly variable, and Mora-Urpí (1984) cites percentages of oil in the mesocarp as between 13–61%. Similar situations have been noted for seje (*Jessenia bataua*) by Blaak (1983) and for macaúba (*Acrocomia aculeata*) (Lleras & Coradin, unpubl. data).

The high genetic variability not only guaran-

Table III

Production estimates for individual plants of some neotropical oil palms. Data from several sources

Species	Fruit Weight/ kg	% pulp	% kernel	% oils Pulp	% oils Kernel	% oils Fruit	Oils/kg Pulp	Oils/kg Kernel	Oils/kg Plant
Acrocomia aculeata	125	45	10	60	65	25	25.0	7.0	32.0
Astrocaryum jauari	9	37	23	45	36	—	+1.4	+0.7	2.1
Attalea exigua	13	—	—	28	62	18	1.2	0.8	2.0
Bactris gasipaes	100	to 98	to 60	30	30	30	to 15.0	to 9.0	24.0
Jessenia bataua	30	10	59	23	1	17	4.0	—	4.0
Manicaria saccifera	7	—	37	—	57	—	—	1.2	1.2
Mauritia flexuosa	200	—	46	12	—	—	24.0	—	24.0
Maximiliana maripa	70	+66	+10	15	50	—	5.0	2.0	7.0
Oenocarpus spp.	30	10	62	—	—	—	4.0	—	4.0
Orbignya cohune	100(?)	—	10	—	50	5	—	5.0	5.0
O. phalerata	35	+30	+9	—	50	4.5	—	1.6	1.6
Scheelea excelsa	50	19	18	—	—	—	—	3.0	3.0
S. liebmanii	92	—	4	—	50	2	—	1.8	1.8
S. macrocarpa	100	—	—	—	—	—	5.4	7.5	12.9
Syagrus coronata	7	—	—	—	+66	—	—	3.0	3.0
Ynesa colenda	300	—	15	—	50	7.5	—	23.0	23.0

tees that estimates presented here will become obsolete once sampling is done systematically, but also will permit, for most of the species, selection of germplasm for specific purposes. Within some species, it will probably be possible to select either for a high proportion of kernel (laurics) or of pulp (oleics), with the secondary products constituting important sources of additional income.

To adequately determine the economic feasibility of oil-yielding palms, it is also necessary to compare their yields with those of some traditional oilseeds such as soybeans (*Glycine max*), groundnuts (*Arachis hypogaea*) and sunflowers (*Helianthus annuus*). Table IV presents some palms for which data are available under three different hypothetical planting densities when compared to some important cultivated oilseeds. It is here considered that densities of 150 individuals per hectare are possible for practically all palms, while higher densities will depend on the species in question.

As evident by the estimates, even at the lowest planting density proposed (150 plants/ha), many species have potentials that surpass the mean yields of most oilseeds: 500 kg of oil per hectare is not an uncommon yield for oil palms even when estimates are based on observation of wild populations without breeding or appropriate agricultural practices. This yield is very close to the genetic and agricultural limits of what can be achieved with monocultures of traditional oilseeds. It is clear that, as in the case of the oils, strong arguments exist to show that several neotropical palms have yields that are equal or superior to those of traditional oilseeds.

One of the major causes of the rapid, devastating advance of the agricultural frontier in the tropics has been the mechanized implantation of monocultures planted primarily for their oils. As evident in Table V, tens of millions of hectares of the best agricultural land are dedicated to the production of oilseeds with species that have mediocre yields when compared to palms, and this area increases every year. We are thus witnessing the rapid substitution of native stands of obscure perennial oil species for well researched annual oilseeds. Thus, the world faces a situation in which the most promising long term sources of oil are being decimated in favor of other alternatives. To fully understand this phenomenon, it is necessary to briefly review the state of extractive exploitation in the Americas.

III. Traditional Exploitation Systems

Up to 30 or 40 years ago, most of the oils consumed in Latin America were either of animal origin (lard) or from extractive exploitation of native perennials. This was mitigated by three

Table IV

Estimated yields under three different planting densities for some neotropical palms when compared with some traditional oilseeds

Species	150 Plants/ha Oleics kg	150 Plants/ha Laurics kg	200 Plants/ha Oleics kg	200 Plants/ha Laurics kg	400 Plants/ha Oleics kg	400 Plants/ha Laurics kg	Age first crop
Palms							
Acrocomia aculeata	3750	1050	5000	1400	10,000	2400	4–6
Astrocaryum jauari	210	105	280	140	560	280	—
Attalea exigua	180	120	240	160	480	320	—
Bactris gasipaes	1500	800	2000	900	4000	1800	3–4
Jessenia bataua	600	—	800	—	1600	—	—
Manicaria saccifera	—	180	—	240	—	480	—
Mauritia flexuosa	3600	—	4800	—	—	—	—
Maximiliana maripa	750	300	1000	400	—	—	8–11
Oenocarpus spp.	600	—	800	—	1600	—	—
Orbignya cohune	—	750	—	1000	—	—	16
O. phalerata	—	240	—	320	—	—	8–15
Scheelea excelsa	—	450	—	600	—	1200	—
S. liebmannii	—	270	—	360	—	720	16
S. macrocarpa	—	1125	—	1500	—	3000	—
Syagrus coronata	—	450	—	600	—	1200	—
Ynesa colenda	—	3450	—	4600	—	—	10–12
			Oleics/kg/ha				
Others							
Glycine max							Annual
Helianthus annuus			500				Annual
Arachis hypogaea			500				Annual

basic factors; the human population was considerably smaller, limited areas were planted with annual oilseeds, and perhaps most importantly, transportation systems were rudimentary.

With few demands, and little outside competition, fairly rustic regional solutions were adequate, and many small oil industries, based primarily on native regional resources, flourished. To cite some examples, for a long time Barcellos, on the upper Rio Negro, had an oil industry using *Astrocaryum jauari* as raw material. As can be evidenced by Pesce's (1941) treatise, Belém had several factories which processed *Astrocaryum murumuru* and a few other Amazonian species, while Maranhão and Piauí had many small industries based primarily on babassu. In Paraguay, as far back as the 1850's small industrial plants were processing totai (*Acrocomia totai*) fruit.

With the upgrading of the transportation network throughout Latin America after World War II, coupled with the planting of millions of hectares under annual oilseeds, the situation changed dramatically. Since most annual oilseeds were processed by modern, more efficient methods, their oils were cheaper to produce than those of most perennials. In addition, adequate transportation systems with ample distribution networks guaranteed that they could favorably compete with locally extracted oils. This led to the demise of many small local industries. Of those that have managed to survive, many have done so mainly by switching from processing fruits of native perennials to annual oilseeds.

Figure 1 presents an overview of overall production of some extractive species in Brazil between 1953 and 1981. As may be observed, with the exception of babassu (*Orbignya phalerata*) there has either been stagnation, or production is in steep decline. Note that some palms such as macaúba (*Acrocomia aculeata*) and murumuru (*Astrocaryum murumuru*), will rapidly lose all of their importance as extractive sources of oil if present trends continue, while species such as tucúm (*Astrocaryum vulgare*) and licurí (*Syagrus coronata*) which presented rates of increase similar to those of babassu during the 1960's, have also entered a state of stagnation. Reports

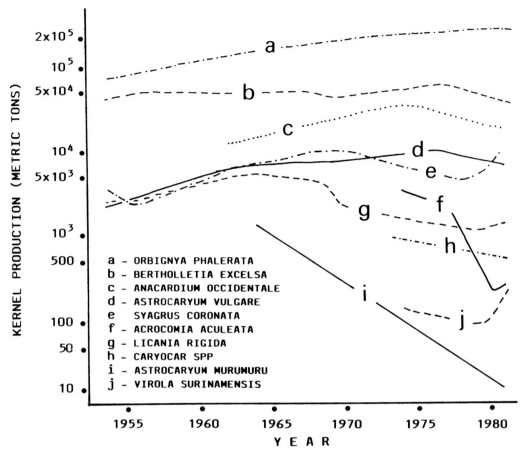

FIG. 1. Extractive production of kernels of some important species in Brazil between 1953 and 1981. (Source: IBGE, 1953/1983.)

for the last three years suggest that even in the case of babassu, production is decreasing (Rogério Igel, pers. comm.).

An analysis of the situation with respect to babassu may point out yet another cause for the rapid elimination of traditional extractivism. Figure 2 presents the evolution of extractive exploitation in northeastern Brazil during this century, compared with population increase during the same period (Lleras, 1983). The 97% correlation (significant at the 0.01 level) obtained between the two shows that increments in kernel production are, over the years, directly related to population growth, and not to any other factors such as increasing market demand. Furthermore, it is estimated that up to 53% of the rural population in the states of Maranhâo and Piauí depend on extraction of babassu kernels as

an important source of family income (Anderson & Anderson, 1983; Lleras, 1983; Pick, 1985). When prices paid per kg of clean kernels are followed over time, they are found remarkably constant: roughly US$0.15 in local currency from 1952 to present (Lleras, 1983). However, in the interim the buying power of the dollar has decreased constantly, and in real terms a kilo of babassu kernels buys less every year.

Although babassu probably constitutes the most acute example of dependency on an extractive resource, Figure 1 may reflect similar situations for all extractive species at present. At current market prices, continued exploitation of these resources in the traditional manner may simply not be worth the effort.

Latin America has a relatively meager tradition of management of natural populations of its

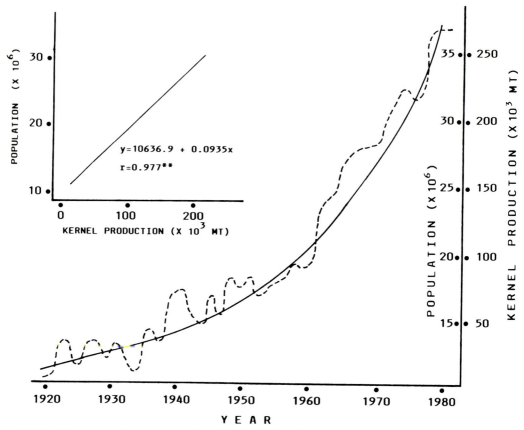

FIG. 2.   Comparison between population growth in the Brazilian Northeast with increase in babassu kernel production between 1920 and 1980. Continuous line, population; dotted line, kernel production. In-set: correlation between population growth and increase in kernel production.

promising perennials, and domestication is at best incipient or wholly nonexistent. With the exception of pejibaye (*Bactris gasipaes*), practically all neotropical palms are exploited exclusively through traditional extractive systems that may, in fact, contribute to the depletion of the resources themselves. Thus, seje palms (*Jessenia bataua*) are usually cut to facilitate access to the fruit bunches (Balick, 1982), and a similar situation seems to be the norm for *Mauritia flexuosa* in Peru (Bohórquez, 1976).

It is evident that these traditional systems, which are becoming economically less and less attractive over the years, are doomed to disappear. If no viable alternatives are offered in terms of management or domestication of native resources, these too will rapidly be eroded.

There is a common misconception that palms are attractive alternatives for planting on land that is marginal for agriculture. However, the opposite seems to be true. In the cases of both *Acrocomia* (i.e., Markley, 1956) and babassu (Anderson & Anderson, 1983; Markley, 1971) a strong correlation exists between presence of these species and prime agricultural land. In fact, it is possible that many of the palm species that form fairly pure stands have done this by invading areas that were opened for agriculture in the past. Obviously, once mechanized monocultures are introduced into a region, they are targeted towards the best available soils, and one of the criteria used to identify these is the presence of certain palms.

Massive stands of palms of many species are thus prime targets for elimination with the encroachment of the agricultural frontier, and in the past 20 years innumerable populations have been destroyed. In 1952, Novaes estimated that between 200,000 and 400,000 hectares of macaúba existed in the state of São Paulo, Brazil, and similar figures were cited for Minas Gerais as recently as 1983 by Wandeck and Justo. However, during our current research with macaúba, we have found that in São Paulo, with the exception of a few relict patches, macaúba has been eliminated, together with the rest of the native vegetation. For Minas Gerais, a very rough estimate suggests that presently, less than a fourth of the area reported by Wandeck and Justo (1983) still has macaúba (Peter Griffee, pers. comm.; our observations).

The situation is even more critical with babassu. In spite of being protected by law in the states of Maranhão and Piauí (Brazil), clearcutting of natural stands appears to be increasing exponentially in these two states (Anderson & May, 1985).

In 1977 we were able to observe that the agricultural frontier in Brazil had reached parallel 13°S. Today, it roughly extends to parallel 9°S, with the consequent destruction of the native vegetation. Referring back to Table V, it is fairly obvious that most of this land has gone into soybean culture.

IV. Future Perspectives

Considering that even with this massive destruction of natural vegetation, the continent as a whole cannot meet basic oil requirements, it is predictable that if present trends continue, we will have to choose between producing food or oil crops, as available arable lands will not be sufficient to meet both needs. In fact, while record agricultural productions are cited year after year throughout Latin America, the amount of food produced per capita has been in constant decline for the past two or three decades. Given these circumstances, it is most likely that we will have to resort to vegetable oils for fuel in the future, and thus be forced to choose between eating or having adequate industry and transportation.

It is obvious that any alternatives that can serve both purposes at the same time will have to be given top priority in the future, and as has been shown in this paper, many species of neotropical palms may meet this requirement. As oil crops, they have potential yields that are many times higher than traditional oilseeds. Furthermore, most species are amenable to intercropping with foodstuffs such as maize, rice, beans, greens and fruits, with oilseeds such as peanuts, soybeans and castorbeans, with many forages or even with species of special agro-industrial interest, such as guaraná or black pepper (Johnson, 1983).

The gradual substitution of the enormous areas presently planted in oilseeds by much more productive consociates, will also permit much better living conditions for human rural populations. This, in turn, will tend to reverse the huge social problem presently created with the mass exodus from rural to urban areas where adequate employment opportunities do not exist.

Finally, the gradual decrease in the deficit between demand and availability of oils through the redefinition of agricultural practices and production systems should also slow the rate of destruction of natural ecosystems, which would, at least, give us time to occupy these untouched areas in a more rational, less destructive, manner.

Viewing palm oil production at a continental level, and comparing the almost laughable quantities of oil contributed by palms as compared to other oilseeds (Table V), the above may seem overly optimistic. However, many countries have the capacity to plant millions of hectares in oilseeds year after year and to increase the areas planted by several hundred thousand or even a million hectares annually (Table V). It stands to reason that these countries also have the technical conditions to make the switch to perennial oilcrops and to reach satisfactory solutions within a few decades.

Although other by-products were not considered, these cannot be ignored. For example, all evidence indicates that the future of babassu (*Orbignya* spp.) as a viable economic proposition is dependent on integral utilization of the fruit (Anderson & Anderson, 1983; Pick, 1985 and many others). If pejibaye (*Bactris gasipaes*) is considered primarily as a source of laurics, apart from selection for material that is also rich in pulp oil, it is possible to select for starch, and Patiño (1977) notes that 2.2 kg of pulp yield 1 kg of flour. Similar options are possible for other species.

Furthermore, practically all kernel feed cakes have fairly high protein value with concentrations cited between 19% for pejibaye (Mora-Urpí, 1984) to 27% for macaúba (Novaes, 1952; Wandeck & Justo, 1983). Although these figures are somewhat lower than those of some oilseeds such as soybeans, palms certainly surpass most tra-

Table V

Production and areas planted (where data available) with some important oil species in the last decade. Data for corn are for all uses and not just oils. (From FAO, 1983 and IBGE, 1953–1983).

Species	Region	Production/1000 MT				Area Planted/1000 ha			
		1974–1976	1982	1983	1984	1974–1976	1982	1983	1984
Palms									
Coconut (copra)	World	4449	4764	5061	4626	—	—	—	—
	Latin Amer.	224	227	223	198	—	—	—	—
Kernels	World	1392	2210	2144	2416	—	—	—	—
	Latin Amer.	287	321	309	316	—	—	—	—
African Oil Palm									
Oleic oils	World	3186	6301	5913	6767	—	—	—	—
	Latin Amer.	113	203	224	235	—	—	—	—
Babassu (kernels)	World	220	—	—	—	0	0	0	0
	Latin Amer.	220	—	—	—	0	0	0	0
Other oilseeds									
Corn (seed)	World	333,671	448,107	347,636	448,027	123,261	125,748	118,524	131,256
	Latin Amer.	37,908	47,515	46,204	51,146	24,507	25,310	24,996	28,280
Castorbean (seed)	World	873	888	922	1029	1541	1580	1415	1623
	Latin Amer.	429	223	199	225	480	495	303	407
Cotton (seed)	World	23,631	27,955	27,885	33,224	—	—	—	—
	Latin Amer.	2836	2422	2290	2714	—	—	—	—
Rapeseed (seed)	World	7917	15,060	13,959	15,920	9086	12,963	12,535	13,646
	Latin Amer.	13	32	17	17	50	32	19	20
Linseed (seed)	World	2406	2844	2256	2466	5732	5382	4622	4900
	Latin Amer.	524	720	687	632	630	989	843	813
Soybeans (seed)	World	58,076	92,253	79,318	90,591	37,798	52,186	48,941	52,181
	Latin Amer.	11,077	18,714	20,206	23,202	6684	11,182	11,378	12,636
Groundnuts (seed)	World	17,830	18,241	19,021	19,836	18,920	18,509	18,570	18,227
	Latin Amer.	993	820	675	731	884	569	477	451
Sunflower (seed)	World	10,307	16,183	15,483	16,451	9114	12,982	12,813	13,721
	Latin Amer.	1010	2066	2458	2509	1271	1796	2002	2107
Olive Oil	World	1721	2125	1746	2092	—	—	—	—
	Latin Amer.	48	15	18	19	—	—	—	—
Sesame (seed)	World	1792	1883	2111	2132	6037	6213	6395	6327
	Latin Amer.	234	146	216	197	449	264	373	373

ditional oilseeds when yields are considered per hectare.

V. Research Priorities

From the above, it is obvious that many neotropical palms have considerable potential as economically viable sources of oil. However, available data are insufficient, not only for the species cited in this paper but for many others that may prove to be equally interesting in the future. Furthermore, the few data that exist are not wholly reliable.

It is here proposed that the first research priority be the unequivocal identification, with ample scientific evidence, of which species have true potential as oil palms. We cannot continue to propose theoretical potentials without reliable evidence. For this, it will be necessary to establish an international cooperative program to carry out a survey of neotropical palms that have promise for oils.

Obviously, it is impractical to carry out a survey of all possible neotropical oil palms. Priorities must be established, and we consider that the genera cited in this paper constitute a good starting point. However, within the limits imposed by logistic and financial considerations, as many other species as possible should be tested.

A standardized methodology must be adopted, to permit comparisons not only within a species under different ecological conditions or in different countries, but also between species and genera. As a first step in this direction, a general descriptor list for palms with all relevant items must be prepared. Available experience with macaúba, babassu and especially pejibaye, should make it possible to define these descriptors in a relatively short time. Another important aspect is adoption of standardized methods for fruit component analysis. Complete interaction between all teams involved in a program of this kind is also essential, and it is advisable to establish a common training scheme for all participants. Frequent exchange of researchers between teams is also to be recommended.

Another important point is how to proceed with those species for which a potential is shown. As a second priority, efforts should be directed towards research on management of native populations.

It has been shown in this paper that past efforts have been predominantly directed to studies in traditional extractive systems. It has also been shown that these systems are declining. There are, then, two main options for future sustained palm utilization: rational management of natural stands or domestication. We favor domestication, because we suspect that extractivism, even in the form of rational management of wild populations is doomed to disappear. However, there are factors that must be considered for each individual species when defining priorities.

For example, babassu (*Orbignya phalerata*) and aguaje (*Mauritia* spp.) cover extensive areas and play a very important role in the subsistence of large rural populations. Both take over ten years between planting and first fruiting. Ignoring extractivism to promote domestication would have a series of grave social consequences. Under present circumstances, it would be very difficult to replace these species in terms of family budgets with other sources of income (May et al., 1985). Furthermore, an existing resource, important because of its abundance, would be lost. Finally, the long time between generations in these species implies that breeding practices will only show long term results.

In the long run, these species and others in similar situations should probably be domesticated. However, higher priority must be given to rationalizing extractive exploitation to produce short-term results for the hard-pressed rural population.

Another clear case is that of species for which domestication is the obvious alternative. Pejibaye (*Bactris gasipaes*) exemplifies this very clearly. No wild populations are known, and it has a series of intrinsic characteristics that facilitate domestication, such as high yields, high genetic variability and precocity of flowering and fruiting. Macaúba (*Acrocomia* spp.) also fits into this category, with traits similar to pejibaye, and with a fairly restricted potential for extractive exploitation.

An intermediate situation, which probably includes the greatest number of species, is also found. Species in this category are not as markedly definable in terms of characters leading towards domestication, and have modest potentials for extractive exploitation. Although ultimate efforts should be towards domestication, they also offer alternatives for management of native populations while domestication is taking place. The *Jessenia–Oenocarpus* complex exemplifies this group.

Rational management of extensive natural populations can only be considered at species and regional levels. No overall approach is possible, as problems are intrinsic to the complex interactions of the species, the environment, and man. However, past experience has shown that it should be approached within modest, technically well-founded programs. As evidenced with babassu (i.e., Pick, 1985) grandiose schemes have only led to monumental failures, and it is fairly evident that overly ambitious programs can only lead to equally disastrous results. Within the scope of this paper, it is impractible to enter into details on extractive management of native populations, as individual situations require detailed analysis with particular solutions.

A. DOMESTICATION

Most of the species that serve mankind have been under domestication for millennia in a very slow, gradual process, and we have few examples of recent domestication. However, two examples can be cited to show that significant advances can be obtained in a relatively short time. These are rubber (*Hevea brasiliensis*) and, of more interest to this paper, the African oil palm (*Elaeis guineensis*). In this last species, within 80 years it was possible to go from the wild plant to domesticated crop, during which time yields increased from 300 to an average of over 4000 kg of oil/ha. Considering that native populations of *Elaeis guineensis* are not exceptionally productive nor particularly precocious, and that the majority of the achievements were obtained without current technology, it is reasonable to expect that major advances are presently possible, within even shorter periods, for species that are more precocious and have higher yields in the wild than native populations of the above-cited species. However, if future efforts are to be successful, domestication must be tackled in an integrated fashion. Piecemeal research, without a very clear definition of global objectives, must be avoided if significant results are expected before most of the native resources are totally depleted.

When the Centro Nacional de Recursos Genéticos—CENARGEN/EMBRAPA was faced with the need to propose new alternatives as crops for the future, it was realized that little could be accomplished without coherent domestication programs. Coradin and Lleras (this volume) present a model that was developed as basic to domestication of neotropical perennials at CENARGEN, and that is currently being carried out, with US-AID support, for macaúba (*Acrocomia* spp.). In this unified scheme, research activities range from assessing genetic resources in the wild to industrial processing, without neglecting socio-economic aspects, which are considered of great importance if domestication of these species is to serve a lasting social purpose.

It is obvious that due to the broad range of any program of this kind, no one institution, and possibly no individual country, will have the capacity to work on its own. Cooperation between institutions, at the national and international levels, is essential if we intend to domesticate neotropical oil palms. Much needs to be done, but through decisive cooperation, there is no reason to believe that we cannot find ways to utilize these great native potential sources of oil in a rational, non-destructive manner.

VI. Acknowledgments

We wish to thank Drs. Michael J. Balick (New York Botanical Garden Institute of Economic Botany), Gustaaf Blaak (Food and Agriculture Organization of the United Nations), and Rogério Igel and Peter Griffee (Grupo Ultra) for helpful discussions and information. Data for this paper were partially obtained while doing research on projects 02380022/0, 02381117/8, 02384003/6 (Programa Nacional de Pesquisa de Recursos Genéticos), 03683040/4 and 03683041/2 (Programa Nacional de Pesquisa de Energia) of the Empresa Brasileira de Pesquisa Agropecuária, and Agency for International Development grants DAN-5542-G-SS-2093-00 (pejibaye), PDC-5542-G-SS-5034-00 (macaúba) and DAN-5542-G-SS-1089-00 (babassu).

VII. Literature Cited

Abreu, S. F. 1940. O côco babaçu; e o problema do combustível. Instituto Nacional de Tecnologia, Rio de Janeiro. 91 pp.
Acosta-Solis, M. 1971. Palmas económicas del noroccidente Ecuatoriano. Naturaleza Ecuatoriana **1(2)**.
Anderson, A. B. & E. S. Anderson. 1983. People and the palm forest. Final report to USDA Forest Service. Washington, D.C. 157 pp.

———— & P. H. May. 1985. A palmeira de muitas vidas. Ciência Hoje **4(20):** 58–64.

Balick, M. J. 1979. Amazonian oil palms of promise: A survey. Econ. Bot. **33(1):** 11–28.

————. 1982. Palmas neotropicales: Nuevas fuentes de aceites comestibles. Interciencia **7(1):** 25–29.

Blaak, G. 1983. Economic prospects for oil extraction from fruit of the seje palm as a rural industry. 10 pp. (typescript).

————. 1984. Procesamiento de los frutos de la palmera cucurita (*Maximiliana maripa*). Pages 113–117 in Palmeras poco utilizadas de América tropical. Food and Agriculture Organization of the United Nations/Centro de Agricultura Tropical Para la Investigación y la Enseñanza, Imprenta Lil, San José.

Bohórquez, J. A. 1976. Monografía sobre *Mauritia flexuosa* L. et F. in Simpósio internacional sobre plantas de interés económico de la flora Amazónica. Instituto Interamericano de Cooperación para la Agricultura. Informes de Conferencias, Cursos y Reunioes **93:** 223–248.

Bondar, G. 1938. O licuriseiro (*Cocos coronata* Mart.) e suas possibilidades na econômia Brasileira. Bol. Inst. Centr. Fomento Econ. Bahia **2:** 1–18.

Braga, H. C. & D. C. Dias. 1968. Aspectos sócio-econômicos do babaçu. Instituto de Oleos, Rio de Janeiro. 87 pp.

Clement, C. R. & L. Coradin. 1983. Peach palm (*Bactris gasipaes* H.B.K.) germplasm bank. Report presented to the U.S. Agency for International Development (USAID). Manaus. 121 pp.

Coradin, L. & E. Lleras. 1988. Overview of palm research on domestication in Latin America. Adv. Econ. Bot. **6:** 175–189.

Costa, J. T. M. (In press). Sistemática das palmeiras neotropicais—Situação atual. In Anais do 36° Congresso Nacional de Botânica.

Food and Agriculture Organization of the United Nations. 1985. FAO Monthly Bulletin of Statistics. 8(1–3). FAO, Rome.

Glassman, S. F. 1972. A revision of B. E. Dahlgren's index of American palms. J. Cramer. Leuterhausen.

Gonsalves, A. D. 1938. O babaçu na economia nacional. Diretoria de Estatistica da Produção. Rio de Janeiro. 86 pp.

Hernández-Xolocotzi, E. 1947. La *Scheelea liebmanii* Becc. (coyol real o corozo): Su distribución y producción. Anal. Inst. Biol. 18: 43–70.

Instituto Brasileiro de Geográfia e Estatística. 1953–1983. Anuário estatístico do Brasil. Fundação Instituto Brasileiro de Geográfia e Estatística, Rio de Janeiro.

Instituto Estadual do Babaçu. 1981. Mapeamento das ocorrências e prospecçâo do potencial atual do babaçu no estado do Maranhão. Companhia de Pesquisa e Aproveitamento de Recursos Naturais/Fundação Instituto Estadual do Babaçu, São Luís. 67 pp. + appendices.

Johnson, D. V. 1983. Multi-purpose palms in agroforestry: A classification and assessment. Int. Tree Crops J. **2:** 217–224.

Lleras, E. 1983. Situação atual e perspectivas do babaçu. Report to CENARGEN/EMBRAPA. Typescript. 25 pp.

———— & L. Coradin. 1984. La palma macaúba (*Acrocomia aculeata*) como fuente potential de aceite combustible. Pages 102–122 in Palmeras poco utilizadas de América tropical. Food and Agriculture Organization of the United Nations/Centro de Agricultura Tropical para la Investigación y la Enseñza, Imprenta Lil, San José.

————, D. C. Giacometti & L. Coradin. 1984. Areas críticas de distribución de palmas en las Américas para colecta, evaluación y conservación. Pages 67–101 in Palmeras poco utilizadas de América tropical. Food and Agriculture Organization of the United Nations/Centro de Agricultura Tropical para la Investigación y la Enseñanza, Imprenta Lil, San José.

Markley, K. S. 1956. Mbocayá or Paraguay coco palm: An important source of oil. Econ. Bot. **10(1):** 3–32.

————. 1971. The babassu oil palm of Brazil. Econ. Bot. **25:** 267–304.

Martin, G. & P. H. Guichard. 1979. A propos de quatre palmiers spontanés d'Amérique latine. Oleagineux **34(8–9):** 375–381.

May, P. H., A. B. Anderson, M. J. Balick & J. M. F. Frazão. 1985. Substince benefits from the babassu palm (*Orbignya martiana*). Econ. Bot. **39(2):** 113–129.

Mora-Urpí, J. 1984. Ei pejibaye (*Bactris gasipaes* H.B.K.): Origen, biología floral y menejo agronómico. Pages 118–160 in Palmeras poco utilizadas de América tropical. Food and Agriculture Organization of the United Nations/Centro de Agricultura Tropical para la Investigación y la Enseñanza, Imprenta Lil, San José.

Moses, T. 1962. Palms of Brazil. Principes **6:** 26–37.

Novaes, R. F. 1952. Contribuição para o estudo do coco macaúba. Escola Superior de Agricultura Luiz de Queiroz, Piracicaba. 86 pp.

Patiño, V. M. 1977. Palmas oleaginosas del Pacífico. Cespedesia: 23/24.

Pérez-Arbelaez, E. 1956. Plantas utiles de Colombia. Camacho Roldán, Bogotá, 832 pp.

Pesce, C. 1941. Oleaginosas da Amazônia. Rev. Veterinária **2:** 1–128.

Pick, P. J. 1985. Babassu (*Orbignya species*): Gradual disappearance vs. slow metamorphosis into integrated agrobusiness. Report prepared for The New York Botanical Garden Institute of Economic Botany. Bronx, New York. 56 pp.

Spruce, R. 1908. Notes of a botanist on the Amazon and Andes. Vol. 1 (A. R. Wallace, ed.). Macmillan, London. 518 pp.

Wandeck, F. A. 1985. Oleaginosas nativas. Aproveitamento para fins energéticos e industriais. Estudos Gessy Lever série Brasileira **1:** 1–30.

———— & Justo, P. G. 1983. A macaúba, fonte energética e insumo industrial. Sua significação economica no Brasil. Report presented to Gessy Lever. 52 pp.

Aguaje (*Mauritia flexuosa* L. f.) in the Economy of Iquitos, Peru

CHRISTINE PADOCH

Table of Contents

Abstract

Exploitation of minor forest products has played an important role in the economic history of the Peruvian Amazon. However, the importance of these products in local commerce has yet to be examined. This article discusses the role of the fruits and other products of aguaje (*Mauritia flexuosa* L. f.), a naturally occurring palm, in the economy of Iquitos, Peru. It is shown that *Mauritia* fruits are collected and sold in large quantity and are locally processed into a number of products. Trade in the fruits and related products provides employment and income for a large number of area residents, most of them women. Compared with commerce in other regional products, aguaje appears to offer an exceptional opportunity for economic advancement to women. Destructive harvesting practices are threatening continued supply of the fruit.

Key words: forest products, *Mauritia,* palms, marketing, Amazon, Peru

Resumen

La extracción de productos forestales diferentes a la madera ha jugado un papel importante en la historia económica de la Amazonía Peruana. Sin embargo, todavía faltan estudios sobre la importancia del comercio local de dichos productos. En este artículo se discute el papel de frutas y otros productos del aguaje (*Mauritia flexuosa*), una palmera silvestre, en la economía de Iquitos, Perú. Se muestra que las frutas de *Mauritia* son extraídas en grandes cantidades y procesadas localmente en diferentes productos. La comercialización de las frutas y otros productos da empleo e ingresos a una considerable población de la region, en su mayoría, mujeres. En comparación con el comercio de otros productos regionales, el aguaje ofrece una oportunidad excepcional a las mujeres de mejorar su nivel económico. Las prácticas destructivas empleadas para cosechar la fruta amenazan el abastecimiento del aguaje en el futuro.

I. Introduction

In the economic history of the lowland Peruvian Amazon and of Iquitos, its commercial center and largest city, forest products have figured prominently. The great rubber boom, which end-

ed about 1914 and which virtually built the city, was based on the exploitation and export of rubber derived from several natural forest species (*Hevea brasiliensis* Muell. Arg., *Castilla elastica* Cerv.). Many other minor forest products, among them gums (balata, *Manilkara* spp.; leche caspi,

Couma macrocarpa Barb. Rodr.), natural insecticides (barbasco, *Lonchocarpus utilis* A. C. Smith), and essential oils (rosewood, *Aniba roseaodora* Ducke), were exploited and exported, providing employment and economic gain, however undervalued and shortlived, for both the rural and urban populations of the region.

Apart from these well-known export items, there are many minor forest products including fruits, fibers, resins, medicinals, and special woods, which have been and continue to be important in the internal trade of the region. Several studies have shown that the harvesting of these products provides an important source of income for members of the many small rural communities found along the area's rivers (Hiraoka, 1985; ONERN, 1976; Padoch, 1987; Padoch et al., 1985; San Román , 1975). However, except in the case of rubber, little information is available on the contribution that minor forest products make to the urban economy of the area.

This article outlines the economic role played by aguaje (*Mauritia flexuosa* L. f.) in Iquitos, the city where the fruits and other products of the palm are processed, bought, and sold. Apart from plantains, which are the dietary staple in Iquitos, aguaje is without doubt the most important fruit that appears in the urban market. Although it is not processed on an industrial scale, and is exported from the region only in minimum quantities, the fruit provides employment and income for a surprising percentage of the city's population, particularly its poor and its women. Aguaje is also unusual among fruits marketed, because unlike those of other species, its fruits are locally processed into a number of saleable products. And in the mythology of the city, aguaje occupies a special place as well; it is an aid in love magic and the subject of both traditional myths and outrageous modern claims.[1]

In discussing a product that is not an important export, and in describing its urban rather than rural role, this article attempts to emphasize and quantify an aspect of the economy of Amazonian forest products that has yet to be appreciated in the literature.

The data presented were gathered during the course of a year and a half's study on the economic importance of native fruits in the Iquitos region. Data were collected by interviewing vendors and processors on all levels of the trade, as well as by frequent observation of marketing activities.

II. Urban and Rural Patterns in the Northeastern Peruvian Amazon

The city of Iquitos, which has a population of approximately one-quarter million people, serves as a commercial and government service center for an enormous area of Peru's lowland Amazon region. Downriver from the port, only the towns of the border offer any commercial competition to Iquitos. Upriver, only Pucallpa, Yurimaguas, and Tarapoto offer substantial commercial outlets in the lowland area, and each of these is many days away by river; there are no long-distance roads. Thus, any products produced for sale along the Amazon, the lower Napo, Ucayali, and Marañón Rivers, as well as their innumerable large and small affluents, tend to make their way to Iquitos' ports and markets. At present, the economic situation of the city is unfavorable. The timber trade is on the decline and the sawmills and plywood factories, which once employed many and brought considerable money into the local economy, are closed or are operating at only a small percentage of their capacity. Exploration for and exploitation of petroleum, the other large employer in recent years, is also stagnant and offers employment to few.

But Iquitos continues in its traditional role as a place to buy and sell. Retailing and small-scale wholesaling yield employment and income to a large percentage of the city's poor and underemployed.

The rural population served by Iquitos is composed largely of small farmers who are also part-time forest product extractors, fishermen, hunters, and at times wage laborers. In most cases subsistence production predominates over production for the market. However, virtually without exception, every producer living within a radius of a week's travel to the city participates to some extent in the local market economy.

Although since the 1950's agriculture has become economically more important than forest product extraction in the region, when many residents of the northeastern Peruvian Amazon need

---

[1] Perhaps the most outrageous is the recent rumor, which is widely believed, that aguaje fruit cures AIDS.

to earn a little cash, they turn to the forest. Among the most important exploitation zones are the poorly drained areas where several economically important palms grow in abundance (see Kahn, this symposium). Of these palms, which include huasaí or chonta (*Euterpe precatoria* Mart.) and ungurahui (*Jessenia bataua* (Mart.) Burret), aguaje (*Mauritia flexuosa*) is harvested in the largest quantities for sale in the markets of Iquitos.

III. Zones of Commercial Aguaje Extraction

Within several days' travel of Iquitos, particularly in the extensive low areas between the Ucayali and Marañón Rivers, as well as in the drainages of the Tigre and Chambira Rivers stretching north from the true left bank of the Marañón, there exist large areas known as *aguajales,* forests dominated by *Mauritia flexuosa*. In its study of the natural resources of an area of 5,500,000 hectares surrounding the city of Iquitos, a team from Peru's Oficina Nacional de Evaluación de Recursos Naturales (ONERN) estimated that 1,900,000 ha or 34.6% of the wooded area included in the study was aguajal, or swamp forest in which *Mauritia* and *Euterpe* represented 80% of the trees found (ONERN, 1976, p. 87). While this may be somewhat of an overestimate, the aguajales within several days' travel from the market by small boat are indeed enormous, and they exist on very poorly drained lands rarely used for other purposes.

The aguajales from which the great part of Iquitos' supply comes are located on the Marañón and its lower affluents. A significant amount, however, also comes from swamps along the Nanay River, Napo, and areas bordering the Amazon and Ucayali. Aguajales located less than a day's travel to the city are now generally very poor in fruit because of destructive harvesting practices; palms are generally cut down to harvest the fruit. The maximum distance from Iquitos of commercially workable aguajales generally depends on the rapidity with which the fruit spoils and the slowness of river transport. Since aguaje fruit will stay fresh for only about five to six days, some areas now being harvested—those on the Chambira River, for example—represent the actual outer limits of commercially harvestable

aguajal. Small cargo boats, often powered by *peque-peques* (highly reliable but slow, air-cooled outboard motors), need about four days to reach the market. The faster public cargo boats or *lanchas* reach Iquitos more quickly, in approximately two to two and a half days, but aguaje spoils rapidly in their unventilated cargo holds.

While almost all aguaje palms in the area are naturally occurring, there are some planted trees, particularly those found near houses. Farmers know that aguaje can be successfully planted both in well- and poorly-drained soils, however cultivation is minimal. Many still believe that the aguajales of the region are an infinite resource and therefore planting is unnecessary.

IV. Aguaje in the Market

Throughout Iquitos, on streetcorners and in markets, and dark red, scaly, fruit of aguaje is sold. Most fruits are ellipsoidal in shape, although occasionally almost round ones are seen. They vary considerably in size; 5 by 3.5 cm (see Fig. 1), however, can be considered average dimensions for fruits marketed in Iquitos. The fruit's dark red to brown pericarp is composed of overlapping rhomboidal scales. It covers a mesocarp—the only part eaten—which is rarely more than 3 mm thick. This mesocarp tends to be acid and oily, and varies in color from bright yellow to deep orange. The darker colored fruits are often less acidic and are preferred by consumers. Most of the fruit's volume and weight consists of a large seed, which is discarded.

In Iquitos aguaje fruit is sold in several forms: raw, *maduro* (ripe, that is, made soft by soaking it in lukewarm water for a few hours), as *masa* (that is, the pulp mashed and the seeds extracted), as *aguajina* (a drink), as *curichi* (a frozen drink in a plastic bag), as *chupetes* (popsicles), or as ice cream.

In the raw form the fruit is usually marketed either in the boat that brought it to port or in the port itself, by the "50-kg sack," which tends to weigh somewhat less than 50 kg and usually contains approximately 1000 fruits. Once the fruit has been sold in the port area, it may be resold, still in the 50 kg sack, to another vendor—whether wholesaler or retailer—or it may be divided and sold in similar quantities and/or in processed form.

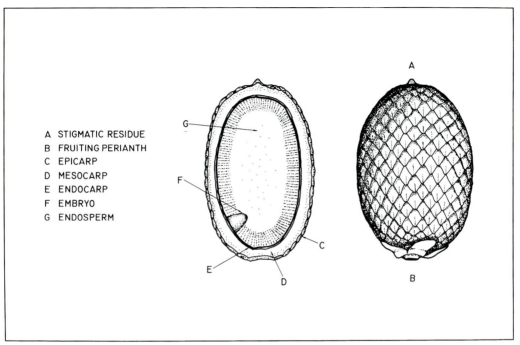

A STIGMATIC RESIDUE
B FRUITING PERIANTH
C EPICARP
D MESOCARP
E ENDOCARP
F EMBRYO
G ENDOSPERM

FIG. 1.   Longitudinal section and exterior of mature aguaje (*Mauritia flexuosa*) fruit (1.5×). Drawn by E. J. Hammond.

When aguaje apears in the market (as opposed to the port area) it is usually sold in *bandejitas* or small basins that on average contain about 50 fruits but whose size and capacity vary enormously. Occasionally the fruits are resold raw in very small cups or small baskets.

On the edges of the market area, but more usually on street corners away from the active marketplaces, aguaje is sold in its "ripe," softened state in quantities of four to eight fruits, usually in a plastic bag and partially or completely peeled.

Within the market, aguaje is also sold as *masa* in plastic bags said to contain "one kg" or "half a kg." These bags are actually never weighed; buyers judge, rather, the size of the bag. The *masa* is made of "ripe" fruit that has been mashed, the seeds extracted, and the resulting paste packed in plastic. Masa can be used by the housewife to prepare aguajina, a drink made by mixing the paste with water and sugar. The prepared drink is also sold at stalls in the market as well as in juice bars and restaurants located throughout the city.

Masa or *aguajina* are also the bases for making a variety of frozen desserts: *curichis, chupetes,* and ice cream. The first, an easily made treat that requires only *aguajina,* very small plastic bags, and a freezer, tends to be sold by people from their homes. The sale of *curichis* is especially common in *pueblos jovenes,* the poorer parts of the city. The making and selling of chupetes requires more knowledge and equipment and most such "popsicles" are turned out in small factories and are hawked from insulated wheeled carts by male street vendors. Ice cream tends to be manufactured and sold by more professional operations and sold in more expensive surroundings. Although other flavors are also used in the manufacture of these frozen products, in all three forms, aguaje is by far the favorite flavor, and especially with *chupetes* (which are produced in much greater volume than ice cream), all other flavors are considered a substitute. Many people would not even consider eating a *chupete* of any other flavor.

The aguaje palm also provides other products which appear in the market. The most important

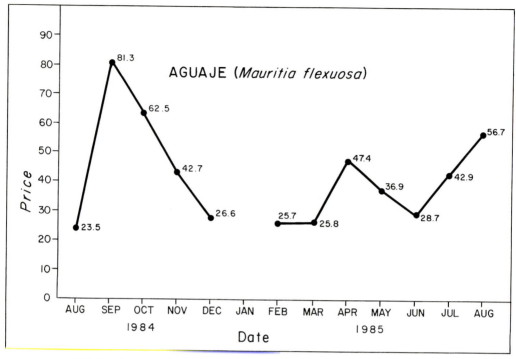

FIG. 2.   Average price in Intis of a 50 kg sack of aguaje. Drawn by B. Angell.

of these secondary products are *esteras,* screens made of dried sections of the petiole tied or woven together with strips of tree bark. Such *esteras* are used as room dividers in houses, as walls and roofs for market stalls, and for other temporary construction needs. In a few cases, *esteras* have been attached to more solid walls and painted or shellacked to lend a "rustic" touch to restaurants, bars, etc.

Another market product that is harvested from aguaje palms are *suri,* larvae of beetles (*Rhynchophorus palmarum* L.) that burrow into dead and fallen trunks. Suri are sold in the market both alive and fried in their own fat. These very oily delicacies are highly prized by many and fetch a rather high price both raw and cooked (Hiraoka, 1985).

In other parts of the Amazon Basin, several other products using aguaje fruits and fiber are made and sold.[2] While the variety of commercial

products made from *Mauritia* in the Iquitos market may appear limited when compared with production in some regions of Brazil (G. Prance, pers. comm.), the amount of processing that aguaje undergoes in the Peruvian Amazon is highly unusual for a fruit of the area. No other fruit is sold in so many different forms.

The many ways in which aguaje is sold in Iquitos accounts to some degree for the large quantity consumed. Also important in explaining the level of consumption is cultural preference, Iquiteños definitely have a taste for aguaje. The eating of a few "ripe" fruits is a daily necessity for many, and such snacking accounts for the consumption of a significant percentage of the total quantity bought and sold in the city. Although I was not

Amazon and in other parts of tropical Latin America, aguaje fruits, fibers, starch and other plant parts are used to manufacture a variety of household products that are rarely or never seen in the market. The indigenous Warao of the Orinoco delta use perhaps more parts of the Mauritia palm than any other group. They are believed to be the only people to use the starch found in the trunk of the palm (Heinen & Ruddle, 1974; Wilbert, 1972).

[2] In this article only the aguaje products sold in the markets of the Iquitos area are discussed. It should be mentioned, however, that in both the lowland Peruvian

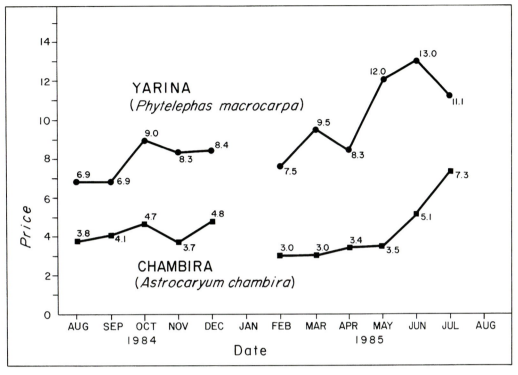

FIG. 3. Average price in Intis of two popular palm fruits. Drawn by B. Angell.

able to verify exactly the amount that arrives in the city on any particular day, through numerous interviews and much observation, I arrived at a reliable estimate of 15 metric tons as the daily demand for the fruit in the urban area.[3] Often the demand is not met completely and the price rises accordingly.

The very high and constant demand for aguaje also marks it as unusual among local fruits. Usually there is a period of relative scarcity of aguaje from mid-August to mid-November due to seasonality in fruiting; the price often rises by 100% or more during these months. However, an unusual scarcity of aguaje occurred in 1984, and

sent the wholesale price soaring to extraordinary levels (see Fig. 2).

As is evident from Fig. 2, the average price for a 50 kg sack increased almost four-fold from August to September. In the first week of September some buyers were paying six times the previous week's price for a sack of aguaje. This pattern of extreme rises does not occur with other palm fruits (see Fig. 3) nor with virtually any other fruit that we have studied in Iquitos. The very strong and relatively inelastic demand for aguaje is explained by the fact that a small but significant processing industry relies on the fruit for its raw material. And, of course, the great liking that Iquiteños have for the fruit also accounts for their willingness to pay high prices.

V. The Structure of the Aguaje Trade

Not only are the urban consumers of aguaje many, those that are involved in marketing the fruit in various forms figure in the hundreds. The

[3] This estimate is based largely on interviews with wholesalers who deal in aguaje. Those wholesalers who agreed to estimate the quantity of aguaje that can be sold each day in Iquitos (some refused to even guess), consistently suggested approximately 300 sacks as the daily demand. Observations of price changes during periods of scarcity and abundance tended to confirm this estimate.

chains of actors involved, including the gatherers in the aguajales of the Marañon, the retailers in Iquitos, and the many intermediaries, are often long and complex and it is impossible to precisely count the number of people who handle the fruit in some way. I shall merely attempt to sketch the flows, estimate the numbers of traders, and describe some of the urban actors.

In a regional study done by ONERN, an attempt was made to describe the structure of the aguaje trade (1976, pp. 252, 253). The short sketch fails to convey the complexity of the average operation, ignoring for instance the importance of contracts in aguaje collection and marketing. The marketing chains by which aguaje arrives in the city markets, not only end but also begin in Iquitos. The chain often starts with large-scale dealers or wholesalers. These important dealers, whom I believe to number about eight, are all urban residents, although many of them have important ties to the major source areas. Several of them once lived in the area of the Marañon, Tigre, or Chambira, and many may have some relatives—real or fictive—who continue to live in the harvesting zones.

Since *Mauritia* is considered an important forest product and is commercially exploited, The Ministry of Agriculture's Department of Forestry and Fauna began in the last several years to require that all persons who intend to harvest the fruit commercially obtain a license to exploit a particular extent of forest and pay a tax. The necessary paper work and prepayment of 5% of the tax must be done in a Ministry office in Iquitos or Nauta. Few small, rural-based extractors wish to engage in the bureaucratic complications and therefore few ever obtain their licenses; this strengthens urban control over the aguaje trade. Most large dealers in Iquitos do get exploitation rights to an area of aguajal. An estimate is then made of the weight of fruit that will be harvested from the specified area and the concessionaire is allowed to bring that amount—usually 50,000 kg over two years—into the ports of Iquitos.[4]

The larger, as well as some smaller, wholesalers, after receiving official permission to harvest the fruit commercially, usually make contracts with and advance money to a number of extractor-contractors who actually live in or spend most of their time in the palm swamp zones. These contractors then hire harvesters or subcontract to others who harvest or employ harvesters. The contractors must see that the fruit is collected quickly, so that it reaches the city in marketable condition.

When Doña N. controlled most of the aguaje market in the 1960's and early 1970's, in partnership with another merchant, the partners had extraction contracts with approximately 20 extractor-contractors at a time. Today few dealers have the capital or the courage to take on such a large, dispersed, and therefore risky operation; few now advance funds or have contracts with more than eight or ten extractors.

Aguaje is taken downriver to market by the contractor in his own boat or the fruit is sent by *lancha*. The delivery of fruit to the dealer who did the contracting is not always a straightforward transaction. Although many dealers insist that they personally would never try to buy someone else's shipment of aguaje (or of any other product), in reality much aguaje is not bought by the person for whom it was intended. Other dealers who arrive at the boat earlier—many actually take boats out to meet *lanchas* before the cargo boats arrive in port—and those who offer a price better than that which was earlier agreed upon, often succeed in buying the product that supposedly is owned by another major dealer. Everyone involved in aguaje marketing has seen his or her products disappear and

ñon should be inspected and taxed at Nauta, a town near the mouth of the Marañon. However, even at that point boats pass at all hours and certainly many do not choose to stop and get inspected and taxed.

The official records on exactly which areas are being harvested by the commercial dealers also cannot be trusted to accurately reflect reality, since inspections of the source areas are not done. It is virtually impossible for a Forest Guard to know where a particular sack of aguaje was harvested once that sack appears in Iquitos. In order to buy aguaje harvested from any area other than one's official concession or to import more than one's stated limit one must pay an extra fee in the port. Understandably, buyers are not particularly eager to disclose where their fruit actually came from; often they do not even know its point of origin themselves.

---

[4] In reality, the large aguaje dealers in Iquitos tend to import a good deal more fruit than is legally allotted to them. Since inspection of all arriving shipments is extremely difficult, with boats unloading at many points along Iquitos' riverfronts, and at all times of day or night, the Forestry and Fauna guards necessarily miss many shipments. The aguaje coming down the Mara-

some have actually left the business because of this very problem.

Some dealers occasionally travel to the harvesting area to supervise part of the work and to ascertain that their contractors are not cheating them. The very largest Iquitos dealer however, a woman who on many days controls about half the aguaje that arrives, boasted to me that she had not been up to the Marañon in 11 years. She chose to report this fact since it indicates that she has had no trouble in maintaining her chain of supply of aguaje. Her boast could not match that of the above-mentioned, now retired "Queen of Aguaje." The now very wealthy Doña N. (see p. 220) recently told me that in all her days she has not even seen an aguajal; her power had been so great and far-reaching and her operation so trouble-free.

Some fruit that arrives has no predetermined buyer and may be bought directly from the boat by wholesalers or retailers. In order to buy directly from the boat and thus at a slightly lower price, however, a retailer must be both brave and astute; she must often jump on to the boat before it is well docked and must then literally fight with wholesalers for her sack. The transaction usually is completed very quickly because of the fierce competition and, thus, the buyer must know how to judge the quality of the fruit with just a glance at the few uppermost examples.

Once the fruit is in Iquitos, it must be packed into sacks, if it is not already so divided, and then must be transferred from the boat to the dealer's storage or selling area. The difficulty, cost, and number of people involved in this transfer depends on the point of arrival of the cargo boat and on the prevailing state of the market. As the Amazon at Iquitos annually rises and falls an average of about 8 meters, the configuration of the ports and unloading and selling areas varies greatly during the year. At low water, most dealers have their stock stored somewhere close to the main port known as Venezia. When the water rises, that area becomes totally inundated (hence Venezia) and dealers work out of houses and basements well up the hill toward the market of Belén. At such times their sacks of fruit usually must be transferred first from the cargo boats to smaller vessels which can maneuver through the flooded streets of Venezia to an area of dry land and from there a carrier must lug the sacks up to the current selling area. For such an operation,

the dealer must usually pay 4 or 5 Intis per sack or approximately 5–10% of the total wholesale price at which the fruit is sold.

Arriving at the wholesale marketing area, aguaje is displayed in open 50 kg sacks and retailers come to buy the product by the sack. A few wholesalers may also buy aguaje at this point and transport the fruit up to the market area proper or to some other location where he or she will also sell it by the sack. However, the great majority of people who buy in the wholesale marketing area are retailers, who include those who sell the product in the raw state but in smaller quantities, as well as those who process the fruit in some way. At times these retailers also sell to other retailers. For instance, many of streetcorner sellers of "ripe" fruits buy the raw fruit in quantities of less than a sack, i.e., in retail quantities. Makers of *chupetes, aguajina* and ice cream often also purchase their aguaje, not as fruit, but already processed as *masa,* adding another link to the marketing chain.

In summary, between the swamp where it is harvested and the market, streetcorner, or ice cream shop where it is consumed, aguaje has usually passed through a large number of hands, and a considerable number of people, including harvesters, contractors, shippers, carriers, wholesalers, retailers, and processors have made part of their daily income from handling the fruit. Although I have mentioned some rural folks in our discussion, I have also shown that the extraction and marketing of aguaje is definitely urban based and controlled. As I shall discuss in a later section, the urban population that is employed in aguaje processing and marketing is surprisingly large. As a source of employment for the city's populace, particularly of the economically humble and of women, aguaje is unequalled by any other fruit.

The marketing chains involved in the commercialization of the two other *Mauritia* products that appear in Iquitos' markets: *esteras* and *suri,* are far simpler. Screens made of the petiole of aguaje tend to be made in areas quite close to the city. One center is the village of Gallito, just about an hour and a half upriver from the city by small *peque-peque.* The manufacturers of screens in Gallito (once fruit gatherers) harvest an aguajal that has been so ravaged by years of fruit collecting that now virtually no fruit-bearing female trees can be found there. Situated quite close to the city, they usually bring in their *esteras* in their own small boats; paying cargo costs would cut their profits greatly. *Esteras* are usually marketed directly to the owners of several general equipment stores that are found near the port area of Belén. Some manufacturers of *esteras* have long-lasting quasi-contractual relationships with store owners; others sell to whomever offers them the best price. The store owners then retail the screens to the public.

In the case of the beetle grubs, *suri,* most sellers come from villages close by the city and thus retail directly the product that they harvested and prepared. As was mentioned earlier, *suri* are sold both alive and fried.

VI. The Marketers of Aguaje

I have mentioned that the major dealers in aguaje probably number eight, with five of them women. The preponderance of women at the rather large-scale wholesale level is a highly unusual feature of the aguaje market. While women predominate as marketers in Iquitos, larger wholesalers of other products are almost invariably men. These major aguaje dealers on the average probably work with about I./7000 to I./10,000 (over $400 to somewhat over $500) in capital. One woman, Doña J. probably turns over a good deal more in her transactions; she is backed by one of Iquitos' major traders, who once worked in aguaje but now pursues other interests.

In addition to these larger dealers, Iquitos' ports and markets are crowded with wholesale buyers who operate with much more modest funds. The majority of such dealers do not specialize; they buy aguaje from time to time if a particularly good opportunity presents itself. Since they are however, a non-localized, ephemeral and highly changeable group, I found it impossible to count these smaller wholesalers who operate with funds ranging from about $100 to several hundred dollars.[5] The most I can offer is my opinion that at the least thirty such people buy aguaje on occasion by the sack, to then resell it, again in wholesale quantities.

---

[5] Many small wholesalers work with less than $50 in capital. These very minor merchants, however, probably rarely buy aguaje because of its price and the competition from other wealthier buyers.

Market retail vendors tend also to be a flexible group, changing the produce in which they deal with the varying prospects for profit that each item offers. Counting such vendors on various days in various parts of Iquitos' three major and five minor markets, I estimate that on any day 50 persons are selling raw aguaje fruit in the market in retail quantities; 25 sell *aguajina,* and 25 sell *masa.* Every one of these vendors is a woman.

On the streets of the city and in the markets one would probably find a daily average of 210 women selling "ripe" aguaje, and approximately 100 men selling *chupetes,* which are usually of aguaje. In addition, about 25 people would be working in *chupete* factories with aguaje and another twenty or so would be making and selling aguaje ice cream. At least ten other women would be making *masa* in their homes for direct sale to other businesses. Unfortunately, I cannot make any estimate of the number of *curichi* sellers in Iquitos; as I mentioned above, these tend to be very small home-based operations. Nor can I count the boatmen, cargo carriers, and other transporters who also handle aguaje.

Even with the missing data, I can confidently state that in the city, where I have found more than 75 species of fruit sold commercially, one fruit employs and supports, at least partially, a population of over 500 breadwinners, many of them with large families, and most of them of modest economic resources.

While I found it impossible to estimate the incomes of all the folks involved in the aguaje trade, I can present several brief examples of the benefits that aguaje selling can bring to vendors.

Doña N., whom I have characterized before as the former "Queen of Aguaje," now owns a gasoline distributing business, including a fleet of trucks and a gas station. Daughter of a street vendor of aguaje, she confirms that wholesaling aguaje indeed made her rich, providing her with the capital to operate her present business. In about twenty years as Iquitos' major aguaje buyer and wholesale merchant, Doña N. accumulated a fortune equivalent to what in the area is normally associated with major drug-dealing and other unsavory occupations.

Don B., a well-known streetcorner vendor of aguaje ice cream—he sells no other flavor—is another economic success who built up considerable wealth selling an aguaje product. Starting penniless as a young boy, Don B., now in his sixties, has sold the same product on the same street corner for 46 years. Although he continues to sell every day, Don B. owns a very large brick house, a small store operated by his daughter and wife, and a rooming house with ten rooms. He has also managed to educate seven children in the local university.

A more common story is that of Doña R., a street corner vendor of "ripe" aguaje. Mother of six children, she has managed to support them with only occasional help from a wandering common-law husband. Doña R. does not live in luxury, but, after 11 years in the business, she is completing a brick house in one of the outlying sections of the city. I estimated that her net income on good days topped I./200 or about $11.50, which was eight times the government minimum wage and more than some domestic servants earn in a month. Doña R. is an experienced and very hardworking street vendor who sells about a sack of fruit a day. Although the income of many other street vendors may be lower, anyone acquainted with the aguaje business will confirm that it offers considerable opportunity for profit. It can however, be a risky business as well. Quality of a sack of fruit is difficult to judge and the purchase of a bad sack now and then may result in an important setback. In order to enter and remain comfortably in this type of trade minimum capital of about I./500 ($28.90) is probably necessary.

VII. Conclusions

As I have described it, the trade in *Mauritia flexuosa* is a complex one, with contracts and obligations that link the urban center with isolated palm swamps and small villages, and various types of middlemen, processors, and retailers playing a role in the commercial network. The economic importance for rural areas of this trade is considerable but has not been discussed here. I have outlined instead the role that aguaje plays in the urban area where control over the trade is centered and where the fruit is processed, bought, and sold. It is in the city of Iquitos where most of the money used in harvesting the fruit originates, where most of the profit stays, and where decisions about how much to collect and when are largely made. I have suggested that the numbers of urban residents involved and the

economic benefits that they gain from the aguaje trade are substantial and particularly impressive when compared with the trade in other fruits.

To anyone familiar only with commerce in major export items and industrial processing operations, these claims may appear unjustified, the number of vendors small, and their incomes pitiful. However, it should be remembered that aguaje is almost purely a locally appreciated and consumed product. It is exported in only minute quantities; a few bags of *masa* go to Lima to be sold to homesick Iquiteños now living in the capital. Iquitos offers a very limited market for any fruit; its population is modest in size and generally poor in income available for non-staple foods such as aguaje. In processing aguaje, nothing more sophisticated than a blender and freezer is used. In this context, the economic role of the fruit in the urban center appears to be exceptional indeed.

Another aspect of the aguaje trade should be emphasized: at all levels of the business, women tend to predominate. The few examples that Iquitos offers of women who have managed to accumulate considerable wealth very often feature aguaje. In Iquitos, there are many mothers with several children who have been abandoned by their men, and in many cases these families constitute the truly poor of the city. Many active and retired street vendors were abandoned by husbands but managed to support their families alone, educating their children, and building comfortable if modest houses from the profits accumulated by selling aguaje. The "aguajera"—the woman who retails aguaje—is one of the stock characters of Iquitos, and the aguajera whose five children are all university graduates and now support their mother in comfort is one of the city's most often-repeated success stories.

While only a very few have become wealthy in the aguaje trade, we have mentioned that commerce in this fruit does offer an opportunity to women to move beyond the most basic subsistence level. To deal successfully in the trade, a buyer must have a good knowledge of varieties, seasons, and possible defects in the fruit. She must also be willing to take some chances, to work hard, and must accumulate some capital if the risks involved are to be weathered. Other products, such as plantains for instance, are less demanding, but they offer less opportunity for gain as well.

Precisely why women have been so successful in reaching the upper levels of the aguaje trade is not clear. One of the large traders suggested that since all retailers of aguaje are women, female wholesalers have an advantage as they know how to treat other women. However, since retailers of most other plant products are also women, this explanation seems to leave the question unanswered.

The complex and populous aguaje trade is built upon the harvesting of a forest product that slowly, but without doubt, is becoming less available in the urban environs. While aguaje is not about to disappear from the Peruvian Amazon, the percentage of fruit-bearing trees in swamps near the city has fallen greatly, affecting the cost of extraction and all subsequent levels of the trade. Some change in harvesting methods will have to be made if the trade is to continue in its present form, and especially if use is to increase, and export of the fruit is to pick up as many hope.

It is difficult to predict the effects on marketers and the urban economy if costs of transport of aguaje increase greatly and less fruit arrives in the market. Most women now engaged in the aguaje trade will obviously not fold up their operations and cease to be traders if aguaje is no longer available. A notably flexible and risk-taking group, these women will find other products to market. However, the particular opportunities that aguaje offers to the industrious and adventurous are important to Iquitos women. They would be adversely affected if the trade were to change.

VIII. Acknowledgments

The research on which this article is based was funded by a grant from the Exxon Corporation. The field work was carried out as part of research agreements between the Institute of Economic Botany, New York Botanical Garden and two Peruvian institutions: the Instituto de Investigaciones de la Amazonía Peruana and the Centro Amazónico de Antropología y Aplicación Práctica. I wish to thank Santiago Arévalo Tamani and Miguel Pinedo-Vásquez for their aid in all phases of the research, and innumerable aguaje vendors for their great kindness in answering my questions and correcting my misconceptions. I also wish to thank several functionaries of the Ministry of Agriculture, Department of Forestry and Fauna in Iquitos and Requena, in particular Mr. Manuel Cubas. I am also very grateful to Kate Clark, Wil de Jong, Andrew Henderson and Michael Chibnik for reading and commenting on the manuscript.

IX. Literature Cited

Heinen, H. D. & K. Ruddle. 1974. Ecology, ritual, and economic organization in the distribution of palm starch among the Warao of the Orinoco delta. J. Anthropol. Res. 30(2): 116–138.

Hiraoka, M. 1985. Floodplain farming in the Peruvian Amazon. Geogr. Rev. Japan 58 (ser. B, No. 1): 1–23.

Oficina Nacional de Evaluación de Recursos Naturales (ONERN). 1976. Inventario, evaluación e integración de los recursos naturales de la zona Iquitos, Nauta, Requena y Colonia Angamos. Lima.

Padoch, C. 1987. The economic importance and marketing of forest and fallow products in the Iquitos region, Peru. In W. M. Denevan & C. Padoch (eds.), Swidden-fallow agroforestry systems in the northeastern Peruvian Amazon. Adv. Econ. Bot. 5: 74–89.

———, J. Chota Inuma, W. De Jong & J. Unruh. 1985. Amazonian agroforestry: A market-oriented system in Peru. Agroforest. Syst. 3: 47–58.

San Román, J. 1975. Perfiles históricos de la amazonía peruana. Ediciones Paulinas, Lima.

Wilbert, J. 1972. Survivors of El Dorado. Prager, New York.

Uses of *Euterpe oleracea* Mart. in the Amazon Estuary, Brazil

JEREMY STRUDWICK AND GAIL L. SOBEL

Table of Contents

Abstract

Euterpe is a New World palm genus distributed from Central America and Dominica in the north, throughout South America to southern Brazil. A major source of heart-of-palm, several species of the genus are so utilized, currently the most important being *E. oleracea*. This graceful, multi-stemmed palm is widespread and common in the Amazon estuary of Brazil, where it is known as 'açaí.' Here it is abundant in the forest margins along the wateredge of the many rivers and islands. Its importance to the inhabitants is reflected by its dominance in the forest gardens surrounding their riverside homes. Its frequency and its multi-stemmed, self-regenerative habit allow it to support a large palm-heart industry in the region. Its fruits are used to make the 'açaí' liquid, a basic and major element of the diet of thousands of local inhabitants. *Euterpe oleracea,* its habit and habitat, and its major and minor uses, based upon field observations in Belém, Ilha das Onças and the island of Marajó in the state of Pará, Brazil are discussed and illustrated. Every part of this palm seems to be utilized in some way by the local people, from roots to stem, leaf sheaths to apical meristem, inflorescences to seeds, etc., but we have emphasized the use and processing of the palm for açaí and the palm-heart industry.

Key words: *Euterpe,* açaí, ethnobotany, palm hearts, palms, Amazon estuary

Resumen

Euterpe es una palma del Nuevo Mundo distribuida desde America Central y Dominica en el norte y a lo largo de Sudamérica hasta el sur de Brasil. La fuente principal del palmito, varias especies del género son utilizadas así, siendo la más importante *E. oleracea*. Este elegante palma cespitosa está ampliamente distribuida y es común en el estuário del río amazonas donde es conocida como "açaí." Aquí es abundante en las márgenes del bosque a lo largo de las riberas de los muchos ríos e islas. Su importancia para los inhabitantes se refleja en la dominancia en los jardines boscosos que rodean las casas a orillas del río. Su frecuencia y su hábito cespitoso y auto-regenerativo, permiten la existencia de una gran industria de palmito en la región. Sus frutos son utilizados para hacer "açaí," un líquido que es elemento prinicipal y básico en la dieta de miles de habitantes locales. *Euterpe oleracea,* su hábito y hábitat, y sus usos mayores y menores, basándose en observaciones

Advances in Economic Botany 6: 225–253, 1988
© 1988 The New York Botanical Garden

de campo en Belém, Ilha das Onças y en la isla de Marajó en el estado de Pará, Brasil son discutadosy e ilustrados. Todas las partes de la palma parecen tener su uso por parte de la gente de la localidad, desde las raíces y tallos, vainas foliares y meristema apical, hasta las inflorescencias y semillas, etc., pero hemos enfatizado el procesamiento del líquido 'açaí' y la industria del palmito.

I. Introduction

Euterpe oleracea Mart. and its uses were studied during a trip to the Amazon estuary (Brazil) from late September to November, 1984. The species, widespread in the Amazon Basin, is better known to local inhabitants as "açaí" (pronounced ă-sigh-ee) and plays an important part in their daily life and in commerce. *Euterpe* species are New World palms. The 18 (Moore, 1973) to 49 (Glassman, 1972) species are distributed from southern Brazil, northern Argentina, Paraguay and Bolivia in the south and throughout the width of South America to Central America and Dominica in the north. They occur from sea level up to relatively high altitudes for palms (ca. 3000 m), and occupy a variety of habitats from Amazonian várzea forests to the tops of Venezuelan tepuis.

The genus *Euterpe,* recognized as one of promising economic value, is in need of research (FAO, 1983; NAS, 1975). Various species are exploited for heart-of-palm and some may be threatened because of this (for example see Balick, 1976). Taking heart-of-palm from a single-stemmed species kills the palm. Açaí, unlike its south-east Brazilian relative *E. edulis,* has more than one stem and thus regenerates after cutting. The palm-heart industry in Brazil thus now involves much greater use of açaí in the Amazon estuary than formerly. Its worth is approximately $120 million annually with both internal and export value. Açaí, a vigorous palm, appears to have the potential for repeated and multiuse cropping. Its frequency and some of its uses in an 'agroforestry' situation were touched upon in a previous paper (Anderson et al., 1985) based upon work done on Ilha das Onças, one of the sites visited for the research discussed here. Brief references have been made in the English language literature to some of the different uses of *Euterpe,* by Wallace (1853) and others. *Euterpe* has been mentioned various times as a source of heart-of-palm (e.g., Balick, 1976; FAO, 1983; Hodge, 1965; NAS, 1975). However, these works have not treated the multiple uses of *E. oleracea* or gone in depth into its ethnobotany. Due to the importance of *Euterpe* in Brazil the majority of studies are in Portuguese. Many of these focus upon the heart-of-palm industry and deal with preservation and canning (e.g., Andrade & Belda, 1976; Zapata & Quast, 1975), and cultivation and growth (e.g., Amaral, 1973; Bovi & Cardoso, 1975) among other subjects. Certain studies, such as those by IDESP (1974) and Calzavara (1972) have focused upon açaí's agronomic potential. This latter study is probably the most concise and comprehensive summary of the uses, commercial importance, nutritional composition, productivity, ecology, botany and agronomy of açaí. However, there is little in English on this palm of such importance not only locally, but also as an export. The taxonomy and the ethnobotany of the genus as a whole remain poorly understood, yet these aspects should be clearly understood in order for proper conservation measures to be taken for both germplasm and species as appropriate. The original observations presented here are intended to not only bring *E. oleracea* to the attention of the English speaking public, but to give a picture of its use and local importance in the Amazon estuary, Brazil.

II. Study Area

The places visited lie within the Amazon estuary. Several rivers converge here, emptying into the Atlantic Ocean in the north-eastern corner of Brazil between the states of Pará to the south and Macapá to the north. The principal city and main port of the region is Belém, the capital of Pará. It lies at the mouth of the River Guamá near its confluence with the River Acará. In the estuary of these two rivers and across a wide channel from the Pará mainland, where Belém is situated, lie several islands. Directly across from Belém, about 2.5 km, lies the Ilha das Onças. Beyond these islands lies the island of Marajó (about 40 km at its nearest point to the northwest of Belém). In between is a wide channel, often rough and dangerous for the smaller boats traversing it. This channel carries to the Atlantic Ocean, via the bay of Marajó, the vast amounts of water pouring out from the southeastern corner of the Amazon basin—not only from the rivers named above but also in great volume from the river Tocantins at the southwestern end of the channel and the river Pará at its western end. This whole water mass is heavily tidal.

The vast island of Marajó forms the northern bank of the channel, situated as it is between the estuaries of the already mentioned rivers to its south and the Amazon River to its northwest and along its northern shore. It is more narrowly divided from land along its western extremes, mostly by the river Jacaré. Very roughly rectangular in shape, it is about 250 km from east to west at its widest point and about 185 km from north to south at its longest point towards the west. Our observations were made in Belém, the Ilha das Onças, along the southwestern and western shores of Marajó and from here along rivers penetrating towards the center of the island. Specifically, our boat followed a course from Belém and Ilha das Onças westward along the channel south of Marajó and the river Pará to the town of São Sebastião da Boa Vista on the southern shore of Marajó. A few days were spent here and in a nearby forest and savanna. We continued north-westwards to Breves, up the river Breves. Northwards of Corcovado, we followed the rivers 'Furo dos Macacos' and Aramá, eventually looping around into the river Anajás, which flows westward from well into the interior of the island. It took us to Anajás and we then followed the river Moções about six hours or so upstream to the small river 'Igarapé Frances.' This was our innermost penetration of the island and we traced the same route to Belém. Various stops were made along the way to study the different aspects of the açaí palm and its uses.

III. Description of
Euterpe oleracea (Açaí)

Açaí is multi-stemmed, pinnately leaved and with distinct, smooth, green to yellowish crownshafts below the leaves (Figs. 1, 2). The palm may be short (ca. 4 m at first flowering in some cases, depending on local conditions) to tall (over 30 m), but the stems always remain relatively slender. Sometimes green in younger portions, they are predominantly light gray to light grayish-brown in color, occasionally with lichens making light patterns on them. A small or sometimes more elongate ring of aerial roots can often be seen around the base of the trunk. These roots sometimes have small wart-like protrusions on them (called pneumathorhizes by De Granville, 1974). The young roots may be bright red in color. Inflorescences may be present singly or several at a time, borne at a slightly erect angle at first or somewhat lower when weighted down by fruit later on. Inserted at the top of the trunk, below the crownshaft, they are often clearly visible. From the central stiff axis of the inflorescence the many erect rachillae (inflorescence branches) splay out at various wide angles after bursting from the inflorescence sheaths, forming a broad, sparse shape, ca. 60 cm long (Fig. 3). The predominant color in the inflorescences seen from ground level is the whitish-gray to light buff color of the rachis and rachillae. The flowers are small (ca. 5 mm across) but quite attractive up close. The main color in both male and female is a palish purple to maroon. Fruits are globose, ca. 1.5 cm across, green when young and usually a darkish purple when mature (Fig. 4). They each contain one seed, accounting for most of their volume, and are surrounded by thin, but coarse and stringy fibrous sheaths. Around these lie the outer coat, a thin, dryish but slightly oily coating, giving the fruits their purple color.

One of the most characteristic features of açaí is the way in which the leaflets of its pinnate leaves seem to droop almost vertically downwards. Its appearance was most vividly described by R. Read (pers. comm.) who said that its drooping leaflets give the appearance of falling rain. The name Euterpe translates from the Greek as 'forest grace' (Hodge, 1965) and is an appropriate name, considering its beautiful appearance.

IV. Habitats of
Euterpe oleracea

The majority of the region visited is tidal, due to the influence of the Atlantic. Açaí, especially

FIGS. 1, 2.   FIG. 1. *Euterpe oleracea* in Marajó rural garden, showing multiple stems, pinnate leaves and graceful habit. FIG. 2. Crownshaft of *Euterpe oleracea* formed from the leaf sheaths.

prevalent on the banks of rivers, grows abundantly in the area in the várzea (seasonally flooded), and in certain mud-bank/island situations. It appears to need some kind of firm ground beneath it and several times was seen growing behind a belt of *Montrichardia* sp. (Araceae), which has a woody stem which can withstand the daily tidal flooding while it bears its arrow-shaped leaves at its apex above water. While *Montrichardia* grows in the mud, behind it the ground is higher, more permanent, not always subjected to daily flooding, and supports açaí. Another palm, *Mauritia flexuosa,* occupies similar swampy habitats and can often be seen growing in association with açaí or close by, but apparently in areas somewhat further from the influence of the main rivers than açaí. In one place, on an island opposite S. Maria at the confluence of the rivers Jacaré, Furo dos Macacos and Aramá, a clear and striking zonation of the three species was observed. Toward one end of the narrow island a dense zone of *Montrichardia* covered the tidal water edge. Behind lay a thick

zone of açaí in similar abundance, and on the slightly more protected ground grew a forest of the tall, thick-trunked, *M. flexuosa* with its crown of massive palmate leaves and huge scaly-fruited infructescences. All the land was fairly low and probably flooded to some degree at one time or another. What was so particularly striking was the fact that all of these plants were growing in practically pure stands with only slight mixing on the edge of the *Mauritia* and *Euterpe* zones. It appears likely that these three plants might form a mechanism for colonizing mud or sand banks. The seeds of açaí were seen floating in abundance after removal of their outer flesh at S. Sebastião da Boa Vista and it therefore seems highly probable that they might be adapted to rapid colonization of such river areas since germination was also observed to be rapid. Just beyond the *Mauritia* zone and taking the position of açaí and *Montrichardia* on the other shore of the narrow island was a stand of *Rhizophora* sp. trees with their long stilt roots anchoring them to the ground beneath the waters edge.

FIGS. 3, 4.   FIG. 3. Inflorescence of *Euterpe oleracea* showing its position below the crownshaft and its simple straight rachillae. FIG. 4. Marble-sized dark purple fruits of *Euterpe oleracea* in ceramic bowl dyed inside with *Licania* sp.

Besides its frequency at the water's edge açaí is common within the low lying forests where it can be occasionally seen growing to 30 m or more, protruding from the canopy. At the water's edge, especially on the river Moções in the interior of Marajó, it was noted that the tall açaí stems would bend way out over the water, then twist upwards, as if reaching for the light. It was not ascertained whether this was purely in response to the light or whether it could have been initiated by the tall palms partially falling over in heavy floods. Given plenty of light, as in some riverside situations, or where planted in the open, or where surrounding forest vegetation is cleared, açaí forms a vigorous but lower growing palm which bears its inflorescences much closer to the ground. In one instance, where planted, the daughter stem of a sturdy young plant bore its fruit less than 2 m from the ground.

V. Association of *Euterpe oleracea* with Rural Riverside Homes

One of the most striking things about açaí, especially noticeable from a boat, is the tremendous frequency and abundance with which it is found around the small and scattered dwellings which nestle between the surrounding flood-plain forest and the river. These are the dwellings of the 'caboclos' (rural peasant farmers), who inhabit the region (Fig. 5). Such areas, away from Belém, constitute the majority of land along the rivers in the parts we visited, along with unpopulated forests. A typical garden we visited was like a grove of açaí with the house nestling between it and the river. Raised walkways led from the house to the toilet and other points outside. The rivers of the area are mostly fairly wide and this dwelling, as with many others, sat right on the edge of a broad expanse of muddy or 'white river' water. Because the area is tidal, a raised walkway or small pier was constructed out from the front of the house to allow one to pass from a boat to a wooden walkway leading to the house. The raised walkways of about 1 m around the açaí garden allow for the seasonal flooding when the rivers of the Amazon estuary area rise considerably. At other times of the year the ground is not flooded daily. In front of the house a kitchen garden, another common characteristic of the region, was present. For this a platform con-

structed from açaí trunks laid side by side to give a large square floor, raised on wooden posts like the pier, etc., to keep it above high water levels, was built. All areas of the house and surrounding buildings are similarly raised from ground level (Fig. 14). The kitchen garden itself consisted of baskets and other containers (such as an old canoe) with plants such as tomatoes, and other vegetables and herbs.

The heavy concentration of açaí around dwellings appeared to be caused by their inhabitants, by their clearing other trees (allowing açaí to predominate, since it forms a natural part of the surrounding vegetation), by their planting it, by discardment of seeds, or all these methods together. The close association of the riverside dwellers and açaí is evident from its many uses and importance to them. A good example is the making of the açaí liquid. In this operation the person may stand right next to their açaí garden, using the fruits and simultaneously casting out the seeds to perhaps become new plants for future harvest (Fig. 6), or for other uses mentioned later.

VI. The Açaí Liquid

The principal use of açaí palm to the local people is for the production of a liquid. Açaí, as the liquid is called locally, is a variably thickish (depending on how it is prepared), usually dark pinkish-purple (sometimes yellow) kind of cold soup prepared from the fruit (Fig. 7). It is usually not drunk, but eaten with a spoon, and forms a major and basic part of the diet of many of the numerous inhabitants of the region. Those who consume it often appear strong and full of energy. Conversations with, and observations of, individuals and families showed it to be loved and desired by the very young to the very old. Short periods without it appear to result in a kind of 'withdrawal symptom,' since a craving is developed for it (at least in certain cases). The crew of our small boat were good examples of this since, on more than one occasion, they diverted our course without any prior warning off on some unexplained course, ending up in a scramble to the riverbank and up an açaí palm with good ripe fruit ready for making açaí, to fulfill their cravings. There is a popular consensus and saying in the region, that when one is without açaí one feels a lacking or emptiness in the stomach.

FIG. 5. Picturesque grove of 'açaí,' showing the typical close association with rural riverside homes.

Açaí forms such an important part of the diet that up to 2 liters of it can be consumed by an individual in one day. It is eaten for breakfast, dinner or lunch or all three. It is said popularly to be strong in iron, and consumption of the liquid appeared to turn human feces black. In a nutritional analysis of the liquid, Motta (1946) noted an Fe content of 0.0009%. Its taste is unique, difficult to describe, but roughly creamy, metallic and slightly oily. Some newcomers like it immediately (Balée, pers. comm.). After trying it several times the senior author felt he was developing a taste for it. Its taste is perhaps more acceptable to newcomers when presented in some other recipes, to be described later.

The açaí liquid is so popular that there are special establishments in small and large towns which make and sell it. These are denoted by the presence of a red, usually wooden or metal sign on a post outside (Fig. 8). Sometimes "AÇAÍ" is written on the sign, but the convention is so much a part of daily life that this is often not done. Crowds or lines sometimes form to vie for the end of the day's supply.

The majority of the inhabitants of the region (particularly outside Belém) are poor, many existing only by subsistence farming of forest products, animals, etc., and use açaí heavily. Nevertheless, açaí is not a product looked upon as being only for poorer peoples, but is popular throughout all socioeconomic levels (Fig. 9). Since açaí is such an abundant plant in the region and produces so bountifully, it is natural that local people should use açaí's products so much, especially one, such as the açaí liquid, which can assuage much of the poorer people's daily hunger needs. Many of them make their own açaí from the many trees around their dwellings or occurring in the forests. No wonder then, that it is seen in such abundance around these dwellings. Mixed with either river shrimp, farinha, sugar, biscuits, other items, or combinations of these, it forms the basis of their diet. Many people eat it alone or with sugar, while the addition of farinha (manioc flour) and sugar is also very popular (Fig. 10). Some people sell the fruits in larger markets, such as that of Belém, for money to buy other things. In Belém the fruits arrive in the dawn hours by

FIG. 6.   Marajó woman making the açaí liquid right next to the 'açaí garden,' where she casts out the seeds.

$\longrightarrow$

FIGS. 7–9.   FIG. 7. 'Açaí branco' (left) and 'açaí preto' fruits and liquids. FIG. 8. A large açaí store in Belém, with the typical red açaí sign. FIG. 9. The use of açaí seedlings as a table centerpiece and young plants (background) as containerized ornamentals for indoors or outdoors, and the naming of this Belém Hilton International restaurant after açaí, illustrates the plants' popularity in the region among all socioeconomic levels.

FIGS. 10, 11.   FIG. 10. Typical ingredients mixed with açaí (right) are sugar and farinha (manioc flour), as seen here. FIG. 11. Large baskets of açaí fruits awaiting processing into the açaí liquid in an açaí store. These were purchased earlier at a Belém dawn market after harvesters brought them in by boat from the surrounding region.

FIGS. 12–14.   FIG. 12. An electrically powered metal açaí liquid-making machine in a modern açaí store in Belém. FIG. 13. An electrically powered, belt-driven machine in a rural riverside home on Ilha das Onças. FIG. 14. Typical setting in a caboclo dwelling in Marajó for manual açaí liquid making.

the basketload from the surrounding regions. During the period of this study a large quantity was coming from Ilha das Onças. It is then often bought directly by the owners of the açaí-making stores (Fig. 11). The larger such operations are, the more sophisticated the machine or method used to make the liquid.

The açaí-making operation basically involves the removal of the mesocarp from the seed. It is then mashed up fine with varying amounts of water, to make the thickish liquid. There are different ways of carrying this out. There are wooden grinding machines turned by hand to remove the edible coating from the seed, and different kinds of metal ones. One of the larger stores visited in Belém had three very modern machines in use. These were of metal, powered by an electric motor and driven by a belt (Fig. 12). The açaí fruits are poured in top and the liquid comes out the bottom. What happens to all the leftover seeds will be discussed later. In one of the larger rural houses visited outside Belém there was a similar machine in use for the family's needs (Fig. 13).

In the stores the liquid is often sold in liter plastic bags. Alternatively, customers bring their own containers to be filled up. In one of the more sophisticated stores, at the time we were in Belém, there were three qualities of açaí being sold. The qualities depended on how many times it had been passed through the machine for fineness, how thick and creamy it was or how much diluted with water. The prices were approximately 30, 45 and 75 cents (U.S.) per liter. There is an all-year-round harvest and supply of açaí, which we were informed by store owners and market people was due to different seasons of maturity of the fruits in different regions. At some seasons it was said to be more expensive than at others in Belém, attributable to the fact that it is locally scarcer at certain times of the year and must be brought in from greater distances.

Two kinds of the açaí liquid are found, of which the purple kind, 'açaí preto,' is by far the commonest. On occasion a yellow kind can also be found (Fig. 7), known as 'açaí branco.' We were informed the latter is also made from açaí (*E. oleracea*) and shown a multiply-trunked plant which fit its description and was used for 'açaí branco,' although it was not fruiting at the time. Some people much prefer one of these two kinds to the other. In one town two neighboring families were found, one of which had only 'açaí preto' in their garden, the other with only 'açaí branco.' Both had recently planted all of their plants or had clumps of seedlings ready for transplanting. A strange story concerning the two different colored kinds is popular in parts of the region. It is said that when planted next to açaí preto the fruits of açaí branco also become purple. Pires (pers. comm.) notes that individuals of açaí branco occur in the wild among stands of açaí preto and that there is a possibility that this might be a recessive genetical trait appearing in only a fraction of the individuals produced from seed. Such an explanation may account for why people would have this concept, since on planting yellow fruited seeds, a high percentage of purple fruited individuals might result.

The home-made liquid is prepared altogether differently than as described above, using the hands (Fig. 14) Some argue that açaí tastes better made this way and that this could be due to the salt from the hands. To obtain fruits, ripe infructescences are located from the ground. Men or boys usually climb the trees. To do this a 'peconha' (climbing belt) is usually fashioned in the forest. This climber's belt goes around the feet and is used to help secure the grip of the feet to the trunk as it is climbed. One way of making it is from the strong but flexible fallen leaf sheath of *E. oleracea*. This method was demonstrated in Ilha das Onças. By twisting and bending a section of this around the knee it can be knotted into a secure loop about 25 cm in diameter forming the peconha. The making of an alternative kind of peconha, from the leaf, and their method of use is described in greater detail and illustrated in the heart-of-palm section.

Once the tree has been climbed, the ripe infructescence is cut off at its base and the climber descends with it. The fruits are then shaken or stripped from the rachillae and placed in a basket or burlap bag to be carried back to the house. Next, some water is warmed (Fig. 15) and placed in a large, low, wide ceramic or metal bowl (Fig. 4); the former tempered by bark dye from *Licania* sp. ('Caripé', Chrysobalanaceae). The fruits are placed in the warm water for a short period (ca. half an hour) to help soften the mesocarp

(Fig. 16), and to remove any dirt or debris, which floats or sinks in the water. Next comes the hard work, which in this manual mode of preparation we only observed being done by women. The junior author participated in some of the açaí liquid making activities and can verify that it is hard work. The fruits must be vigorously worked by the hands to loosen and remove the softened mesocarp from the seed. After removing the water the initial pulping of the fruits takes place in the large bowl (Fig. 17). After much of the mesocarp has been pulped, a sequence of two hand made sieves are used (Figs. 18, 19). The first used and larger-meshed of these is called the 'caroceiro.' The second, finer-meshed sieve is called the 'paneira fina,' and is used for making a finer pulp or liquid from the unmashed portions of the açaí flesh already passed through the caroceiro. Beneath the paneira fina a large bowl is placed to collect the açaí liquid. Both seives are square, approximately 50 cm by 50 cm, with narrow cross-strips woven at right angles with slight gaps between them to give a mesh with the desired straining effect (Fig. 18). Those documented had a framework of two dowel-like pieces on each of four sides, making a total of eight altogether, onto which is woven the inner mesh which acts as the sieve. The outer 'dowels' are placed to alternate along their overlapping ends with the dowels from the proximate side giving strength and rigidity. This rigid framework sits upon the rim of the container beneath, which catches the açaí liquid.

Similarly, as the two strainers sit one upon the other while the fruits are first being mashed through the caroceiro, their similar size and outer frames allow the user to mash vigorously on the mesh part since the two frames, along with the wide bowl rim beneath, give good total stability and rigidity (Fig. 20). The inner mesh is interwoven with the ends of each cross-weave piece looped and knotted around the dowels to secure it. From its double loop around the dowels each piece is woven into a finishing area beneath and just inside the frame. It is bent back and cut to give a neat, secure finish. On both sieves the frames were made from pieces of the palm locally called paxiuba (*Socratea exorrhiza*), slightly rounded in cross section, ca. 1 cm wide, and dark brown in color. The cross-weave strips were very light brown on one side and somewhat darker on the other. Certain strips were woven with the reverse side showing, dividing the mesh visually

FIGS. 15–18. FIG. 15. Warming water to soak açaí fruits. FIG. 16. Açaí fruits soaking in warm water in ceramic bowl to soften the mesocarps. FIG. 17. Initial mashing of the açaí fruits after softening of the mesocarps. FIG. 18. Caroceiro (left), showing general construction of both this and the paneira fina. Close up of cross-weave (right) of the caroceiro made from Arumã (*Ischnosiphon* sp.) showing ca. 1 cm square holes which retain the açaí seeds but allow flesh to fall through.

into four equal squares. In the paneira fina the strips were ca. 5 mm wide. The space left between the weave was about 1–2 mm wide, giving a fine straining effect. Where the mesh had been worked the most in the center the pieces had become worn in width and thickness, and because of this the space between them had increased. After prolonged use some get holes worn in their centers and need replacing. The plant from which these strips are made was locally called Arumã (*Ischnosiphon* sp.). We were informed of the names of plants used for these items by their owners and users. The caroceiro had its cross-weave made from slightly wider strips of Arumã than those used for the paneira fina, with much wider (ca.

1 cm²) gaps left between them. This allows all the flesh removed from the açaí fruits to pass through while retaining all the seeds. The word caroço in Portuguese actually means fruit pit (stone or seed) so the meaning of caroceiro is the "item used for removing the seeds," exactly what it does.

The flesh is removed from the seed by rapidly kneading, moving and energetically working the fruits with their softened skins on the caroceiro. As noted above, during this operation the caroceiro sits on top of the paneira fina which in turn sits on the rim of the bowl (Fig. 20). In the process of making açaí, the hands and lower wrists of the woman become covered by the purplish-

FIGS. 19–22. FIG. 19. The two square hand-made 'sieves' used for making the açaí liquid by hand. The caroceiro (left) is used first, the paneira fina (with a finer mesh) is used last. FIG. 20. The caroceiro, positioned on top of the paneira fina which sits on the rim of the liquid container. The fruits can be vigorously mashed upon this firm framework. FIG. 21. Fruits being mashed a second time in bowl to remove any persisting mesocarp. FIG. 22. Mashing açaí mesocarp flesh in the paneira fina to produce the thick liquid.

pinkish mush which she is vigorously creating. A limited quantity of water is poured over the seeds and caroceiro-mesh to wash more flesh through to the paneira-fina below. Any liquid run-off is caught by the bowl beneath and can be collected and passed over the mush again to avoid too much dilution with water. After as much flesh as possible has been strained through the caroceiro the seeds are placed back in the original bowl. Here they are worked vigorously a second time to remove any persisting mesocarp (Fig. 21). They are then returned to the caroceiro where the cleaned seeds are retained after everything else has been passed through. The flesh is further vigorously sieved through the paneira fina, the caroceiro having been put aside (Fig. 22). This results in an even more mushy purple mass which eventually, perhaps after passing more than once through the mesh, and after pouring more liquid

over it, is all passed through to the bowl beneath as the final thickish soup-like açaí. Enough for one day's family consumption is made on a daily basis.

VII. Use of the Açaí Liquid as a Base for Other Products

Besides its great and primary use as a subsistence food, the açaí liquid can also be made into a variety of other products. The most well known and popular of these is a regionally popular purple ice cream (Fig. 23). This is also available as 'açaí branco' ice cream which can be made from the purple fruits (Pires, pers. comm.). Due to its great regional popularity and the fact that the açaí palm characterizes much of the surrounding region's appearance, the Belém Hilton Hotel has even named a fine restaurant after the plant

FIGS. 23–26. FIG. 23. The popular purple açaí ice cream. FIG. 25. Açaí mousse. FIG. 26. Belém Hilton International pastry chef creating açaí chocolates.

('Restaurante Açaí'). Here are available such other items as an açaí milk shake and mousse (Fig. 25). The Hilton chef (Fig. 26) has created these and a variety of other delicious items (Fig. 27) using the açaí liquid as a base. These include açaí chocolates (Fig. 26) and a rich açaí gâteau (Fig. 28). Being more similar to modern Western foods, these products make a more subtle introduction to the unique taste of açaí for the person unaccustomed to the native cuisine, than does the liquid alone.

VIII. Use of the Seeds

Once defleshed, the light brown açaí seeds (over 1 cm in diam.) remain, fresh and washed clean with water. The area where the açaí liquid is made is often the open kitchen or back 'porch' (Figs. 6, 14) common to many of the rural riverside dwellings. Right outside is usually forest or a garden area. Much of the time animals are kept in this garden area, either penned up, tethered in the open, or running free. Many of them eat the açaí seeds and there is usually an abundant supply, often just dumped right onto the ground outside the area of preparation. Pigpens are often built in this area, and the seeds can be dropped right from the caroceiro into the pen for the pigs to feed on (Fig. 29). The quantity of seeds, which seemed to be the principal food of the pigs, is great, and anywhere we visited there were always piles of them either waiting for the pigs or being munched on.

Everywhere that açaí is made seeds are left over in great quantity, especially where the liquid is made for commercial sale. In Belém the seeds could be seen, piled up in huge quantities, near every açaí-making store, filling sheds especially constructed for them or waiting in large trash containers—not for a garbage man to collect but to be taken away for other uses (Fig. 30). A very rich soil to grow plants in is made from rotted-down açaí seeds, and widely used in the region. The organic soil formed, after composting them for some time, is a dark blackish brown when moist. Especially popular in the rural riverside homes where they make their own soil (Fig. 31), it is widely used for the plants in their kitchen gardens.

The abundance of seeds left over for these purposes is easy to understand, considering the vast quantities of açaí produced and consumed, cou-

pled with the fact that the seed coat flesh from which it is made is a relatively small part of the fruit. The seeds (over 1 cm in diam.), are about the size of a marble. When present in the large numbers resulting from making the liquid, they soon heap up wherever they are dumped, making large mounds (Fig. 30). In the very warm, moist climate of the region they soon sprout, and at the rear of houses where açaí is made, indeed, any corner where the seeds sit for any time, there is a profusion of sprouting seeds and seedlings (Fig. 32).

IX. Use and Extraction of Palm Hearts from *Euterpe oleracea*

Besides the açaí liquid, the other main product from açaí is palm heart. *Euterpe oleracea* is currently the world's principal source, with the Amazon estuary being the principal producing region. Factories both large and small and of varying degrees of sophistication are found situated at the edges of rivers (Figs. 33, 34). Here palm hearts are brought in by boat for processing, bottling or canning, then transported to Belém or elsewhere, where many different labels are applied. Depending on the quality, some are exported while others are consumed in Brazil. The better and less fibrous quality generally goes for export. France is the major world importer of palm heart (ca. $8 million annually), while the United States imports about $2 million annually.

There is a large internal market for palm heart in Brazil and a variety of dishes can be found in Brazilian restaurants. Although the taste of the raw heart is quite bland, it has a soft, artichoke-like texture and a pleasant, weakly acidic taste after canning. It is often served as a salad either alone or on a bed of lettuce, and can be made into a delicious hot cream soup resembling cream-of-asparagus in taste but creamy white in color. Palm heart pizza is another common preparation, where it is chopped, cooked and served on United States-style pizza (tomato sauce and cheese) slices. This was also recently observed in an Argentine owned pizzeria in New York City. In another recipe found in Belém, palm hearts were prepared within a thin pocket of dough, empanada style.

The palm heart itself consists of the tender, whitish immature leaves. Once removed it is a flexible cylinder about 60 cm long by about 2–3

FIGS. 27, 28.   FIG. 27. A variety of products made from the açaí liquid. 'Açaí' Restaurant of the Hilton International, Belém. FIG. 28. Rich gâteau ('torta de açaí') made with the açaí liquid and decorated with fruits and parts of rachillae.

FIGS. 31, 32. FIG. 31. Marajó woman demonstrating rich, dark organic soil for growing plants made from leftover açaí seeds. FIG. 32. Seedlings sprouting profusely in shaded alley behind açaí store in Belém.

cm in diameter (Fig. 35). In *Euterpe oleracea* it is neatly packaged within the cylindrical crown-shaft (Fig. 2), lying at the very center. The outside of the crownshaft consists of the outermost and oldest leaf sheath which, beneath the point of attachment of the petiole, spreads out to encircle the crownshaft for most of its length with a coarse, green to yellow, fibrous sheath. Within are concentric layers of younger and younger leaf sheaths (Fig. 36). Within this tough protective casing lie the still smaller, immature leaves, yet to emerge. Less fibrous the younger they are, only the youngest in the very center are edible. When the edible portion (free of any fibrous tissue) is very narrow, they may be kept for Brazilian consumption. Some foreign markets will also accept a certain degree of fibrousness in texture, others will not.

Various palm heart management and harvesting methods are employed, which may be tied into domestic or commercial systems aimed at sustaining a supply for the future. Regeneration of *E. oleracea* appears rapid, both vegetatively by multiple shoots produced from the base and by rapid germination of numerous seeds on the forest floor. These factors, along with the frequency of the palm in riverside forests of the region, appeared to give a potentially abundant supply of palm heart. In some cases palm hearts are harvested by independent individuals cutting down every stem of sufficient size to yield a saleable heart. However, in order to sustain a steady supply from one area it would appear that selective cutting of only a certain number of stems per individual is preferable, comparable to the selective pruning of any plant where stems or parts are removed to allow other parts to develop more strongly. In the case of açaí a double benefit occurs through this method since the stems cut yield the current harvest. Furthermore, since *E. oleracea* is such a frequent and important component of várzea forests and river/forest margins

←
FIGS. 29, 30. FIG. 29. Pigs feeding on discarded açaí seeds. FIG. 30. Heap of açaí seeds piled up outside açaí store to be taken away for other uses.

FIGS. 33–35.   FIG. 33. A palm heart factory in São Sebastião da Boa Vista, Marajó. Note layers of discarded açaí leaf sheaths (left foreground). FIG. 34. Women at dock cut leaf sheaths off palm hearts brought in by boat. FIG. 35. Cutting the flexible 'true' palm heart into sections, which sit in a bath of water, salt and citric acid to await canning.

FIGS. 36, 37. FIG. 36. Stack of cut palm hearts in the forest. Note their concentrically arranged fibrous sheaths which must be removed to get the edible heart. FIG. 37. Palm heart worker holding the crown including the whole crownshaft which he has severed from an açaí trunk he has climbed.

of the region, such controlled cutting could be of significance in conserving both soils and native forests.

To harvest the heart the entire stem may be cut down with an axe or the harvester may climb up and cut through the base of the crownshaft with a machete in order to bring down the entire crown (Fig. 37). To climb, a quickly made 'peconha' (climbing belt) is fashioned in the forest.

One method using the leaf sheath of açaí was described previously. Another method demonstrated by palm heart harvesters involves the use of a fresh green açaí leaf, still attached to the crown (Figs. 38–42). Here, a leaf is selected (at ground level) from an açaí crown. While still attached to the crown it is twisted along its length so that a strong cord about 2–3 cm in diameter is produced by the many leaflets twisted around

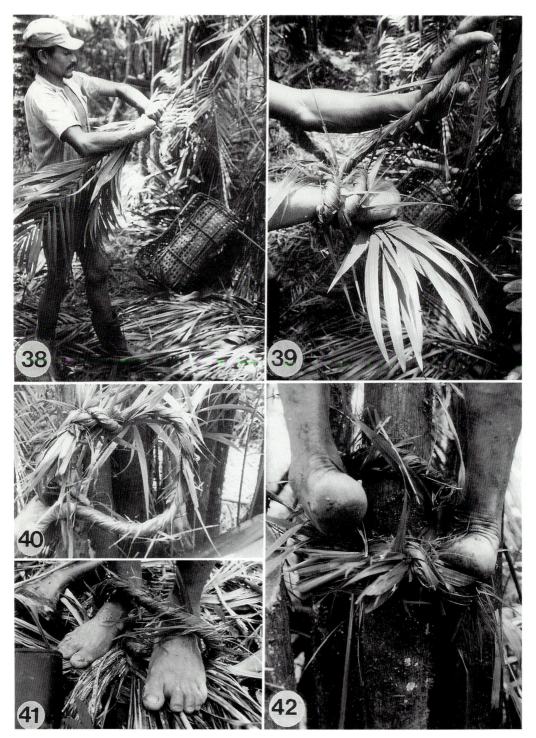

FIGS. 38–42. FIG. 38. Making a peconha (climbing belt) from an açaí leaf still attached to the crown by twisting the leaflets around the rachis. FIG. 39. Twisting the twisted leaf around the wrist. FIG. 40. The peconha made from the twisted, then knotted, leaf. FIG. 41. The peconha is positioned toward the back of the feet. FIG. 42. Using the peconha to climb the açaí trunk.

FIGS. 43–45.   FIG. 43. The cylinder containing the palm heart severed from the crown. It consists of the crownshaft area and the basal two or three leaf bases. FIG. 44. Removing a leaf sheath by cutting along its length with a machete. FIG. 45. With several sheaths removed, the palm heart, still with some inner leaf sheaths covering it, is ready for its journey to the factory.

FIG. 46. Cans filled with palm heart sections waiting to be sealed.

around the base of the outermost leaf sheath, the lowermost two or three leaves are cut off, using a machete, leaving only the very base of the petioles protruding. The remaining part of the crown is severed by cutting through the cylinder of leaf sheaths just above this (Fig. 43). To remove the petiole stubs and encircling leaf sheaths, the latter are cut along their length, one at a time, opposite the petiole, so that the entire piece can be removed (Fig. 44). The procedure is repeated, but with several of the fibrous leaf sheath cylinders retained to avoid bruising and discoloration of the tender hearts during transportation to the factory from the forest (Fig. 45). The heart must be preserved for three days or more in this way while the workers remain in the forest. At the factory other workers may be employed to strip off more leaf sheaths at the unloading jetty (Fig. 34). The final and innermost coarse sheaths are only removed when inside the factory, revealing the tender central cylindrical hearts. These are immediately cut into uniform 10 cm sections. To do this a wooden cutting block may be used with divisions along one side into which the cutting knife slots, thereby cutting the exact sized pieces desired (Fig. 35). These are then placed in a water, citric acid and salt bath (Fig. 35), then transferred into cans with this solution (Fig. 46). The cans are then machine sealed. Finally, the cans are left in a bath of steaming hot water for sterilization before boxing up for shipment out and subsequent labelling.

X. Use and Potential of *Euterpe oleracea* in Horticulture

Horticulturally, the açaí palm is of great potential value. Its slender multiple stems, along with its graceful, vertically pendulous leaflets make it extremely ornamental. Riverside areas where stands of açaí occur are thus attractive and where groves occur around riverside dwellings a particularly ornate picture results (Fig. 5). In Belém açaí is frequently planted in gardens, even in apparently sandy soils away from any open body of water. Here again it makes a beautiful ornamental tree. It grows naturally in both open areas and forest shade. However, individuals in the open, with increased light, appear more sturdy, more attractive, and may produce inflorescences at relatively low heights (2 m or less).

the rachis (Fig. 38). Standing away from the crown it is then twisted several times around the wrist enabling the person to walk in toward the base of the leaf (Fig. 39). It is severed and strongly knotted to form the climbing belt (Fig. 40). To climb, the two feet are placed through the belt which is held toward the ankles and the ball of the foot with the feet slightly apart (Fig. 41). The climber places his feet around the narrow trunk (perhaps 15 cm wide) using the two sides of the belt at the back of his feet to help grip the trunk (Fig. 42). The tree is shimmied up in small hops using the two hands together which can easily grip around the narrow trunk to pull the climber upward. Between each hop the feet are secured in place with the use of the peconha.

Once the crown has been brought down, the cylinder containing the palm heart is cut away (Figs. 43–45). After severing the crownshaft

FIGS. 47–50.   FIG. 47. Marajó woman holding seedlings of açaí branco taken from her garden. FIG. 48. Fallen açaí leaves used as a mulch around a *Musa* c.v. FIG. 49. Discarded infructescences used as a mulch around the base of *Theobroma cacao.* FIG. 50. Two fresh açaí leaves woven together to begin a carrying basket. Note the two rachi (at top).

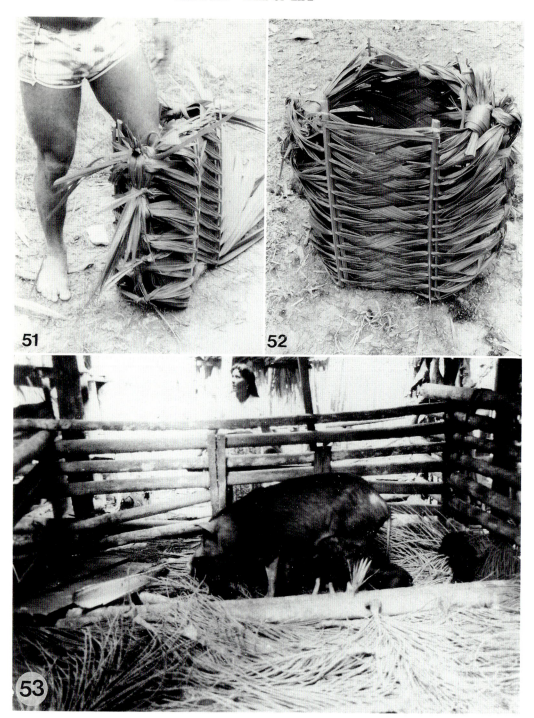

FIGS. 51–53.   FIG. 51. The outer pinnae knotted together to make the basket's sides. FIG. 52. Completed carrying basket from açaí leaves. FIG. 53. Pigpen with bedding of discarded açaí infructescences and fencing made from açaí trunks.

FIG. 54. Palm heart harvesters walking on path on muddy forest floor made from açaí trunks laid side by side.

Germination of fresh seed discarded after açaí making appears rapid and profuse in the hot humid local conditions. In the Belém Hilton small plants were used in tubs on patios or indoors while the seedlings with their bifid leaves made an interesting and unusual centerpiece for the tables (Fig. 9). Outside Belém cultivation was also noted in some gardens. In one case seedlings of both açaí branco (Fig. 47) and açaí preto were being grown.

Besides using the tree horticulturally, the use of various parts of the plant in horticultural practice is also worth noting. The use of the composted seeds as an organic soil has been discussed above. The numerous leaf sheaths left over outside palm heart factories (Fig. 33) are also valued by locals for the dark organic soil they produce on decomposition. Both the leaves (Fig. 48) and the infructescence skeletons left after removal of the fruits (Fig. 49) are used as a mulch around the bases of other economic plants, the former under *Musa* c.v. and the latter under *Theobroma cacao* for example.

XI. Other Uses

Green açaí leaves may be rapidly woven into baskets in the forest by experienced hands (Figs. 50–52). Two leaves are laid down on the ground with their rachi slightly separated. The pinnae of the adjacent sides of the leaves are interwoven to unite the two (Fig. 50). The entire structure is then bent into a square-cornered 'U' shape with the two rachi thus forming four uprights and the already woven section forming the base and two sides. The free pinnae are then woven and knotted together (Fig. 51) to form the completed basket (Fig. 52). Carrying straps are fashioned from plant material such as stringy bark and broad leaves, such as from *Musa*, may be placed inside to help hold in fruits or other items collected in the forest. The açaí leaves are also woven tightly around objects such as game caught in the forest, so that they can be carried home. The use of leaves and leaf sheaths as climbing belts has been discussed above. The spent inflorescences with their many stiff but flexible, simple rachillae are used as brooms and fashioned into dolls. They are commonly used for bedding for the pigs in pens in the riverside dwellings (Fig. 53).

The trunks of açaí, fairly constant in width along their length (perhaps 15 cm), smooth and without persistent leaf bases, are usually in plentiful supply around forest dwellers' houses. They are widely used for fencing (e.g., pigpens, Fig. 53) and flooring. They are used for the floors of outer areas of the houses, raised perhaps 1 m from the ground to allow for the seasonal flooding of the riverside areas. On these floors tasks such as açaí making might be carried out (Fig. 14), or the kitchen garden may be located. The trunks are also laid out several wide along stretches of muddy várzea forest floor to form a drier path and more secure footing for carrying palm heart out of the forest (Fig. 54).

XII. Conclusion

In this paper some of the major and minor uses of *Euterpe oleracea* have been touched upon. The palm is clearly important in many ways to the local inhabitants, particularly as a significant element of their diet. It plays a substantial role in the economy as both palm heart and the açaí liquid. Beyond this, its frequency and ecological niche suggest that it plays a major role in certain Amazonian estuarine ecosystems. In this role it could be of value in future Amazonian conservation efforts. Such efforts could also be argued for because of its economic values. *E. oleracea* is a very wide ranging species. Since it is shown here to have such a high degree of importance in the relatively limited study area, comparative studies throughout its distribution, including the Guianas and Venezuela, are merited.

XIII. Acknowledgments

Funding for this project was provided by Projeto Flora Amazonica (NSF grant BSR 8106632), which Dr. G. T. Prance made available to us. During the course of this study the senior author was supported by an Andrew Mellon doctoral fellowship with the Institute of Economic Botany, New York Botanical Garden and the junior author by a doctoral fellowship from the Herbarium, New York Botanical Garden. Our special thanks for enthusiastic and friendly help go to Marilac Raiol, Melissa Lawton, Jose Maria Reis, João Valdir Canella, Wilson Carvalho Barbosa and Mauricio Albuquerque. We also wish to thank Nina and Peter Schaepe, Adaute, Agostinho Cardoso Dias, Rafael Cabral and the Hilton International, Belém. Patricio Mena provided the Spanish abstract.

XIV. Literature Cited

Amaral, D. I. 1973. Nota preliminar sobre teste de germinação do palmito (*Euterpe edulis* Mart.) no Rio Grande do Sul. Bras. Flores. **4(16):** 62–63.

Anderson, A. B., A. Gely, J. Strudwick, G. L. Sobel & M. G. C. Pinto. 1985. Um sistema agroflorestal na várzea do estuário amazônico (Ilha das Onças, Município de Barcarena, estado do Pará). Acta Amazonica, Supl., **15(1–2):** 195–224.

Andrade, J. O. de & M. C. R. Belda. 1976. Estudo bromatológico comparativo entre palmito enlatado e "in natura" (*Euterpe edulis* Mart.). Revista Agric. **51(2):** 75–82.

Balick, M. J. 1976. The palm heart as a new commercial crop from tropical America. Principes **20:** 24–28.

Bovi, M. L. A. & M. Cardoso. 1975. Germinação de

sementes de palmiteiro (*Euterpe edulis* Mart.). Bragantia **34**: 29–34.

Calzavara, B. B. G. 1972. As possibilidades do açaizeiro no estuário amazonico. Bol. Fac. Ci. Agrar. Pará, Belém **5**: 1–103.

De Granville, J. J. 1974. Aperçu sur la structure des pneumatophores de deux espèces des sols hydromorphes en Guyane. Cah. ORSTOM. sér Biol. **23**: 3–22.

F.A.O. 1983. Palmeras poco utilizadas de América Tropical. Informe de la reunión de consulta organizada por FAO y CATIE, Turrialba, Costa Rica.

Glassman, S. F. 1972. A revision of B. E. Dahlgren's index of American palms. Cramer, Germany.

Hodge, W. H. 1965. Palm cabbage. Principes **9**: 124–131.

IDESP. 1974. Instituto do desenvolvimento economico-social do Pará: Perspectivas para o Aproveitamento Integral do Palmeira do Açaí. Série Monografias 14. Belém, Brazil.

Moore, H. E. 1973. The major groups of palms and their distribution. Gentes Herb. **11**: 27–141.

Motta, S. 1946. Pesquisas sobre o valor alimentar do açaí. Anais Assoc. Quím. Bras. **5(2)**: 35–38.

NAS. 1975. Underexploited tropical plants with promising economic value. National Academy of Sciences, Washington, D.C.

Wallace, A. R. 1853. Palm trees of the Amazon. John van Voorst, London, England.

Zapata, M. M. & D. G. Quast. 1975. Curvas de titulaçao do palmito doce (*Euterpe edulis* Mart.). Colet. Inst. Tecnol. Aliment. **6(1)**: 167–187.

The Brazilian Fiber Belt: Harvest and Management of Piassava Palm (*Attalea funifera* Mart.)

ROBERT A. VOEKS

Table of Contents

Abstract

Piassava palm (*Attalea funifera* Mart.) is endemic to the coastal restinga forests of Bahia, Brazil. Its durable, water resistant fiber has been commercially exploited since the 1500's, first in the fashioning of ship's anchor ropes and later in the manufacture of brooms and brushes. Although still destructively exploited on unattended land, piassava is increasingly being protected and managed as a valuable perennial crop. The leaf fiber is harvested either seasonally or on a continuous basis, depending on the competing interests of the cutters and land owners. Management strategies for piassava habitat include: 1) benign neglect, 2) burning, and 3) planting. During burning, piassava's deep subterranean stems escape the flames, allowing this species to survive and numerically dominate the post-fire environment. Although widespread, the use of fire to "improve" piassava habitat is temporally infrequent. Land owners began planting on an experimental basis in the 1970's. Although geographical differences in fiber quality are recognized, planting is carried out exclusively with seed from local sources.

Piassava fiber exports have steadily declined since the beginning of this century due to over-exploitation and competition with other natural as well as synthetic materials. This situation has been aggravated by the rising value of the U.S. dollar. Export losses have been more than balanced, however, by the growing demand for piassava fiber within Brazil.

Key words: palm, piassava, Attalea, Bahia, rainforest, fire

Resumo

A palmeira piaçava (*Attalea funífera*) é endemica nas matas de restinga da faixa costeira do estado da Bahia, Brasil. Sua fibra (durável e resistente 'a água) tem sido explorada desde o início do século XVI, sendo primeiramente usada para amarras de embarcações marítimas e depois na confecção de vassouras e escovas.

Embora com uma exploração destrutiva nas áreas em que se encontram abandonadas, as piaçaveiras são cada vez mais protejidas e manejadas como uma planta de valor econômico.

A extração da fibra acontece no decorrer do ano, ou somente numa estação dependendo dos interesses na competição entre tiradores e fazendeiros. Os tipos de manejamento no habitat das piaçaveiras são: 1) sem cuidados especiais, 2) com roçagens e queimadas, e 3) plantacões. Embora muito comum, o uso do fogo "para melhorar" o habitat das piaçaveiras é feito infrequentemente. Durante as queimadas os caules subterraneos escapam das chamas, garantindo a sobrevivência da espécie e também proporcionando a piaçaveira numéricamente o domínio da área após o fogo. O sistema de plantio foi iniciado pelos fazendeiros por volta de 1970, em fase experimental.

Embora tenham sido notadas diferenças na qualidade das fibras de diferentes regiões, foram usadas somente sementes do próprio local em cada plantação.

A exportação da fibra piaçava tem caido consideravelmente desde o início deste século, decorrente da competição com outras fibras naturais e também com os muitos materiais sintéticos. Situação essa agravada pelo aumento dos valores do dollar (E.U.A.). Contudo, enquanto os pedidos de exportação diminuem, aumentam a demanda e o consumo da piaçava dentro do Brasil.

I. Introduction

The exploitation of leaf fiber from piassava palm (*Attalea funifera* Mart.) represents one of the first and longest running economic activities in the New World. By 1587 the Bahian plantation owner Gabriel Soares de Sousa was able to report that ". . . for ship's cables this land has another answer, the beard of some wild palms . . . from which one makes ropes that are very strong and that never rot, [and] that there is a large quantity in the forest . . ." (Sousa, 1938, p. 425). It was the unique ability of this natural filament to withstand long periods of immersion in salt water that led to the popularity of piassava anchor ropes among trans-Atlantic mariners (Camara, 1789; Lapa, 1968). During the colonial period, this purely extractive enterprise was carried out throughout the range of *A. funifera,* and even into the southern range of its shrubby relative *A. acaulis* (Maximiliano, 1940). Principally an occupation of the pacified Tupiniquim and Aymore Indians (Spix & Martius, 1820), piassava collection was early the principal industry in the Captaincy of Ilhéus, surpassing sugar, cotton and coffee in value (Silva Campos, 1981). It was the chance discovery of its utility in broom and brush manufacture, however, that led to the extensive and destructive exploitation in the latter 19th century (Dodge, 1897). Growing from literally nothing in 1840, the export of this new and popular fiber to Europe peaked in the early 1880's at over 8000 tons per year (Associação Comercial da Bahia, 1867–1940). To fiber merchants in Europe, the term piassava became synonymous with any long-stranded palm fiber. To this day several unrelated species share this indigenous South American Indian name, including *A. funifera* and *A. acaulis* from Bahia, *Leopoldinia piassaba* from Amazonia, and even some African fiber palms.

The collection of Bahian piassava fiber was observed first-hand by Booth (1889, p. 239), who wrote that "The present mode of obtaining it is to cut the tree down, and pull the fiber from the trunk afterwards, a very foolish proceeding . . ." Such destructive methods, responsive to intense international demand, resulted in palm depletion, increasing costs, and eventual replacement on foreign markets by cheaper African fibers (Kiddier, n.d.).

While continuously declining during the 20th century as an export item, piassava fiber production has risen sharply in the last few decades, contributing significantly to Brazil's efforts at economic self-reliance. The increasing role of piassava in the national market has led some fazendeiros (or farm owners) to manage this palm on a sustainable basis. Thus, as a native species with economic value throughout the history of Bahia, piassava provides an example of our changing perception and means of exploitation of rain forest resources. This paper describes the present state of management, harvest and economic worth of piassava palm. It is based on fieldwork carried out in Bahia from May 1984 to Sep. 1985.

II. Geography and Botany

Piassava inhabits a north–south belt near the coast of Bahia, Brazil (Fig. 1), from about 13° to 17°S latitude (Silva & da Vinha, 1982). The mean annual temperature ranges from 23–24°C, and the mean annual precipitation is on the order of 1800–2000 mm. The summer (Jan–Mar) is characterized by convective rainfall activity, whereas the winter (Jul–Sep) regularly receives showers from the passage of cold fronts along the coast (Sa et al., 1982). Thus, although relatively distant from the equator, the Bahian littoral does not experience a dry season.

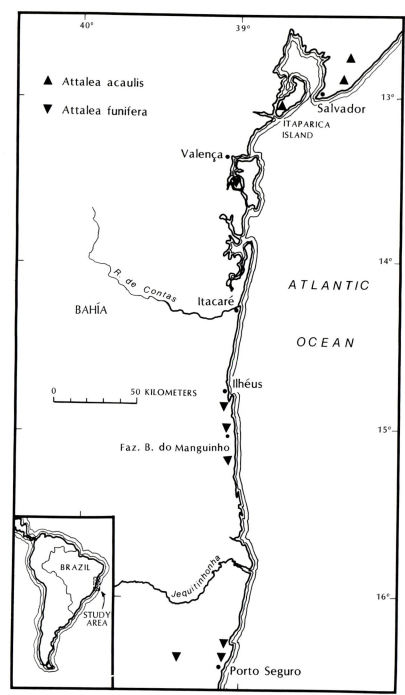

FIG. 1. Distribution of Piassava. Symbols represent collections made by the author and housed at the Herbarium, Centro de Pesquisas do Cacau, Itabuna, Bahia. *Attalea acaulis* (the shrub form of *A. funifera*) is included because it is known by the name piassava, its fiber is harvested, and its independent taxonomic status is questionable.

Topographically this region consists of a series of nearly level Pliocene/Pleistocene surfaces, gently dipping towards the sea. Although dominated by latosols, these landforms in places exhibit an apron of sandy, podzolic soils around their flanks (Braun & Ramalho, 1980). Porous, acidic, and low in exchangeable bases, these siliceous soils sustain a slightly-dwarfed evergreen "restinga" forest association, of which piassava palm is a member.

Piassava reaches a height of 12–15 m. Its leaves extend over 9 m in length; leaflets, which are 50–60 cm in length and aggregated, begin 3–4 m from the leaf base attachment (Bondar, 1942). The fiber extends along the leaf rachis and attaches to the stem. Inflorescences are fragrant, simply branched, and massive, attaining a length of nearly 2 m. Individuals are largely sequential hermaphrodites, with strictly male expression yielding to increasing female expression as the palm grows and enters the rain forest canopy. Flowering and fruiting are continuous throughout the year, with a flowering peak during the summer (Dec–Feb). Pollination is apparently carried out through deception—with pistillate stigmas mimicking staminate flowers—by a host of mostly specialized insects. The fruit are avocado-sized drupes, with thick, hard endocarps protecting 1–3 seeds. Bunches may attain 50 kg in weight (Voeks, 1985; in press).

III. Fiber Collection

A razor-sharp machete and a garfão (forked wooden ladder) comprise the tools of the fiber cutter. The garfão, which is used to scale the palm, is fashioned on site from a 5 to 8 m tree. The bark is stripped away, as are most of the branches. The base of one branch near the tip is spared, resulting in a small terminal bifurcation which is leaned against the upper trunk of the palm to provide balance. Notches are often cut along the length of the garfão to provide toe holds. A fastidious climber may inlay strips of wood in the notches, producing a delux garfão.

Harvest is carried out by a barefoot man who first carefully ascends the garfão, hand-over-hand for balance (Fig. 2). Once in the crown, he hacks a tiny wedge out of one of the older leaves, near its junction with the trunk. Due to its own weight, the 9 m frond sags into a horizontal position, thus providing a working platform. While work-

ing, the cutter normally keeps one foot on the trunk side of the wedge to prevent the entire frond from collapsing under his weight. Where piassavas grow closely together, the frond is cut so that its tip eases into the crown of the adjoining palm, thus forming an inter-palm scaffold for the cutter. In this way, he can move swiftly from palm to palm without ascending and descending.

The fibrous material, which early in the life of the palm consists of a protective sheath over the terminal bud, eventually forms a tight mass of 4–5 m wire-like strands binding the leaf rachis to the leaf base. Also collected is the borra, a paper-thin fiber that binds the strand fiber together. Extraction is accomplished by severing the two points of fiber attachment for each rachis and tossing the mass to the ground; this is repeated for all the leaves that have separated from the terminal bud. A third grade of fiber called toco is also removed. Toco is thick and stiff, grows flush with the trunk, and is extracted in short 0.5 m lengths.

Once the fiber has been stripped from the palm the process of separating, bundling, and transport can proceed. The strand fiber is manually separated from the borra by grasping the mass of fiber in one hand and peeling away the strands with the other (Fig. 3). While the borra is heaped on wooden slats for drying in the sun, the strand fiber is temporarily set aside. When sufficient strand fiber for a bundle has accumulated—usually about 3 arrobas (45 kg)—lengths of borra are twisted by hand into cordage and layed out in four parallel lines about 0.5 m apart. Next, with a whip-like motion, the strand fiber is arranged on top of and perpendicular to the borra cord. The short pieces of toco fiber, which have been tied together with pieces of borra twine, are then placed in the middle of the developing molho (or fiber bundle). The two cabeças (or ends of the strand fiber) are next tied into tight bundles with the outer two lengths of borra, and then folded over so as to meet in the middle. The molho is completed by securing the two remaining pieces of borra twine around the middle of the bundle, resulting in a transportable package of piassava fiber.

After drying, the borra is sold to local thatch makers, who clean, trim, and weave it by hand into an attractive and water repellant roofing material.

A division of labor exists in cases where fam-

FIG. 2.   Young fiber collector on working platform leaf.

FIG. 3. Fiber cutter separating the strand fiber from the paper-thin borra.

ilies look after the piassava fazenda. The scaling of the palms, stripping of the fiber, and fashioning of the molhos is carried out by the men and boys. Fathers teach this craft to their sons at an early age, and ten year old boys are said to climb and cut as well as their fathers. Neither are preoccupied with injury. Once mastered, the continuous clambering up and down trees becomes quite mechanical. Women and the younger children often gather the fiber from the bases of the trees and separate the borra from the strand fiber.

IV. Negative Effects of Harvest

The degree of harvesting damage to piassavas on managed fazendas depends on the attitudes of both the owners and the cutters. Paid by unit weight, the cutter maximizes his earning power by removing any leaves or reproductive structures that impede fiber extraction. Carried to an extreme, however, such destructive exploitation may diminish the continued productivity of the fazenda. The unspoken compromise that seems to have developed between workers and owners is that the cutters kill only one or two living leaves for use as working platforms. Since these leaves are usually the oldest and closest to death, their loss poses the least threat to the health of the tree. I have seen a cutter remove as few as 0.95 living leaves per palm (n = 28) during a day. He accomplished this by chopping down mostly dead or dying leaves for use as working platforms. This low figure is unusual, however, and probably reflects "good" behavior exhibited in my presence.

While in large measure protecting the valuable leaves, cutters show less regard for the reproductive future of the palms. The woody botão (or incipient flower spathe), emerging from between the leaf attachments, is a hindrance to fiber extraction and is always cut away. The developing fruits, which dangle below the canopy on massive infructescences, may or may not be cut off. If ripe, the entire bunch of fruit will probably be carted home for food. There the husks are hacked away with a machete and the tasty seeds are eaten raw or rendered into a rich cooking oil.

Although much of the prime piassava habitat is managed, many owners of restinga do not harvest the fiber on a regular basis and do not employ caretakers. Often such areas are too small or distant to be adequately overseen. In these cases, piassava is nearly always collected by fiber poachers, whose methods are often very destructive. Besides cutting all the growing spathes and developing bunches of fruit, they may kill 2, 3, or more of the living leaves. In the worst scenario, when the palm is particularly tall, poachers fell the entire tree in order to strip its fiber. This type of destructive exploitation on unattended land, which was common in the 19th century, is tending to limit the distribution of piassava to carefully managed properties.

V. Management

As a native of the local rain forests, piassava need not necessarily be managed in order to reap economic returns. The term management, however, will be used in a broad sense, including any level of habitat manipulation carried out to maintain and improve present and future piassava productivity or quality. Since much of the piassava habitat is privately owned, any vegetation modification (or lack of it) will be assumed to represent a conscious decision on the part of the owner as to what is best for his farm.

Piassava fazenda management falls into three general groupings, including: 1) benign neglect, 2) burning, and 3) planting. As will be shown, the boundaries between these strategies are somewhat arbitrary, and more than one strategy may be used on a single fazenda. Benign neglect entails little more than an annual harvest of the piassava fiber-mass from the native restinga. No seeds are planted nor is the vegetation manipulated in any way. This old second growth forest, or capoeirão, presents special difficulties for the fiber cutter. The high number of tree species translates into a large distance between piassava trees, necessitating the hauling of fiber often formidable distances for cleaning and packaging. The few scattered piassava plants per hectare also means that the total fiber production for the individual fazenda will be low. In addition, individual piassavas tend to be quite tall in capoeirão, thus adding to the time required to clean a tree. For the fiber cutter, who is paid per unit weight, these can be important considerations.

This management option is often the preferred choice of small scale farmers, who are unable to survive the hiatus in income resulting from burning or planting. This option also represents the best strategy for inaccessible parcels of land on expansive fazendas, particularly if, as is often the case, fiber collection is only a secondary economic activity (Ferreira et al., 1985). With profitable and prestigious cacao occupying the best lands, the potential contribution of piassava to the farm economy is minimal, and may not justify careful attention. In addition, there seems to be a general perception on the part of fazendeiros that fiber farming is a lower class endeavor. In Bahia, "o cacau é ouro." Thus, economic considerations notwithstanding, time spent on piassava management may represent time wasted for the wealthier fazendeiro.

Management by fire of rain forest palms—including piassava—is widespread among folk societies in the New World tropics and provides a classic example of plant cultivation without invoking domestication. By sparing those trees perceived to be valuable, shifting cultivators are assured an orchard-like stand of desirable species without further forest modification (Alcorn, 1981; Posey, 1984). Examples of palms that are managed by this or similar techniques include: guagara (*Manicaria saccifera*), jirot (*Socratea* sp.), jira (*Socratea durissima*) and conga (*Welfia georgii*) in Panama (Gordon, 1982); coyal (*Acrocomia mexicana*), corozo (*Orbignya* sp.) and palma real (*Scheelea liebmannii*) in Tabasco, Mexico (Heizer, 1955; Johannessen, 1957; West et al., 1969); and babassú (*Orbignya martiana*) in Brazil (Anderson, 1983).

Piassava farms are most often managed by fire. The belief that torching the forest somehow improves piassava regeneration is widespread and has been so at least since the turn of the century (Bondar, 1942; Moraes, 1911; Valeriano, 1934). Now as in the past, piassava farmers recognize three post-fire successional stages. The patioba stage encompasses the unproductive period from seedling emergence to when the leaves are just large enough to produce fiber. The bananeira stage takes in the period from when leaves begin to produce fiber to when the trunk begins to appear. The coqueiro stage, which covers most of the productive life of the palm, starts with the emergence of the trunk and ends with the death of the individual.

Burning is carried out in the summer, after the vegetation has been hacked down and allowed to dry in the sun, and in general resembles a typical slash-and-burn process. Previously standing piassavas are spared. The key to the value of burning, however, lies with the ability of piassava seedlings to quickly dominate these charred patches. With their deep subterranean stems protected from the surface flames, young piassavas lose only a few above-ground leaves. They are thus one of the few forest tree species able to survive the effects of fire. With little competition, high sunlight, and a flush of post-fire nutrients, piassava seedlings quickly send up new leaves, eventually forming a relatively dense stand (Voeks, 1987).

Although the most ubiquitous management tool, the act of burning is most advantageous when carried out but infrequently. This is the case because several unproductive years create a serious economic hardship for small farmers. Whereas the long-term goal is increased yield, the short-term outlook is no yield whatsoever. More important, because natural forest succession is gradual, burning need only be repeated as often as piassava density drops to uneconomic levels. On one large piassava fazenda near Ilhéus, for example, extensive burning was carried out in the 1930's in order to increase the number of palms. Fifty years later, piassava still forms dense and in places monotypic stands, surrendering completely to other forest trees only on the patches of clayey soils. Thus, although geographically widespread, management by fire need be repeated only occasionally.

After burning, fazendeiros plant a crop of manioc, thus supplying a quick economic return while waiting five to eight years for the piassava to enter the productive bananeira stage. This root crop is cultivated only once, however, because the post-fire soil fertility is believed to quickly diminish. Other fiber farmers avoid planting manioc in the belief that it desiccates the soil and thus prejudices future piassava productivity.

A variation of palm management by fire occurs where the conversion of forest to pasture, particularly common in southern Bahia (Leão, 1982; Mori et al., 1983), has led to the unintentional joint exploitation of cattle and piassava. Quick to recolonize these disturbed areas, piassava palms give a distinctive signature to this simplified landscape. The economic emphasis, however, is clearly on the ruminant grazers; consequently, little attention is paid to careful management of these weedy invaders and in the course of being harvested many are literally pruned to death.

Early in this century fire appears to have been the only means of piassava management (Valeriano, 1934). Bondar (1942, 1943) outlined the failure of early planting schemes—particularly resulting from bruchid beetle infestation of seeds—and proposed a planting strategy to eliminate this problem. The first systematic planting of piassava seeds, however, was not carried out until the 1970's near Valença. The stimulus for this planting may have been the recent success of African oil palm (*Elaeis guineensis*) cultivation in the region. Moreover, while demand for piassava fiber within Brazil was rising, this once common palm had been largely eliminated from the region since the late 1800's (Booth, 1889). Regardless of the impetus, these early experiments were successful, and were noted by a fazenda owner near St. Cruz Cabralia, who initiated his own planting projects in the mid-1970's. A third fiber farmer, also impressed by these early attempts at cultivation, has recently begun planting near Olivença. The following observations summarize the trial-and-error methods used at the latter two fazendas.

Fruits were collected from the ground or directly from fruit bunches on nearby trees. Near Olivença the pulpy mesocarp of the fruit was removed prior to planting in order to avoid termite attack. Fazendeiros were cognizant of problems with infestation by bruchid beetles; one avoided the situation by selecting only freshly fallen fruits or cutting ripe uninfested bunches, whereas the other took no precautions. In open capoeira (early second growth vegetation), the St. Cruz Cabralia farmer planted two fruits in plots spaced 3 m apart. The capoeira was not burned. In his early attempts, he slashed, planted and burned; germination results using this method were, however, unsatisfactory. Much better germination was obtained by slashing, planting, waiting one year, and then burning. In this way, the young stems became safely ensconced below the soil surface and away from the heat of the fire. The fazenda owner in Olivença achieved best results using a slash, burn, and then plant sequence.

Only nearby piassava populations were used as seed sources; no effort was made to transport seeds from better areas or to select seed from better trees. Although there are conflicting opinions, people who work with piassava perceive variations in fiber quality. Fazendeiros both in the far south and north of piassava's range indicated that the strands are stronger in the central part of the range, near Ilhéus and Olivença. Fiber merchants were divided in opinion. On a local scale, several informants pointed out that fiber collected in dense forest was of better quality than that from open, disturbed sites. Thus, the recognition of different quality fibers has yet to be translated into any level of selective breeding.

VI. Fiber Harvest Schedule

Fiber from managed land is collected by traveling crews or by families that reside on the property. In the former case, teams of workers collect the fiber on an annual basis, moving from one fazenda to the other throughout the year. This situation is most common on large fazendas. In the latter case, resident cutters serve both to harvest the fiber and protect the palms from fiber poachers. Where the cutters are residents, harvest scheduling takes on two forms: 1) the family cuts fiber during a prescribed season and survives on these earnings for the balance of the year, or 2) fiber is continuously extracted throughout the year, thus providing year-round occupation for employees.

The timing of piassava fiber harvest is biologically flexible. Unlike fruits, nuts, and seeds, which have a fixed season of collection, piassava extraction is little constrained by biology. Draped below the fronds, the web-like strands neither rot nor fall to the ground; rather, each palm acts as a temporary storage unit, with the filaments available for extraction when the schedule of the collector permits.

The date of the first harvest of an area is said to dictate the timing of subsequent annual collections. However, the actual harvest schedule more often depends on the conflicting interests of the owners and the cutters. On one fazenda near Porto Seguro, for example, the employees reside on the property and extract fiber on a continuous basis. The fazendeiro would prefer winter harvest, believing the biological stress of leaf removal during the dormant season to be negligible; summer harvest is thought to cause a higher death rate in piassava trees, or at least lead to diminished leaf production the following year. However, in this case the need for reliable labor transcends biological considerations.

Fiber extraction on large fazendas is normally carried on an annual basis, although I have seen 18 months pass between harvests due to labor problems. Such postponements occur when fiber cutting crews are delayed at one job, thus forcing arrival at subsequent fazendas to be put off. Labor shortages also take place when cutters are redirected to cocoa culture chores, which always take precedence over piassava activities. A special case of labor availability determining the seasonal harvest schedule occurs on the island of Itaparica, near Salvador, where fiber gathering activities are linked to the slack period for fishermen. Idled by the diminished winter catch, fishermen seasonally switch their attention from fish to fiber.

A further factor that determines fiber harvest timing is the Bahian perception of climate; winters are thought to be cold and wet, summers warm and relatively dry. Since an equal quantity of fiber harvested in the winter will be damper and thus heavier than that cut in the summer, on economic considerations alone, cutters prefer winter work whereas merchants would rather buy in the summer. On the other hand, Bahians abhor what is perceived to be the uncomfortably cold winter temperatures; this factor in addition to the increased danger of falling from rain-slicked palms motivates cutters to work in the summer. Thus, labor shortages, conflicting interests, environmental perceptions, and the frequent relegation of piassava collection to a secondary economic activity results in piassava harvest being carried out throughout the year.

VII. Fiber Sales

The movement of piassava fiber from fazenda to manufacturer is carried out by three types of businesses: 1) small independent establishments, 2) fazendeiro-owned firms, and 3) large export houses. Independent establishments are common, may be short lived, and negotiate small quantities of fiber. Such operations, which are mostly owner run and operated, serve to facilitate the flow of raw fiber. Molhos as well as unbundled fiber are purchased, cleaned, rebundled, and sold on consignment to Brazilian broom and brush manufacturers.

Fazendeiro-owned firms usually sell untreated fiber directly to broom and brush manufacturers, who agree to purchase a predetermined quantity of fiber per year. Shipments are picked up by truck at the fazenda. In a special case, the owner of a large number of geographically separated cocoa and piassava fazendas maintains a fiber distribution center in Ilhéus. There he prepares fiber from his own fazenda as well as that purchased from others. The fiber is cleaned, separated into thickness grades, chopped into various lengths (Fig. 4), and shipped to broom companies in São Paulo and Porto Alegre.

International sales are carried out by two export houses—one in Salvador, the other in Ilhéus. Although it buys piassava from throughout the hinterland, the Salvador firm focuses on the fiber-rich region around Valença. The Ilhéus exporter procures fiber from the southern part of the state, beginning in Itacaré to the north, and extending to Canavieras in the south. This division of the piassava fiber-shed results for the most part from the natural north-south break in the flow of goods caused by the unbridged Contas River near Itacaré.

Both the Salvador and Ilhéus exporters clean, grade, cut, and bundle their product prior to shipment to European ports. The Salvador exporter ships out of the home port, whereas the relatively slow traffic at the port of Ilhéus requires that the Ilhéus exporter forward some shipments inland by truck to Salvador for later overseas transport. Interstate movement of piassava is exclusively handled by truck transport.

VIII. Current Economic Trends

Three changes highlight the recent economy of piassava: 1) a dramatic increase in fiber production and local use, 2) the near disappearance of fiber exports, and 3) the growing local popularity of fiber as a roofing material.

The annual production of Bahian piassava is shown in Figure 5. Notable is the gradual but consistent increase in production beginning in the 1950's; by the later part of the decade production had doubled, and by the 1970's, it had quadrupled. The leap in production from 1973 to 1974 is suspiciously abrupt, suggesting a change in the method of data collection. Nevertheless, assuming that the most recent figures are accurate, the state-wide production has grown over 10-fold in the past three decades. The cause or source of this upsurge is not evident, although it may be related to the intensive piassava farm management practices that began in the 1970's in the Cairú–Valença–Ituberá fiber-shed.

The data for piassava exports from 1938 to the present are plotted in Figure 6. Also shown are the values of piassava exports in US$ after 1969. These data serve to underline the continuous annual decline in piassava exports, with yearly tonnage figures presently on the order of 3% of those one century ago. Whereas the recent value of exports has largely remained steady, piassava as an export commodity is clearly disappearing. This decline in international demand is contrary to the surging fiber production figures (Fig. 5); whereas in the 1940's and 1950's, annual export was on the order of 60% of total production, this figure slipped sharply after 1975 to less than 1%. Although the specific source of this burgeoning national consumption is not clear, piassava brooms and brushes are manufactured and used throughout the country. It is the rare abode whose floors and backyard are not kept clean with piassava brooms, and in most cases the streets as well bear witness to the strength and resilience of this palm product. Thus, piassava has made the transition from export cash crop to integration into the national market. These conclusions are not in accord with the observation by Ferreira et al. (1985) that most Bahian piassava still is exported.

Although the bulk of piassava fiber is still bound for the broom and brush market (Bondar, 1942; Silva & da Vinha, 1982), piassava borra fiber has found a lucrative market in Bahia as a thatch material. Once cast off as trash or utilized only by the lower classes, this material is now employed principally for weekend beach cabanas and the chic homes of the well to do.

I further examined the present status and future prospects for piassava on the international market by mailing questionnaires to European importers. Excepting Holland, all the respondents stated that they are importing smaller quantities of piassava than in the past and that in the future they expected this trend to continue. The Holland firm indicated that imports would remain stable. This decline in importation is related to the high cost of piassava fiber in comparison to other natural fibers and particularly plastic monofilament. Lack of competitiveness

FIG. 4.   Piassava fiber in Ilhéus distribution center. This fiber has been cleaned, graded, cut and bundled for sale to a broom manufacturer.

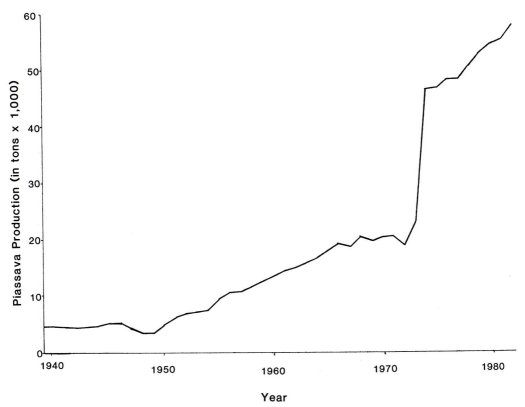

FIG. 5. Annual Piassava production. Data are taken from the annual reports of the Instituto Brasileiro de Geografía e Estatística.

of piassava, according to importers, has been aggravated by the rising value of the U.S. dollar relative to other currencies. Thus at the same time that devaluation of the European and Brazilian currencies has occurred, the price of piassava has been maintained (through mutual agreement of the Bahian exporters) in U.S. dollars, with the result that each successive year the equivalent quantity of European currency purchases fewer and fewer bundles of piassava. This situation acts to enhance the competitive ability of other natural and synthetic fibers, to the detriment of piassava imports.

Piassava fiber does not lack for competitors. Respondents indicated that they import piassava-type fibers from several sources, including Sierra Leone, India, Sri Lanka, Java, Mexico, Venezuela, Nigeria, and Manaus, Brazil. Bahian piassava is known as a high quality broom material, able to maintain elasticity in wet conditions better than the African fibers (Whitford, 1954). Nevertheless, the high prices demanded

for Bahian piassava have, in part, forced broom and brush manufacturers to mix this product with other inferior grade fibers. The export of Bahian piassava fiber is thus witnessing its final episode. Instigated by destructive exploitation in the mid-19th century, the competition with cheaper natural fibers as well as plastic monofilaments has slowly eliminated the foreign market. At the same time, the dramatic rise of the domestic market is largely compensating for the vanishing demand overseas.

IX. Future Research

Although it has been a distinctive element in Bahia's economic landscape for over four centuries, piassava has yet to receive much attention from researchers. This situation promises to improve with the recent efforts initiated by botanists and agronomists at the Centro de Pesquisas do Cacau.

In view of Brazil's need to generate income

FIG. 6.   Piassava export quantities and values. The sources for the period 1938 to 1969 are the annual reports of the Instituto Brasileiro de Geografia e Estatística, which combined *A. funifera* fiber export quantities with those for Pará piassava (*Leopoldinia piassaba*) from the Amazon region. In order to estimate the approximate value of Bahian piassava exports alone, I reduced the summed figure by 20%; this figure reflects the 5 to 1 ratio of Bahian to Pará piassava exports reported during years when both figures were listed. The export tonnage and value in U.S. dollars for 1970 to 1984, which were culled from recent Promoexport records and their latest annual report (1983), include Bahian piassava exclusively.

through exports and, at the same time, address the growing needs of a largely landless rural population, I suggest the following three lines of research. First, many piassava fiber collectors and fazendeiros noted that the fiber from some regions was of higher quality than that from others. This should be investigated, with the aim of developing palms that yield better quality fiber and in higher quantities. Second, agroforestry experiments should be initiated using various combinations of piassava grown in conjunction with other food and cash crops. Since these sandy soils do not sustain cocoa, such small scale endeavors focusing on piassava as a cash crop would not compete with more lucrative uses of the land, and thus could serve as a means of providing meaningful and sustainable occupation for landless folk. Third, improvements should be made in the overseas advertising of this and other palm products. In the case of Bahian piassava, waning interest by foreign countries appears to be as much related to poor marketing as to competition with other commodities.

X. Acknowledgments

This research was funded by a Fulbright Exchange Fellowship, a University of California, Berkeley, Regent's Fellowship, and a Center for Latin American Studies Travel Grant. I thank Hilgard O'R. Sternberg and Herbert G. Baker for guidance during the project, James J. Parsons as well as three anonymous reviewers for constructive criticism of the text, and Maureen DeCoursey and Janira Voeks for field assistance. I am particularly grateful to Luiz Alberto M. Silva, Sergio G. da Vinha, and Talmón Santos from the Centro de Pesquisas do Cacau for advice, assistance, and for introducing me to Bahia.

XI. Literature Cited

Alcorn, J. 1981. Haustec non-crop resource management: Implications for prehistoric forest management. Human Ecol. **9(4):** 395–417.

Anderson, A. 1983. The biology of *Orbignya martiana* (Palmae), A tropical dry forest dominant in

Brazil. Ph.D. Dissertation. University of Florida, Gainesville.

Associação Comercial de Bahia. 1867–1940. Wilke, Picarde, Co.: n.p.

Bondar, G. 1942. A piassaveira e outras palmeiras Attaleaineas na Bahia. Bol. Ins. Cent. Fomento Econ. Bahia **13:** 1–73.

———. 1943. A piassaveira e o segredo de sua reprodução. Chácaras & Quintais **67(6):** 739–741.

Booth, W. S. 1889. Bahia piassava. Kew Bull. Misc. Inf. **34:** 327–342.

Braun, O. & R. Ramalho. 1980. Geomorfologia da Bahia. Revista Brasil. Geogr. **42(4):** 822–861.

Camara, M. F. 1789. Ensaio de descripção fízica, e econmica da Camarca dos Ilheas na America. Mem. Econ. Acad. Real Sci. Lisboa **1:** 304–350.

Dodge, C. R. 1897. A descriptive catalogue of useful fiber plants. U.S. Dept. of Agric. Rep. No. 9.

Ferreira, M., E. L. Oliveira & M. S. Barboza. 1985. A piaçava na Bahia. XXXVI Congresso Nacional de Botánica, Abstracts.

Gordon, B. L. 1982. A Panama forest and shore: Natural history and Amerindian culture in Bocas del Toro. The Boxwood Press, Pacific Grove, California.

Heizer, R. W. 1955. Primitive man as an ecologic factor. Kroeber Anthropol. Soc. **13:** 1–31.

Instituto Brasileiro de Geografia e Estatística. 1946–1982. Anuario Estatistico do Brasil. Conselho Nacional de Estatistica, Rio de Janeiro.

Johannessen, C. L. 1957. Man's role in the distribution of the Corozo Palm (*Orbignya* sp.). Yearb. Assoc. Pac. Coast Geogr. **19:** 29–33.

Kiddier, W. n.d. The brushmaker and the secrets of his craft: His romance. Jonathan Cape, London.

Lapa, J. R. 1968. A Bahia e a carreira da India. Nacional, São Paulo.

Leão, S. 1982. The evolution of agricultural land use patterns in the State of Bahia, Brasil. Ph.D. Dissertation. University of Western Ontario.

Maximiliano, Principe de Wied Neuwied. 1940. Viagem ao Brasil. trans. Editora Nacional, São Paulo.

Moraes, P. de. 1911. A piassabeira: A extinção dos piassabaes naturaes e a sua necessaria cultura. Chácaras & Quintais **3:** 15–16.

Mori, S. A., B. M. Boom, A. M. Carvalho & T. S. Santos. 1983. Southern Bahian moist forests. Bot. Rev. **49(2):** 155–232.

Posey, D. A. 1984. A preliminary report on diversified management of tropical forests by the Kayapó Indians of the Brazilian Amazon. *In* G. T. Prance & J. A. Kallunki (eds.), Ethnobotany in the Neotropics. Adv. Econ. Bot. **1:** 112–126.

Promoexport. 1983. Comércio Exterior da Bahia: Exportação Segundo Firmas, Mercadorias e Países de Destino—1983. Salvador, Bahia.

Sa, D. F., H. A. Almeida, L. F. Silva & A. C. Leão. 1982. Fatores edafoclimáticos seletivos ao zoneamento do cacaucultura no sudeste da Bahia. Revista Theobroma **12:** 169–187.

Silva, L. A. & Vinha, S. G. da. 1982. A piassaveira (*Attalea funifera* Mart.) e vegetação associada no Município de Ilhéus, Bahia. CEPLAC/CEPEC, Ilhéus, BA, Brasil. Bol. Técn. No. 101, 12 pp.

Silva Campos, J. 1981. Crônica da Capitania de São Jorge de Ilhéus. Nacional, Rio de Janeiro.

Sousa, G. S. de. 1938. Tratado Descritivo do Brasil em 1587. n.p.

Spix, Von & C. P. Von Martius. 1928. Atravez da Bahia: Excertos da "Obra Reise in Brasilien." Trans. P. da Silva & P. Wolf. Impresa Oficial, Bahia.

Valeriano, C. 1934. A piassaveira. Bahia Rural **1(10):** 293–296.

Voeks, R. A. 1985. Preliminary observations on the reproductive ecology of the piassava palm (*Attalea funifera*). Anais Acad. Brasil. Ci. **57:** 524–525.

———. 1987. A biogeography of the piassava fiber palm (*Attalea funifera*) of Bahia, Brazil. Ph.D. dissertation, University of California, Berkeley.

———. (In press). Changing sexual expression of a Brazilian rainforest palm (*Attalea funifera* Mart.). Biotropica.

Webering, V. A. 1937. Notas sobre a piassaveira. Bahia Rural **5(49/50):** 1828–1830.

West, R. C., N. P. Psuty & B. G. Thom. 1969. The Tabasco lowlands of southeastern Mexico. Coastal Studies Institute, Louisiana State University, Tech. Rep. No. 70, 193 pp.

Whitford, A. C. 1954. Miscellaneous plant fibres. Pages 439–483 *in* H. R. Mauersberger (ed.), Textile fibres: Their physical, microscopic and chemical properties. John Wiley & Sons, New York.

Worldwide Endangerment of Useful Palms

DENNIS V. JOHNSON

Table of Contents

"Because of its diverse applications and its economic importance, the palm family ranks among the top three of all plant families, the other two being the Gramineae (grasses)—including corn, wheat, and rice—and the Leguminosae—beans, peas, and many other foods, also many medicines. Yet the palm family is surely the most threatened of all major plant categories."

Norman Myers, *The Primary Source,* 1984

Key words: Palms, conservation, endangered species

I. Introduction

The Palm family consists of 200 genera and approximately 2600 species, according to the most recent classification by Uhl and Dransfield (1987). A family of great diversity, it is as old as any other group of flowering plants, and has been intimately associated with the rise of human culture. The great majority of palm species are native to the tropical regions of the earth, but their occurrence is neither uniform in population numbers nor species diversity. Certain palms occur in dense, virtually pure stands and constitute in themselves the forest, whereas others are common or uncommon plants of the understory vegetation in tropical rainforests. As for diversity, the Asian tropics are the richest, followed closely by the American tropics; Africa is a distant third.

Wherever in nature palms occurs in proximity to human populations, they have provided a wide array of useful products. By product group and in order of importance, they are as follows: Food—in the form of edible fruits, edible seed oil, sweet or fermented beverage as well as sugar from the sap, palm hearts, and stem starch. Fiber—from the leaf, petiole or leafbase for weaving, ropemaking, brushes and the like. Building materials—furnished by trunk wood, petioles, and leaves used for thatching. Fuelwood—from the trunks, petioles and leaves. Folk medicines—derived from the fruit, sap, leaf wax, and roots. In a number of cultures, as recorded by ethnologists, these palm products and/or the trees themselves have assumed magico-religious significance, and rituals are associated with them. This is almost always the case in cultures where a palm has come to be considered a "tree of life." The multiple utility of palms is without question.

Currently we have a fairly accurate idea of the numbers of palm genera and species, but what we know about their utility to humankind in the past, present or future is inadequate. Because it is inadvisable on the basis of our present incomplete knowledge of the Palmae to deem any one species as lacking potential value, any assessment of the worldwide endangerment of useful palms must make the assumption that none should be excluded.

Thus far, very little research has been directed toward the conservation status of palms. Moore (1977) provided the first and still the most comprehensive treatment of the subject. His findings furnished much of the original information on the Palmae for the database of the Conservation Monitoring Centre (CMC), of the International Union for the Conservation of Nature and Natural Resources (IUCN), located at Kew Gardens.

Advances in Economic Botany 6: 268–273, 1988

Without access to this unique centralized database on the conservation status of the world's flora and fauna, the present study could not have been undertaken.

In this paper, I discuss briefly palm conservation; report on the conservation status of threatened palms, and a recently-completed utilization and conservation project in the New World; make a preliminary assessment of the conservation status of threatened palms, and planned conservation research in the Old World; and conclude with some suggestions as to where future palm conservation efforts should be directed.

II. Palm Conservation

As used here, the term "conservation" is not employed as a synonym for "preservation." In other words, it implies neither that palm conservation precludes utilization of palms in the wild, nor that palm fanciers should be restricted in their quest for exotic species to cultivate, provided that wild populations are not threatened. Since palms have long been associated with humankind in nature, it would be highly artificial (and futile) to advocate, under the guise of any conservation program, that the human linkage be weakened or broken.

An estimated 83% of all palm species are found only in the wild (in situ) and have never been cultivated. Clearly, from a conservation standpoint, it is the survival on earth of these palms which is of greatest concern. Accelerating rates of forest clearing to convert land into agricultural production, pastures, as well as for mining activities, hydroelectric complexes, or other purposes, threatens the future survival of a host of plant and animal species, palms included.

Virtually all of the remaining 17% of palm species exist both in situ and ex situ, in the wild and under cultivation. At least a rudimentary knowledge of the growth habits and/or requirements of about 450 species comes to us from the nursery trade, private gardeners, botanical gardens, arboreta, public parks, as well as from the plantation cultivation of palms and the management or utilization of wild trees. A very few truly domesticated palms exist only under cultivation and are distinct from their wild progenitors. The best example is provided by the date palm (*Phoe-*

nix dactylifera), a species which has never been found to occur in the wild.

The creation, in 1984, of a Palm Specialist Group within the Species Survival Commission of IUCN has enabled conservation efforts to be focused on this important family.

III. Threatened New World Palms

Initial research on the in situ status of palm species in Latin America and the Caribbean was carried out in 1985–1986, as an activity of the Palm Specialist Group, through a palm conservation and utilization project supported by the World Wildlife Fund–U.S. Because of the breadth of the undertaking, it was necessary to focus the study on the most threatened palms, that is, those which had been assigned an IUCN world category of either Endangered or Extinct. (IUCN definitions are: Endangered: "Taxa in danger of extinction and whose survival is unlikely if the causal factors continue operating. Included are taxa whose numbers have been reduced to a critical level or whose habitats have been so drastically reduced that they are deemed to be in immediate danger of extinction." Extinct: "species which are no longer known to exist in the wild after *repeated* searches of the type localities *and other known or likely places*." Lucas & Synge, 1978.)

When the project began, a list was obtained from the CMC which contained 46 Endangered and 2 Extinct palm species. The study of this group of palms led to reclassifying the two Extinct species to Insufficiently Known, for reasons of uncertain nomenclature. Through a combination of additions and deletions, the number of Endangered palms in the region of study was reduced from 46 to 43. Table I lists these palms as well as two other species which occur elsewhere in the New World.

Table I reveals some interesting patterns. A total of 26 different genera are represented among the 45 palms. Five genera account for 20 of the Endangered species: *Attalea* (5), *Ceroxylon* (5), *Coccothrinax* (4), *Chamaedorea* (3), and *Copernicia* (3). Of the 45 species, 41 are endemic to a single political unit. Of the latter, Colombia leads with nine, followed by Cuba with 7, and Brazil and Peru with six each. From the standpoint of endangerment, it is critical to note that

Table I

Endangered New World Palms[1]

[IUCN World Category]

Genus and species	Distribution
Acrocomia sp. (*Acanthococos emensis*) Toledo	Brazil
Attalea burretiana Bondar	Brazil
A. crassispatha (Martius) Burret	Haiti
A. septuagenata Dugand	Colombia
A. tessmannii Burret	Peru
A. victoriana Dugand	Colombia
Bactris militaris Moore	Costa Rica
Brahea berlandieri Bartlett	Mexico
B. edulis Watson	Mexico
Ceroxylon alpinum Bonpland	Colombia
C. crispum Burret	Peru
C. latisectum Burret	Peru
C. verruculosum Burret	Peru
C. weberbaueri Burret	Peru
Chamaedorea amabilis Wendland ex Dammer	Costa Rica
C. metallica Cook ex Moore	Mexico
C. pulchra Burret	Guatemala
Chelyocarpus dianeurus (Burret) Moore	Colombia
Coccothrinax borhidiana Muñiz	Cuba
C. crinita Beccari	Cuba
C. pauciramosa Burret	Cuba
C. victorini León	Cuba
Copernicia ekmanii Burret	Haiti
C. humicola León	Cuba
C. occidentalis León	Cuba
Cryosophila cookii Bartlett	Costa Rica
C. kalbreyeri (Dammer ex Burret) Dahlgren	Colombia
Geonoma hoffmanniana Wendland ex Spruce	Costa Rica
Itaya amicorum Moore	Peru, Brazil
Jubaea chilensis (Molina) Baillon	Chile
Lytocaryum insigne (Drude) Toledo	Brazil
L. weddellianum (Wendland) Toledo	Brazil
Mauritiella pacifica Dugand	Colombia
Neonicholsonia watsonii Dammer	Costa Rica, Panama
Oenocarpus circumtextus Martius	Brazil, Colombia
Parajubaea torallyi (Martius) Burret	Bolivia
Reinhardtia koschnyana (Wendland & Dammer) Burret	Costa Rica, Nicaragua, Panama, Colombia
Roystonea elata (Bartram) Harper	Florida, USA
Sabal bermudana Bailey	Bermuda
Schippia concolor Burret	Belize, Guatemala
Socratea hecatonandra (Dugand) Bernal	Colombia
Syagrus acaulis (Drude) Beccari	Brazil
S. pseudococos (Raddi) Glassman	Brazil
Thrinax ekmaniana (Burret) Moore	Cuba
Wettinia castanea Moore & Dransfield	Colombia

[1] Based on a printout dated 1 Aug 1985 provided by the Conservation Monitoring Centre, and information contained in the final report of the WWF-US project entitled: Economic Botany and Threatened Species of the Palm Family in Latin America and the Caribbean.

four palms (*Itaya, Jubaea, Neonicholsonia* and *Schippia*) are monotypic, that is, each genus contains only a single species. Thus, in these cases, species loss means loss of the genus as well.

Results of this WWF project have demonstrated the value of generating current and more detailed information about the most threatened of palms in the New World. In so doing, it has created baseline data upon which conservation action plans can be designed for individual palm taxa and particular countries.

IV. Threatened Old World Palms

The conservation status of Old World palms remains to be studied. However, a project is under development as a parallel effort to the investigation in Latin America and the Caribbean. A proposal has been submitted to the World Wildlife Fund–International for a two-year study of the conservation and utilization of palms in India, Malaysia, Indonesia and Philippines, which also is to be focused on the most threatened species. This project, also under the aegis of the Palm Specialist Group, will consist of sub-projects led in each country by members of the Group. As part of the project development a list of all Old World Endangered and Extinct palms was provided by the CMC. Table II contains the 45 Endangered and 1 Extinct species. It needs to be emphasized that Table II represents a working list. Apart from a verification of the validity of binomials and current status, the list has not been refined and is therefore provisional.

Examination of Table II reveals that 23 genera are represented among the 46 palms. Compared to the New World, threatened palms are more highly concentrated within a few genera. Together, *Pritchardia* with 13 and *Hyophorbe* with 4 account for 17 of the 46 species. Endemism is also high, especially on islands, with 44 of the species occurring only in a single political unit. The Hawaiian Islands account for 13 endemic species, followed by Madagascar with 12 and Mauritius with 4. The number of Endangered monotypic palms in the Old World (9) is more than twice that of the New World. These are: *Beccariophoenix, Halmoorea, Kentiopsis, Masoala, Medemia, Neoveitchia, Pelagodoxa, Pritchardiopsis,* and *Tectiphiala.*

A single Old World palm, *Pritchardia macrocarpa,* is classified as Extinct. However, it may well represent a false extinction resulting from uncertain nomenclature. Robert W. Read's planned study of native Hawaiian palms will resolve the problem. It must be added that this particular palm is not totally extinct; a single specimen is in the collection of the Foster Garden in Honolulu (Hodel, 1980).

It is anticipated that the proposed project work in India, Malaysia, Indonesia and Philippines will identify additional palm species which merit the Endangered category.

V. Conclusion

Although the provisional worldwide conservation status of palms has been revealed to be serious, there is some justification for optimism. A total of 91 palms are seriously threatened, about equally divided between the Old and New Worlds, but it is encouraging to note that thus far we cannot confirm any total extinctions. It must be emphasized that the findings of this study are preliminary. Our knowledge of the in situ status of many palms is fragmentary; some species currently classified as Endangered are listed as such because they are poorly known and little collected.

An impressive amount of systematic research in association with doctoral dissertations and the preparation of new floras is being carried out worldwide on the Palmae. Increased interest in the economic development of certain palms has also led to important new studies, such as the two books on Southeast Asian rattans by Dransfield (1979, 1984). These investigations have made invaluable contributions to the body of knowledge about the Palm family and greatly facilitate palm conservation project work.

On the basis of what we now know, future worldwide palm conservation efforts could best be directed toward two groups of palms. The first group is those palms which solid evidence indicates are on the verge of extinction in the wild. Examples are *Attalea crassispatha* in Haiti and *Pritchardia* spp. in the Hawaiian Islands. The second group consists of the 13 Endangered monotypic palms, which includes *Medemia argun.* This palm occurs only in Egypt and Sudan; it is the most threatened in the world, for it has reportedly not been seen in the wild since 1964 and is nowhere in cultivation. Monotypic species deserve special attention because of the greater overall loss of palm genetic diversity any extinction would represent.

With respect to being able to attract conservation support and attention, the Palm family is admirably well placed, in part because the utility and beauty of palms are almost universally ac-

Table II

Endangered and Extinct Old World Palms[1]

[IUCN World Category]

Genus and species	Distribution
Areca concinna Thwaites	Sri Lanka
A. subacaulis (Beccari) Dransfield	Sarawak
Synonym *Pichisermollia subacaulis* (Beccari) Monteiro-Neto	
Beccariophoenix madagascariensis Jumelle & Perrier	Madagascar
Ceratolobus glaucescens Blume	Java
C. pseudoconcolor Dransfield	Java, Sumatra
Chrysalidocarpus pembanus Moore	Pemba Island
Dictyosperma album Wendland & Drude ex Scheffer	Mauritius, Reunion, Rodrigues
Dypsis louvelii Jumelle & Perrier	Madagascar
D. mocquerysiana Beccari	Madagascar
Halmoorea trispatha Dransfield & Uhl	Madagascar
Hyophorbe amaricaulis Martius	Mauritius
H. lagenicaulis (Bailey) Moore	Mauritius
H. vaughanii Bailey	Mauritius
H. verschaffeltii Wendland	Rodrigues
Kentiopsis oliviformis (Brongniart & Gris) Brongniart	New Caledonia
Latania loddigesii Martius	Mauritius
L. lontaroides (Gaertner) Moore	Reunion
Lavoixia macrocarpa Moore	New Caledonia
Marojejya darianii Dransfield & Uhl	Madagascar
M. insignis Humbert	Madagascar
Masoala madagascariensis Jumelle	Madagascar
Medemia argun (Martius) Wurttemberg ex Wendland	Egypt, Sudan
Neoveitchia storckii (Wendland) Beccari	Fiji
Orania longisquama (Jumelle) Dransfield & Uhl	Madagascar
Pelagodoxa henryana Beccari	Marquesas
Pinanga acaulis Ridley	Pen. Malaysia
P. adangensis Ridley	Thailand
Pritchardia aylmer-robinsonii St. John	Hawaii
P. elliptica Rock & Caum	Hawaii
P. eriophora Beccari	Hawaii
P. gaudichaudii (Martelli) Wendland	Hawaii
P. hillebrandii Beccari	Hawaii
P. kaalae Rock (2 varieties)	Hawaii
P. kahanae Rock & Caum	Hawaii
P. lanaiensis Beccari & Rock	Hawaii
P. macrocarpa Linden ex Andre (EXTINCT)	Hawaii
P. munroi Rock	Hawaii
P. napaliensis St. John	Hawaii
P. remota Beccari	Hawaii
P. schattaueri Hodel	Hawaii
Pritchardiopsis jennencyi Beccari	New Caledonia
Ravenea madagascariensis Beccari (2 varieties)	Madagascar
R. robustior Jumelle & Perrier (2 varieties)	Madagascar
Tectiphiala ferox Moore	Mauritius
Vonitra fibrosa (Wright) Beccari	Madagascar
V. utilis Jumelle	Madagascar

[1] Based on a printout dated 12 Apr 1986 provided by the Conservation Monitoring Centre.

knowledged. Through the combined efforts of the Palm Specialist Group and the International Palm Society, and with support from individuals and conservation organizations, we have the opportunity to maintain the full diversity of this unique plant family for future generations to use and enjoy. A beginning has been made. To achieve our goal we must maintain the momentum by developing detailed action plans to save endangered species before we find ourselves faced with outright extinctions.

VI. Acknowledgments

This paper is based, in part, on work undertaken for a project entitled "Economic Botany and Threatened Species of the Palm Family in Latin America and the Caribbean," supported by the World Wildlife Fund–U.S. I extend special thanks to Linda McMahan and Jane MacKnight of the Plant Program for their support and assistance. Michael J. Balick and Robert W. Read participated in the project and made significant contributions to it. Without access to the computerized data of the Conservation Monitoring Centre, none of this research would have been possible and I am indebted to Hugh Synge for his generous cooperation.

VII. Literature Cited

Dransfield, J. 1979. A manual of the rattans of the Malay Peninsula. Forest Department, Ministry of Primary Industries, West Malaysia.

———. 1984. The rattans of Sabah. Forest Department, Sabah.

Hodel, D. 1980. Notes on *Pritchardia* in Hawaii. Principes **24**: 65–81.

Lucas, G. & H. Synge. 1978. IUCN plant red data book. IUCN, Gland, Switzerland.

Moore, H. E. Jr. 1977. Endangerment at the specific and generic levels in palms. Pages 267–282 *in* G. T. Prance & T. S. Elias (eds.), Extinction is forever: The status of threatened and endangered plants in the Americas. New York Botanical Garden, Bronx, New York.

Uhl, N. W. & J. Dransfield. 1987. Genera Palmarum, a classification of palms based on the work of H. E. Moore, Jr. The International Palm Society.

Index to Common Names

Page numbers with an asterisk (*) indicate pages with illustrations or maps.

Index to Scientific Names

Page numbers in **boldface** indicate primary page references. Page numbers with an asterisk (*) indicate pages with illustrations or maps.